The Elysian Fields of Information Technology

A People Path to Technological Value

MARK K. ALLEN

The Elysian Fields of Information Technology
A People Path to Technological Value

Copyright © 2009 Mark K. Allen

ALL RIGHTS RESERVED. No part of this book shall be reproduced, stored in any retrieval system, or transmitted by any means, electronic, mechanical, photocopying, recording, or otherwise, without written permission from the publisher. No patent liability is assumed with respect to the use of information contained herein. Although every precaution has been taken in the preparation of this book, the publishers and author assume no responsibility for errors or omissions. Nor is any liability assumed for damages resulting from the use of the information contained therein.

International Standard Book Number: 978-0-578-00132-6

Library of Congress Catalog Case Number: 1-132860791

Printed in the United States of America

First Printing: February 2009

Trademarks

All terms mentioned in this book that are known to be trademarks or service marks have been appropriately capitalized. The publisher and author cannot attest to the accuracy of this information. Use of a term in this book should not be regarded as affecting the validity of any trademark or service mark.

Warning and Disclaimer

Every effort has been made to make this book as complete and as accurate as possible, but no warranty or fitness is implied. The information provided is on an "as is" basis. The author and the publisher shall have neither liability nor responsibility to any person or entity with respect to the loss or damages arising from the information contained in this book or from the use of any CD or programs accompanying it.

Cover Design and Page Layout
Mark K. Allen

For more information contact:
Real Enhanced Decision Technology, LLC
Post Office Box 802
Kelso, WA 98626-8825 USA
Phone: 360.423.2847
Email: tefoit@realenhanceddecicions.com
Internet: http://www.realenhanceddecisions.com/EFOIT.aspx

TABLE OF CONTENTS

INTRODUCTION 3

Humble Beginnings 5
   A Hero and Mentor 7

Addressing Requirements 9

The Technology Spark 11

A Vision 12
   Vision Cycle Diagram 13

A Reality 14

IT Department Infrastructures and Business Perceptions 15
   IT Employee Infrastructures 15
   IT Software Infrastructures 17
   IT Hardware Infrastructures 18

About this Book 19

Why I Wrote This Book 20

Who this Book is For 22

Chapter 1: INFORMATION PEOPLE 25

The IT Human Element 25

   High School Diploma vs. College Degree 26

   The Enterprise Level IT Environment 29

   The Big Business Level IT Environment 30

   The Small Business Level IT Environment 31

   The Startup Level IT Environment 33

   The Players 35

   IT Organization Charts 36
     CIO 37
     CTO 37
     IT Director 37
     Software System Architect 37
     Data Architect 39
     Network Architect 40
     Project Manager 40
     Team Lead 41
     IT Business Analyst 41

TABLE OF CONTENTS

    Programmer\Analyst 43
    Database Administrator 43
    Network Engineer 44
    Software Tester 44
    Technical Writer 45
    The IT Consultant 45
    Software Engineer 46

Software Engineer Personality Types 47
    The Artistic 48
    The Egocentric 48
    The Realist 48
    The Caretaker 48
    The Politician 49
    The Conservative 49

The Human n-Tier Diagram 49

Summary 50

Chapter 2: CAPTAINS AND CREWS 53

The Right IT Leadership 53

Enforcing the Chain of Command 58

Securing an Objective 61

The Need to Know 64

Auditing Leadership Integrity 67

Speaking the Same Language 69
    The importance of XML 70

Adapting IT to the Business 73

Keeping IT in Check 76

Invoking IT Discipline 79

The Impact of IT Team Tools 81

You Get what You Pay For 83

Changing the IT Mindset 86

Building the Right Morale 87

Taking IT to War 91

Training the IT Warrior 94

Dealing With 3rd Party Vendors and Consultants 97
    The Money Loving Consultants 101
    The Client Loving Consultants 101

    The Balanced Consultants 102
        Choosing the Balanced Consultant 103

Summary 103

Chapter 3: COMMUNICATIONS 105

IT and Business Communications 105

Gathering Business Intelligence 106

Centralizing Business Intelligence 109

Streamlining Business Intelligence Software Systems 111

Liaisons 115

Managing Analyst 116

Lead Analyst 117

Business Analyst 118

Technical Analyst 119

Analytical Team Relational View (without Lead Analyst) 120

Analytical Team Relational View (with Lead Analyst) 121

Setting Expectations 121

Understanding the "Bottom Line" 123

The Tao of Integrity 125

The Right People 127

Ten IT Commandments 128

Summary 130

Chapter 4: THE POLITICS OF INFORMATION TECHNOLOGY 133

A History of IT Politics 133

What's at Stake 134

Is There a Liar in the House? 137

Working with Adversaries, Enemies and Friends 140

Types of Politicians 143

Types of IT Power 144

Avoiding Political Suicide 147
    Communicating with Executive Management 148
    Common Political Mistakes 149

The Double Edged Sword 151

IT Funding 154
  Scenario One: 155
  Scenario Two: 155

Information Control 156

Summary 161

Chapter 5: BUILDING THE SHIPS 163

Making the Right Decisions 163
    Build vs. Buy 165

The Importance of a Physically Separate Development Network 168

Give the People What They Need 170
  Service Oriented Architecture (SOA) 171
  Software as a Service (SaaS) 172
  Distributed Software Systems 175

The Software Development Lifecycle (SDLC) 180
  The Product Vision 182
  The Product Plan 183
  Product Development 191
  Product Testing 192
  Product Deployment 194
  Product Support 195

Change Management 195

Black Box Management 198

Computer System Security 201
  Threat Modeling 202
  Data's Journeys 202
  What Hackers Do 204
  STRIDE 208
  Basic Threat Modeling Rules 209
  Threat Modeling Results 212
  DREAD 213

Software Research and Development (SR&D) 214

Intellectual Property and Software Patents 216
  Summary 221

Chapter 6: READY FOR CHANGE (RFC) METHODOLOGY 225

Introduction 225

Popular Software Methodologies 226

The Problem with some Software Methodologies 230
  Why is Building Software So Difficult? 232

The Ready for Change (RFC) Method Set 233
  RFC Tools 237
  RFC Communications 240
  RFC Communication Protocols 241
  Why use RFC? 242
  Who is involved in RFC? 244
  RFC Documentation 246
  When to use RFC 248
  The Virtual Office? 249
  RFC Philosophy 251

Changing the "Old School" Location-Based Management Mindset 254

Building for the Unknown 256
  The Re-Use Factor 259

Summary 263

Chapter 7: THE HADES OF INFORMATION TECHNOLOGY 265

Introduction 265

Why Software Projects Fail 269
  Lack of or Poor Software Testing 269
  Lack of Change Management Processes 270
  Scope Creep 270
  Poor Project Software Estimation 271
  Poorly written or no Project Requirements 271

Poor Leadership 272

The Stupid Factor 275

Friendship over Facts 278

Complacency 280

Complacency View 282

Overcompensation 282

Inappropriate Encounters 283

IE Scenario 284

Non-Technical People Making Technical Decisions 284

Refusing Responsibility 286
  Business Courses to Solution 287

Summary 287

TABLE OF CONTENTS

Chapter 8: WELCOME TO THE ELYSIAN FIELDS 289

The State of Perpetual Forward Motion 289
    Are there problems in the Elysian Fields? 293

Elysian Fields Project Examples 295
    The Personal Computer (PC) 295
    The Modem 299
    TCP/IP and the Internet 299
    Email 302

Physics of the Elysian Fields 305

Laws of IT Physics 308

Elysian Field Requirements 310

Shapes of the Elysian Fields 311
    Reuniting Church and State 313
    The Technical Evangelist 317

Elysian Fields Vision Quest 320

Artificial Intelligence (AI) 321

The Singularity 324

Point of no Return 327

The Greatest Elysian Fields Projects 329
    Enemies of the Elysian Fields 336
    Friends of the Elysian Fields 339
    Changing the Return on Investment (ROI) 342
    Summary 346

EPILOGUE 351

BOOK REFERENCES 355

INTERNET REFERENCES 357

INDEX 361

ABOUT THE AUTHOR 385

DEDICATION

This Book is for:

Anne, Sheryl, Miora, Xena, Veronica, and Sequoia

Anne taught me kindness.

Sheryl teaches me tolerance.

Miora teaches me acceptance.

Xena teaches me patience.

Veronica teaches me perseverance.

Sequoia taught me about unconditional love.

ACKNOWLEDGEMENTS

I would also like to express my most sincere gratitude to my friends and colleagues:

Somnath Banerjee, Tom Upchurch, Leah Blackburn, Jim Nichols, Robert McConnel, Mark Meyer, Judy Otto, Ronald Mayslin, and especially *Katherine M. Yackley.* Your support, intellect, wisdom, and friendship both personally and professionally have been truly inspiring and has meant more to me than I can say. I am lucky to know you. Thank you so very much!

- Mark

INTRODUCTION

For those of you who are unfamiliar with the mythical realm of the Elysian Fields, it is the ancient Greek equivalent of "Heaven". Below are dictionary definitions of this mystical place called The Elysian Fields:

- [noun] a heavenly place (peaceful and beautiful) where those who are favored by the gods can go when they die

- **In Greek mythology, the final resting place of the blessed chosen by the gods**

- **Elysium. In Greek mythology, the abode of the blessed, paradise. Situated at the end of the world it is here that those chosen by the gods are sent to**

If I were to imagine this mysterious place of beauty, my vision would most likely be different from yours, as it would be based on my own most intimate wants and desires. Take a moment to imagine what The Elysian Fields would be like for you as if it was real, and examine the following questions:

1. What would you do for entertainment?
2. How would you make sure that you obtained what you wanted and needed?
3. Who or what else would you like to accompany you?
4. How would you communicate your thoughts and ideas?
5. What special powers or abilities would you like to have, if any?
6. Whom would you want to talk to the most and what questions would you ask them?
7. What Earthly deeds do you believe awarded you entry into the Elysian Fields?

History has taught us that the pursuit of paradise usually costs its adventurer something that is significantly important to him or her. This could include a variety of things such as:

- A loved one
- A physical possession
- A task that could lead a person to financial and or moral bankruptcy

Either way, many believe that the pursuit of "paradise" or the "Elysian Fields" during their lifetime is well worth the price, as long as someone else pays for it. However, there are people

INTRODUCTION

who believe in working hard to achieve their own "Heaven on Earth" and are willing to share the trials and tribulations of their journey within a team or group. Whether you use the words "paradise" or "Elysian Fields", they refer to a state of bliss, great delight and or peace, which is comprised of different elements based on the group, organization or individual describing it. In this book, the noun "Elysian Fields" does not refer to as an "after death" reward, but as technological platform that can be obtained by an individual or team. The mere concept that a technical equivalent of paradise could exist in relation to information technology is an argument that some seasoned IT professionals might consider absurd due to its constant evolution. The very nature of technology is the fact that it is always changing. Its core essence is a constant state of growth that drives civilizations to always explore, learn, invent, innovate, and desire more. New discoveries must constantly rise from previous ones so that the medium can advance. However, a counter argument can be made that the state of perpetual change within technology is in itself is indeed platform. Also, that there are several specific higher levels of this domain that many organization fail to achieve, with the Elysian Fields being the highest. This would signify a powerfully efficient yet effective level of competency, that could enact precisely the required changes consistently, just as a car produces carbon emissions from its exhaust when the engine is running. The bottom line is that the ability to produce the required growth in a competent and reliable manner when and where ever needed is paramount. To some, this viewed as a state of technological "perfection". This final state is a great and seldom realistic goal that many organizations set out to conquer. This objective is pursued after for many different reasons. Some companies are driven by capitalistic greed and the ultimate quest for the "unfair advantage". Other non-profit based businesses' motivations lie in solving a particular global, regional, or local problem or issue they are working to help resolve. Most of the time, technology is the primary tool used to carve the way to the Elysian Fields.

We have seen various exceptional technological teams throughout history reach the Elysian Fields. For instance, American President John F. Kennedy made landing on the moon a primary national goal in 1961. At that time, he made his now famous statement:

"I believe that this nation should commit itself. To achieving the goal, before this decade is out, of landing a man on the Moon and returning him safely to the Earth. No single space project in this period will be more impressive to mankind or more important for the long range exploration of Space."

In 1969, a man landed and stepped foot on the Moon for the first time in human history. The Apollo Moon Landing Project was undoubtedly a landmark Elysian Fields project that will remain as a monument to human achievement forever.

If the Elysian Fields are supposed to be a form of "Heaven", then why should we worry about anything if we could ever get there? If there is a lesson that should be learned about successes in Software Engineering it is that, those achievements will most definitely change. IT departments would have to work hard to stay in the Elysian Fields if they could ever even get there to begin with. We live in an age where new technology seems to emerge every week and IT departments must always be aware that this new offering might be the breakthrough that gives their business the "unfair advantage". This is a point of stress for many IT Departments and Business folks as they are constantly bombarded by the media with "the next best technical thing" that will take them to the top of their industry. This situation has many businesses asking their IT organizations questions such as:

- Why can't we update our software applications quickly to reflect to changes in our business?

- Why can't our websites all link to each other and share data with "real-time" updates that everyone can report on?

- Why are so many of our business processes still manual?

- Why does our closest competition, who company size and revenue match our own, have better and more effective technology than we do?

- We are increasingly losing our competitive edge each quarter with our current technology, how can we prevent this?

- How do we begin to gain the "unfair advantage" in our industry using technology?

It is logical and normal to wonder or even worry about things we don't know about or understand. The more we know, the better we can plan and that helps to alleviate certain anxieties. I generally have some concerns whenever I start a new IT project with a client because I am usually waiting for the usual "challenges" that show up before too long. There are always problems within a project from the usual suspects (Software Engineers or the occasional IT Manager, Team Lead, or Consultant).

Humble Beginnings

I was born in North Philadelphia, a poor ghetto neighborhood in the 1960s. At that time, "North Philly" was considered by many national and local newspapers to be one of the worst neighborhoods in the country. One of my earliest childhood memories was playing outside when I must have been maybe 5 or 6 years old. As I sat on the steps of our row home in the middle of our block, our neighbor, who may have been approximately 70 years old, had just turned the corner at the top of the block, and began walking towards me on the same side of the street with a bag of groceries under his arm. His name was Mr. Pennington and he used to call me "Buster". He always had a smile on his face and took time to talk to me frequently. This person was always kind to the children on the block and he used to give us some of his spare change so that we could buy candy from the corner store. I really liked Mr. Pennington a lot. He was like a "grandfather figure", as I never had a grandfather. As Mr. Pennington continued to walk down the street towards me, I can remember that he began to smile as he saw me sitting on the steps of my row home starring back at him. Behind Mr. Pennington, a shadowy figure began to emerge slowly, jogging, but moving much faster than it initially appeared to be. Soon the object became clear, as Mr. Pennington moved even closer, now maybe six or seven doors north of me. I could now see that the jogger clearly. He was a young teenage boy, approximately 17 years old, and wore a soft cloth hat, and he had caught up with Mr. Pennington and was attempting to pass the man on the left side of the narrow sidewalk. Just when it looked as if the young jogger would pass Mr. Pennington, the teenager bumped the man with extreme prejudice, knocking him onto the sharp cement house steps below him. Mr. Pennington's bag of groceries fell to the ground. The bottles and other contents of the grocery bag crashed and liquid spilled all over the pavement and into the street. Mr. Pennington lay on the steps of the house above him on his right side breathing heavily, mouth open, glasses broken and now laying on the steps under him. Mr. Pennington's face clearly displayed great pain, mixed with shock and humiliation. The teenage jogger had stopped and was standing over Mr. Pennington with a slight smile of satisfaction. The jogger made a gesture to the man that I could not hear, and Mr. Pennington reached into his back pocket and handed the jogger his wallet. As the tall teenager stood over this kind old wonderful man and casually robbed him, I then got up from the grey and white cement steps of my house and ran inside to tell my mother what I had just seen. This was one of my earliest and most clear memories in my neighborhood. Although these thoughts were of a negative nature, I had many other good many memories as well, but this particular scene was the nature of the place that I lived in when I was a child. North Philadelphia was indeed a dangerous place and as I grew up, I would bear witness to and be a victim of more violent crimes than I care to remember. For young children in our neighborhood, gangs were a major problem. The threat of being attacked or robbed was more of an expectation than a fear whenever my brothers and I would have to walk across our neighborhood for any reason.

When I was a very young child, I thought it was important to have a father who lived at home with his family. The father I wanted did not have to get up every day and go to work, he just needed to be there at home for us, to protect and teach us. Many of the children in our neighborhood had fathers that stood or sat on the corner of the block all day and drank, talked, or gambled, but they were they were available when needed. If a child had to talk to their father, they knew where he was most of the time. Just the fact that a child's father was not far away also offered a certain level of protection for that kid in regards to potential harassment, theft and fights with peers or even adults.

My best friend in kindergarten, Charles, had a father and a mother at home. His father went to work every day and his mother stayed at home to care for their home and little sister. His dad would even drop him off at school occasionally, which I thought was amazing. Charles's father appeared to me as a tall, big and strong man with a deep voice. He did not say much because he had a serious look that did not warrant much speech. Since Charles lived on the street adjacent to mine, my mother would let me go around the block, play with him, and even have dinner with his family sometimes. Whenever I went to Charles' house, his mother was strict with us and the atmosphere in their resident was one of discipline and no nonsense. Charles' mother scared me at times, as she was very different from my own mother and not nearly as kind. Charles was generally a very good and well-disciplined boy at the time and I completely understood why after visiting his home. When I look back on my earliest childhood, I realize what a profound affect not having my father around at all had on the lives of my three brothers and me today. From my earliest perspective as a very young boy without a man to guide and mentor him, I felt that a major part of my life was missing, and Charles's family helped me to see that even more clearly.

My father had been in jail at that time and had been for all of my youth. The fact that he was in prison was like some deep dark family secret that no one on my father's side of the family wanted to talk about. I knew and felt that it made my immediate family different in more ways that were readily apparent because my father's family treated my Mother, brothers and I like "Outcasts" because of the things he did. In addition, whenever I was questioned by anyone about what my father did for a living, or where he was, I became embarrassed and would often lie about it. The environment that I grew up in as a young child demanded a strong father figure but the fact was, that there was no man at home who could protect my me and my brothers from the bad elements of our neighborhood. There was no good male figure to teach us how to be men, which meant as boys we were on our own and had to figure this complex process out for ourselves. Some of my friends and relatives say that they do not remember their early childhood days when they were between 5 to 9 years old. Those years are some of the most influential years of a person's life. I believe they may actually remember those times, but they don't want to for their own reasons.

A Hero and Mentor

My mother's name was Anne Allen. She was an honest, hardworking, single parent who got up every day and walked approximately 10 city blocks to work when I was a young child. She was an attractive, heavyset woman who took great pride in her appearance and had a wonderful smile and unforgettable laugh. Mom above all was a truly a nice, kind, caring and loving person who was in turn, loved by her friends, family, and co-workers. She worked at Messiah College in North Philadelphia for 30 years. Whenever I visited her job, the students would constantly talk about how nice she was and how much they liked her. She worked hard to keep her home clean and as safe as possible. Mom never drank, smoked cigarettes, or used drugs. My mother never had various men coming over to the house spending the night like some other women in the neighborhood. That kind of scenario never happened in our house. My mother would on rare occasion, have a boyfriend who would visit for maybe an hour or so, and then leave. She was a Christian woman who made her faith known to anyone who was interested and was a strong role-model for both boys and girls alike.

Anne Allen was born into, and grew up in poverty. She was the oldest of 8 children in a 2-room house with dirt floors in Lancaster, Pennsylvania. She said that during many winters when she was a child in elementary school, that if the local Mennonite Church had not brought their family food, they would have starved to death. She would also tell me how she

INTRODUCTION

only had one dress to wear to elementary school and her mother made it. As a child my family was poor but not to the level of poverty that my mother grew up in. We always had enough to eat and had decent clothes to wear, many of which came as charity donations from our church. My mother raised three boys independently on a secretary's salary without the help of a husband or child support of any kind. That task invoked strength, discipline, determination, faith, and a great love. I can remember when I was of pre-school age, she would drop me off to our neighbor, Ms. Elizabeth, before going off to work. This woman seemed to be a good person as I can recall but was somewhat of a rough around the edges. The one problem I had was that after my mother left for work, Ms. Elizabeth would lock me in her basement for what seemed like hours each morning and then let me out just before lunch. I hated this process as it felt like she was punishing me for something I did not do. I could feel that my mother did not want to leave me there, as she would always stay as long as she could and hug me before she left for work. As soon as she found another caretaker on our street for me, I was transferred and much happier afterwards. My mother always put her children first, no matter what the cost or situation and this fact never seemed to change.

Every Sunday mom got us ready for church and off we all went. The church we attended was "Diamond Street Mennonite Church" which was approximately three blocks from our home. Church was the major place outside of our home were my mother tried to instill in her children a sense of faith, honor, kindness and a sense of morality. It was important for me to see that she was a living example of this, and as a child on through adulthood, it had a profound effect on the person that I became. Mom was not a college graduate but she was a wise and intelligent woman with modest hopes and dreams. She was driven by age old, time tested values that she worked hard to teach and instill in my siblings and me. It took years for me to understand from childhood and well into my late 20s, exactly how Anne Allen gave weight to the following words:

- **Honesty**
- **Loyalty**
- **Respect**
- **Kindness**
- **Patience**

To some people they are just words, but to my mother, the meaning of these words were simply who she was. Practicing these values across the board made her accountable for the inspiring role model she was, in both her personal and professional lives. Everyone can learn something meaningful from the positive example of Anne Allen. She was a strong, independent, intelligent, forgiving, kind, honest, patient, and loyal mother, person and friend. I work hard every day to be half the person she was, and her wisdom and life experience has helped guide me in almost everything that I do. I have had other male mentors in my life, namely Ronald J. Sider (Professor, Author, and Evangelist) and Freeman Miller (Bishop, Mennonite Church, Philadelphia, PA) who have helped me a great deal and taught me what it was to be a responsible man through mentoring and by example. I am forever in their debt. They both knew my mother and were her friends for decades. Let me be clear, Anne Allen was my hero and the primary constant in my life from which I drew strength and courage. When she passed away in May of 2000, it changed my life in ways I cannot describe. At this point, I believe that I understand now that life if not most important thing; it is how you live it. To be lucky enough to have a mother and friend like Anne Allen at any time in this world, is a great and powerful gift that I will be thankful for through the end of my days.

After my mother died, I began to ask myself, how do I apply her powerful concepts and values in a world that does not largely seem to make them a priority? This was especially true in the world of business and technology where cash is king and revenue is the bottom line. There are thousands of books currently available that can teach a person how to program computers in many different software languages, but this is not one of them. This is a book about people and technology, "Information People". Information Technology is Information People. The best technology for the best situation in the world is nothing if you do not have the right team to understand, implement and support it.

Addressing Requirements

What makes this book different from the rest of the technology book genre is that I will discuss and show you topics that many people in IT will not or cannot in a simple, straightforward manner. Along with this, I will explain common and specific topics from both a Software Engineer's and a Businessperson's point of view. Through explanations and diagrams, I will then offer solutions to problems from both views that meet in the middle as an attempt to help the Information Technology and the Business employees who have to interact with one another to better understand and communicate during the Software Development Lifecycle (SDLC). This is critical for businesses in order to posses the best chance of meeting their objectives. Much of the information in this book had not previously been compiled into a single resource that was readily available, and was scattered throughout many different websites, books, articles, whitepapers, and presentations. Generally, Information Technology books and technical whitepapers focus on a few related core topics at a time. Some of those categories include:

- Software Development Languages, theory, and functionality

- How to develop software

- Database creation and management

- Project Management

INTRODUCTION

- Business requirements gathering and documentation

- Software Project Cost Estimation

- Software Methodologies

Some of the challenges with these resources is that they are not always simple to understand or easy to read for IT and or the business. The Elysian Fields of Information Technology takes a different approach to addressing this issue. Based on almost 2 decades of "real world" IT experiences, and a basic vocabulary, this book offers effective solutions for some of the most common, serious and traditional authentic problems that hold many IT projects hostage or put them at a high risk for failure. The Elysian Fields of Information Technology also puts IT into perspective by focusing on the business first and showing how projects must be able to be traced back to the business owners who commissioned them. This book works to build a better understanding of the relationships of businesses and their IT organizations. Correcting misunderstandings through identification, communication, respect, controlled politics, and common sense is a primary objective of this resource. Information Technology is ultimately about people and this book speaks primarily from that human element, not a technical one. It is the human team that uses the tool called "Information Technology", and in every aspect of the industry that must constantly be addressed.

The following are two definitions for "team":

1. **[noun] two or more draft animals that work together to pull a vehicle**

2. **[noun] a cooperative unit**

It's not hard to guess which definition most businesses would want to be identified with. In order to become a cooperative unit, the group must first be able to communicate with each other in a common language. The unit will then have the ability to understand each other and must then work to achieve a culture if they have not already. From that, the group can begin to establish a common goal or objectives that benefit the unit. Conquering the vision of a unit takes sacrifice and commitment from all members. This is where good leadership becomes paramount in order to keep a team focused, hungry, educated and united.

For every successful small to mid level IT project there are hundreds that fail or never make it passed conception. Then, there are the expensive Enterprise level projects that are unsuccessful. These projects can end up costing their respective companies millions of dollars or more. Businesses that than can afford to waste tens of millions of dollars on an unsuccessful IT project or projects can never complain that money was an issue in their failure. Whereas, many small to mid level projects could make that claim. In many IT Project scenarios, time is more of a factor than money (but not always) when it comes to successfully completing an IT project. A fine balance must be maintained in this regard.

Information Technology and its Business counterpart belong to the same company but are part of different worlds entirely. In many businesses, the two entities simply hate and or misunderstand each other, which have led to relationships that lack in basic "trust". Some of these companies are handicapped when it comes to communication and hence do not understand what each other's goals are or what their partner is doing. This is their environment and history but is does not need to be. The more those businesses grow and the longer they incubate that kind culture, the harder it is for them to change for the better.

The Technology Spark
I first became interested in technology when I was approximately 8 years old. My mother bought me a toy computer. It was a motorized box that you could put various proprietary cards into a slot the back of the unit and the two simulated tape reels on the front would slowly spin to pictures of the subjects printed on those inserted cards. I would setup a makeshift computer network operations center behind our couch in the living room and pretend that I was a secret agent. My friends and I would also make computers out of cardboard and old scraps of paper to achieve the same imaginary goals.

My favorite TV show as a child was about a bionic man. The fact that a doctor could put a man back together, after a major accident that lost two legs, an arm, and an eye and make him better than he was before intrigued me. I, along with many millions of kids across America wished that we were bionic too so that we could do all of the cool things that this character did, like running at sixty miles per hour and lifting cars. My two older brothers watched reruns of a popular science fiction show about a space ship that was on a five-year mission to new worlds, and as I got older, I began to join them and watch those shows too. My fascination with technology skyrocketed from that point on. I became spellbound by Gene Rodenberry's vision of the future and joined the many science fiction fans and dreamers who wanted to travel the stars in a space ship at "warp speed". A well-written science fiction based story, television show or movie had my attention, loyalty, and passion.

When I was a teenager, my neighbors purchased one of the early Radio Shack computers. They gave me an open invitation to their home to use it whenever I wanted, and that was one of the best invitations I ever had. This was of course very different and far more sophisticated than the arcade video games that I had been playing at that time. I felt empowered when I typed in the "print" command and hit "Enter" and saw the sentence I had typed previously scroll across the screen repeatedly. Soon after, my best friend's family purchased a Compaq home computer. He and I would stay up all night playing games on that computer and discovering some of the other programs he purchased for it. I began to understand and see firsthand the power of the PC, and how it could potentially change the world.

My first experience working with computers professionally was as an end user in the United States Navy. I did some data entry for the Transient Personnel Office at Naval Base Norfolk, VA in the late 1980s before I was honorably discharged. After leaving the Navy, I started a sole proprietorship. My first company was an independent record label called "Powercoat Records". I was lucky enough to have made some extra money with this project, releasing a few music cassette tapes and recording local artists' demos in my small home private recording studio at that time. During this period, I was able to marry two of my passions, Music and Technology. I built a 64 Track MIDI Studio that I called "Allensound MIDI" and was able to have a couple releases reviewed by several music magazines such as "Home and Studio Recording" along with many other national and foreign alternative music publications. I also enjoyed limited international independent and college radio airplay by radio stations looking for fresh new independent recording artists. During the late 1980s and early 1990s, Allensound MIDI was a state of the art home recording studio and I had a great time working with that project as it taught me a lot about business and technology. With the recording MIDI studio concept being relatively new and primarily synthesizer and drum machine based, I had to do a lot of my own music keyboard synthesizer sound programming. I could not afford the "top of the line" star endorsed electronic instrument patches, so I began to develop my own. When I worked with other musicians or when they visited my recording studio, they would ask where I bought my synthesizer patches (programs). When I told them that I had written the patches, they wanted copies for their own synthesizers. These opportunities soon spilled over into my business software as well and that is how I was introduced to my first programming languages. I had purchased used copies of software development applications at yard sales and was astounded by how easy it was to use software to keep track of my clients and customers. As you can imagine my thirst for more technical knowledge then led me to more advanced languages and applications.

Like so many other Software Engineers in the early to mid 1990s, I was a quick convert from the older languages because of how much easier and faster the newer technology was. During the 1990s, Visual Basic grew to be the most widely used business programming language in the world and I worked on many client server applications, as did many of my colleagues during this period. In 1999, I converted over to, and began working primarily as a Web Developer and continued to evolve learning new technologies as they were released. That has comprised the bulk of my IT project work ever since.

A Vision

A vision for a harmonious business and technology relationship has always been a simple yet very elusive one. Many organizations fail to achieve a good relationship with their technology departments and vice-versa for many reasons. In order to establish a good working partnership, the business and IT must first learn to:

1. **Set or acquire logical, smart goals that are rooted in the best interest of the company and its employees.**

2. **Use or create intelligent and intuitive liaisons between business and technology departments that can communicate and translate all company information fluently to either side.**

3. **Discover and exploit the common ground that business and technology people share.**

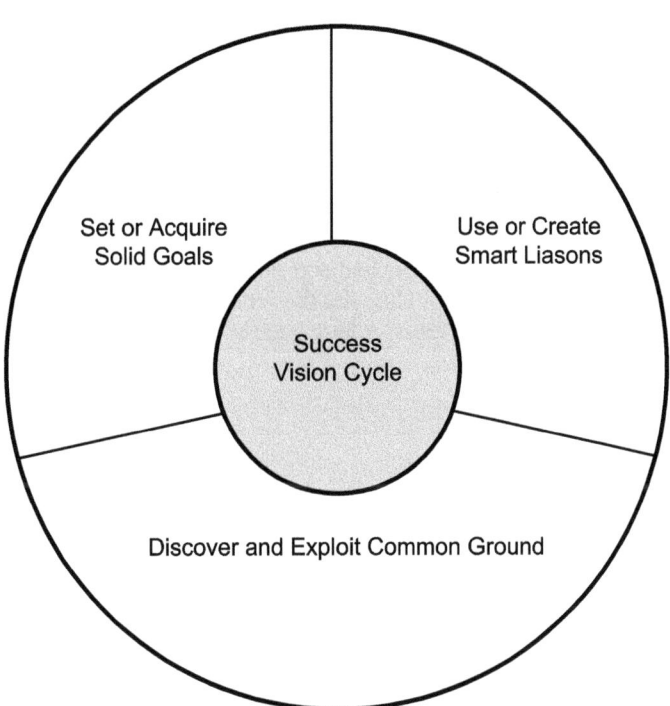

Vision Cycle Diagram

A good example of such a vision is a fictional but effective one. Let's take a look at the popular television series about a crew in a ship lost deep in outer-space searching for their way home, which is one my all time favorite television programs. On the show, the lost spacecraft was a Star Ship that, due to an accident in space, was sent instantaneously more than thirty thousand light years from Earth. At the same time, a different Star Ship that was comprised of an insurgent Captain and his crew, that the primary spacecraft was perusing, were also sent to the same place during the incident. The insurgent ship was damaged beyond repair after the accident and the primary spacecraft had sustained heavy casualties among its crew.

In an unexplored area of space known as the "Delta Quadrant", 30,000 light years from Earth, facing new and uncommon threats, with a strong desire to return to Earth, the primary spacecraft's Captain (Katherine) made the insurgents a special and necessary offer. Since her spacecraft was the only working Star Ship, Katherine asked the insurgents to join her crew, and for their ship's Captain to become her First Officer. This was a risky move to say the least, as both crews were strong enemies. From the perspective of the primary spacecraft, it would take everyone almost seventy years to get home and both crews would have to work together as one if they were going to even come close to achieving their goal.

Katherine vowed to do whatever she could to get the crew back to Earth without violating her oath as a Space Academy Officer or the Military "Prime Directive" (Military Rules of Conduct). After eight long years of traveling through unknown space, dealing with friendly and hostile alien species, along with the deaths of several crewmembers, Katherine met her objective by returning her ship and her crew back to Earth.

As the Captain of her ship, Katherine also served as her crew's Mother, leader, confidant, protector, and disciplinarian among many other things. She had accomplished something that no other space Captain in Military history had ever done, and survived to tell her story. How did she do it? Why didn't she give up? How did she get both the Military and insurgent crews to work together and become one crew? A look back at the Vision Cycle Diagram will help answer these questions.

A Reality

While the adventure of the lost starship was a compelling story, we are not flying around in Star Ships equipped with replicaters, transporters, and holodeck technology. We have not yet conquered disease, poverty, or war on Earth. At this moment, those goals may not be attainable in our short lifetimes. However, it may be impossible for our grandchildren's children, but a great deal would have to change in the world of politics, religion, finance, and technology to make it a realistic goal within the next century or two. I believe that politics is a natural adversary of technology. Technology is widely viewed by too many big businesses today not as a way to make the world a better place but as a way to get rich, control people and environments, and bully foreign governments. This type of attitude will have to change along with many other factors before we could ever realistically start to enter The Elysian Fields of Information Technology on a global scale.

From a world perspective, The Elysian Fields of Information Technology would need to begin to take on a new meaning. With this, our goals would now start to become more common and mainstream. For instance, if there was no more war, poverty, hunger or disease, we might start to accomplish:

- How the human race could start to use more of our brain's capacity and its processing power to find solutions to our problems and evolve

- How to further enhanced human physiology and the ability to repair any life threatening injuries

- Colonization of the Moon and Mars along with space travel that anyone could afford

- The ability to make all manufactured goods one hundred percent recyclable
- The ability to provide energy using safe and renewable and clean power sources

This is just the tip of the iceberg. Many others and I believe that all things that human beings can imagine are possible. The challenge is, we just don't know how to do all of the things human beings can imagine…yet.

IT Department Infrastructures and Business Perceptions

Employee, hardware and software infrastructures can vary significantly between businesses. However, it is important to note that some factors are constant in organizations that have a high level of productivity and are considered "successful". Below are some of those factors:

1. The right people performing the right tasks
2. The best possible software tools to support number one
3. A sound IT hardware platform (network) which support numbers one and two

A separate and dedicated IT hardware platform (network) will also avoid negatively affecting the business platform (network) or company software production services. These aspects go a long way towards influencing how a business perceives its IT department, processes, and personnel. IT must not be disruptive and provide reliable and effective services.

IT Employee Infrastructures

As with any project, the wrong people doing the right things, the wrong people doing the wrong things, and the right people doing the wrong things can all lead to chaos. This management issue is critical for almost any team to get control of. For example, good requirements gathering processes are needed for a new IT software project that is about to get underway. A Software Engineer is assigned to the task that has little to no experience with business analytics, as opposed to an experienced Business Analyst. The business grows frustrated with the requirements process and IT as a whole. The organization also begins to question the competence of IT in relation to understanding their needs as a business.

These types of management issues and gaps are commonplace in many IT Departments. Some of the reasons for this are:

- Revenue Limitations
- Time Constraints
- Lack of IT Management Experience and Training

INTRODUCTION

- Corporate Politics

Below is a sample diagram of an IT employee structure for a small to mid-size business:

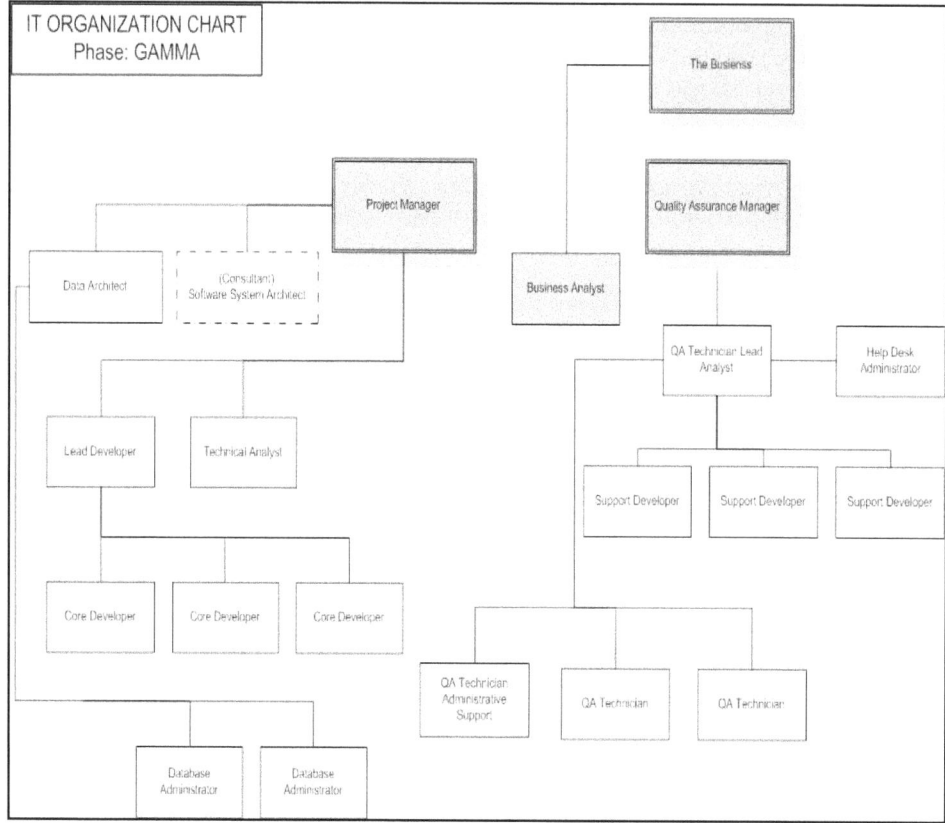

Next, are some of the critical IT Project positions. These IT jobs and others will be in more detail in the next chapter.

1. **Project Manager – Insures that project deadlines and objective are met. Insures that project members have what they need to perform their assigned tasks**

2. **Software System Architect – Designs software systems and sets standards and processes for software system development based on business requirements**

3. **Data Architect – Designs databases and sets standards and processes for data management based on business requirements**

4. Business\Technical Analyst – Gathers requirements, develops, maintains, and provides project documentation and business information

5. Software Developer – Develops, tests, builds and supports software applications according to software system architecture and business requirements

6. Database Administrator – Creates, test and maintains databases and data storage processes according to data architecture and business requirements

7. Quality Assurance – Insures IT products and services met or exceed established business quality and integrity metrics.

IT Software Infrastructures

Using the best possible tools for a given task is an important factor in the successful and timely completion of that task. The software selection for IT Projects on the market today vast, and IT Departments are often subject to revenue, hardware, and software support limitations. It is critical that software development tools must be selected that will best support the software development lifecycle and the organization's IT software development methodology.

Some organizations simply cannot afford the expensive enterprise software system application suites with their licensing and support fees, which may support their development requirements. However, it is still possible for those companies to build their software systems in-house following a Software Development Lifecycle (SDLC) process that yields predictable results.

Below is a list of IT software solutions that are required for most small and large software application projects:

1. A documentation, presentation, and notification (communications) software application

2. Project Management Software

3. A Software Application Development Solution

4. A Database Application

5. Application Testing Software

6. A Bug Tracking Application

INTRODUCTION

Without any one of the software solutions listed above, it would be more difficult to attempt an in-house IT development project that required it. Each tool contributes significantly to a particular phase of the SDLC process. Since the SDLC can at times be a linear process, the inability to complete a particular phase could result in delaying or the total inability to move on the next phase thereby halting the entire process. This would maximize project risks and the organization's return on investment (ROI).

IT Hardware Infrastructures

Developing IT software system projects on business networks is risky and not recommended. With this, IT project software development should be separated from business networks to avoid the risk of adversely affecting those networks and business ROI. For example, confusion regarding IT development, testing, training and production environments by business employees, IT, and third Party Consultants has been an ongoing problem. A critical mistake in this arena could cost an organization, in some cases, hours or days or more of lost revenue due to the system not being available (or corrupted) and or the number of resources needed to resolve the problem.

For years, many businesses have failed to effectively measure the productivity of IT accurately or at all. Comprehensive analysis of this issue has resulted in extensive global studies and the polling of business executives in various industries both large and small. The resulting data supported the fact that IT can be generally classified into four different types of departments. Those types consist of:

1. **IT Organizations that are focused on Markets**

2. **IT Organizations that are focused on Operations**

3. **IT Organizations that are focused on both Markets and Operations**

4. **Unfocused IT Organizations**

Important keys to understanding how an organization's perceives their IT department lies partly in how closely aligned the objectives of business executives and IT truly are. If the business has plans for their future that greatly differ from those of IT, and the technology involved will not support the business plan, then the organization's perceptions in this regards will most likely be more negative. Another key point in understanding an organization's IT perceptions is discovering exactly where business executives see the value in IT. Does the value lie in the data? Is there intellectual property that exists somewhere that can be exploited? This information is critical for IT to identify and analyze. Do the IT objectives present a significant return of investment to business executives? Businesses are always interested in the bottom line, which is usually revenue related. IT exists ultimately to make an organization more profitable, in whatever way that may be.

In many cases, the answers to the IT Perception questions analyzed may be the determining factor in whether or not a specific IT project is outsourced or developed in-house. How good an IT Department is, in most cases, is irrelevant. The business perception of that IT Department is what ultimately matters.

Technology professionals should never forget that IT is a relative new comer to business within the history of modern technology. For thousands of years, trade has been transpiring among many factions of human beings without the benefit of computer systems. If computers were to disappear tomorrow altogether, businesses would adapt, continue, and find new and different ways to remain competitive in their respective industries.

Many in business today still struggle with why such high levels of IT is needed within the companies when they see such little return on investment from them. If a business perceives that IT is blocking the path to company growth and prosperity, then IT will have no value to that organization. If this turns out to be the case for your IT department, then IT layoffs may be right around the corner. Achieving a better understanding of IT Infrastructures and Business Perceptions is increasingly significant for anyone who is a part of the Software Development Lifecycle (SDLC). This knowledge serves to help that cycle perform more effectively and increase IT return on investment.

About this Book

This book is about building and understanding productive relationships between businesses and their Information Technology organizations. This is because businesses in general need to make it to a state of positive technological and effective perpetual change, if they have not done so already. It is also about maintaining those relationships in a healthy way, using industry standards and proven best practices. Above all, it is about implementing forward thinking, common sense practices in regards to technology in business. This means breaking many traditionally held company practices of holding to certain political values that simply don't work in Information Technology and business relationships. This book is about implementing effective positive change using sense, once thought to be common and can be again, if a business has the courage to do what is required in the pursuit of success for their technological endeavors. I have talked to hundreds of IT folks that included Managers, Software Engineers, and DBAs over the last decade about what they felt were the primary reasons IT projects fail. A vast majority of the commentary from these professionals were amazingly similar. When these individuals generally spoke of the IT projects that they were a part of that they knew were successful, the resulting themes and project pulse lines were virtually the same. Some of the major success factors ultimately amounted to:

- Proper project planning

- The right people, performing the right tasks, at the right times

INTRODUCTION

- Egos being held in check

- Project Politics were controlled

- Having enough revenue to get the job done

The human factor in regards to IT projects is often talked about as being a major issue, but "team chemistry" can often be ignored when choosing an IT project team. This book also addresses these critical subjects as well.

The Elysian Fields of Information Technology is a difficult place to find and the path is not always clear because people can sometimes be difficult to understand and work with. It can be even harder to stay in a good path if you can ever find one. This book is designed to be an "aid" or "roadmap" that may be needed at times in a person's (or group) career just as any other resource book could be. I will try to cover as best I can what most of the other technical and or business related books do not, and provide insight and solutions to help businesses and their IT Departments to find and maintain their own "Elysian Fields".

From its inception, computer hardware has continued to be more advanced than the software that runs it. The two are logically well married for obvious reasons. Many of the topics covered in this book apply to computer hardware and network engineering business relationships as well. My software background forces me to acknowledge that IT Project objectives are met successfully, and work out the best when everyone in IT works as a team. If that team trusts and respects one another, even if they do not like each other, the possibilities can be endless. Everyone on the "proverbial boat" must be rowing in the same direction in order for success to be achieved.

Why I Wrote This Book

I initially began writing this book out of sheer frustration with the failure of IT and business managers to make good decisions in order to complete IT software projects successfully. I have had the consistent misfortune of being a part of many projects that have been:

- **Managed by people who had little to no leadership or managerial skills**

- **Managed by people who did not understand the SDLC**

- **Managed by people who did not understand people**

- **Managed by people who were obsessed with controlling the thoughts and actions of their subordinates and exercising their power over them**

- **Managed by people who were more interested in advancing their careers than achieving a win on the project that they are tasked with leading**

The politics, egos and ignorance involved in management can be stifling to software production within an organization. Greed, ignorance, selfishness, politics, and power hungry managers are the natural enemies of Information Technology advancement and to the business that hired them. One of the many problems with developing software is that too many companies hire good (or great) software consultants, pay them a staggering amount of money, and then ignore that consultant's well-researched and competent advice in regards to fixing or elevating their company's technology. This has been an epidemic in IT as this feedback has been consistent from hundreds of business and IT professionals that I have spoken with over the years. Ultimately, there is very little that any good consult can do in this regard because businesses govern themselves and do not have to take advice from any consultants they hire, even though in many cases they should.

The basic lack of IT knowledge, experience, and understanding rarely stops business professional from making technical decisions that they believe are competent when in reality, they are truly disastrous. This is because many business managers do not understand how IT works or even care about it, and view software development as a foreign or simple task. This is not unexpected because without the proper IT training, many software projects can appear falsely to be much easier than they really are when viewed from a very high level. In situations like this, when a software project fails, IT usually takes the blame which makes matters even worse. This is because in all too many cases, expectations are set for IT, and it is not IT that is setting the expectations. When it comes to technology, professional Engineers are the ones who must set the expectations for the users. This is an important pulse echoed throughout this book and a major reason for its existence. Businesses provide the software system requirements, IT engineers work to transform those business requirements in reliable software systems and set the expectations in regards to that part of the process. This basic concept in IT has become decimated, convoluted, and ignored due to politics, ego, power and ignorance by a great number of large and small businesses in the IT industry. Watching businesses struggle and become stagnated because of their own technology when they have good IT project teams, tools, and revenue is truly sad. There are small businesses that exist all over the world, who are able to accomplish impressive technological achievements in the same industries as their larger competitors with less than half of their rival's resources. Good, strong, experienced, competent and wise management is a key.

It seemed for a long time that I always managed to end up on the right projects with the wrong management. In some cases, the projects that I worked on burned venture capital at a rate faster than the "Space Shuttle" burned fuel on its way to orbit. As expected, the project failed, largely due to mismanagement, which led to lack of funds. Rarely have I seen or have been a part of a project that had failed because of poor software engineering or tools, but that does happen on some projects. Projects are usually unsuccessful because a team or individual at the beginning stages fails to research, develop, and plan a strategy to produce what is required by the business.

By the time you finish reading this book, whether you're a business or IT professional, you will hopefully gain a new and or different insight as to human factor that greatly affects the development of business technology today. With this, maybe you can then work to reduce the high level of politics, ego, and ignorance that plague the success of so many IT projects. The IT industry is weighted down with a high rate of unnecessary risks that are "people" related. As the saying goes, if you are not part of the solution, you are part of the problem and never has this been truer than in an IT project. The industry must significantly reduce its problems as soon as possible so that it can ultimately help us to save, and improve our way of life before it is too late.

Who this Book is For

The Elysian Fields of Information Technology was written for the following groups:

- Information Technology Professionals who want to build the needed relationships with each other and their business counterparts to insure software project success

- Information Technology Industry Professionals who want to build a successful career and better understand the business

- Information Technology Industry Professionals who have had technology problems in regards to peers in the workplace

- Information Technology Industry Professionals who want to overcome the stigma of past failed software projects and use that knowledge to make future projects a "win\win" for both IT and the business

- Business Professionals who deal with Information Technology on a regular basis who want to build the needed relationships with their IT counterparts to insure software project success

- Business Professionals who want a better understanding of IT

- Business and IT Professionals who want to get projects completed successfully to generate additional revenue and use that revenue to move to the next level of success.

- Business and IT professionals who ultimately want to evolve beyond the politics, greed, and bad decisions that ruin many professional relationships and continuously foster IT project failure.

- Business and IT professionals who want to use best practices, logic, and common sense to build the best possible technical solutions that will give their organizations the unfair advantage in their industries.

24

Chapter 1: INFORMATION PEOPLE

The IT Human Element

Information Technology should be called "Information People". Its people who ultimately design, plan, develop, implement, manage, support and destroy technology. People also create and solve all technology problems. There is no technology without people to create and consume it. People who work in the Information Technology industry are a largely misunderstood lot and in many cases by their own leaders and peers.

Information Technology departments are the places in most companies where one might go to find the "techies" or "geeks". Movies and television have perpetuated certain stereotypes of IT people over the years. Unfortunately, many IT people have done little to dissuade the media's negative stereotypes. At the center of the stereotypes are usually the Software Engineers or "Developers" as they are referred to internally. This unique group of employees traditionally has a reputation for being weird, geeks, difficult to work with, immature, rude, anti-social, and nerdy (just to name a few). They have also traditionally been the last group in most businesses that you would want to make angry or upset. In many companies, the Developer group's combined IQ level is mind boggling to say the least; however, sometimes it can also be overwhelmingly disappointing. Yet, many IT software projects usually run past their deadlines, are over budget, or fail altogether. IT Project failures can decimate a business or in some cases, destroy it but IT is generally the highest paid section of a business. Expectations and stress levels run high on many software projects, as the return on investment must significantly exceed the expense of the project in order to justify it.

There are those who believe that you can put a group of five or more extremely intelligent IT people in a room and they could design and build anything according to their skill sets. The truth of the matter is that in general, you might experience a technology ego war of epic proportions if you made this a regular practice. Many IT Software Engineers, Software System Architects, IT Directors and CIO's (Chief Information Officers) are primarily a group of highly stressed individuals who fight to keep up with ever changing software and hardware technologies. IT people deal with two critical constants on a technology level among many others. Those being:

1. **The less IT gives to the business, the less the business expects from IT.**

2. **The more IT gives to the business, the more the business wants and expects from IT.**

These basic rules seldom change. As a competing business strives to come up with new and more efficient technical ways to try and gain the "unfair advantage" in their corner of the industry, all other businesses must meet or beat the other's advances in order to survive.

Good IT departments within the industry are not democracies. In most cases, IT organizations are setup as dictatorships with only the stark illusion of a democracy from time to time. In the some of the worst IT shops, the chain of command is nothing more than a food chain with Software Engineers living at the bottom. In these "dog eat dog" workplaces, Software Engineers fear for their jobs the most. Confusion, mistrust, anxiety and bad management are ramped. If this type of IT environment achieves any level of success, it is usually minimal and or short-lived, and the Software Engineers involved generally do not get the credit they want and deserve. The IT turnover rate is high in these scenarios with little done by way of retention to keep the employees who actually add to value to the company.

I have worked with three businesses that have had "flat" IT management command structures. Two of the three company's IT Departments had been disorganized, and could almost be defined as chaotic. Communication was poor, there was no project plans, and even with regular meetings, no one knew what anyone else was doing. The third company's IT department had the same issues as the first two I mentioned. However, the difference was, at some point, a person stood up, took control of the anarchy, and then organized the team. The leader in effect, became the project manager. When this person took the reins, the other team members followed because of the strong and competent leadership displayed and the team eventually became more successful.

High School Diploma vs. College Degree

The buck stops here. In most cases, IT projects that fail are not lead by people with High School Diplomas. The same can also be said for the successful IT projects. However, what makes IT different from many other areas of an organization is that knowledge and experience are usually equally or more valued than a College Degree. While a College and or more advanced Degree in Computer Science may be preferred or necessary to achieve executive management status, it does not mean that individual is the best person for the job or that they will even be able do it. Many developers agree that some of the most talented among us only have only High School Diplomas, and these folks are generally not Executive Management. The same is also true that far too many IT employees with College Degrees are some of the most unreasonable and or senseless people in the industry. A surprisingly large number of IT people do not have Degrees that have anything to do with Computer Science. In my experience, I have known working IT people with Degrees in other fields such as:

- Finance

- Theology

- Psychology

- Geology

- Education
- Political Science
- Hospital Administration
- Art
- Music
- Journalism
- Business
- Law
- Marketing

It is quite possible that I have known IT people with more varied Degrees than the ones listed above. Some of the folks whom I have worked with that have held the Degrees listed above were very good at their IT jobs. Computer Science Degree or not, it all comes down to the individual and how competent they are.

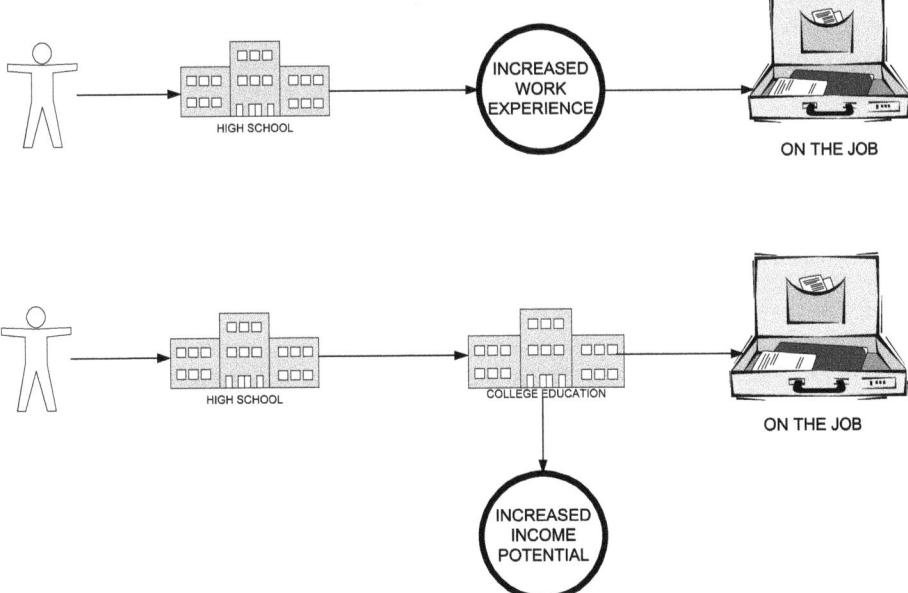

IT people are most often products of their environments. A mismanaged, chaotic, visionless IT environment generally produces employees of the same mindset through the process of basic submission. These employees may have tried to invoke change numerously through the years in their positions to no avail. Through this, some have become cynical, lacking the true belief that "real" change will happen during their tenure. Over a long period, they can no longer imagine a well-managed, organized, IT department with a clear vision that has a great chance of influencing its employees in a positive manner. It is important to note; if there is even one negative minded, malicious IT employee, the entire IT group is at risk. For example, a basket of fresh apples cannot make a rotten apple fresh again. The rotten apple always makes the other apples decay more quickly if not promptly removed. For people in general, this rule is the same and can have devastating results if left unmanaged.

IT Project success and failure begins and ends with people. Unfortunately, the IT industry still places most of its attention on the tools instead of the people who use them. Various metrics are utilized to identify why projects fail, and why projects succeed along with which tools are the best for any given task. You can have the best tools on this planet for a simple task and you will most likely fail in your project if you do not have the right people. Some say that if you do not hire the right people that is not a problem because you can train them later. I believe that is where most IT hiring people put the ROI (Return on Investment) at risk. It is true that we all have to learn somewhere and sometime, but the best IT people are hungry. If an exceptional IT person is not familiar with a tool or they do not have experience with a specific product, they will have to learn about it on their own time in order to stay competitive. That IT person cannot afford to wait for a company to hire them in order to get the experience they need with a tool. This sets the right person apart from the wrong person. Almost every company offers free demos of their development product(s) along with in-depth technical information. Using their demos, you can usually find out enough about a product to impress folks that might quiz you about it, that alone a job interviewer who might seek experience from you in regards to that same product. The best IT folks always stand out even if they have the desired experience or not. They are a thirsty lot, a self-motivated crowd that waits for no one to teach them what is new in technology and how it works. They always find out themselves first. Surprisingly, there are a number of people in the industry who are not technical. These folks just want to make a living like everyone else. Some are good people doing the best they can but many of them are not true IT people in regards to understanding the technology they work with. These people must be managed within a project correctly. In most of the projects that fail, you can usually trace the failure back to the wrong person in the wrong position making the wrong decisions. This is plain and simply an epidemic. Especially in Information Technology, where people are always the greatest asset and the greatest liability.

On every level in IT people are often different. They think on entirely different scales and their goals may be abstract. For instance, Software Engineers working at Startup business are primarily concerned with building an IT infrastructure for the company. The business may consist of ten to twenty employees. Developing that company's first commercial product is a primary agenda item. Other items on a Startups IT agenda might be:

- Building a company website

- Building a company intranet

- Building or enhancing existing software to meet specific and or critical business needs

- Building a company culture

- Building a positive industry presence

Either way, the mindset is that of getting the business technology of the ground and starting a good culture within the company, which can be a difficult thing to do at any level. While on the other hand, an Enterprise businesses IT department may be gearing up to refactor an application that has been in use for three years or more that affects five to ten thousand concurrent users. The IT infrastructure is already in place and the IT department consists of seventy or more Software Engineers. Time is generally a major concern in this scenario as training thousands of existing users will have to take place among other tasks such as:

- Gathering project requirements

- Building a project plan

- Building a project team

There is one common denominator in Information Technology and is shared by every employee on all levels. That common denominator is revenue. Money is the primary driving force behind almost every business IT project. On each level of business, money shapes how information technology projects are executed and anything else is rarely viewed as being more important. The more money you have to spend on a project, the more risk is involved. With increased revenue, the more successful the project has the potential to become.

The Enterprise Level IT Environment

Generally, and enterprise level business can have tens thousands of employees all over the world. Depending upon how large an enterprise business is the IT department could have hundreds or more developers. Software projects at this level could also have many hundreds of IT and business people working together in different offices, regions, or countries.

One of the biggest enterprise projects that I worked was a CRM (Customer Relational Management) implementation for a global company. The software was to be implemented in Ireland, England, India, and the United States. The Project team consisted of Business and IT employees from all of the aforementioned nations. After I joined the project, I learned from another employee that our project was not the first to try to achieve our objective. A year prior, another IT CRM project team had been assembled and failed to meet the objectives the first time. On the current team, I was working as a Senior Programmer\Analyst along with two others who held the same titles as I. The three of us started searching for any documentation that remained from the previously failed project. On an obscure server, buried in unrelated files, we found a directory of documents containing information about the previous project. To our surprise at that time, most of the documentation in those directories was embarrassingly poorly written. In addition, for the size of the former project, there were little more than six or seven documents remaining. It was our speculation at that time that, in order to avoid any shame, the previous regime might have made it a point to hide or destroy any evidence of their demise.

There were at least three employees that I was aware of that were from the previous project who were now working on the current project with us. The other programmer analysts and I had problems with the previous project employees who were now on the team. The previous project employees seemed to have a personal stake in the success of the current project and tried to gain control of meetings and discussions whenever possible. After several months of working on the project, I found that I was then working in an intensely political environment. New project employees began showing up every two weeks. Approximately every six weeks after my first two months of service, a Project Manager was fired by senior management or quit the project voluntarily. I began to spend more time in meetings than working on my project tasks as my time in meetings averaged three to five hours a day. After awhile, I found myself spending the major part of my non-meeting time bringing new project managers up to speed on the internal workings of the corporate mess.

Enterprises businesses are tough IT environments to work and survive in. Many employees can tend to feel like things and not people in climates such as these. However, many IT employees love this environment and being a part of a huge team. Although not all Enterprise level IT projects are big, for some, there is a great deal of security to be had working for an enterprise level company. The rewards of a successful project on this level can lead to significant bonuses, grand promotions, senior management recognition or nothing at all. The competition on this tier can be, and is most often fierce, as special recognition can also be quite rare for the individual.

The Big Business Level IT Environment

At this level, a company's employee count could range from five hundred to thousands of employees. Depending on the organization's business model, the company is gearing up to take a step into the enterprise realm. In many businesses at this level, there are major projects currently underway to make that happen. This can be a seriously tense IT environment as they try to stay the course while attempting to move the company up to the next level. A big IT project at this point in a company life cycle is usually a make or break project and jobs are on the line in IT and the business.

My experience with a company trying to make the move to enterprise was a primarily a lesson in politics. The business invested tens of millions of dollars in a huge IT project geared towards moving the company to enterprise and the project was a failure in the fact that the company still had the very same IT limitations as they did before the project began. They had achieved no real objectives through their technological efforts. I refer to this project as "Little Washington, D.C." due to its high level of political competitiveness, gridlock, and waste. Everyone had an agenda and these goals clashed constantly in meetings and on everyday tasks. This environment was an IT soap opera with all of the respective actors, and I was caught up in the stage with all of the drama. This was one of my biggest professional mistakes to play this game of politics. I learned more about IT working on "Little Washington, D.C." than I have on any other project that I had ever been a part of thus far.

"Little Washington, D.C." affected my IT personality a great deal and forced me to deal with people and the business in a whole new light. I was able to see firsthand the negative affect dark politics had in a big business IT department. The affects were devastating to the project and team in regards to the resulting power plays. The IT department became more about who could grab the most power than completing actual project with success. This was the dark side of projects that some people know all too well and try to avoid.

I have had other experiences working with big business IT departments that were creative, fun, and successful. Either this was a time in IT where creativity was welcomed, or it was usually a "stay the course" environment in which a big change was not warranted to reach enterprise. This stage is where IT stars are created. It is where the hardest pushes in technology for a company must be considered, planned, managed, and implemented only if necessary. Many companies die in this stage, and IT are the culprits that killed them in too many instances. Trust at this level from a business towards IT is in many cases hanging by a thread as the business looks towards technology to give them the tool(s) they need to compete on the next level. IT career friends and enemies are made at this point, and many of those people you might never forget for the rest of your life, even if you want to.

The Small Business Level IT Environment

Small businesses make up the bulk of all businesses in the United States. I have worked with many small businesses over the years and they have been a critical training ground for me. Some companies had as little as ten employees and others had as many as a hundred and fifty people. This is usually a hardworking environment with IT employees taking on various roles as needed.

Although the goal of a large number of small businesses is to become big businesses, some small businesses are very happy to stay that way. These companies are not interested in competing in larger arenas and their business models are more focused towards a particular niche. The companies that are successful in this endeavor have generally become very adept at making a good deal of money without threatening big businesses. They are able to operate under the radar and avoid having big businesses move in a take a piece of the action or all of it.

There are many IT napoleon complexes in this realm with valid excuses as to why. Some of the reasons for this are:

- Many successful years of successfully exploiting a niche

- The ability to offer better customer service than bigger businesses that may want a piece of the action

- Gaining the trust and loyalty of the business

- Having developed well-oiled IT processes that are time proven and validated

Small business IT can be a tough environment because many are "family or friend-based" arenas. One small business that I consulted with consisted 80% of employees that had known each other for approximately twenty years or more. Being a consultant in and environment like this was a new experience for me. The employees were some of the nicest folks I had ever met but the feeling around the company was very "cult like" and a bit scary. The owners were of a "new age" mentality and very suspicious of people in general who did not share their "unique" outlook completely, which left me too wonder about them far too often. However, I agreed with and found many of their ideas refreshing, especially some of the owner's view regarding traditional IT shops and their employees. The owner was outwardly critical of IT shops that were not like his "new age", free spirited, flat managed company to a fault. Ironically, he not could see that he was acting like the people he criticized and ultimately hated. There was no influencing this tightly controlled environment without the CIO changing his mind voluntarily, and that did not seem likely while I was consulting with that particular company.

Small businesses are a great environment because of the extreme differences that exist on this tier. Small businesses are some of the best training environments for new IT employees because they deal with many of the same problems as their larger counterparts. Critical IT project deadlines, new technology, and customer support are paramount at this level as well as the larger tiers. The bureaucracy may not be as intense in this realm, which may provide some IT employees a chance to breathe while they learn and grow. However, some may argue that smaller technical environments can be even more stifling with little room for error.

The Startup Level IT Environment

Working to get a business off the ground is one of the toughest tasks to accomplish. Sometimes ranging from one to fifty employees, the startup business phase is most often a trying and stressful experience and one of the most creative. It is a fact that most new companies are unsuccessful. Many fail due to insufficient capital and or improper business planning. The birth of IT in a new business can often be sheer chaos. Depending on the company, a brand new IT department can go in many different directions. This environment is not for the faint of heart. Overtime, uncertainty, and new challenges are the norm. In some cases, receiving your paycheck on time or even at all is just a part of the job and definitely not the good part.

I am going to explore this topic in more detail than the others for the following reasons:

- I have worked for five different startups so far in my career. All of the startup companies that I have worked for had different missions but started out with many of the same problems.

- Most companies never make it past the "Startup" stage largely due to inadequate financing.

- IT Startup environments are the usually the most chaotic IT environments because those companies are trying hard to establish themselves.

The first startup I ever worked with was a small consulting company. The owners left a larger company that they were working for and took several other employees with them to start their company. At the time that I signed on, they were in desperate need of a Software Engineer. Their employees were generally nice but somewhat aloof. I worked for them for several months but decided to move on due to their inability to pay me the salary negotiated on my contract when I joined the company. In addition, this particular company lacked a cohesive vision and the financial foundation to expand. They had the same number of people when I joined the company as when I left the company.

The second startup I worked with was an "integrity challenged" environment from the very beginning. This was yet again another consulting company. The Principal's primary focus was to squeeze as much overtime out of their employees as possible to further their own economic success, which is not unusual by any means. This is essentially the goal of a great deal of businesses, but this particular company lacked the necessary tact in making its startup employees feel like they had a share in that company's future potential successes. The biggest problem with this business was that group of owners left their former employer where they had comprised their previous IT department. This is because their former employer, an Enterprise company at the time, was forced to hire these folks back as their new IT consulting company after they left due to the fact they were the former core intellectual property owners. This consulting company's first client was a reluctant and unhappy one for good reasons because their former employees, who were now their new consultants, basically held them hostage. Like many of the startups that I worked for, this company was in desperate need of a Human Resources Department or at least an HR representative. The company's principle lack of integrity would to trickle down to the employee level on many occasions. The absence of expertise in this area created a serious liability for the Principals and exposed an inept level of competence in the regards to how employees, and along with their own clients, were treated.

In the late nineties, during the now famous "Dotcom" era, I was offered what I thought was a great contract with a Dotcom startup with serious potential. This company had leadership with a clear vision and a business plan that relied on developing innovative technology. The IT team at this company was one of the most intelligent and finest that I have ever worked with. The IT team worked like a well-oiled machine to deliver one of the first products of its kind. A secure electronic Internet content delivery software application. This was an amazing environment where I gained a tremendous amount of education regarding Information Technology and how to work as a team and independently within this realm. This company was very significant to my career because at that time, I made a crucial decision that would affect the rest of my IT career. That decision was a simple yet pivotal one. At that time, I was a Senior Developer and not working on anything of any consequence on the project. A call went out from the CIO to the Development Team for a volunteer to work on a critical piece of the current project, it's Business Rules Engine (BRE). A day went by and no one answered the CIO's challenge. I struggled within myself to answer the call as I questioned my skill set and technical ability to meet this challenge at that time. The Development Team had a stronger belief in my ability to perform this task than I did and some began to question why I did not stand up and accept the critical task. I was in a situation that I did not care for, I was between a rock and a diamond, and it was time for me to "put up" or "shut up" technologically. After serious thought and consideration, I then emailed the CIO and carbon copy the entire team that I would write the Rules Engine component of the application for the project. I promptly purchased the technical books that I needed to ramp up on the issue at hand, and tackled the assignment head on. I successfully completed the design, coding, and implementation of the Ruled Engine component. The rest is history. To this day, I have the respect of the team members of that project that I am still in contact with and was hired to several other projects as a result. That project forever changed how I think of technical ability, skill sets, resolve, and mentality in relation to technical challenges. My new positive outlook and unwillingness to hide behind a façade opened a brand new world of thought and provocation that inspired me to always do my best and to help others on my team to do the same. I was not interested in feeding my ego but maintaining the level of confidence that everyone needs in order to reach for their goals, stay focused and not give up.

The Players

When choosing the members of any Information Technology Team, politics and friendships in making the team selections, and the members that are evaluated for hire can be a dangerous liaison. If the Manager doing the hiring is able to keep an objective outlook and hire team members who did a good or great job then that generally works out best for the team. However, in many cases, some IT managers tend to hire people that either they know well, look good on paper, test well, or just people they "trust". These may not always be the best people for the job at hand, and can lead to serious political problems later down the road with that project. For instance, I worked for a large company that hired a consultant who was a friend of the Director of Development. They paid the consultant almost three times as much as the Senior Developer who was the Team Lead, and the consultant only worked approximately two to three days per week. This consultant also wrote very poor software, which after code reviews, lead other Developers on the team to question the consultant's competency as a Software Developer. The consultant was allowed to manage full-time employees at the company, and make decisions in regards to the project that he was never held accountable for. This lead to poor team morale, along with several volatile confrontations between team members and that particular consultant.

Another example of a bad hiring practice is a job interview that I conducted in which the company was searching for a Database Administrator. I knew that the person being interviewed for the position was someone that the owners of the company that I was working with wanted to hire regardless of the results of the interview. This was because they had worked with this candidate previously and had developed a personal relationship with them that had nothing to do with how good of a Database Administrator they might be. I was very careful during that particular interview. In addition, I did discover through my interview with the person that the candidate's skill set was not up to par with that of even a Junior Database Administrator and that the person in question would not be a good fit for the position. After the interview, I relayed this information to my Principals and they hired candidate regardless of my recommendations. A month later, that same company hired a new IT Director who was also a former boss and family friend of the newly hired Database Administrator. Soon after, one of my Principals informed me that the newly hired Database Administrator had complained that I "talked down" to them and that made them "feel bad". This made for a very uncomfortable working environment for me in particular when I was only doing my job. Because this person was not qualified for the position in which they were hired, they had to undergo constant "on the job" training that added to the stress of the team and impeded the progress of the project significantly.

The main point here is that the IT players can be a very volatile crew, and personal relationships in this arena can be a "double edged" sword. There were some friends that I have worked with in the past who were awesome Engineers and easy to get along with. However, others took advantage of my friendship, and did not do the best job that they could manage at the time because they thought they could get away with that. This hurt our friendship and forced me to re-evaluate my views in regards to working with friends in an IT or any other work-based environment. IT Players need to be selected in a manner in which trust and friendship are weighed equally along with qualifications and experience. One way to accomplish this is evaluating a candidate's over ability to produce in difficult environments, insisting upon good and unbiased references (even from the candidates that you know), using objective job interviewers (not you), and then taking their advice.

IT Organization Charts

IT Organizational Charts vary from company to company dependent upon the size and mission of the specific organization. The following Organizational Chart is intended to provide an example of how a large company or even an enterprise may be structured.

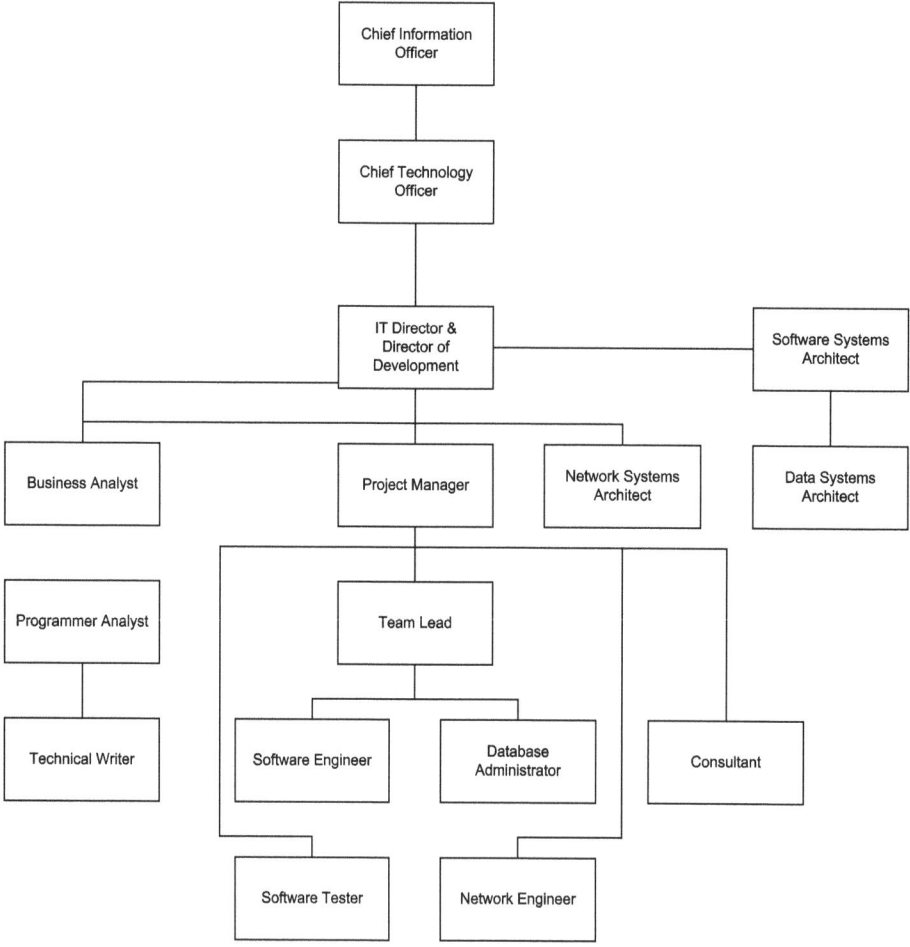

CIO

This Chief Information Officer is responsible for the leadership and strategy of a company's ability to deliver information and along with its assets. CIO's must possess expertise in high-level technology, their business, their respective industry, and be able to deal equally with all entities. A company that that hires a CIO makes visible commitment to focus on the most efficient IT management attainable. This executive position establishes a visible mission to support how information is:

- **Acquired**
- **Handled**
- **Supported**
- **Delivered**

CIOs can help different companies in various ways. The benefits that a CIO provides to a company largely rely on the reason why the company hired them initially.

CTO

This is an executive in relation to the CIO and this office is generally established at a medium to large organization. CTOs (Chief Technical Officer) report to CIOs. A CTO directs the use of technology in company-developed software and the technology based services that are sold to clients. In most cases, a CTO is more technical than a CIO. Since a CTOs primary focus is on that of technology and not the business, the CTO can place more attention on technological research and development that helps the business make better choices.

IT Director

This executive position is to plan and direct the Information Technology of a company, including the implementation and management of information processing systems, networks, office automation, and telephony and telecommunications systems. IT Directors also manage information technology purchasing, facilities, equipment, space, staffing and training. They also oversee and ensure that IT processes and software are developed and implemented in a logical manner.

Software System Architect

The Software System Architect is a relatively new position in the IT community. The roles and responsibilities of a Software System Architect vary significantly from business to business. Like building Architects, the Software System Architect's task is to design and facilitate the creation of software based on requirements. IT Software System Architects design software systems to meet human needs. They also write the standards documentation that Software Engineers follow when developing a product.

As a member of the World Wide Institute of Software Architects (WWISA), I subscribe largely to their definition of a Software System Architect's roles and responsibilities. I see their definition as a logical one and they explained it in a simple and clear manner.

Below, this definition is described in more detail and the same is also posted on the WWISA website (http://www.wwisa.org/wwisamain/role.htm):

- *PHASE 1: Pre-Design Phase*

  The architect listens to understand the scope of the project, the client's key design points, requirements, and expectations. The architect also studies the context of the project - the entire enterprise of which the project is a part. Client resources are assessed, such as the financial and intellectual capital available, and the problems the client needs to resolve. The architect identifies possible solutions available through technology and organizational, management, and product changes. A design direction begins to take shape, with the architect and client collaborating and refining their understanding until a shared vision emerges. Broad budget and schedule objectives are set.

- *PHASE 2: Domain Analysis*

  The architect undertakes to thoroughly understand and document the areas (domains) for which the system will be built and to learn the client requirements in detail. The desired behaviors of the system are outlined. The architect assesses the client's business and technology environment, and the interplay with scope. The domain terms and concepts are accurately defined.

- *PHASE 3: Schematic Design*

  Architectural-level designs depicting the domain characteristics and technology structure are prepared. The look and feel of the system - user interface style - is designed. Prototypes are built at this point, if they are needed. Migration and risk assessments are performed.

- *PHASE 4: Design Development*

  The architect continues the expansion of detail and design refinement to converge on the final design. All the domain and technology design drawings - that is, what the client needs to validate that the requirements are met - are finalized at this stage.

- *PHASE 5: Projects Documentation*

  The architect focuses on the requirements of those who will construct the system. The construction process, the roles of the team members, and the construction sequences are documented. The construction guide, user interface style guide, and test guide are written. The architect specifies tools and methodologies, as needed. All the details needed by those who will build the system are completed.

- *PHASE 6: Staffing of Contracting*

    The architect assists in identifying the actual builders of the system. For projects that are outsourced, bids are submitted to outside contractors and potential participants are evaluated. The architect assists with contract details and in assessing cost. Sequences are arranged and contracts signed.

- *PHASE 7: Construction*

    The architect's supervisory role during construction ensures that the client's vision is understood and executed. The architect reviews construction-level designs to the degree dictated by the complexity and vicissitudes of the construction process. The architect conducts design reviews and analyzes problems and change requests. The architect designs the accepted changes, assesses the impact on overall design and cost, and sequences the changes. The architect participates in testing and acceptance reviews to the extent the client desires.

- *PHASE 8: Post Construction*

    The architect assists the client with the project rollout and the migration to the new system. The architect can be involved with the training of system operators and users, as needed. The architect assists in warranty issues and ongoing maintenance procedures.

For more information about the World Wide Institute of Software Architects, go to their website:

http://www.wwisa.com

Data Architect

Data Architects develop data related architectures that increase a company's revenues in many of the following ways:

- By providing accessible, integrated data

- Improving productivity through efficient and effective management of data

- Create and document the data architecture through the gathering of requirements and existing data related processes from business and or client users

- Facilitate and document discussions on appropriate business data and its usage

- Ensure all data related components are properly created, integrated, implemented, and managed

- Coach the IT team on the value and implications of data, its use, and ramifications

- Educate users on the value of data and its associated attributes

- Provide support and verify quality assurance and data integrity through all stages of implementation

Network Architect

The Network Architect designs the business computer network. This includes but is not limited to:

- All computer hardware and its security

- Network related software

- Network access methods and protocols

Usually, a network engineering team must exist from the initial start of a company that plans to use IT Services. In light of this, The Network Architect may reside within this primary team and be an intricate part of the overall Architecture team.

The Network Architect focuses on the lower-level transport protocols and the standards and technologies for enabling system qualities via network command and control structures. They evaluate, select and purchase the company's networking hardware and software while managing the overall network topology. The Network Architect designs, builds, implements, and manages the network operation center (NOC) command and control structures for network event monitoring and trouble ticketing.

Project Manager

A Project Manager's job is primarily that of a servant and politician. A Project Manager's sole purpose is to does whatever it takes to make sure that IT Team members have the tools and environment they need to get their tasks completed. They constantly work to resolve issues that may negatively affect a team's productivity and ability to meet their timelines. A Project Manager should be unobtrusive and only visible when problems with the team arise. Without a good Project Management, the risk of a team missing project deadlines and the project going over budget increase dramatically. Usually on small projects, Project Managers deal directly with all members of the software development team. With many larger projects, there is often a lead developer or lead analyst to report directly to the Project Manager. This role should never be taken lightly as this person must be good at doing many different jobs simultaneously, organized, deadline driven, work well with others, and be a solid communicator.

Traditionally, the Project Manager spends a lot of time in meetings with the business as well as some technical ones in which many try to avoid. Some liken this role to the Conductor of a Symphony Orchestra, who keeps the timing of the musical composition and ensures that all of the musicians start and end playing what they are supposed to at the right times. It can be almost impossible to have a successful project with a poor Project Manager, although it must happen on rare occasions, that is a team I would work hard to avoid.

Team Lead

A Team Leader actively participates in the work of the IT Team by assisting the Project Manager and or the Software System Architect. The Team Leader manages the team's work on a lower level, allocates resources, and resolve complex technical problems requiring a high degree of knowledge of a specific interest. A Team Leader provides advice on technical issues and or technical direction that is significant to the software's specific programming or overall functionality.

They also must have well-developed and reasonable personality, communication skills, and political savvy with the ability to figure out complex technical issues. Decisions made at this level may have a major impact on the operation of a Software Project. Team Leads could be required to represent the company on specialized information in regards to technical issues related to the software project.

IT Business Analyst

The IT Business Analyst ensures that the company software systems are physically strong enough to handle the current and future business requirements. They must have a comprehensive understanding of complex business processes from an IT perspective. This is necessary to create and or recommend solutions or upgrades to the processes in question. The IT Business Analyst must be able to assist with large and sometimes difficult software application implementations. They should know their industries inside and out and always be aware of what the competition is doing in order to better position their businesses for the proper innovations that could potentially give them the unfair advantage. Good analysts are usually intelligent and creative people with a passion for understanding how processes work and how to make them better.

It is important to stress that the Business Analyst is one of the most important people in the software development process. They are the gatekeepers of the business processes and in most cases, advise management as to whether or not a software project should even be attempted to begin with. This advisory position in a business can save a company a great deal of revenue if implemented and utilized properly. Analysts can be very effective when organized into small structured teams of three to five team members that report to an analytical managing entity.

Chapter 1: INFORMATION PEOPLE

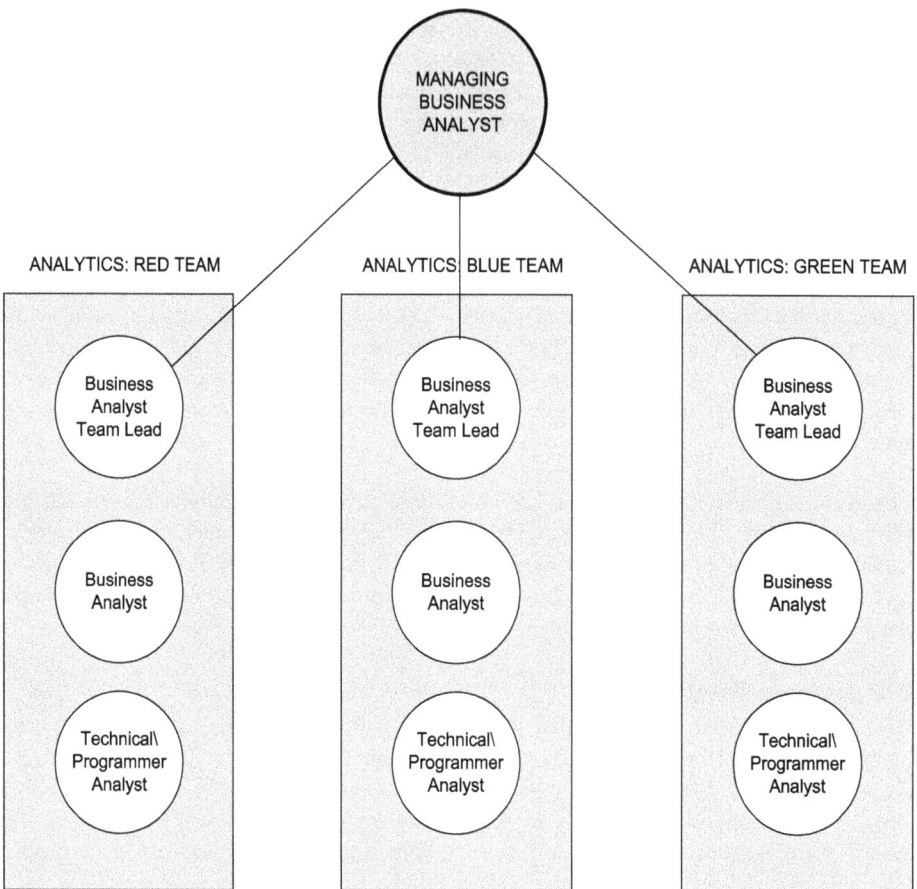

The diagram above is dynamic and can be adapted to almost any size of business. An analytical team of this structure can scale as a company grows and be reconfigured for various types of tasks.

Below are some examples of how different analytical teams can be utilized within a business:

- **Analytics RED Team** – Exclusive Tasks: Work with IT Development Team to assess business needs in regards to new Software Applications

- **Analytics BLUE Team** – Exclusive Tasks: Assess industry past and current trends Document and Report findings on a weekly basis

- **Analytics GREEN Team** – Exclusive Tasks: Focus on Research and Development. Work with Architecture team on new ideas, innovations, and intellectual property

The IT Business Analyst will assess new and current client needs, and document client and business requirements and processes. They will also produce and update Functional Specifications, use case, and other process oriented documentation. The Business Analyst will know everything about the business and is a liaison and translator between the business and IT. They are also the company librarians, brain trust, and industry experts.

Programmer\Analyst

The Programmer\Analyst provides technical software systems analysis as well as develops and implements new and or existing software systems. Programmer\Analysts work to improve business software systems and assist with the testing of those systems. Their analysis helps to develop new tools and resources needed by software system users.

This analyst will also work with or also be a part of the Software System Architecture Team. Technological Research and Development are an area of focus and in some cases a primary task. In addition, this Analyst is an important liaison to the Business in regards to the IT Development Team. They help to translate the language of technology into the language of business. This is a vital part of the communications process in an age where many businesses still view the language of technology as ancient Latin.

Database Administrator

The Database Administrator is responsible for the design and management of data systems. This role implements database software and related utilities that meets the business requirements outlined by the company's Data Architect and Business Analyst.

It is important to note that the Database Administrator is the keeper of the company's raw information. They make sense of all data that is aggregated by Software Systems. This is a crucial part of the Business Analyst Team and requires accurate reports in order to make the right business decisions. If a financial report is not correct, the repercussions could lead to additional revenue loss. For example, if an accounts receivable IT Development report shows significant losses over the last several quarters, a CFO (Chief Financial Officer) may decide to restrict or cut revenue from the IT budget. However, if that report was inaccurate, IT funds for an important development project that could enhance ROI may not be awarded the finances to be initiated.

Chapter 1: INFORMATION PEOPLE

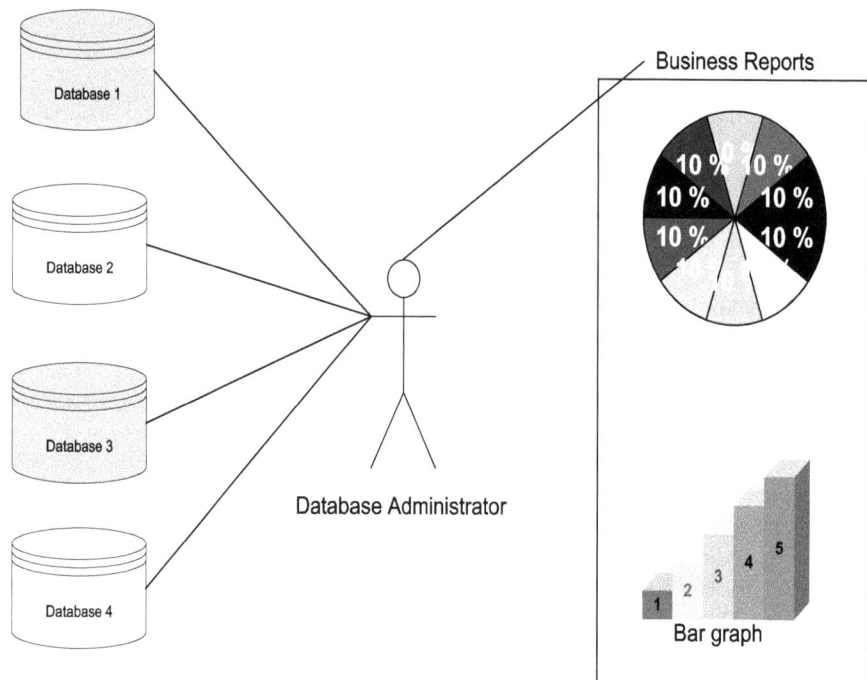

Network Engineer

The Network Engineer is responsible for the implementation and support of Local and Wide Area Networks (LANs and WANs). Network engineers usually work to implement large heterogeneous networks based on the design and requirements provided by the Network Architect, and have significant expertise in implementing and administering network hardware and software.

Software Tester

The Software Tester's primary focus is on how a software application might be used. Any personal views that a Software Tester might have about how to use the application that they are testing are irrelevant. The business requirements must be tested, not opinions. The Software Tester's creates test plans and scenarios from documented business requirements that work to expose unhandled software application errors. They work with Software Engineer usually in an iterative fashion in order to correct errors before an application reaches the production environment and is consumed by the business.

Generally, a Software Engineer is only as good as their Testing Team. A Software Engineer cannot correct bugs that they do not know exist. Software Testing Teams that derived sound testing process and who pay attention to detail are the front lines for a company when it comes to Quality Assurance in software performance.

Technical Writer

The Technical Writer is responsible for authoring hardware and software documentation for a company's in-house software systems or in some cases for third-party vendors. The Technical Writer's primary responsibility is to produce documentation for the user. The produced documentation's foremost goal is to help or teach the user how to work with a software application. Technical writers must have a strong understanding of technology and superb writing and communication skills.

Technical Writers also create the training materials that is used to teach users. Naturally, this information must be accurate as the repercussions of inaccurate documentation on users can lead to faulty data aggregation. This problem can then further progress to reports being unreliable and business decisions being made from those reports.

Without documentation, there is no written history. We learn from the written word, which is passed down from generation to generation. Software Development projects are no different. It is critical in many cases to have a document describing the "why" and "how" things came to be in a company in regards to its technology and overall processes. This written history is important for analytics and can be used to assist in decision making in order to avoid making the same mistakes repeatedly. Making the correct decisions the first time in business based on the errors of the past can save a great deal of time and money.

The IT Consultant

IT Consultants (or 3rd Party Contractors) are not employees of the companies that hire them and must never be treated as such for reasons of state and federal law and logic. Their tasks can vary significantly and can include any of the job descriptions listed previously and then some. Consultants are generally hired to help because there may be regions of a project where significant gaps in resources, experience or tools exist and cannot facilitate certain critical tasks. In addition, the extra help may not be needed on a permanent basis so outsourcing specific jobs could be deemed logical from a revenue standpoint. In many companies, IT consultants are some of the least respected members of the IT Team while being the most experienced and knowledgeable concurrently. This can put a noticeable strain on the business\consultant relationship for many reasons.

The following are some of the reasons why:

- Consultants are usually paid higher salaries than permanent company employees.

- When a project is a success Consultants share largely in that success. If the project is outsourced, Consultants can get all of the credit for that project.

- When a project fails, Consultants are free to move on to a new project while the IT Team employees have to stay and deal with the business repercussions.

- Consultants are hired on a temporary basis to fill a void in the IT Team for a given project. However, many consultants hired for short term projects end up working for the companies that hired them for years or in some cases, indefinitely.

Software Engineer

IT Software Engineers build company or commercial software from business requirements. The Software Engineer has been historically the most difficult position to work with in the IT Department. IT Management has often described working with Software Engineers as "Herding Cats". This is because cats like to do what they want to do when they want to do it, with few or no exceptions. Software Engineers are very similar, and are a very creative group. They often feel about the software applications that they write with the same pride and affection as an artist would a painting or in many cases, how a mother or father might feel about a child.

Software Engineers have a strong effect on society as the programs they write are integrated deeply into our daily lives. Some software applications require forethought like for instance, using an ATM machine. Other software programs do not solicit thought, such as the software systems that are invoked when you start a new sports car. The level of control that is given to Software Engineers in this respect is enormous. Generally, society does not question the software that runs the hardware they use everyday. By in large, the software, and the hardware that runs it is drastically underutilized and its far-reaching effects are not fully realized. Hollywood has long been keen on showing the public where our Information Technology endeavors can lead us. Movie trilogies like "Terminator" and "The Matrix" paint a picture of a bleak future where the software and hardware technologies that humans created eventually become "self aware" and begin see humans as inferior. These scenarios right now are Science Fiction and make for great entertainment. However, many Software Engineers have been, and are currently, working on projects that are leading up to making some of our worst science fiction, "computers taking over the world", fears a reality.

Software Engineers are strong "on the fly" decision makers and can make hundreds or even thousands of decisions in the course of developing a software application depending on the size of the project.

There are many variables to consider in the design stage of a software project, for example:

- What are the Business Requirements?

- Will the software be an internal or external facing application?

- What are the security concerns?

- What other software applications will the primary product need to communicate with and what are the hardware requirements?

- Will the software application be a client or web application?

- Which Operating System will be used or does it matter?

- Which development language is best for the project?

- What will the project timeline look like?

- Which Software System Architecture: Is it best to use a Design Pattern?

- How must the project be documented?

- Which development methodology is best for the project?

The above are only a few questions that need to be answered before and during the life cycle of a development project. These questions only scratch the surface and the underlying questions that accompany this list are numerous and are equally, if not more, important. Software Development is a highly specialized, technical, skill that requires a great deal of patience, tenacity, analytical ability, and time. You do not necessarily need to be a genius to be a great Software Engineer, although some intelligence does help significantly.

The stress factors for Software Engineers are can be significant. After the project budgeting, planning, provisioning, meetings, and analytics, it comes down to the Software Engineers ability to build the application within the specified timeline designated. If the software cannot be built and or implemented, the project will fail. This is the bottom line and the final truth. Nothing else about the project matters if the primary business requirement objectives cannot be met.

Software Engineer Personality Types
Software Engineers are an eclectic group of individuals who are generally difficult to understand. Like all highly specialized, industry specific workers, they have distinct trade personalities. I have attempted to break down the most common personality types from this group in to six basic categories. These sub-sections describe on a high level the behaviors of most of the Software Engineers you are likely to encounter. In most cases, you can get an idea of which type of Software Engineer you are working with by being patient and studying

their behavior. It is also very likely that you may meet or inadvertently have to work with Software Engineers who are a combination of two or more of the personality types listed.

It is always good to know what type(s) of Software Engineer you are working with or which kind may be on your team. Analyze these Team Members carefully. In some cases, the results of the analytics in regards to the Engineers on your team will give you a good indicator as to how your software may work internally and may be supported after implementation. It is important to note that there are many combinations of the Software Engineer personality types described. Be careful not to try to group all Software Engineers into just one or two categories, as this may be somewhat rare for many IT environments. However, it is possible to have an IT department that is comprised of a particular type of Software Engineer based on specific hiring preferences and guidelines but there is usually an exception to the rule when it comes to personality traits in this area.

The Artistic

This Software Engineer most likely is a strong music lover and plays one or more musical instruments. They may also play or have played in a band and would gladly give up their technical careers for a future playing music. This is usually a secret dream. This Engineer is also an expressive person and it shows in their code. They generally do not follow the crowd and have a strong identity or work hard in some way to have one. Most Software Engineers are artistic in one way or another and seek this career path as a means of expression.

The Egocentric

This Software Engineer sees themselves as a smarter and more experienced Engineer than most others in their Development department. No matter whom you may be or what you have done, this Engineer has some advice for you on how you can do things better. They are very much into working the politics of the business and strongly lobby members of the IT leadership whom they think are most likely use their ideas and further their causes. Leadership is the ultimate goal for this Engineer and anyone who stands in his or her way should be ready for war. They also have a strong sense of "self entitlement".

The Realist

This Software Engineer usually has a plan rooted in logic and time tested processes. They will not agree with or adhere to ambiguous technology strategies or "wild, wild, west" cowboy\cowgirl development methodologies. This Engineer is not a risk taker and is more concerned with having a job tomorrow than trying out the "next big trend" in software development during a project. New technology must make sense always to this Engineer or they are not going to use it. They are astute and driven primarily by certain experiences.

The Caretaker

This Software Engineer puts themselves in a position help other team members. They are usually popular and the well-liked members of the development team. In some cases, these

Engineers are abused by way of other team members in regards to assumptions that they will perform tasks that most other team members don't want to do. By in large, this Software Engineer is often one of the most trusted members of the development team.

The Politician
This Software Engineer is more interested in building strategic alliances within the business than they are working with technology. This Engineers goal is ultimately to move up the corporate latter to the executive realm. A large part of the time, this Engineer does the least amount of work on the team and in many cases shares significantly in any project milestones and successes. Primarily a people person, this engineer is deft at picking and winning their IT wars, battles, and partnerships. They are always watching, analyzing, and thinking about whom and what they are going to use to get to the next level of where they need to be.

The Conservative
This Software Engineer believes that the current technology is great because they feel they have reached an expert level with it and do not want the current technology to change due to their comfort level. Change is feared, because it generally means that they have to step outside of their "safety zone". Learning a new technology or process is unattractive and threatens their current way of life. This Engineer is usually the last to learn new technology and in many cases the most skeptical of new technology because they don't know anything about it or may not even want to understand it. They weigh primarily of the side of "newer does not always mean better" and generally do not have the proper mentality for Information Technology.

The Human n-Tier Diagram
The n-tier (n = 3 or more) Software Design Architecture has been a popular and successful model for software development to emerge from the client-server era. In short, a tier (or sometimes called a layer) is referred to as a group of objects that work together to meet a subset of requirements. These objects are autonomous, and work in relation with other independent objects in other tiers to fulfill an umbrella or parent requirements list.

I have developed a diagram that shows IT People in an n-Tier setting. When a particular architecture is successful and is able to withstand the test of time there is a good chance that it can be utilized in areas other than where it was initially conceived. If people use software and are productive in their tasks, then their processes should further enhance that software.

The following is a diagram of how information people can do just that:

USER INTERFACE TIER	ANALYTICAL TEAM: MANAGING ANALYST BUSINESS ANALYST PROGRAMMER ANALYST (REQUIREMENT GATHERING)
APPLICATION TIER	DEVELOPMENT TEAM: SOFTWARE SYSTEMS ARCHITECT PROJECT MANAGER TEAM LEAD SOFTWARE ENGINEER (BUILD SOFTWARE FROM REQUIREMENTS)
DATA TIER	DATABASE TEAM: DATA ARCHITECT DATABASE ADMINISTRATOR (MANAGE DATA BASED ON REQUIREMENTS)

The User Interface Tier is the primary area where information is aggregated and displayed by the Analytical Team. The Application Tier is where software is designed, coded, tested, and implemented by Software Developers. The Data Tier is where Database Teams process and store aggregated information for corporate reporting systems and business intelligence.

Summary

One of the many common misconceptions about Information Technology by non-IT individuals is that if a person works in IT, they do not have to deal with employees in other departments very often. This is no longer the case. Software Engineer and business employee silos were largely the case from the 1950s through the mid 1990s. Since then, new software methodologies and technology has exploded and expanded at a rapid pace and has forced increased collaboration between the business and IT. New software processes have been created and implemented to support enhanced technology and business process relationships. Because technology constantly changes, and organizations must stay on the cutting edge of technology in order to stay competitive in their industries, new requirements for IT had emerged. These updated requirements in most cases demanded that projects be implemented faster and more effectively to save time and money. This meant that sometimes communications had to be optimized, and Software Engineers had to work directly with their business partners to get the requirements they needed to complete their assigned tasks. Traditionally, Software Engineers are not trained to estimate, gather and document software requirements and have to learn this vast new skill on the job. This has placed a considerable strain on IT projects as this gap often goes unaddressed due to time and or financial constraints, which creates somewhat of a paradox. A vast number of Software Engineers should never be made to work with business users because they don't have the inter-personal skills for it. Furthermore, any business that assumes that untrained individuals can successfully gather, document, and maintain business requirements may not have the good sense to build anything correctly. The following old saying is an important truth in this regard:

Never argue with an idiot, they will only bring you down to their level and then beat you with experience.

Many businesses and IT Departments are constantly trying to find new and better ways to work together as this marriage is essential for technological success in most organizations. It is extremely important to understand that technology is nothing without people just as the personal computer is just a box of junk without the electricity that powers it. If you think Information People first, then you will usually have IT in the right and proper perspective from the very start.

"Seek not good from without: seek it from within yourselves, or you will never find it".

- *Epictetus, (Greek philosopher, AD 55-c.135)*

Chapter 2: CAPTAINS AND CREWS

The Right IT Leadership

This is where is all starts and ends. The leader is ultimately responsible for the success or failure of their teams and their efforts. Leadership is expensive in the fact that he or she cannot please everyone nor should a leader ever try. Attempting to please either the right people while keeping all others at bay, comes at a price, personally, professionally or both. There is no way around that fact and the "buck" stops at Executive Management and always should. Managers and Directors alone usually do not always have the power to get major IT changes sold to and implemented with the business. In some cases, they also lack the basic core capacity and leverage to get the funding needed for large IT projects. Executive Management has this power. Directors and Managers need these individuals on board in order to make large, and critical changes happen within the organization. IT Executive management, depending on the size and type of the business, may consist of one or both of the following Officers that we discussed previously:

1. **Chief Information Officer (CIO)** – This Executive controls how information is input, processed, stored, and retrieved within a business. All IT software architecture, data warehouses and applications fall under their responsibility. The role of the CIO can be a very stressful position, as business expectations are high when it comes to their software applications being stable and reliable. CIOs also have the difficult task of trying to explain to the rest of the Executive team in simple terms why software and hardware systems must be built, upgraded, maintained or discontinued. They must further work to convince their fellow Executives to give them the money to make these things happen periodically. A CIO works to implement, expand and exploit new and existing business related Internet, Intranet, and Extranet solutions.

2. **Chief Technical Officer (CTO)** – This Executive is the caretaker of the direction that technology takes within an organization. In some larger to enterprise level businesses, a CTO reports to a CIO and is more of a Director level role. In mid-sized to smaller organizations a CTO may be the only IT Executive in charge of IT. In this instance, the CTO most likely would assume the same role as a CIO.

It is imperative that a CIO or CTO have unquestionable integrity. This means that an ideal executive on this level must have the best interest of their business and IT team at heart at all times. This is important because dishonesty or questionable ethics is the "kiss of death" when it comes to technology and requesting funds for it. The primary tool that a CIO or CTO has in working with their colleagues and the business is "trust". The average business individual has no idea or cares little about the inner workings of the technology that they use every day. A business must trust IT when they say that a software or hardware platform will or will not do what they need it to do. Many business people pay attention to technology news from a variety of sources (internet, radio, television, magazines). In many cases, they will have questions or may argue their point if they are told by IT that a process or the specific software functionality requested cannot be implemented. Business people can occasionally be more perceptive regarding technology than many IT people realize. They will eventually see and hear news stories of their competition doing something technologically innovative that they cannot do at that point in time. With this, leaders must be truthful as to why the organization does not have the technology that they need in order to be more competitive. Furthermore, those leaders must be always be ready to share their objective with business people who need to be aware of it, and that vision had better be a solid one.

Good IT Executive Leaders must be able to do the following:

1. Create a logical technological vision and inspire other to buy into it

2. Create a technical plan based on their vision and enforce it

3. Hire the right people and get out of the way

4. Fire the wrong people and make examples of their failures

5. Learn from their mistakes

6. Know when to go to war for the right ideas and when to back off. They understand that they must live to fight another day

7. Keep the best interests of the organization at heart first, and use IT to make that happen with honesty and integrity

8. Tell the truth and answer questions directly and assuredly

9. Listen! This includes meeting with employees at the lowest levels of an organization to hear their concerns first hand. The Leader compares this information with that of the reports submitted by their officers for integrity.

10. Understand and manage politics on any level professionally

11. Find intelligent and loyal advisors

12. Identify who their friends and enemies are

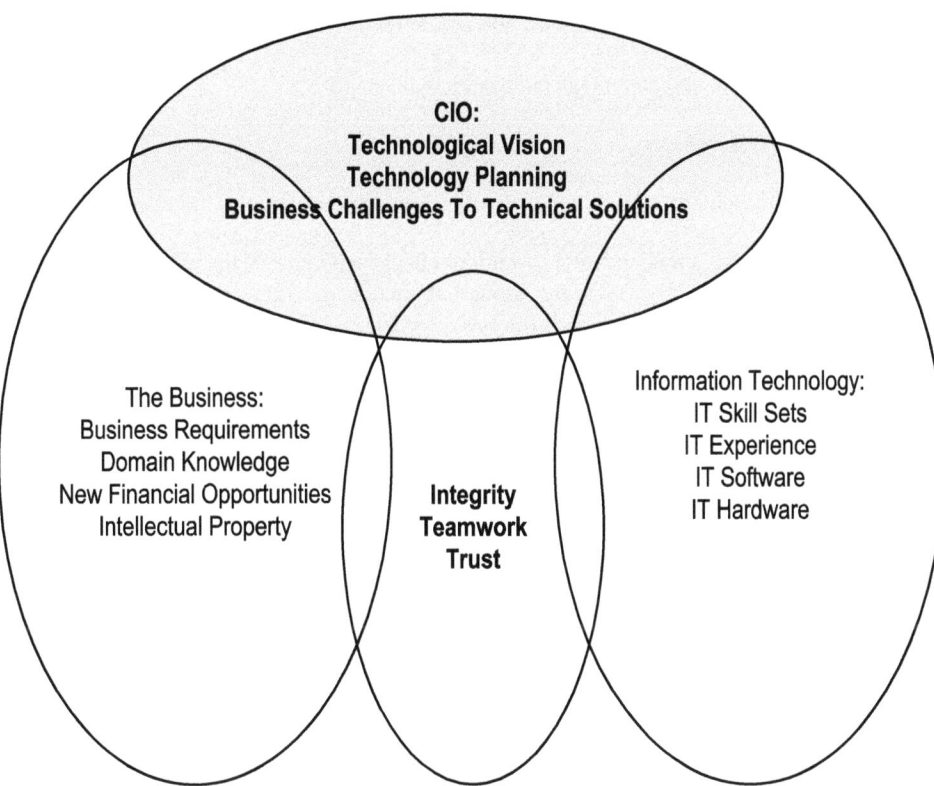

Bad IT Executive Leaders are plagued by one or more of the following:

1. Lack of a logical technological vision and the inability to inspire other to buy into it

2. Lack of a technical plan

3. They hire the wrong people and get out of the way

4. They fire the right people and wonder why they can't get things done

5. Fail to learn from their mistakes

6. Fight the wrong battles and don't know when to quit

7. Keep the best interests of themselves at heart first, and use IT to make that happen

8. Tell the truth when it serves their best interests and answer questions indirectly

Chapter 2: CAPTAINS AND CREWS

9. Listen to what they want to hear and ignore the rest

10. Contribute to and encourage politics on many levels

11. Enlist poor advisors

12. Lack the inability to know the difference between their friends and enemies

Bad IT leadership has a tendency not to want to change anything. Many like to find processes that they believe work and are easy enough to maintain. After that, the leadership will generally stay the course even though the business demands change over time. This may be due to incompetence, fear, inexperience, bad advice or a combination of all four. This often leads to a vicious cycle of confusion, frustration, hesitation with no elation. Leaders that fall into this type of trap are often guilty of repeating the same flawed processes and expecting different results. This is the definition of "insanity" but many in management don't see it from this perspective. Good IT leadership stays poised and ready for change. They understand that if their organization's technology is not constantly upgraded than it is stagnant. If a company's technology is dormant, then its future is dismal or already dead.

Both good and bad executives can have large egos. A healthy ego is a necessary tool that is needed in an IT Executive's war chest in order to inspire, lead, foster confidence in their team and themselves. However, the executive leader's ego should never obstruct the leader's ability to do their jobs or deal with their peers and the business. Egos have always been a "double edged" sword that can be as helpful as it can be harmful simultaneously. IT is not a democracy, it is a dictatorship. Good IT Executives do not pretend that this is not so, and they work to earn the trust of their organization and IT team through vision, logic, planning, competence and discipline. Effective IT processes are worthless without the discipline to carry them out. IT executives must enforce the software development lifecycle and their management team's ability to be effective with that process. If this cannot happen then the risk of software project failure increases dramatically.

I once worked for a CTO for a short time who tried to give his IT team and me, the illusion that his environment was running as a democracy. He had a small business that had found a niche with their software product and did very well financially within it. The CTO had a habit of making statements like "I hire people that are smarter than me", but he had an enormous ego and would only listen to ideas if they were what he wanted to hear or the ones that he planted. His Democracy was a farce because he constantly reminded me how much smarter and more accomplished he was than I, and everyone else. Since he hired me because I had more experience than anyone did on his team at the time, I could only assume that he really did not believe that the employees he hired were actually smarter than he was. His IT department was unlike any other that I had ever seen or heard of previously. They had their own language with definitions for well-defined IT terms that meant something different from the standard industry meanings. Since they did not use industry standard terms and definitions, the CTO and his team simply made up their own. I spent most of my time at this company confused, and trying to figure out exactly what the IT employees were talking about and trying to achieve.

Next, I found out that all of the developers that he had hired had never worked for any other IT department previously. The CTO had hired them all from other industries and taught them to develop software himself. For example, one of his IT developers used to be his Gardener. With this practice, the CTO was effectively able to control and manipulate his IT department and invoke strong loyalty from his team. The CTO would also make it a regular habit to tell his IT department how smart and good they were even though they were a substandard team who used old technology and knew very little about the IT industry outside of their company. A good point to all of this is that his team seemed to work well together. Most of them had known and liked each other for many years before they joined the organization so that may have contributed to their success as a team. I knew that my days working with this type of anomaly were numbered and that I could not stay there. This is because I realized that over time I would slowly unlearn critical IT lessons that I needed keep so that I could continue to learn and grow in the industry.

Shortly after I made that decision, the CTO blew up at me in a meeting when I exposed a major risk in his technical plans. Not only was this professionally embarrassing to me, but it unveiled the true character and personality of the CTO. He became even angrier with me when I began to make improvement suggestions to his software in meetings as a direct result of his earlier requests. This man turned out to have serious control issues and through my long conversations with him, he revealed to me that he truly thought that he was a great man who truly believed that he could do anything he wanted in life. The CTO had a strong IT background and often scoffed about how much he hated traditional IT and all of the damaging egos that he had been subjected to. This seemed to have contributed significantly to his own sour feelings, and why he wanted, and enjoyed the "special" IT environment that he had created within his company. This may have been that CTO's version of the Elysian Fields but it was certainly not mine, and that's just fine.

The problem with this person was that he had become what he hated about IT the most, and sadly, he could not see that. His own ego prevented him from understanding why he hired me in the first place, which was to help him and his company. His ego prevented him from listening to new ideas and concerns that he needed to hear from the objective consultants that he hired. The CTO ended up blaming me for being "closed minded", and just like all of the traditional IT people that he had so many problems with. This was a uncomfortable and unfortunate situation in which I learned a lot from the experience of going through it. These types of situations are strong learning opportunities and should not be ignored. This taught me that there are many types of leaders and environments even though they may be very different and somewhat odd; they can work sometimes if the circumstances are right. However, I do not recommend that you join an organization like the interesting CTO's business or any company like it, unless you are in desperate need of a job.

Chapter 2: CAPTAINS AND CREWS

Enforcing the Chain of Command

You might remember a popular television commercial that opened with several cowboys riding their horses out on the open range. One might think that the cowboys were herding hundreds of cows or buffalo in the hot unforgiving sun. As the camera panned back the cowboys were not herding cows or buffalo, they were herding cats, and they looked to be about a thousand or more. The cats were everywhere and the cowboys were scrambling to try and keep them all together and going in the right direction. The cowboys were failing at this, and the cats looked to be winning the battle of wills and perspective. The commercial was hilarious and the term "herding cats" became a popular one especially when people spoke of IT management.

The "Chain of Command" is usually associated with military command structures. Authority flows downward from top to bottom through executive roles or military ranks by a command system. In this system, one's accountability is directed to their superior. It is important to understand the concept that in a chain of command structure, a higher ranking person does not necessarily have the authority to issue commands arbitrarily. For instance, in a business, if a manager needs something done by an employee of another department, they are expected to make a request to the manager of that department first. That manager must then make the decision to contact the employee within their own chain of command in order to comply with the original request. Power, authority and responsibility lesson the lower you go down a chain of command structure. Managers at the lowest levels are ultimately responsible for notifying senior level managers of project issues, concerns, milestones, successes and failures. For a chain of command to be effective, it must be unified and orders must be followed and not questioned. This means that there should never be more than one manager per IT employee for a given IT task. No other lines of command should ever conflict with the primary one.

Software Developers are generally very creative and or artistic people. Many of them are also musicians and artists who enjoy role-playing and video games and are members of different Period and Science Fiction groups when they are not at work. Creative people have a notorious reputation for being hard to manage, and in some instances, simply difficult to deal with in general. They can usually have issues focusing on assignments that they are not strongly interested in, and quite often have many thought processes going on in their heads that may have nothing to do with their immediate tasks. This is one of the reasons why IT leaders must run a tight ship during projects. There can be as many different ways of doing things in IT Software Projects as there are people involved and they all may not be necessarily bad ways of getting the project implemented. Managing IT can be a tough challenge because of these reasons and even more so if the manager involved is working for a large organization that has a Project Team of 150 or more employees. Keeping creative people focused on their tasks is an art form in its self and catering to them will in most cases wear a manager down. In situations such as these, it may be better for an IT manager to be "respected" and "feared" more than "liked" by their subordinates.

Enforcing the chain of command is a critical element in IT management because of the types of people involved. IT Projects usually require a good deal of thought an planning and IT team members sometimes have their own ideas of how an IT project should proceed regardless of how they are told it is going to progress. These ideas in some cases turn into tasks by certain strong willed, creative individuals and that can take a software project off the progressive track that it needs in order to be successful. A project manager must not only be aware of such potential problems but must have the power, authority and backing by the IT chain of command to correct the issue before it jeopardizes the success of the project. Subverting the chain of command can have dire consequences and should only be done in extreme circumstances. The Repercussions of this act can lead to a variety of problems for whoever chooses to invoke it from company IT Directors, all the way down to members of the help desk team. Some of the fallout from employees jumping the chain of command might include:

- The employee who subverted that chain of command being fired

- The manager of the employee who subverted the chain of command being fired

- Other employees developing the mindset that it is ok to subvert the chain of command

- Management beginning to appear weak to its employees

- Chaos

However, sometimes subverting the chain of command may be a good idea and a necessary thing to do. In such cases, a good command structure may not always punish and employee for doing so. Actually, if the action saves the company significant time, money or embarrassment, the employee who broke the chain of command may be rewarded by senior management. Some good reasons for doing this are as follows:

- Reporting a manager who is breaking the law or company rules at work

- Reporting an employee who is breaking the law or company rules at work and a manager ignores continued reports made to him or her of the matter

- A health and or safety issue exists that is ignored by a manager after continued reports to him or her of the matter

- A legal issue exists that is ignored by a manager after continued reports to him or her of the matter

- A major product and or project flaw exists that could derail a project exists that is ignored by a manager after continued reports to him or her of the matter

Great care must always be taken whenever an employee decides to subvert that chain of command in IT. In many cases, what may appear to be an issue of importance may not be a problem after all. This discovery may be a part of a higher project plan that the employee may be unaware of and may not have the need or be authorized to know about. Many organizations work on a "need to know" basis. Not all IT managers may be aware of the information that their employees discover by accident, or may learn from other employees who gossip and share information about subjects that they should not. Discoveries such as these may not always be something that you should be quick to tell your boss's superiors about, so using good judgment in these types of situations is mandatory.

A typical IT Chain of Command for a larger organization might look like this:

1. CEO
2. CIO\CTO
3. IT Directors
4. IT Architects (Software\Data\Network)
5. IT Managers (Project\Development\Network)
6. IT Team Leads (Development\Network)
7. Software Engineers, Database Administrators, Technical Analysts, Network Administrators, Testers
8. Technical Writers
9. Support Desk

It is important to note that a company IT chain of commands structure can vary greatly based on the size and type of an organization. However, the previous example should give you a good idea of how a chain of command structure might affect an IT department and how the hierarchy manages IT roles. Ex-military personnel seem to do very well due to their former training and the discipline needed to survive in a military environment. Veterans understand the importance of discipline and what can happen to a soldier or sailor who lacks and or fails to acquire this critical attribute. The military environment in most cases can be most unforgiving of individuals who do not, cannot, or will not follow orders. These service members can be punished for this in many different ways, which include:

- A reduction in rank and pay

- Restriction to base

- Jail time

- General Court Marshall

- Administrative or Dishonorable Discharge from Military Service

With this in mind, after military service, working the private sector can seem to be simple. On the contrary, it can sometimes be more difficult for someone coming from a more disciplined and structured military environment to the private sector. Since the penalties for non-compliance may not be as severe in the private sector as it is in a military, employees may be able to get away with offering a lower quality of service in regards to their tasks. Sometimes individuals with strong military backgrounds don't get along with people of non-military background at work because they do not respect their work ethic, and level of discipline that they may apply to getting their jobs done. I have seen this in IT on many occasions and there is usually a deep rift between these types of people that often cannot be repaired. The chain of command can help in issues such as these by providing common ground in direction and working hard to insure that each and every IT project member feels value in their roles and responsibilities.

While discipline is a high priority in an IT chain of command, it is also important for this structure to allow all IT project members to show their initiatives. In most cases, this is why employees are hired to begin with. New and good ideas are a source of strength in an IT department and in projects. This means that egos must be "held in check" by all concerned and managed carefully. A chain of command that allows good ideas to go unnoticed or readily ignored losses a valuable commodity needed for growth and sustenance.

Securing an Objective

Every business must have an objective or the organization has no idea of where it is going. If an organization does not know where it is going then it will go nowhere fast. In business, if you are not growing then you must be dying, and the same is true of technology. Well thought out and logical objectives help to set focus and having a good direction is critical to survival. The objective must be attainable and should be attacked incrementally. One of the reasons why so many fail to meet their goals is because they try to conquer their objectives all at once. For larger objectives, milestones should be set and worked up to. A larger milestone might be a goal that can take years to reach, so clear attainable smaller steps in this process helps all players involved to better focus.

Chapter 2: CAPTAINS AND CREWS

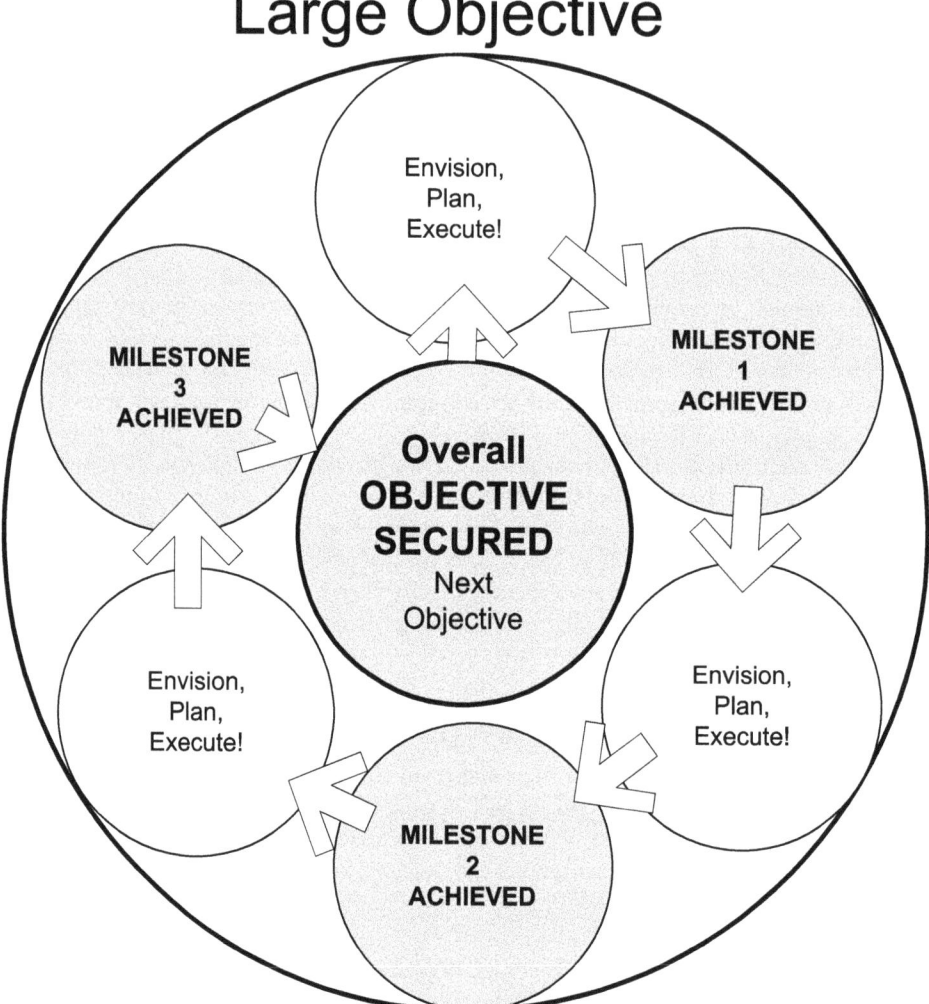

What are you trying to achieve as an IT department? This question does not pertain to what type of software you are trying to build or what kind of company you support. The core focus of the question is:

1. What level of quality of service are you and your IT Team trying to deliver to your business?

2. What goals or milestones is your IT team trying to achieve?

3. Do you have a plan as an IT service for how you deliver your product?

4. What is your team's ultimate objective in IT; what do you want to achieve as a team?

These questions are important because they work to flush out problems in direction with IT team strategies for cohesion. Every team no matter how large or small should have a mission statement and all employees should have it memorized. It is good idea to have IT employees recite the department mission statement at their performance review evaluations to insure that they understand what the team is trying to achieve. Below is an example of an IT mission statement where "XYZ" is the name of the organization.

"The XYZ Information Technology Department exists to serve XYZ and will work hard to gain and maintain the trust of our business partners. We will achieve this by effectively transforming business challenges into timely technical solutions that meet business requirements. Furthermore, we will exploit technology in order to help our business gain the unfair advantage in our industry by procuring intellectual property through innovation. Our service will actively contribute to XYZ's growth and profitability."

The above mission statement is a plain, clear and powerful one. Mission statements should expose the basis for a company and or department's reason for being. A mission statement must also serve to inspire and motivate employees and give them a common reason for working at an organization. It will focus on long-term goals and must always be simply communicated. A plan must exist that serves to facilitate a mission statement and management must also work that plan to make it real. The following is an example of a plan that can be used to implement and enforce technological objectives:

Chapter 2: CAPTAINS AND CREWS

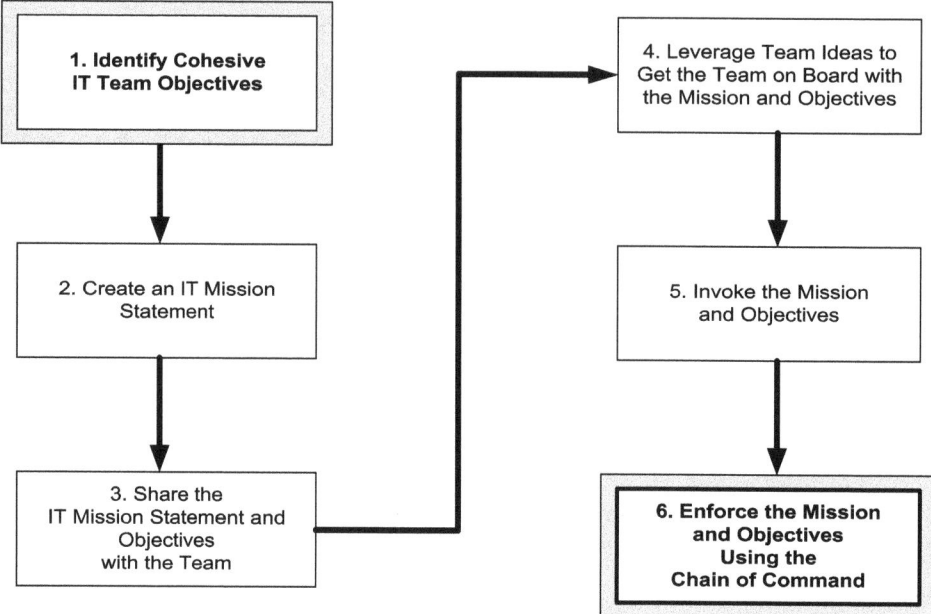

A business and or its IT department can have perfect objectives and the best planning that can be thought out and carefully implemented. However, without the discipline to stick to the process, it all means nothing. We will examine how to invoke IT discipline later in this chapter.

The Need to Know

The rules that govern the "Need to Know" protocol are:

- Any person will not have access to comprehensive information unless that data is need by that person in order to complete their assigned task

- If a person can show and or explain sufficiently why the requested information is needed to complete their assigned task, then they will have access to the requested data required.

The Need to Know Protocol

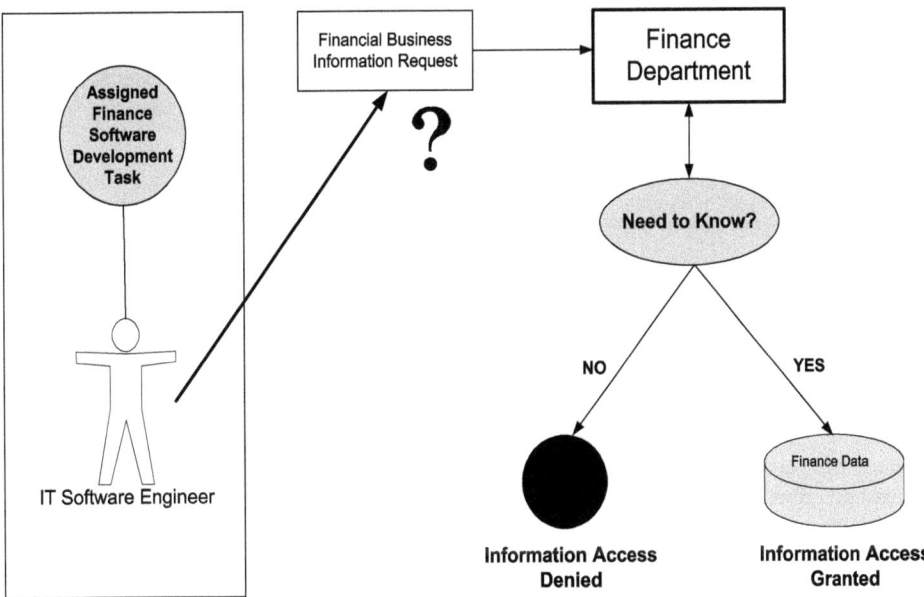

Rules that govern the "Need to Know" are enacted by the vertical and horizontal separation of data access and the responsibilities of employees. This protocol is designed to protect an organization's intellectual property and general information. It also maintains distributed knowledge of a company by Executive Management as this rule is applied to them as well.

Due to the ravenous breed of politics that IT can often muster, in many instances it may not be a good idea to share more information than any one person or group needs to get their jobs done. Sharing too much information can be the starting point for taking a project off course. Not only that, the sharing of information regardless of rules can be dangerous, irresponsible and against the law.

For example, recently a non-profit organization published my wife's name and home address on their website for the public to peruse. Once I discovered this, I promptly contacted the organization and requested that they update the listing in regards to my wife and have the private information removed. I also reminded them they could leave themselves open to lawsuits in relation to mishandling private information. Lastly, I asked them not to share my family's personal information on the Internet again without our expressed permission. The organization was very responsive and polite, and complied promptly and changed their policy on publishing private information on the Internet without the consent of its members. However, after the fact I received a rather interesting email from the organization's webmaster. His letter stated that I should not give out any private information whatsoever if I do not want it to be published. Furthermore, he stated that fact that my spouse gave his organization the private information constituted "permission" to publish the information in regards to the particular organization event in question. Finally, he said that my lapse in responsibility is what created the problem and that I should pay more attention to this in the future. I did not respond to this webmaster's email for the following reasons:

1. The issue had already been resolved

2. A new policy had been implemented to prevent this from happening in the future

3. A new and critical awareness had been raised in management of the potential of future lawsuits and other damaging member ramifications from sharing private member information without the individual's consent

4. The webmaster was not the person in charge of the matter, which was a good thing

Since the webmaster had copied his superior and the rest of his management team on the email described, I felt comfortable enough in the fact that his blatant ignorance in this matter had been well documented. In the webmaster's logic, he made the assumption that any information shared willingly with an organization gave that organization the right to make the individual's information public, if the organization chose to do so. However, his argument violates many state and local privacy laws and is a reckless and dangerous way for an organization to proceed in business. Not only are the organization's members put at risk of harassment, identity theft and unscrupulous marketing companies by sharing their information without their knowledge, but an organization's trust factor gets lost in this type of practice also. Ultimately, my request to the organization was not to remove all of my wife's information from their listing but only the private information that made her personally identifiable. The data that would remain would be general information that anyone browsing their website could safely peruse to get the information they required for the event posted.

A good "Need to Know" protocol is important for keeping order in IT. From our own frame of reference, sometimes we want to know far more than we should in a given situation. When involved in a large and complex IT project that might include hundreds or even thousands of tasks, focusing on your own jobs and processes is usually difficult enough. Too much information can be distracting and sometimes lead to making the wrong or bad decisions because the overall context of the information is not well known or cannot be thoroughly analyzed at that time. One of the continuing issues that I have had to face in IT over the years has been that of disclosure. For instance, an IT Director makes a reference to a new technology tool that IT will use in an upcoming project within a company meeting with several business Directors and Managers. Some or all of the Directors and Managers at the meeting may or may not understand what the new technology in question is or what it does. After the meeting the attending business management then hurries to their PCs to access the

Internet and browse for any data they can find on the new technology and how to use it. From the information compiled on the Internet, some business managers then develop a strong view as to exactly how the new technology the IT Director spoke of should be implemented. In a follow-up meeting with the IT Director, business management, now armed with their Internet article knowledge, begin to take an expert stance on the new technology and or process and invoke a major debate as to its viability and purpose within their organization. The problem with this is that in many cases the new technology tool and its process has already been researched by IT and approved by Executive Management as required by the business. The debate and arguments presented by business management in this regard were predominantly irrelevant due to their failure to understand the core and important technical aspects of why the new technology tool was selected to begin with. Since business management will not support the technical side of the new tools (as it is not their job), it is a waste of time to talk about that subject in a business management meeting or for business middle management to be concerned with internal IT matters that relate to technical processes that do not affect them. This is because they do not need to know about the details of the technology in question in order to do their jobs.

Another example of the "Need to Know" protocol that I can share is when I worked for a company that made special spices and sauces that were used in the foods of some of the largest and most popular fast food restaurants in the world. As I worked on the design of their company's laboratory software that processed and matched the various ingredients needed to create the many spices and sauces, I was told by a company Director that the data I was working with was classified. This was because I was viewing their client's "Intellectual Property" as well as some of their own for their company's products. He also said that not even the Vice-President of the company had permission to see the data that I had unlimited access to, and was working with because he did not need to know that information. The Director then said that he knew this "first hand" because at one time a Vice-President had asked to see the "secret formulas". The Director himself had to deny the company Vice President's request because of the company's active "need to know" policy.

Auditing Leadership Integrity
To find out if your leader has the best interest of their team at heart you must learn their true agenda if they are willing to reveal it. The good news in this area is that hidden agendas usually don't stay hidden for very long when it comes to information technology. At some point, a leader is going to have to execute a plan that will give their team some insight as to what they really want to do and what direction they are heading. For example, I worked for a large company as a Software System Architect and was asked by the CIO of the company to assist with the hiring of a new IT Director. I was excited at the prospect of being able to talk to all of the different candidates that the CIO had screened. Over the course of several days, I and the IT Development Manager had the opportunity to talk with 3 very interesting individuals. The last candidate for the position that we interviewed was a short and quiet man with a strongly confident but unassuming demeanor. As we walked into the interview room,

we were surprised to see that he was already sitting there waiting for us with a pleasant smile. As we began asking him questions, he remained calm, pleasant, kind and soft spoken when answered them. His knowledge of IT was vast with more than 3 decades of experience to back it up. He was able to speak on almost any IT subject and drill down into a level of detail that showed he was unusually intelligent and quite possibly genius. We liked him a lot and with his previous experience as a CTO he seemed like a "must" for the job. Our CIO gave the team few days to decide if we wanted him to lead us and it did not take us that long to agree that we wanted to hire him. We gave our CIO the "thumbs up" on this quiet, intelligent little man and within the week our CIO hired him and we were on our way.

The first week on the job with our new IT team was filled with technical discovery through teaching sessions with our new boss. I also noticed that this man was not really a quiet man at all. This person talked a lot and at great length. When he would call me into his office (which was quite often) he was fairly long winded when he began speaking on a subject that was of specific interest to himself or that was about his past experiences which were too numerous to mention. As the months passed, the more I learned, and his true ego and politics began to emerge. The IT Director began to carve a careful but deliberate political landscape in regards to the IT Development team. He was beginning to make unflattering comments to the IT Development Manager about me, and vice-versa which started to make being in the room with the two of them somewhat uncomfortable. The IT Director did not realize that the Development Manager and I were very good friends who constantly shared information about work. The Development Manager and I had made an agreement to be political allies after learning of the new IT Director's mental games. This turned out to be a great move on our part because as the months wore on the IT Director began to play the IT Manager against me on a serious level. It was very clear at this point that the IT Director was putting together a plan of "divide and conquer" with the development team. Whatever his motives were at that time, serious damage was being done to team morale. As the IT Director began to query additional team members in private, they began to talk to the IT Development Manager and myself about some of the other derogatory things that the Director was saying about all of his subordinates. This man had no idea that his team talked to each other nearly as much as we did. Had he known this, I am sure he would not have tried to decimate his team in that manner.

Finally, The IT Director's true agenda was revealed. It appeared that he wanted to implement a new technology tool that was essentially a beta software product masquerading as a polished and well-tested production application. Also, he wanted a specific consulting company that he chose to implement and support the product. I never discovered exactly what stakes the IT Director may have had in the product or consulting company that he wanted on outsource this work to. The one thing that I was sure of, after all of his political games, was that he did not want his existing IT Development team to do the work. As a result of spending the majority of his time engaging in damaging IT Department politics, the IT Director had little time to get any other significant tasks completed. This fact, along with dismal IT team morale, eventually caught the attention of the CIO and the rest of Executive

Management. The Executive Management team began an in-house audit of the IT Director and questioned the entire IT team. He was not a popular person within his own IT department or with general Business Management as well. This was later brought to my attention by several business managers, who also accused the IT Director of the same "negative political initiatives" that his subordinates complained about. After the Executive Management audit concluded, the CIO fired the IT Director. The damage done to the IT Development team, as a result of this incident, was irreparable. The team suffered a great deal and the turnover rate increased at an alarming rate.

With all of his vast intelligence, the Director failed to realize and appreciate how close his IT team was and how well they communicated. Maybe he did not care about that fact at all, and thought that he could override those types of concerns and push his agenda through at the company before anyone realized what was really happening. Sometimes this is possible depending on the organization. The bottom line issues that lead to the demise of the IT Director included:

- Not having the best interest of his IT team (subordinates) at heart

- Overall lack of integrity which eventually damaged his credibility

- Practicing negative politics within the organization as a whole

- Underestimating the intelligence and abilities of his IT development team

- Bad decision making

- Ego driven management with a strong sense of "self entitlement"

Regardless of what leaders say, and how good their politics are initially, they are always ultimately what they do. A leader's actions define them and through further analysis a determination can be made as to the integrity (or lack thereof) of their command. If a leader's agenda does not work for you after you have learned enough about it, you may want to find another job as soon as you can before it negatively affects your career. Bad and or selfish leader's agendas do not always end well and can have long lasting negative effects on an entire organization if left unchecked.

Speaking the Same Language

Various languages are often based in different ways of thinking that reflects their related cultures. That is why when translating one language to another many common issues arise such as the same words or phrases having very different definitions in the two languages. Another problem is that a word or phrase might not even exist in one of the languages. In this case, a substitution would have to used for the original word or phrase communicated that could give a word, phrase, or conversation a completely ambiguous meaning to the person or group receiving the end result of the message. Whether your painting pictures on a cave wall, pyramid, or typing on your home computer, some basic principles must be in place if you want a wide audience to understand what it is you are attempting to communicate. Some of these principles are:

- The person or group that receives your message must understand the basic idea that you are trying to communicate

- The person or group that receives your message must understand the language that you choose to communicate your thoughts and ideas

- The message must then be as clear and simple as possible to avoid basic misunderstandings

- Common words must be identified that have the exact same definitions to both the message sender and receiver

IT Teams must use the same terminology in order to be successful. This contributes to building a culture within the group. It is important that the terms and phrases be based on industry vocabulary, not created by team members. As a culture is born and begins to grow within a group, it is inevitable that new words and phrases will be adopted that may only pertain to that specific tribe's intellectual property. However, this should be constrained to matters that are non-technical in nature (if and whenever possible) as to avoid confusion by new team members or other IT professionals who may be working with your group. This includes other entities such as consultants and third party vendors. These two groups are usually working hard to escape from the "land of confusion" after first contact with a business client. Further misunderstanding in communication with consultants and third party vendors can cost an organization an amazing amount of time and money and deplete ROI. It is best to follow the "KISS" principle in IT, which means, "Keep It Simple Stupid".

The importance of XML

Before the advent of the large-scale software system integration projects that started in the 1990s, most software applications were not integrated. These siloed applications were often disparate monolithic software systems that served specific purposes and most had no requirement to be interoperable. As hardware and software technology advanced rapidly, new software platforms were developed that enabled new and existing applications to communicate with each other. This was a great thing because businesses could now begin to consolidate their software systems and data into a more uniform interface. The problem with this, however, was deciding on how a new software application would talk to an old disparate one. That is, what language could be used to communicate between the two systems? This is where a new protocol was required and XML was born.

Extensible Markup Language (XML) is a simple and flexible text based format that was originally created to fulfill the requirements of the enterprise level electronic publishing industry. XML is a major player in how various data is exchanged over the Internet and between software applications worldwide. XML is a standard for communications between software systems and their many platforms and operating systems. It is also a standard for describing data compositions, which makes the job of moving those data structures from one place to another achievable. People must still create and identify exactly how the XML composition will look aside from a few basic principles. XML is recommended by the World Wide Web Consortium, which governs the principles of the language. It was designed to describe data and to identify what it is supposed to be. Below are a few simple facts you should know about XML:

1. XML uses Document Type Definitions or "DTDs" or a schema to describe the composition of the XML document (or template)

2. XML was not created to do anything at all and has no functions. XML was created to describe data. It was not designed to permanently store data. That is what a database is used for.

3. XML was created to let anyone be able to use "Markup Tags" to describe their data structure any way they need or want to.

4. Like HTML (Hyper Text Markup Language), XML is also a markup language

Below is an example of an email written using an XML document:

```xml
<?xml version="1.0" encoding="ISO-8859-1"?>

<Email>

    <To>cio@sample_company.com</To>

    <From>mallen@realenhanceddecisions.com</From>

    <Priority>HIGH</Priority>

    <Subject>Information Technology Question</Subject>

    <Body>How do we get to the Elysian Fields of Information Technology?</Body>

</Email>
```

The first line defines the XML version and character encoding for the document. This email message is comprised of a root node <Email>, receiver <To>, sender <From>, priority

Chapter 2: CAPTAINS AND CREWS

<Priority> and message body <Subject>. The information in this document is wrapped up in customized XML tags that I created. Keep in mind that this XML document does not do anything at all. In order for it to mean something, a software application must be developed, or customized to in order to receive, send, view, and or process the message. I created the XML tags that wrap this message just as you can easily create your own using a simple text file. The application that will receive your XML message must understand this structure in order to process the document. Your XML document might look like this:

<?xml version="1.0" encoding="ISO-8859-1"?>

<Message>

    <To>Jim</To>

    <From>Sandy</From>

    <Subject>Financial Reports</Subject>

    <Body>The CFOs financial reports will be ready in the morning.</Body>

</Message>

XML documents can be viewed from all standard web browsers. The following is a screen shot of how the previous XML document looks in Microsoft Internet Explorer from both expanded and collapsed views.

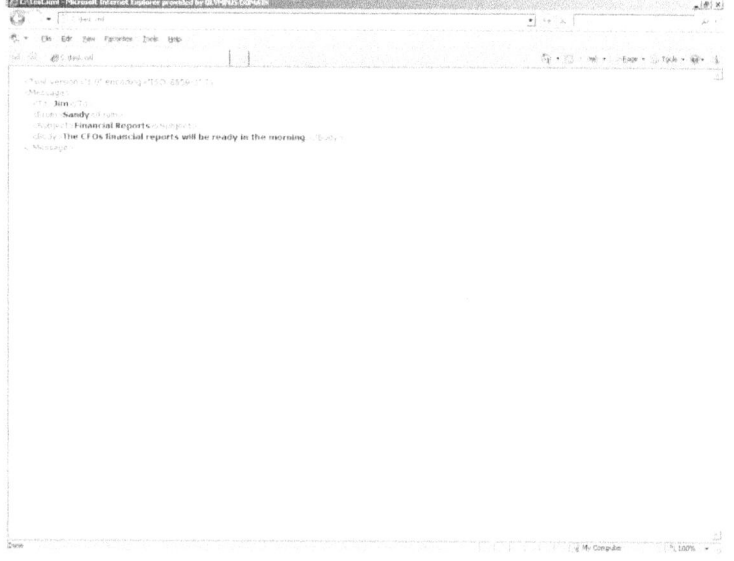

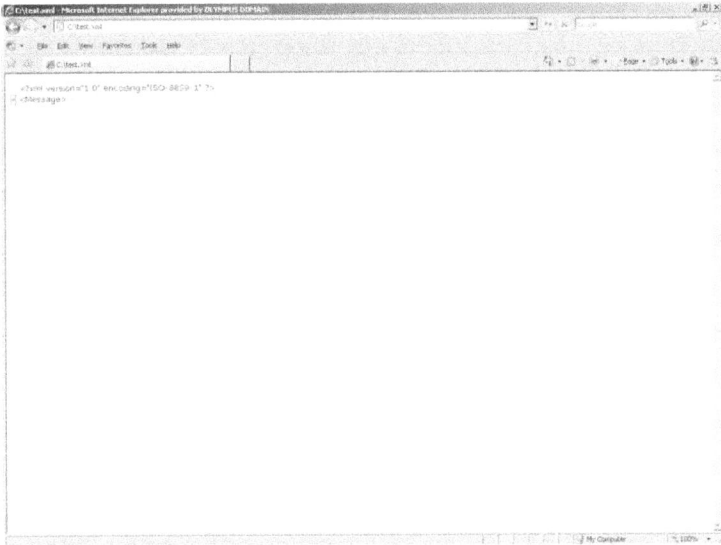

Think of the level of chaos that would encompass the United Nations (UN) if all of the sudden they had no way to translate from one language to another. Think of all of the problems that the UN has now even though they possess adequate translation capabilities and technology. Here's the point; the fact that the various countries that attend UN meetings are able to understand each other lets them focus on higher global matters. XML is able to achieve this solution with distributed software systems all over the world. IT departments must mimic this process and find a common language that fulfills their requirements geared towards successful software project implementations. This can be achieved by:

1. Identifying commonly used IT technical words and phrases used within your IT group

2. Documenting those IT technical words and phrases and publishing them to the IT group

3. Use the IT technical words and phrases in IT meetings and project documentation

4. Updating and re-publishing the documentation to the IT team as needed

Adapting IT to the Business

Up to now, I have talked about how an IT team might be structured but that does not mean that an IT team has to look a certain way. IT teams are supposed to serve the business, nothing more and nothing less. It always amazes me how many IT people I meet from one site to another who don't see themselves as business servants and scoff at that very notion.

Chapter 2: CAPTAINS AND CREWS

These feelings are not just restricted to the IT lower echelon; many in IT management share them as well. There are some core elements that almost every IT team needs. Such as:

- CIO or CTO
- IT Director
- Project Managers and Development Managers
- Software Engineers
- Database Administrators
- Analysts
- Network Engineers

A small percentage of the clients that I have worked for have had IT departments that were established and tailored for the businesses they served. In most cases, they had:

1. **Too many IT employees**
2. **Too many IT employees that were incorrectly structured**
3. **Too few IT employees**
4. **Too few IT employees that were incorrectly structured**

I once consulted with an organization that generated over 40 million dollars of revenue annually. Their IT environment was the worst I had ever seen based on the number of employees the company had, and how critical IT was to them. The company had no:

- CIO\CTO
- Database Administrators
- Analysts
- Software Testers
- or separate Network Development Environment

It was almost impossible to get any IT tasks implemented, that alone, any serious software development done within that type of organization. Despite my best efforts to help them, the company's Executive Management could not conceive of why they needed to hire a Business Analyst even though gathering business requirements for their software projects was one of the company's biggest problems. The company was also fond of telling IT exactly what positions they should hire next without understanding what roles IT needed to acquire in order to support them. Since the IT Development Manager himself did not want to change, this made the situation even worse as this business had no idea of this, and was unwilling to implement the industry best practices for improvements that I suggested. The IT Manager was told by Executive Management to hire more experienced Engineers, but he openly told me that he did not want to do that. As a result, the IT Manager constantly sabotaged any and all attempts made to add more experienced Software Developers to his team.

I once consulted with a startup whose annual revenue was less than $500,000.00. Interestingly enough, they had implemented the following:

- Database Administrator
- Business Analyst
- Software Tester
- Separate Network Development Environment

However, they had no CIO or CTO. This oversight made consulting with this company difficult because the governing and owning Principals had no IT background whatsoever and believed that they could make sound IT decisions regardless. This proved disastrous and frustrating on many occasions when trying to explain to the Principal owners the why and how of IT and what needed to be done to achieve successful IT software implementations. One of the base problems with that startup was that there was no one on the executive management level who could represent IT or had the power to make the things happen that IT needed. Instead, the Principal owners hired a network support manager and placed him in charge of IT development. The Support Manager had no software development experience and constantly fumbled project management tasks to the point of failure. He was eventually fired due to his lack of development management experience and ineffectiveness.

The primary goal in adapting IT to the business is too build a flexible, efficient team that the business needs so that it can operate more effectively. For this to happen, IT must have access to the resources that can study and understand exactly what the business requires. IT Management must also have the power to hire the employees they need to fill the gaps in their team structures. They must also have the proper support in firing the resources they don't require as unneeded help and other overhead negatively affect a business's return on investment. In too many IT environments, management teams place unrealistic expectations on teams that are too small, large or inexperienced to perform the tasks they are assigned. This can lead to frustration from both IT management and their respective teams due to the "Insanity Factor". The Insanity Factor being, management not making the team changes they need to succeed and expecting success regardless, repetitively. Simply put, two or more wrongs don't make a right. If IT management is serious about building software applications that are going to be of use to their business partners, then they should also be committed to making sure they have the right people to do the job.

Below are some of the ways an IT team can be adapted to the business through working with a Business Analyst:

1. Determine what type of software is required and will need to be built

2. Determine what type of skill sets will be required by an IT team to support the type of software to be built. For instance, if the company develops video games, that task will require a Software Engineer that has a different skill set than that of a Software Engineer that would be required for business applications.

3. Determine the level of experience needed by the resources required to do the work. For instance, it would be unwise to hire a Software Engineer who just finished college with little no experience to immediately take over a complicated development task of a Senior Engineer with 20 years of experience.

4. Start with a small team and add the resources required as needed. After analysis, if a project is too large for the current IT team, strongly consider outsourcing the project and hiring additional resources to support that project after it is completed and implemented by the outsourcing team.

Working to keep an IT team flexible to the business should be as water is to the cup that holds it. It must morph to the shape of the object that it has to support. This is not an easy task but it can be accomplished with good and strong management. An IT department that fears change will naturally not adapt and be forced to spend unnecessary time and resources to compensate in one way or another. This practice is commonplace in a number of IT environments and is a path away from the Elysian Fields and the main objective. In order to be successful, IT departments along with their business partners must constantly morph. Businesses must change in regards to customer needs and industry competition. IT must morph in regards to its business. In many cases by understanding the business' industry they are involved in, IT teams can then attempt to be proactive instead of reactive in their growth and maintenance of their company's technologies.

Keeping IT in Check

We looked at the importance of having a strong chain of command in IT, and how managing an IT team can be much like herding cats. However, It does not have to be that way. Having a strong chain of command is essential but without good and well-known rules and processes in place, strong leadership is just not enough.

Tested, proven processes are a key to keeping IT in check. Sound logical rules help to establish and test processes so that business objectives can be met. Those processes must also be:

- **Analyzed**
- **Adapted**
- **Implemented**
- **Enforced**

This is what I call "AAIE" (pronounced "EYE"). AAIE is a mechanism for IT management that works to insure that only the processes and their correct steps are implemented. Invoking processes for the sake of having them makes no sense and is a waste of time and resources. AAIE is an important avenue for identifying if a process is required to begin with. When analyzing a new task, if it has been decided that a process is something that does not fit the needs of the IT department, it must be ignored. Furthermore, if any existing processes fit this scenario, then they must also not be utilized. However, if it is determined by analysts and business management that a process is needed for a given situation, then the new one should be added. New processes must be thoroughly thought through and tested first, before they are implemented. If this does not happen then the results could cost the business significantly in regards to its return on investment. It could also have negative repercussions on IT in regards to how business views the competence of IT personnel in future software projects.

Below is additional AAIE information:

1. The first thing that must happen is an IT department must identify what processes are needed in order to be successful. These would include processes that involve requirements gathering, use case identification and change management.

2. IT Departments must take the relevant steps from the processes they must implement and discard the steps that don't apply to their situations.

3. Processes are of no use if they are not implemented and utilized. To implement a process, it must be documented, published, adopted by the IT team and be subject to review.

4. There must be repercussions if members of an IT team do not utilize the processes that are selected by IT management. Continued ignorance of IT processes for

reasons that are not identified as valid by IT Management, should have a negative effect on performance reviews. If the infractions are either severe or habitual, then the employee should be fired after further review.

Good sound processes and their management are a basis for establishing metrics within an IT Department. Metrics are a way to measure how effective processes are in delivering services and products to business partners and customers. They can also be used to track productivity, resources, and can be trended. This helps IT management to understand how well their team is doing currently compared to how well they have done previously and against the industry. It gives management insight as to how well their team fairs against their most important competition, themselves. No IT employee should have a job for life without constantly reinventing themselves through continued hard work, team participation, task completion, competence and good ideas. Metrics help to support that this remains true.

The quarterly, bi-annual or annual performance review is a necessary tool that is needed for keeping IT in check. IT Performance reviews should always be approached as a learning opportunity and a chance for an employee to get information that will enable them to get better at doing their jobs. However, not all IT folks will see a performance as a good thing. These type of situations generally make people very nervous as they tend to feel that it is themselves personally who are being reviewed as opposed to their job performance. IT employees who get performance reviews that they do not agree with should always have a chance to respond to the results they received. All outcomes from these types of situations must be clear, concise and well documented. This is important due to the fact that performance reviews often determine whether or not an employee will received a promotion, salary increase, more stock or other business benefits and or perks that may be desired. It never ceases to amaze me at just how many IT departments do not implement consistent performance review processes. Excuses for not doing this vary and are far reaching. Some include management being too busy and or not wanting to send the wrong message by making their IT teams feel too "stressed" during ongoing software development cycles. The problem with this type of thinking is that when a bad situation arises with an employee in regards to their performance, then there is no reliable way to track and document it. Without IT performance reviews, no employee performance history can be established. This can be even more of a concern when raises and or promotions are given to some employees for apparently no good reason, when other employees feel that there are no "reasonable" or "fair" metrics by which those types of decisions could be made. This type of situation can then negatively affect morale, which is the opposite result and the very point of why consistent performance reviews are important to begin with. If an IT Department has the time and energy to constantly deal with employees who are disruptive, then they definitely have the time and energy to implement and enforce good processes and rules that work to help the department run more smoothly.

Lastly, it is imperative that the rules that govern IT within an organization be clear and documented for employees. There must be no doubts as to what those rules are so there can be no excuses for the blatant ignorance of them. Games cannot be understood or played without rules, and IT is no different in this regard. In order for IT stay in check, employees must know their boundaries. Without IT rules, chaos takes over and management becomes a "theory" instead of a "practice".

Invoking IT Discipline

Discipline is most often associated in some way with punishment. However, in regards to IT discipline, it is related to the field teaching, learning, and or study. Discipline also means, "To bring under control" or "Training or teaching that molds and corrects moral character and or mental faculties". This is exactly what must happen in environments for success in the business to take root technologically. I have always been in favor of running projects more in a military fashion because many things in an IT project "must" happen and cannot always be open for debate. For instance:

- IT project requirements must be documented and published to the appropriate team members

- IT software systems must be documented both functionally and technically

- IT software systems must be properly tested by trained testers who have approved test plans for the software involved

In many IT departments, some or all of these critical areas are often neglected or sacrificed due to project time constraints. However, there always seems to be enough time to figure out and fix a problem with a software system under extreme circumstances when something goes wrong with it. With a military type of command structure established in an IT department, this would be corrected almost every time or the Superior in charge of the process would be punished through their performance reviews or by other means. This further insures that the discipline needed to make sure that the required processes implemented actually occur.

Good IT discipline is invoked through ongoing training, instruction, and reinforcement. IT environments must be a place of constant learning and mental hunger for wanting to improve upon the current technology and being more effective. Since IT is essentially a "service" this must always be a primary goal when working to meet the needs of the business and its sometimes-demanding customers. This is where self-discipline is critical.

Many IT personnel still work in relative seclusion or in some cases, they work at home or while traveling. These employees may not have someone directly managing them in an office structure much of the time. They must be self-motivated in order to focus on their assigned tasks with very little interaction and complete those jobs independently with success. For IT managers, selecting employees for the privilege of working outside the office should be conducted on a case-by-case basis. Not all personnel possess the qualities and self-discipline to work off-site and get their tasks completed. Many people are easily distracted by television, children, spouses and friends (or other projects) while working at home. In addition, it may be difficult for some to relate their work environment to their home environments as this association must happen for most people to get into the correct mindset to be productive. It is important for IT management not to restrict or limit all personnel to working in the office because a small or large percentage of the team is not able to work at home. IT personnel who are able to work at home without degrading the IT project should be allowed to do so no matter how others feel who have not shown that they can be productive working offsite. This is not a fairness issue, it is a productivity issue. Many people work offsite in various business environments and this trend is growing for a number of good reasons. Some of them are as follows:

1. Companies are trying to be more "green" by letting employees who are able to work at home for one or more days during the week. This lowers fuel consumption and reduces traffic which contributes significantly to "global warming". Traffic is a major problem in most cities and businesses have a distinct opportunity to have a positive effect on this issue if they choose to do so.

2. Working at home often allows employees who have small children to spend more time with them and work "as needed". As long as their assigned tasks are completed on time, in most cases, this is all that matters.

3. Some employees have sick family members that need constant care and attention. As long as their assigned tasks are completed on time, in most cases, that is all that matters.

4. Having employees that work at home also allows business in some cases to save money on energy as that employees PC (Personal Computer), lights, and other electronic equipment can be turned off, as they are not needed during these times.

5. Companies that have space concerns can solve that issue by regaining office space that can be used for new or other employees that must work on-site.

6. Companies may find that they can move to a smaller office or eliminate their physical offices all together.

For environmental as well as productivity reasons, anyone who can work at home and complete their assigned tasks, and not degrade the quality of their projects, should be able to work at home. It is imperative that offsite employees be trained not only according to their company principles in this regard, but will also do the following if it is not already incorporated into the laws of their particular organization:

1. Keep a daily log of all task performed during that day of work at home for purposes of job performance history and audit

2. Be accessible via phone, instant messaging, video conferencing and or email during pre-designated work hours so that members of their team can reach them for questions and meetings. If that person will not be available at any point during that time period, they should let the manager know clearly how long they will not be inaccessible and when they will be available again.

3. Be willing and available to come into the office ASAP for emergencies that cannot be handled remotely during designated work hours

4. Communicate clearly and simply at all times and to promptly contact the appropriate team members if they have any questions or comments that may help themselves or others perform their task more efficiently and or effectively

Training offsite employees in these four basic rules will go a long way to invoke IT discipline both on and off site. Expectations will then be set by both parties as to how to conduct IT business whether or not an employee is actually in or out of the office. It is important to stress that all IT personnel should be trained together periodically (every 3 to 6 months) in IT processes, etiquette and expectations in a grand effort to effect behavior and make practicing implemented organizational processes a habit. Ongoing regular effective training and cross training of personnel is a key to invoking IT discipline on a large scale which is critical to keeping a team on track, focused, skilled and disciplined.

The Impact of IT Team Tools

Having the right people using the right tools is extremely important in making technology work but it is not the only factor in that regard. The correct people involved must also have the intelligence, experience, and wisdom to implement those tools properly. Anyone in IT who chooses their tools irresponsibly based primarily on the sales appeal of those products run the high risk of implementing solutions in search of problems. There is no shortage of IT Departments that manage to do this on a regular basis.

Previously, I had sat down to lunch with an IT manager of a medium size organization to discuss IT strategy and the tools they had chosen to use for his business. I was surprised to learn that this IT manager actually thought the tools he had chosen for his team would help them learn and adhere to the software development lifecycle. He also told me that he thought that upgrading his core third party software platform would solve all of his team's problems moving forward. Since I had worked with this IT Manager extensively in the previous months before this lunch meeting, I already knew what his IT team's major problems were. It was indeed true that his technology was outdated and needed to be upgraded but that was not his IT organization's biggest issue. His team's major problems were that not only did they not use the software development lifecycle or any its principles, they did not even understand it. In this regard, new tools were not going to improve his or the IT team's situation or environment. It was clear to me that they would have the same concerns and issues no matter what tools they had chosen and were using. The IT manager's primary problem was with his people and not the tools they were using. Technology tools within themselves do nothing. They exist only as objects and are agnostic of their environments and users. As Engineers, we make the technology tools effective by applying them appropriately according to the tasks that we are assigned. I made this clear to the IT manager and suggested that he insure that his team be trained in and understand the principles of the software development lifecycle first, instead of spending tens of thousands of dollars on tools that are designed for Software Engineers that have already attained this specific discipline.

A friend of mine worked at an Enterprise whose IT department was floundering due to some bad decisions that their management had made in regards to what tools they had purchased to develop their software with. The problem they were having is that IT management could not find enough Software Engineers who were skilled in the obscure technology they were using. Because of this, their project was continuously delayed, and changed to accommodate this oversight. However, the basic problem was again, not being corrected. Instead of making a choice to use a more mainstream and viable technology that could achieve the same results, the organization's IT management continued to search for resources that were extremely difficult to find to do the work. The level ignorance of the IT managers involved in the behavior described has had a devastating effect on my friend at this company and his level of respect for his superiors, not to mention his morale. The negative repercussions due to the actions of IT management have undoubtedly had major effect on the return on investment of the IT department as well as the business as a whole.

In the right hands, when using effective processes for the appropriate job, IT tools can have a great impact on a software project and or product. Elements of IT software tools that contribute to the overall impact include:

- **Quality Assurance** – The IT tool helps insure that the software system works correctly, is stable, maintainable, and functions according to business requirements.

- **Change Management** - The IT tool helps to document the history of the software development lifecycle from envisioning and planning through deployment and support.

- **Project\Process Management** - The IT tool helps to clarify, focus, and set expectations for IT projects to better meet or exceed business goals.

- **Software\Hardware Architecture** - The IT tool helps to design, code, test, and implement and support software systems.

- **Documentation** – The IT tool serves to record the history of the software project's process, milestones, and results.

- **Presentation** – The IT tool serves to communicate visually, ideas, models, and processes to other project team members.

- **Software and Database** – These tools enable IT software and database engineers to build the product according to business requirements.

- **Communication** – The IT tool is used to send and or display messages to other project members regardless of their physical locations.

The bottom line principle is that IT tools should help talented resources perform their assigned tasks more effectively. If an IT tool does not meet this requirement, then there is no logical use for that tool and it should not be utilized. Many in IT love utilities that have an attractive user interface and include functionality that has little to do with the requirements they need to fulfill. This is known as the "Coolness Factor" and is often ineffective and useless. The "Coolness Factor" also adds significantly to the selection of the wrong tools for a given job and must be avoided at all costs.

You Get what You Pay For

Many organizations are of the mindset that they can drastically cut IT costs by eliminating critical personnel, software, and hardware and still achieve major enterprise level goals with an understaffed IT team, and little to no IT budget and resources. These businesses want results and in most cases, expect to get good or big returns without having to invest hardly anything. When IT personnel are understaffed and have few resources they often have to resort to survival mode, which often produces short-term or "tourniquet" solutions. These types of solutions are not designed to help an organization for the long-term. Short-term "quick fixes" in most cases end up costing a company more money than they would have spent if they would have paid to implement the solution with the proper resources. Cheap short cuts in IT are usually counter-productive and work against what they were originally designed to achieve. This is the fast track to developing reactive software solutions as opposed to proactive software solutions. Effective and efficient software systems that yield good return on investment generally take significant envisioning and planning which takes more time than most businesses can or want to allow. The bigger the software projects the more planning and time is usually required. On enterprise level software projects, "quick fixes" and cheap short cuts are almost never effective and can cost 2 to 3 times more money to upgrade or fix after the software application has been implemented.

I have often seen IT managers hire employees to work on large and complicated projects when they were fresh out of college and or had little to no experience for the roles in which they were selected. The plan was to have those employees "learn on the job" because the company either could not afford to or did not want to pay the high salary of an experienced and senior IT person. While training IT personnel is critical, they must have at least some basic skills and experience at the point of hiring when large and or critical projects are at stake. It is a common misconception that new and inexperienced IT people can always learn on the job in an enterprise project environment. From the very beginning of an enterprise project there are many planning stages where experienced IT personnel are critical for the long-term success of the project. Important questions and tasks must be answered and performed by project team members throughout the software development lifecycle. All members in their respective roles must be able to competently and successfully answer questions that affect many other team members and their tasks. If this cannot happen due to personnel who lack the knowledge and background then their peers can become frustrated and that can negatively affect team morale. This may also force team members to question the competence of IT management for hiring inexperienced IT personnel for important tasks that they are assigned to. Many IT employees' performance reviews and careers hinge on how successful the projects they work on are. Individuals who are learning at these junctions can tend to be "bottle necks" and hold up or stall the software development lifecycle and in turn cost the project and the organization time and money. Critical software projects are not training grounds for new inexperienced and employees. In most cases, companies are investing significant finances and resources in the IT projects that they commission and have little time or room for failure. Inexperienced personnel in the software project implementation process raise the level of risk for failure significantly and businesses must understand this so they can avoid this particular mistake in future critical projects. If IT management wants to hire new personnel who have little to no background working in the roles they are selected, then they must be sent to comprehensive training before they are allowed to work on IT projects independently. Afterwards, they will need to be paired with experienced IT people in their genres so they can be "Mentored" and learn in the field to gain the much needed experience to perform their tasks competently.

A source of never ending astonishment for me is in regards to how many IT departments I have consulted for that do not have separate development environments. The excuse that I often receive as to why this is not implemented is due to the business thinking that this platform is not necessary, so no funds are assigned and budgeted for it. As a result, business-computing environments are mixed with development computing environments, which can be a dangerous marriage. I have seen firsthand and on many occasions, where updates that were supposed to be implemented and analyzed on test computers were mistakenly installed on live business production systems. Depending on the level of change management processes and procedures the organization had in place, this mistake invoked either a major loss of time and money due to business systems being taken offline to correct code and or configuration errors that had to be remedied. All too often, IT software engineers need to utilize software and other network and hardware functionality that the business is currently consuming. Since the business must be up and running at all times in order to remain profitable, having IT on the same network domain only adds to the high risk of imminent:

- IT business network interference and latency due to testing

- Business network and or product down time

- IT software development network bottle necks and decreased bandwidth

- Overall security challenges as Development Networks must be "Open"

For serious development to be able to take root and grow within any IT environment, the software engineering team should have their own personal physically separate development network environment that is less secure and aloof from the business network domain. The IT development network is a "sand box" for the IT team to work with so that does not interfere in any way with the business systems. In this way, IT engineers can:

1. Envision IT Software Projects

2. Plan IT Software Projects

3. Prototype Software

4. Research and Develop software with the network being "Locked Down"

5. Deploy Test Software

6. Test Software

7. Make mistakes and learn from them safely

What this comes down to is that organizations and IT departments must not rely on being cheap and cutting corners to be successful. This usually leads to the exact opposite, more spending and additional processes. Companies and their technology teams who are serious about software development and their technology understand that achieving the results that they need is not always an inexpensive endeavor and that it takes time. In IT, the fast and the furious tend to fail in high numbers and can take many businesses with them. In this era of technology advancements that grow exponentially in relatively short time periods, businesses that may not have been founded on technology can grow into it, and then have that technology ultimately destroy it.

IT is notorious for being the most expensive department within an organization. It also is usually the most misunderstood section of most organizations due to the technology factor. If a business feels that they are not getting what they are paying for from their IT departments, then it may be because of significantly different objectives. When it comes to IT, you always get what you pay for because if you do your homework and get good references you can significantly lower your risk of failure with people. However, if you don't invoke competent research and development processes, and seek out sane referrals from trusted sources, then you definitely get what you don't want but unwillingly deserve.

Changing the IT Mindset

The days of complacency in regards to traditional IT personnel who believe that they will have "jobs for life" is surely coming to an end. With the advent of service-oriented software, many new third party companies are offering software applications as monthly services. Previously, traditional IT departments might have designed, coded, tested and implemented the software that their business now subscribes to. Application Service Providers (ASP) have propagated to the point of offering a great many services. An ASP is a 3rd party business that offers specific services to individuals and organizations over the Internet. They are also known as "On Demand" software companies. This market is already huge and is constantly evolving to meet business needs. Some entities that utilize ASPs include:

- Non-Profits
- Governments
- Private Businesses

ASPs offer a wide variety of services and the numbers of services offered by these types of organizations are rapidly expanding. These services are highly specialized, subscription based, and completed supported by the ASPs that make them available. Updates to existing services are usually offered 2 to 3 times during the year depending on the service organization and if the new functionality implemented is available to all subscribers. Some new features offered by ASPs are not free, and cost an additional fee if a company decides that they want to add the new functionality. Some ASP services include:

1. Customer Relational Management (CRM)
2. Enterprise Resource Planning (ERP)
3. Human Resources
4. Sales
5. Web site hosting, design, management and marketing
6. Educational Training
7. Medical Billing

8. Software Testing

9. Office Software (Word Processing, Presentation, Spread Sheets)

10. Hosted Web Meetings and Video Conferencing

11. Purchase Order Management

12. Financial Accounting

Outsourcing has been an enemy of many traditional IT departments for a long time. Organizations have traditionally outsourced IT projects so that they could use their IT resources to focus on their business core competencies and save on costs. Now and in the future, "in-house" IT must compete with ASPs for their jobs. Teaching software engineers to think in terms of the business and not just technology has become more necessary. This new way of thinking will help to save the jobs of many software engineers who never previously thought of their jobs as being disposable. In many companies, IT must compete directly with ASPs. To do this, IT department's software products must:

- Include Superior Functionality

- Be relatively easy to use and inexpensive to support

- Allow business users some level of extensibility if required.

- Include attractive, simple and effective user interfaces that their business users love.

This can be difficult to achieve but these IT software requirements go a long way towards making it difficult for an organization to decide to outsource a software application to an ASP. This is where working with the business to achieve the best possible requirements and to implement excellent envisioning and planning is crucial. It can be done, but the level of politics that can be involved in this process may be insurmountable within organizations without major executive support. If the leaders of IT cannot cut through the bureaucracy and politics that might burden their projects, their jobs and or careers may suffer as a result.

Building the Right Morale

Morale is important to the financial health and productivity of a company. If employees are not happy then their work usually shows it in one way or another. There is a saying, "Happy people do good work and sad people do bad work". This is far more the case than most people realize especially when it comes to technology where good and or great work is critical for financial success and growth. Many consider good morale to be the hub of productivity, and how others perceive their company, is in many cases, what their employees say about it. If employees are constantly talking about how much they love their jobs and how great their company is, that can go a long way in how that company is valued by many outsiders. This can lead to a continued stream of new clients and business opportunities. Most individuals and organizations like working with people who are willing to "go the extra mile" to help them because they themselves are happy professionally and want to share that with their clients. Every company that wants to get to or stay competitive in their industry must be concerned about the morale of their employees.

It is inevitable that not everyone on an IT team is going to like each other or get along but that really does not matter in the long term. It is always a great thing if a team and can have a great relationship both professionally and personally. However, it is not always realistic or even possible to achieve both. What is most important is the professional relationship and that should always be the primary target. Ideally, IT is not a popularity contest despite the many games that many people play in this field. Developing and maintaining good morale in IT is extremely important in the health and fitness of an organization and its business partners. Employee morale is a fragile entity that must be constantly nurtured and fed. This is something serious enough that if management does not understand it, the result may cost them their jobs. Some of the tools that IT Management can use to build good morale are:

- Frequently hold "Power Lunches" where employees can meet at a local restaurant or coffee shop for instance, and talk about how they are doing and their jobs in an informal environment that is outside of work. People can get to know each other and get a better understanding for what their colleagues are doing and feeling.

- Hire an independent consultant to periodically come in and talk to employees about company or departmental concerns. Have the consultant keep all employee comments unidentifiable and report to management the overall pulse and personality of their personnel. In this case, it is important that any consultant hired to do this be of unquestionable integrity and make it clear to all personnel they talk to that the information that they share will be read by management but will not be personally identifiable. In that way, employees can feel free to share their thoughts and concerns without fear of reprisals from their superiors.

- Watch, listen, and learn. Spend time walking around the office to see and hear what is going on. Look for employee interaction, listen for good communication and hopefully some occasional laughter, and learn about how people are reacting to one another. This periodic exercise can speak volumes to the manager who is willing to be attentive to it.

The following are two diagrams that show the importance and repercussions of both good and bad morale:

In order for management to discover the status of the morale of their personnel, they must talk to them. Management must be accessible to their employees and it is important for those employees to feel at least somewhat comfortable communicating with their superiors. If employees tend to quickly become quiet whenever management enters a room or area then that may not be a good sign. If employees at departmental or company meetings do not speak when given the opportunity that could also be an issue. Employees need to trust their management in order for morale to grow. Management must practice the skill of patience, listening, and good communication in order to disarm nervous or apprehensive employees. In this way, an employee can get the opportunity to know their superior(s) and in turn may be more willing to voice their concerns when a legitimate problem arises or they see a need for improvement in an area that has been overlooked by management previously. The road to building good morale in IT and many other parts of the business are the same. It begins and ends with:

1. **Trust**
2. **Respect**
3. **Patience**
4. **Loyalty**

These four subjects extend deep into many of the attributes that employees want and need. They lead to some of the things that employees want and deserve that include:

1. Good Pay (raises, bonuses, respect)
2. Flexible work schedules (the ability to work remotely is possible)
3. Good company benefits (health insurance, stock, retirement plans)
4. Good vacation, sick day, and holiday plans
5. The right quality tools for their respective tasks

When it comes to technology, necessity is still the mother of invention, but good morale builds greater products. It does this by motivating everyday people to do extraordinary things together. Good morale has the ability to make exceptional teams out of mediocre employees who might not measure up to a group of company all-stars. Since company stars sometimes do not work well together due to the competitive nature of their environments and personalities, they must have a reason or reasons to do so. Having morale at a high level within IT is often the catalyst for getting projects implemented. People are excited to look for the solutions to difficult challenges, as this is essential for Information Technology departments and the reason for the creation of technological solutions.

Taking IT to War

Business is war. Competition is fierce, and as a rule, business usually comes down to either one side gaining and working to maintain the unfair advantage and the other side trying to take it. Weak organizations generally do not eat well and suffer from malnutrition, they get sick and eventually die, while the strong businesses in their industries either assimilate their remains or leave them to the vultures that pick at what is left of the bones of the dead. The vast majority of people go into business to make money and as much of it as possible and that is the bottom line. With this, you have competing organizations within an industry that are literally trying to put each other out of work. With mortgages to pay and families to feed at stake, this is very serious business. Whenever an IT department becomes complacent, all of their competition gets stronger. The longer their self-satisfaction lasts, the more powerful their competition will become if they are constantly learning and growing in their technological pursuits. Eventually, that competition will most likely overtake their complacent adversaries and acquire the larger market share, which will make their company the entity that other businesses aspire to.

There is a revolution happening in Information Technology that has everyone in the industry encapsulated within a race against time and understanding. The more information a business can accumulate, analyze, utilize efficiently and productively will make that organization a virtual powerhouse of intellect and a model for others to follow. A company that can achieve and maintain this goal will also be extremely influential because of their superior technology, processes and sheer domain knowledge because they will have obtained the unfair advantage in their industry and worked through the strenuous political processes that others fall victim to. However, there is much more to this than gathering large amounts of data. The real Information Technology revolution lies in discovering the new possibilities of exactly how all of this new data can be understood. This is a monumental task and a process that constantly demands new information analysts to help decipher. All of this new data is accumulated at such a rapid pace that the sheer volume of the continuous tsunamis of raw information that is gathered this week alone worldwide could take years to analyze. This is the real challenge of the new IT revolution. What does all of this new data from all of the industries of the world mean? Newer and more powerful technology will have to be created and upgraded continuously just to assimilate all of this new data in a faster and more reliable manner.

This task may be most likely best suited for Artificial Intelligence (AI) to pursue. AI will definitely grow to handle a job of this magnitude but there is a real and significant danger in allowing the infinite processing of the world's data by computer systems. A serious question in this regard is; at what point does a computer network accumulate and process enough data to become self-aware? Based on that computer network's established rule set and its ability to change those rules, a complex AI system may decide at some point that it does not want to share all of its information with people or systems. Information filtering at some point is imminent based on the right applied data processing rule set and the constant flow of overwhelming numbers of new waves of data weekly, daily or hourly depending on the

Chapter 2: CAPTAINS AND CREWS

circumstances. With all of this new information to process, what conclusions might a computer network come to draw about human beings in general, our habits, and our personalities. The data exists in various systems today to do this but the technology to assimilate and make sense of it logically is always a work in progress. Learning to make sense of all of the enterprise data that is streaming into an organization is a key reason to take IT to war. The ability for a company to understand the information they are continuously accumulating is essential in their decisions, growth and quest for the unfair advantage.

An IT Department must be trained to understand that if they are not constantly learning and building then they are dying or already dead. Information Technology is a state of perpetual motion where positive change is king, whereas cash is king to the business. All changes must be driven towards adapting to what the business and their clients need. In many cases, IT personnel are oblivious that they have any competition. They get up in the morning, go to work, write some code and go home. They do not connect themselves or their tasks to the business and or any return on investment that may be associated with it.

When IT goes to war, everyone involved must understand the reasons why. Those reasons include:

1. **Giving the business the tools they need to do their jobs to secure the unfair advantage in their industry**

2. **Giving their business partners better and more effective, simple to use, easy to support software applications than 3rd Party vendors can provide**

3. **Providing software solutions that make business processes more efficient and allow business employees to do more and improve the overall financial bottom line**

4. **Increasing the value of IT in the eyes of the business to fight any notion of obsolescence consistently**

5. **Making IT within your particular organization the absolute envy of other IT departments in your industry due to your technology, processes, effectiveness and efficiency and relationship with the business**

6. **Completely and totally obliterating any competition to IT and its business counterparts**

7. **Protecting the organization, its assets, and preserving its right to do business**

It is imperative to understand that the IT war once started, never ends. This is because this type of war is more of an eternal quest than an actual conflict between parties. It is a war against obsolescence. The eternal quest is for a better way of doing things that few others are aware of, with tools that may not have even been thought of yet. This war of the "Quest" lasts for the life of a business. If it were to ever be cut short, an organization's technology would begin to degrade and with that, it would eventually lose its competitive edge or unfair advantage. Once this downward process begins, it is difficult to stop or slow down much like a runaway truck heading down a steep hill into a crowded market full of people. The process, if not averted, usually results in disaster in most instances.

The IT war must be limited to the competition and not internal business colleagues. This is a critical rule that must be enforced at all times. If the IT war were to spill out into the department internally and then to the business the whole purpose of invoking an IT war will most likely backfire. The repercussions of this unfortunate turn of events could readily destroy an IT department and the organization completely as well. It is of the utmost importance that that IT management work as hard as possible to keep their teams focused on their real enemy, which are complacency and industry competition.

Complacency wants:

- **Your Time**
- **Your Attention**
- **Your Morale**
- **Your Ambitions**

The competition wants:

- **Your customers**
- **Your jobs**
- **Your stock**
- **Your money**
- **Your sales**
- **Your complete and total demise**

If management fails to understand why taking IT to war is important, then they may also fail to realize why it is needed by the business in the first place. Finally, I remind you again that business is war, and IT is its "WMDs" (Weapons of Mass Destruction) and that arsenal must always remain armed, ready and aimed at complacency and industry competition.

Training the IT Warrior

Many IT personnel learn their skill sets by playing with various software languages, applications, hardware platforms, and by reading books on their spare time. Others learn "on the job" and occasionally attend specific skill focused training seminars that are paid for by their organizations. Some IT employees learn their trades by becoming apprentices and are mentored by a senior IT person that is well seasoned in the particular area in which they are teaching. Training the IT warrior correctly takes much more than what was previously described. The IT warrior must learn above all else how to think correctly. If this person cannot achieve this task, then they will be of little use to their team and organization. However, if the IT employees can learn to process information with the correct mental discipline, then the IT team has the ability grow into something extraordinary.

What is an IT Warrior? The IT warrior candidate can be a complex and misunderstood individual. Some reasons for this include an attitude of persistence, respect, passion and professionalism. This unique individual is made up of a strong varied composition that includes:

1. A raw passion for learning new and existing technology both on the job and at home
2. Honesty, integrity, and the ability to listen and try new things
3. Just enough ego to boost confidence and enhance job performance
4. Intelligence tempered with wisdom
5. Objective thinking
6. Warranted respect
7. Political knowledge without the practice
8. Amiability
9. Discipline
10. A strong desire to use technology according to "Best Practices" but will adapt when and if it is necessary to do so
11. A strong sense of individuality but can also work well with a team
12. The ability to write and speak simply and clearly when communicating their thoughts and ideas to others

Train IT personnel, especially software engineers, in acquiring the attributes described is no easy tasks. Some of the qualities listed previously are inherited traits such as numbers 5 and 11. The ability think objectively, with a strong sense of individuality but can also work well with a team can be hard to come by in a person. Naturally, it is always best to find candidates who initially match as many of the attributes as possible to train. Since this is not always practical, a plan must be in place for honing the mindset of the IT warrior. It is important to note that the way of thinking in this regard is the most important point. If you can get a person to think in a particular fashion, when you present technological tasks and challenges to them, they need little motivation in finding the best possible solutions. They will also make every effort to learn the skills they need on their own.

When it comes to technology, the brain is, and has always been the best tool for the job. If a task or process, no matter how large or small, can be accomplished just as efficiently and effectively without using technology, then don't use the technology! When it is not needed, technology is just an added layer of complication and distraction that often makes a situation worse. This is because if they are not part of the equation, technological solutions do not need to be supported, which saves time, money and reduces risk. The larger the solution, the more maintenance and resources technology requires. That is why the IT warrior must work smart first and hard second. IT is a thinking person's field as technology and projects in general are often areas of discovery. Many managers believe that the more people you put on an IT project that faster it will be done. That is not usually the case in Information Technology projects, as three people may not think any faster than one person can. Envisioning and planning are the most critical part of an IT projects and is where objectives and planning are "King" and "Queen". After the architecture and organization is established, it is very possible for the rest of an IT project to be completed more quickly according to the requirements because it has direction. Everyone in the project should know what he or she needs to do and have a great idea of how to go about his or her respective tasks. If the IT warrior does not understand how to use their most important tool (their brain) correctly, then they may not be the right candidate for the task. This is what every IT person must be taught to use in the appropriate manner first, accordingly to an organization's requirements, and business plans.

How do you know if an IT candidate has the right way of thinking imbedded within them to become an IT warrior? This can be unmasked or exposed in several ways. Some techniques that can be used are:

- Talk to the candidate and spend some time with them. Find out what they like to do when they are not at work. If their hobbies involve spending a good deal of time playing with and or studying technology that is similar to what they are doing at work, then this would show good IT warrior potential.

- Observe the candidate to find if they can actually work alone and in a team environment. Check the candidate's reputation and talk to their peers to find if they work well with others or if they are popular or not so. Also, recognize who is giving you the feedback about the candidate. This could be a clue as to whether or not politics may be involved and to what degree with the candidate. This analysis could also reveal if the individual has issues with their ego at work as well.

- Listen to the candidate to try to discover their technological views and how they go about their tasks. Do they apply the level of discipline required to be effective in their tasks? Do they speak in terms of "Best Practices" relating to technology or do they want to do things their own way on a regular basis.

- Analyze the candidate's work (or have someone you trust who is qualified to do it) to discover if it is well produced. Did they document their work and if so, is the candidate's documentation subject matter useful, easy to read and to the point?

Good IT warriors are hard to find because they are usually working. An intelligent organization will pay them well and keep in them happy with plenty of benefits. However, a sign of an IT warrior is that their egos are kept in check and they are not "entitlement" minded. True IT warriors are usually innately multi-talent, well versed in their craft, and always willing to grow. In order for a potential IT warrior to learn, they must have incentive to absorb what you want to teach them. In most cases, IT warriors want to learn more about the subjects that are of interest to them and they may not necessarily be the topics you are trying to show them. This can be a major issue so the incentive that you present must be interesting in order to get the attention of the warrior candidate. Because the right incentive must be something that is of significant interest, it is vital for the candidate in getting them on board with what you need them to learn and how you need them to think. This is why a good logical plan must be in place to train the IT warrior effectively. The planned curriculum developed to train the IT warrior must take into account the following:

- It must allow the IT warrior to integrate new ideas with what they already know.

- Focus on one theory and concept at a time and insure that they both deal with problems that relate to what the business is trying to do.

- Training should stay aligned with the "hands on" method of teaching as this is most effective with IT personnel.

- Candidates in the IT realm tend to take criticisms and mistakes personally and this could lower self esteem, which could negatively affect the ability to learn the material.

- The subject matter must be able to withstand challenges from various individuals with differing viewpoints.

- The teaching method utilized should be focused on self-directed learning projects. This will also allow the candidate to learn in a manner that will let them control the time and place in which they review and material and how much attention they are able to give to it.

- Use CDs, DVDs, slide presentations and anything visual to get your subject matter the attention it needs.

- The training environment should be as comfortable and relaxing as possible.

In training the IT warrior, the subject matter that a mentor or executive is trying to teach should be interesting, realistic, and attainable. If not, the IT warrior or the respective candidate could be planning their company exit strategy in the not too distant future. Not only that, but also those very same candidates that were once fighting on your side could very well become your enemies. These enemies are the worst kind, because they most likely know you and your company secrets intimately.

Dealing With 3rd Party Vendors and Consultants

This can be a tough topic for many IT Departments because there are so many horror stories in this realm to recount. A large number of IT departments that have used third party vendors and or consultants have many interesting accounts concerning their experiences in this relationship arena. This is another one of the primary love\hate marriages in the IT industry that is a complicated one full of high and low drama on both sides.

First, it is important to understand that IT consultants (or otherwise known as Independent Contractors) are not employees of the companies that hire them. I make this statement because during my years as an IT Consultant, I have seen IT and business managers at some companies make the mistake of trying to control the hours, environments, and tools of their Independent Contractors. In many cases, the measure of control that a business exercises over their consultants may violate the law of their State in regards to whether the Consultant is indeed an Independent Contractor and not an employee. If Consultants are treated as employees, they may be entitled to specific benefits under the laws of the State where their tasks are being performed. For instance, common Law Factors exists that determine whether or not a Consultant is an employee, and that Contractor may be entitled to certain employee benefits. Some of those control factors include, but are not limited to:

- If the contractor is required to comply with a hiring individual or company's instructions and rules regarding when, where, and how they work.

- If the contractor has established a "continuous" or "unbroken" relationship with a client where the contractor's tasks are performed frequently

Chapter 2: CAPTAINS AND CREWS

- If the contractor's working hours are set by the hiring individual and or business

- If the contractor is required by the hiring individual and or business to work "full-time" for them and not take on other clients

- If the contractor is trained by the hiring individual and or business to perform the duties requested of them

- If the contractor is required by the hiring individual and or business to perform the work on the premises of the hiring individual and or business when the job(s) could be somewhere else

Every State in America has clear guidelines for determining whether an Independent Contractor is and employee and vice-versa. In the United States for more information, contact your State's Labor and Industries Agency as this data is subject to change. In addition, you may want to check to see if your State's Labor and Industries Agency is following the laws it was established to enforce internally as well, you may be surprised at the results of your query. Every employee and contractor should be aware of their State's labor laws and challenge them whenever they are in doubt to insure that they are doing their job.

Unfortunately, I had worked for a State Agency that was responsible for enforcing the rules that differentiate employees from contractors and vice-versa. However, this State run agency did not police itself internally when it came to hiring IT Contractors to work on the projects that they were given revenue by the State Legislature to complete. This agency clearly ignored the laws of their State and treated Independent Contractors on their IT projects as if they were employees by controlling when, where, and how they worked among many other factors. I had even witnessed the firing of a State employee as a clear result of that person filing a complaint about their State Agency treated Independent Contractors as employees without offering them any benefits as required by that State's law. Many IT consulting companies will not complain about State Agencies treating their workers like State employees because they fear the political retaliation it would cause them. Since countless dollars are stake in State IT contracts each year, and biennium, few Independent Contractors want to be "blacklisted" from the opportunity to win these jobs because they "blew the whistle" on a State Agency that was ignoring the labor laws it was created to enforce. Although it might be in the best interest of IT consulting companies to partner with one another to expose the State employees who are abusing them and violating the law, but in reality, this is likely not to happen. This is due to the politics and huge amount of money and control that is at stake for all parties involved so business goes on as usual.

I have spent the vast majority of my career in IT serving as a Software Consultant to many companies ranging from startups to enterprises and this can be a very a tough job. Often times, consultants are setup to be the "fall guys" for failed company projects that were managed incompetently. It is easy to blame an individual or team who are not permanent employees of a company, by permanent employees when things go wrong with an IT software project. Jobs are on the line in many of these instances so that can make it easy for some company employees who may be at fault to accuse consultants for IT project failures. The problem with this is the good consultants who are involved in situations like these are only doing what they are assigned to do by the organization that hired them. They have no managerial power at the company so they cannot effect change nor do they manage anyone on the IT team at their client company. While consulting on a recent IT project, I was blamed by a business Director for missing project deadlines and taking the IT project over budget. The truth of the matter was that the project had taken much longer than expected due to severe "scope creep" by the business that IT management had allowed. The Director that accused me of taking the project over budget had endorsed this "scope creep". As I had no managerial power whatsoever to stop all of the requested changes that flooded every cycle of development, all I could do was to remind the business strongly that their requested changes were taking the project off course. I worked diligently to try to help the business to think in "phases" in order to keep the project timeliness. This was to no avail as company management supported all of the business's requested changes without thinking them through. The Director in question was present for almost all of the business changes request approvals but when he accused me of being the cause of the missed timelines, this fact was suspiciously omitted. Not only did I promptly and professionally remind the business Director and his team of this, I also shared my documentation of the facts that I had compiled to support my position. I heard nothing more of myself being the reason why timelines were not met after sharing my documentation with the Director and his team.

As a general and practical rule, consultants should never manage anyone on the IT team at the business that hired them (with the exception of Project Management). This is often a simple and basic conflict of interest. A bad or greedy consulting company would call this type of relationship "heaven" and could then steer the project in any way they desired and the business would not always know this. In addition, the consultant could embed themselves within an organization and feed off of that company financially like a revenue parasite. The embedded consultant could use their managerial power to:

- Hire additional consultants or other external personnel they desired

- Remove company IT project members that do not serve their purposes

- Stall the project to make more money

- Steer the project to obscure technologies that the consultant has special domain knowledge of in order to create a special dependency on themselves

I once worked for a company on an enterprise level project that at the height of its confusion employed 12 different consulting companies. The burn rate on this initiative was high to say the least. One consulting company did not know what was the other one was doing. This was because the companies generally did not communicate. This was not because the consultants did not necessarily want to talk to each other, it was because most of the personnel involved with the IT project didn't know what to ask each other or who the other project members were. The projects ran in chaos mode for a long time with only the illusion of management.

There is one primary rule that all Software Consultants should follow consistently. That rule is:

- *Good Software Consultants must never suggest to their clients what they "could do"; they must only suggest to their clients what they "should do".*

Software Consultants are "advisors", nothing more, nothing less. Good advisors make "suggestions" only, and never "tell" their clients what to do, ever. This is because they are "Advisors" not the project "Owners". The business always "Owns" the project and is ultimately responsible for it. The business owners can either take or ignore their consultant's advice. Many clients choose to selectively implement parts of the suggestions provided by their consultant's which can sometimes lead to many different problems. One of the biggest issues with this client approach is that when something does not work as they expect it to, companies then want to blame the consultant even though the consultant suggested a good and full solution that would have avoided the issue. Situations like this make a consultant's job far more difficult and sometimes not possible at all. There are few things worse in IT than when a bad Client\Consultant relationship goes on too long. Clients call Software Consultants because they have a service need due to a gap that they are unwilling or unable to fill. Software Consultants are service providers and therefore they should strategically position themselves to provide those services. That is the heart of this type of relationship. When the client no longer has a need (or want) for the requested service, and or the consultant can no longer provide their services adequately, then the relationship must end. However, in all too many cases, it does not.

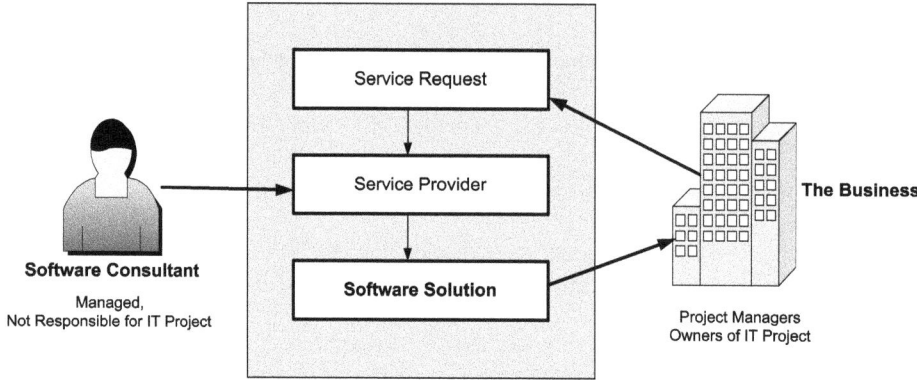

There are three basic types of IT consultants. They are:

1. **Consultants who only care about money**
2. **Consultants who care more for their clients**
3. **Consultants who care about the money and their clients equally**

The Money Loving Consultants

Some Software Consultants don't understand or care about the "big picture". That meaning, all they care about is taking as much money from their clients as they can get. Helping the client is secondary or tertiary. While revenue is important and is always the "bottom line", it is not the only line. Therefore, when a consultant makes revenue their only goal in their relationship with their clients, then their clients will always suffer as a result. Both the consultant and the client will sustain loss when it comes to:

- **Trust**
- **Performance**
- **Future Contracts (Revenue)**

In many cases, the "money loving" consultant will take on tasks that they do not have the skill set to complete successfully. This often times slows projects down and increases the risk associated with a software product's implementation. The slower a project runs, the more revenue they have the potential to make.

Consultants who think and operate this manner also negatively affect their own reputations. In the end, this behavior is counterproductive due to the fact that the ability to acquire future projects depend on the success of current projects. References and word of mouth are critical in a consultant's ability to find new work. Focusing solely on draining a client's finances often times leads to lost future revenue for the consultant among many other undesirables.

The Client Loving Consultants

It is usually a good idea for Software Consultants to keep their relationships with their clients on a professional level. However, many consultants stray from this path for various reasons. On many occasions, I have seen Software Consultants become "best friends" with the people whom their work for. Often this type of Client\Consultant relationship can become a liability for the consultant. For instance, if a client is your friend, it is more likely that they may expect occasional favors from you. Some of those favors might include:

- Working for free

- Working overtime for free

- Expecting you to come into their office anytime they wish. This could include days off and in the middle of the night without pay.

- Calling you anytime they wish with their questions and or problems. This could include days off and in the middle of the night without pay.

- Expecting additional features to their software applications for free.

I have seen the pay of some consultants cut in half because they let their client "friends" take advantage of them. Some Client\Consultant friendship relationships work out very well because the "respect" factor is present and neither party tries to supersede the other. However, this type of relationship is not common and could take years to develop. One should not count on a friendship starting with new clients. Focusing on this area is counterproductive to what should happen in the professional Client\Consultant relationship. That is, the client is requesting a service, and the consultant should be providing the requested service lawfully, as best they can.

The Balanced Consultants

Finding Software Consultants who care equally for their clients as they do for earning a living is not an easy task. Consultants of this type tend to not stay in one place for more than a year or two at the most. This is because a great deal of the time a client does not understand the value of this type of consultant. The balanced consultant will generally not sacrifice what they know is right in industry best practices just for the sake of revenue. They will not deal with a bad client for very long if they can help it. They understand, and recognize when a relationship is not working or will not work out over time. The most important aspect of the Client\Consultant relationship to the balanced consultant is:

1. An interesting project

2. A good working environment with good people

3. A good hourly rate

All of the above, with the exception of number 1, are completely subjective to the needs of the balanced software consultant. These types of firms and the individuals who work for them are not driven or motivated by any single factor. That is because no one issue alone can make the balanced consultant successful. This consultant type understands that when a seasoned organization looks for software consultants, they look for a package not any one attribute.

Choosing the Balanced Consultant

There are some basic attributes to look for when considering working with any software consulting firm. First, it is always critical to get as many references as possible in regards to the consultant, and know what it is that you want the consultant to do upfront. It's hard to find a good consultant if you don't know what you want, so you must have your house in order (project scope defined) before you can expect an consultant to be able to competently help you. If you have done your homework and have outlined the technical services that you need performed, then you should look for the following in a software consultant:

- Solid communication processes. How do they communicate and how effective has it been with their previous clients?

- What are their IT processes and methodologies? How do they implement the Software Development Lifecycle? What other methodologies do they know and work well with and why?

- When problems arise, how prompt have they been to address and correct them?

- Do they have a professional reputation and deliver project deliverables on time?

- How do they adjust to and handle change requests?

- Do they refuse work that they lack the skill sets to accomplish?

- Are their rates reasonable and what is their general project exit strategy?

Depending on the organization's software project scope and requirements, there may be many more questions that would need to be asked. Outsourcing carries a certain degree of risk for most companies. Not being afraid to ask the right questions is the first step in helping to minimize those risks. No third party software-consulting firm has ever made or broken a software project. It is always the organization's management of their projects and consultants that invoke success or failure. This should never be a secret in any Client\Consultant relationship.

Summary

Are you managing your IT team or is your IT team managing you? Are you managing your projects or are your projects managing you? Are you managing your software or is your software managing you? IT crews are subject to their Captains, who are in turn responsible for their crews. The 33rd President of the United States, Harry S. Truman said the following:

- *"I sit here all day trying to persuade people to do the things they ought to have the sense to do without my persuading them."*

Chapter 2: CAPTAINS AND CREWS

- *"It is amazing what you can accomplish if you do not care who gets the credit."*

- *"I never did give them hell. I just told the truth, and they thought it was hell."*

- *"The buck stops here."*

President Truman was one of the most modest Presidents in the history of the United States. However, he made the most critical decision in the history of the human race. After 4 months in office, Truman dropped two atomic bombs, one on city of Hiroshima and the other on city of Nagasaki in Japan during the Second World War. Although he was greatly criticized as a result, this act changed the planet forever by thrusting humankind into the nuclear age. Not only that, the atomic bomb made The United States of America a world super power and ended World War II. Afterwards, Truman put The United States in a position to help other nations (including Japan) and positively affect world policies. He heavily supported the reconstruction of Europe and the creation of Israel, as we know it today. Truman believed in service, not domination, and would not be appreciated for his contributions until decades after his death. His quotes are words to both lead, and live by.

"He that always gives way to others will end in having no principles of his own."

- *Aesop (Ancient Greek Fabulist and Author of a collection of Greek fables. 620 BC-560 BC)*

Chapter 3: COMMUNICATIONS

IT and Business Communications

The "Tower of Babel" was a good story of how devastating it was when groups of people within a city lost their ability to communicate with their fellow citizens. Frustration and confusion mounted in the city because large groups of people who could previously understand each other no longer could. This lead to the breakup of the city due to the fact that city patrons did not want to live and work with people that they could not understand. There were groups of people, however, in the city who did speak the same language. As a result, those people left to start their own new cities and communities.

On March 13, 2007, the United States Navy lost communications with the USS San Juan, a billion dollar nuclear submarine off the coast of Florida. This prompted the Navy to start a major search and rescue operation and begin notifying the families of the submarine crewmembers that the submarine could not be found. Early the next morning, communications with the USS San Juan had been re-established and the officers and crew aboard had no idea that anyone was looking for them. It was widely reported that the USS San Juan had simply missed a pre-scheduled communications period.

When communication is lost with a billion dollar nuclear submarine, one of the major concerns within the military must be that the submarine in question might think that the United States may be under a nuclear attack. As a result, the submarine might then respond by launching inter-continental ballistic missiles (ICBMs) against pre-designated enemy targets after a period. Fortunately for everyone in this case, that did not happen. Just such a scenario was the making of a popular Hollywood movie back in the 1990.

IT and the business must educate each other as to their communication methods, techniques, jargon and syntax. Businesses can help to facilitate this through meetings, training sessions, seminars and even carefully planned company parties. If businesses do not constantly strive for the absolute best levels of inter-departmental communication then it risks becoming stagnant in that regard. If this happens the company's technology also runs the risk of not growing as well. Some reasons for this is are:

- New IT software projects are born from business needs. If the business fails to communicate their needs to IT, there can be no new IT projects that they can use.

- If the business incorrectly communicates its needs to IT then the business risks losing time and money on related IT projects as a result.

The Tower of Babel and the USS San Juan stories teach us how miscommunication and the lack of communication can both have potentially devastating results. Constant education and training in regards to inter-departmental communication within any business is always a good plan. Even a company that is well educated in interdepartmental communications can still have serious problems with IT if it is not structured properly. IT people are not usually business minded and business people are not usually technical. This fundamental difference should never be ignored in any capacity and should always be a point of reference. With this in mind, it is best to have a well-trained, experienced liaison team in place to facilitate, translate, and nurture the relationship between the business and IT. This helps to keep the wrong people from meeting with the right people and vice-versa. It also works to insure that all players concerned are truly on the same page before, during, and after a project.

Gathering Business Intelligence

Obtaining the "unfair advantage" in order to accumulate the most revenue possible is the driving force of business ventures in a capitalistic society. The more a business knows about its own inner working and about what its competition is doing, the better equipped it can be to move forward effectively in their industry. Business communications is much more than just one company department talking to another in meetings or through email and telephone calls. In many cases, business communications are inadvertent, and critical data for IT projects may be relayed through other means. IT plays a major role in the acquisition and analysis of business intelligence from which a company that has established a reliable research and development division can greatly benefit from.

The art of industrial information gathering from a company's competitors, whether obtained legally or in a covert manner, is alive and well. Many businesses collect their information illegally, which is spying, in order to gain an advantage over their competition. While this may be unethical, against the law, and sometimes even dangerous, for some businesses, it is well worth the risk and they will spend surprising amounts of money for that data. This is because obtaining your greatest adversary's trade secrets could either level the playing field between the two of you or give your company the "unfair advantage" over your competition.

Business intelligence is the practice and methods by which industrial data is obtained, analyzed, and used in order to further the cause of an organization, group, or individual.

This practice also enables a company to:

1. Better understand how they are performing in their marketplace

2. Budget and allocate resources more effectively

3. Monitor business drivers

4. Make more informed and better decisions quickly

It is important to note that the practice of gathering business intelligence can be quite broad and can stretch the legal limits of the law. Many businesses have made this act an art form and have also developed processes in which they can operate inexpensively and procure large and detailed amounts of information about their competitors without breaking the law. Some businesses are able to do this by using some of the following methods:

- **General Intelligence** – This is the usual way in which the public gains information about almost anything. This information can be obtained through the Internet, newspapers, television, industry analysts, the company's employees and magazines. Some of the elements that make up general intelligence are:
    - The size of the company
    - The location of the company's headquarters and their satellite offices
    - The number of employees that company has
    - A company's mission statement and basic strategy
    - A company's goals
    - A company's employee turnover rate
    - A company's assets
    - Company products
    - Company services
    - Company press releases
- **Industrial Espionage** – This includes any information about a company that is gathered illegally or through a covert manner. This includes such illegal practices as:
    - Wire tapping
    - Secretly recording business conversations
    - Theft
    - Coercion
    - Blackmail

- Spying
- Bribery
- Internal and external company surveillance

However, depending on the country you reside in, some of the above procedures may be legal in regards to gathering business intelligence.

- **Revenue Based Intelligence** - This form of business intelligence gathering is also based on gathering data from public and readily available sources. However, this occurs more in the national or international arena. This type of information procurement is usually the practice of medium to large companies who have much more to gain or lose than smaller local businesses. The type of information in this realm includes:
    - A company's quarterly and yearly revenue earnings
    - A company's quarterly and yearly revenue earnings broken down by products
    - A company's quarterly and yearly revenue earnings broken down by services

It is important to note that the simple act of gathering data is not intelligence. The process of effectively analyzing the data gathered through the methods above then makes it true business intelligence.

For instance, in 1983 the United States came dangerously closer than ever before to invoking a nuclear war with the former Soviet Union. At that time, the relationship between the United States and the Soviet Union was "extremely stressed" and nuclear war tensions were high. This was due to years of intense information gathering by the Soviets that appeared to point to a conspiracy based on the strong premise that the United States was going to launch a preemptive nuclear strike against them. Although the Soviets had incredibly deft resources and methods of gathering data at that time, unlike the United States and Great Britain, they had little to nothing in place that could effectively analyze it. Therefore, they could only theorize and conspire as to what all of their data meant and make assumptions as to the intentions of the United States in regards to their nuclear intentions, which were based on conspiracy theories. The problem with this is at that time was that it brought the planet to the brink of World War III.

As the United States and NATO (North Atlantic Treaty Organization) were performing military exercises in 1983 that were designed to culminate in a nuclear bombardment of Eastern Europe, Soviet Union leaders were convinced that those military exercises were in fact an actual invasion. The President of the Soviet Union at that time, Uri Andropov, had his country's military on high nuclear alert because of this, and was battle ready to launch a full nuclear counter-strike in response to the perceived invasion by the United States. Although this is an extreme example, it is a good one to illustrate the importance of effective data analysis. Without it, reports are most likely translated into assumptions, theories, and conspiracies and many conclusions can be drawn from that data that have very little or nothing to do with the facts of a matter.

Centralizing Business Intelligence

It always amazes me at to which extent many companies do not share much needed information internally that is requested, required, and important to completing business and client related mission critical tasks. A de-centralized business intelligence structure within an organization can contribute to far less streamlined business processes and hinder a company's ability to make decisions quickly. In 2006, Gartner (a leading IT research and consulting company) conducted a survey of 1,400 CIOs. It reported that IT organizations were becoming more focused on business intelligence in order to deliver services and software solutions to their businesses and customers.

Traditionally, it has been challenging for companies to build or buy software solutions that connect their decision makers and employees to the specific data they need. This is, however, an essential driver in obtaining enhanced business performance and is a goal that every business should work hard to reach and maintain. IT must work with their business partners to build or buy comprehensive reporting environments based on complex business intelligence software systems. This software must be able to aggregate and process data from a number of different sources that contain business and customer related information. These sources include Customer Relational Management (CRM) and Enterprise Resource Planning (ERP) software systems along with data warehouse consumption. Comprehensive but intuitive user interfaces must be used to display the data in a variety of formats so that the same information can be understood by the various decision makers and employees utilizing the business intelligence-reporting environment.

The following is an example of high-level business intelligence system architecture:

Chapter 3: COMMUNICATIONS

Centralized Business Intelligence Layout (High Level)

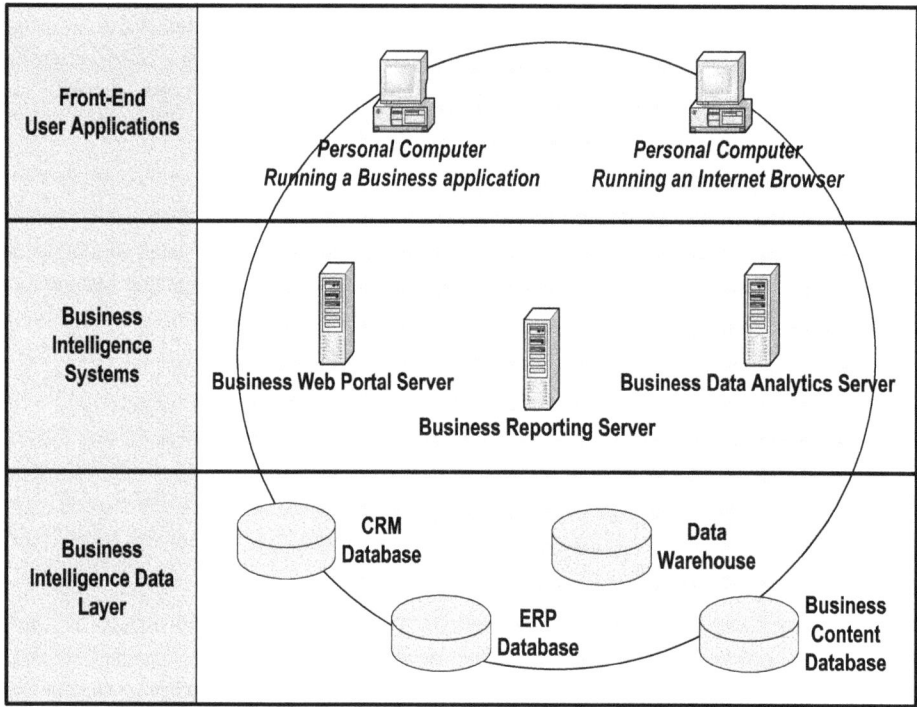

The benefits of implementing a solid, stable, scalable and reliable centralized business intelligence foundation include:

1. Access to a broad spectrum of business data by employees and management

2. Increased and more comprehensive support for executive management

3. Increased and more comprehensive support for employees

Centralizing business intelligence can often expose many problems within an organization that need immediate attention. Insuring that various business departments whose reporting tools are proprietary to their needs, actually integrate with, and work with the reporting systems of other business units is an ongoing challenge. In many cases, large companies internally support databases and even separate data warehouses that are incompatible with each other and are not either supported very well, or may contain data that is no longer useful. Another problem with a business in this scenario is that they are often supporting redundant information throughout their various data structures. This is because repetitive data and outdated information can pose a significant business risk and negatively affect the ability to make strategic decisions consistently.

A centralized business intelligence foundation is also a good platform to see if the company's products and services offered to their customers also work for the business as well. For instance, if as consulting company offers their customers a commercial reporting tool that they develop in-house, then that organization's employees should also use the reporting tool. In this way, employees can provide valuable feedback on the reporting tool and serve as working proof that the product works in a business environment. This is often referred to in business as "eating your own dog food". The company can use this as a selling point to customers, letting them know that they themselves use their own products and services, (hopefully) if they work well. Usually, if a business uses it own products and services, many customers will believe that the product does indeed work and may consider using it too.

Centralized Business Intelligence Critical Data

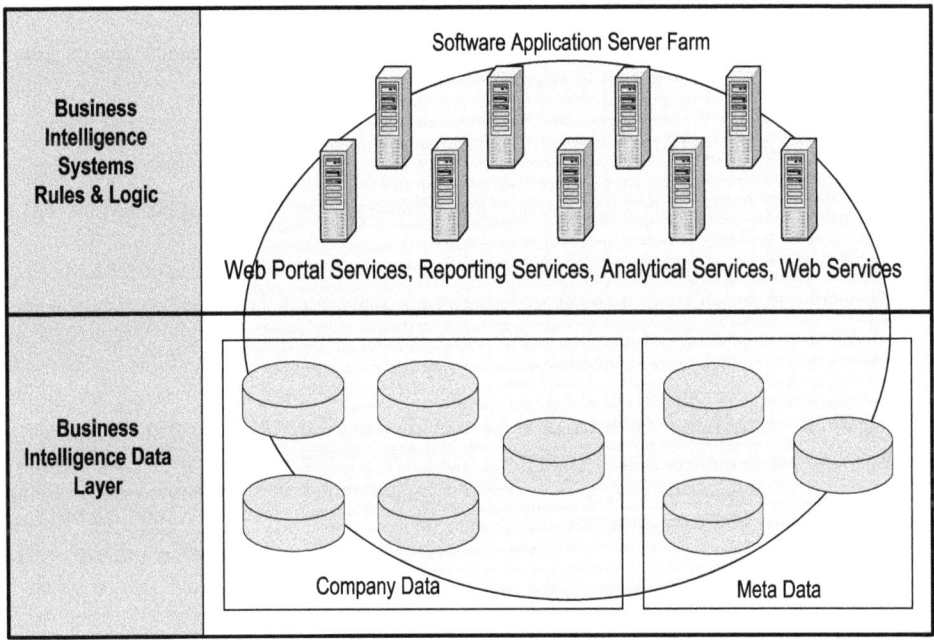

Streamlining Business Intelligence Software Systems

Some large companies internally support software applications and disparate data sources that contain redundant data and information that is no longer useful. This may be true even if the company has centralized business intelligence applications in place. This is because some departments within the company may continue to maintain their own reporting systems. IT organizations seeking to efficiently and effectively build and maintain a corporate business intelligence environment must investigate these scenarios, and eliminate and or integrate these types of siloed systems into the main artery of their organization's business intelligence infrastructure.

The return on investment of doing this includes:

- Cutting the cost and support of unnecessary software systems

- Cutting the cost and support of unnecessary computer hardware

- Freeing up hardware resources that could be utilized elsewhere within the company or sold for additional revenue

- Cutting the cost and support of unnecessary disparate databases

- Cutting the cost of software system development by reducing the number of systems needed for application integration

- Consolidating and targeting all reporting services and applications

- The ability to apply centralized security to business intelligences applications

When business intelligence applications are streamlined, they are much more effective because system security can be increased and better maintained. The best way to insure good application security in this regard is to centralize all business intelligence resources to an area where significant and redundant physical and application related security "best practices" can be applied. It is generally harder for an IT organization to enforce system security if company applications are scattered or distributed all over the business software production network. This is because the ways in which companies can share information is too vast and filled with many security holes, which can be exploited by uninvited and unwanted entities. Many companies also do not have the resources to support and protect disparate business intelligence related systems that have their own security in place. Usually, organizations create extranets that allow their sensitive and target specific business intelligence data to be shared with their employees, partners, and customers on the Internet worldwide.

Centralized Business Intelligence Global Use

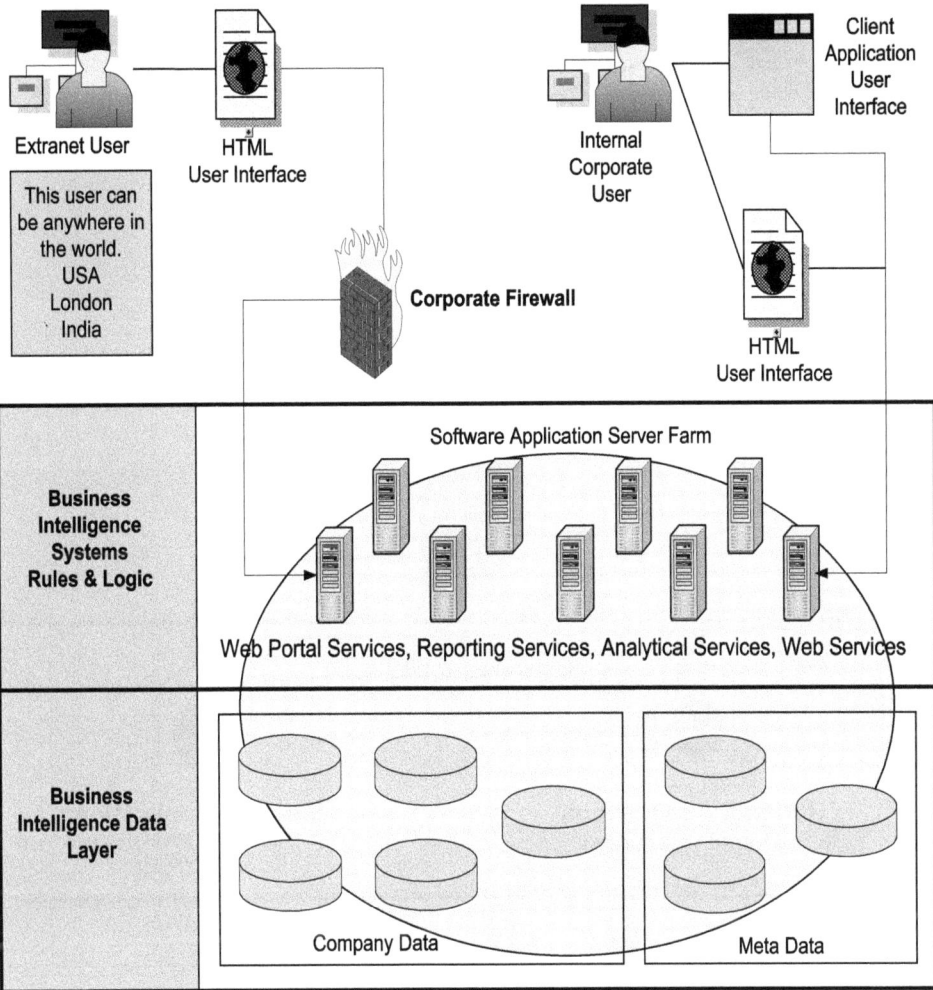

It is also important to understand the use of extranet, intranet, and internet in regards to business intelligence systems. The differences between the three of these domains are based on the level of security applied to each.

Chapter 3: COMMUNICATIONS

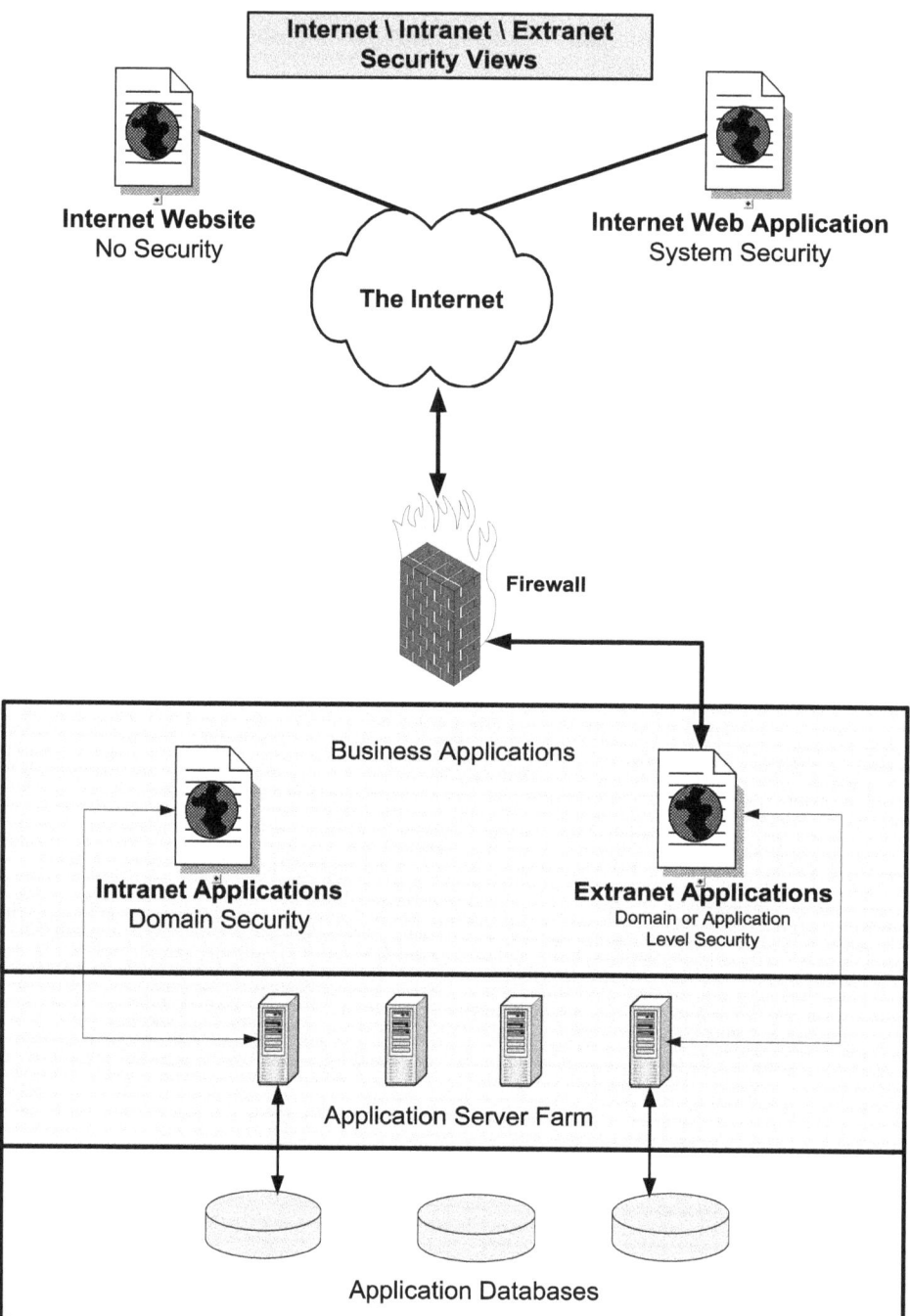

- **Internet** – Web sites and web applications are published and made available to the general public to peruse. Advanced web-based applications that facilitate ecommerce transactions generally include a high level of security. Other web application security is based the user's assigned permissions within web applications they logon to. The Internet can be accessible from Internet or Extranet web sites and web applications.

- **Intranet** - Web sites and web applications are published and made available behind a firewall, within a business, group, or individual's computer network. Security is based on the assigned user's domain permissions granted by the administrator of network they logon to. Intranets are not directly accessible from the Internet. However, in some situations, an intranet can be made accessible from an Extranet if the business requires.

- **Extranet** - Web sites and web applications are published and made available behind a firewall, within a business, group, or individual's computer network. Security is based on the assigned user's domain permissions granted by the administrator of network they logon to. An Extranet is accessible from the Internet.

Liaisons

The Business Analyst is responsible for determining the needs of the business. They assist company stakeholders and decision makers with information discovery and resolve business problems using process orientation. During the Software Development Life Cycle, the Business Analyst serves as the liaison between the business and IT or third party service providers. Common titles for Business Analyst include:

- **Functional Systems Analyst**

- **Functional Analyst**

- **Business Systems Analyst**

- **Systems Analyst**

Companies may differentiate between the titles (or add to them) and related responsibilities for this role but the core duties of this position are virtually the same.

The Business Analyst role within any organization is only as valuable as that business is wise enough to utilize them. A enlightened company that appreciates the value of an effective, experienced analytically sound communications team, and utilizes it effectively in relation to the software development lifecycle has a gold mine in their midst. An ignorant company can fail to realize the importance of communications and analytics by blocking its liaison team from being effective or allowing it to languish has little to no value in this arena.

Make no mistake, the liaisons are the communications hub of a company. They are the librarians, historians, and therapist of the business. Business Analysts monitor the pulse of their respective industries and make it a point to keep the company headed in the right direction. Being the stewards of the company information, Business Analyst in most cases serve as the point people for all departments. This means that the team must be solid, knowledgeable, intelligent and easy to work with.

Analyst usually are among the highest paid groups in a business because of their knowledge base, documentation, reports, meetings, and suffer through more politics than most other business groups. When you need information regarding the state, direction, history or problems of a specific industry, you talk to an Analyst. For example, evening news programs, talk shows, financial insiders, and sports commentators all prominently feature Analysts on a regular basis as the comprehensive experts in their fields.

Great Business Analysts are generally born, not trained. Unmistakably, you can train a person to be a good Business Analyst, but to become a great Business Analysts a person must have a natural passion for:

- Gathering factual and required company and industry data
- Reporting and analysis of factual company and industry data
- What is happening (new innovations) in their respective industry
- Working with company employees to understand their needs
- Producing and maintaining business process documentation
- Facilitating required company meetings
- Assisting with Training

The less passion that an individual has for the above tasks, the more difficult they can be to perform at a high level.

Managing Analyst

An information team must have a leader who can tie all of the company data together and communicate that data effectively to executive management. If a leader is going to play politics within a business, this is definitely one of the people you do not want doing that. A strong bi-partisan, well-spoken and somewhat charismatic individual must fill the Managing

Analyst role. They must pull together, focus and utilize not only their own diverse team, but manage information from different departments along with their processes. Business Analysts are major patrons who must be secured on the road to the Elysian Fields.

The Managing Business Analyst understands that the data that a business generates is the company's past, present, and future history. They understand that all of the data that is gathered by the analytical team must be translated into languages that the business and IT both understand. In order to reach this objective, the following must take place:

- The Managing Analyst must work with the business and the Data Architect to implement a viable Data Warehouse or Data Marts (organized business data).

- The Managing Analyst must work with the business and the Software Systems Architect to implement a comprehensive web-based reporting system. The reporting software system will consume the Data Warehouse or Data Marts.

- The Managing Analyst must be a masterful tactician when it comes to insuring that his team members are in the right places at the right times. This individual will be an expert at separating political information from useful business data from their team.

- The Managing Analyst's primary responsibility is to keep their team focused on what the business needs, and how the business can get what they need in the best way possible for all concerned.

If you are working to take your business to the Elysian Fields, you must have the right people in the right places doing the right things. If the Managing Analyst is not filling the role described, the odds of leading your business to successful projects falls dramatically.

Lead Analyst

Depending on the size and the needs of the business, a Lead Analyst may or may not be needed in all scenarios. Some may refer to this role as a "Managing Analyst". This means that the primary role of the Lead Analyst is to insure the integrity of business requirements.

When many IT and business people refer to the Analyst, they talk primarily about requirements gathering and how important that task is. However, it is important to note that few seem to focus on the integrity of the processes by which those requirements gathered. Who insures that the requirements are correct after they are gathered, signed and documented? The Lead Analyst does before his or her boss ever sees it.

Requirements gathering can easily be a full time job. Universal translation and politics in almost any arena is not easy to manage. This can be a serious issue in requirements gathering. Dealing with various business groups that need technical solutions for some of their problems is usually tough. While the Business and Technical Analysts are busy trying to interpret what the business needs from what the business wants, in many cases there is little time to re-check for errors in requirements and processes.

The Lead Analyst functions as the requirements police. It is not always practical for Business and Technical Analysts to sit with or follow the business people whose processes they must learn and convert to use cases. Lead Analysts are the follow up. They shadow the business people they need to in order to make sure that the processes documented for a given IT project are correct. They are not meant to harass or question the integrity of the employee, but to question and or test the integrity of a business process and its facts. This is because everyone makes mistakes or honestly may forget minor steps of their everyday processes while attending project requirements meetings. This is not unusual in requirements project gathering meetings. In many cases, business people refuse to take ownership of their IT projects. This is because they may be unsure of the related project business processes or they cannot confirm the entire process because it depends on one or more other business people who may be unavailable some, or most of the time.

Business processes and use cases are the law that IT must abide by in order to get technical projects done successfully. If there are no means of law enforcement provided by the business, then the rules can go unheeded. Depending on what the business requests of the analytical team, the Lead Analyst could serve as law enforcement in many different capacities such as:

1. **City Police** – IT project requirements gathering only

2. **State Police** – Business departmental requirements gathering only

3. **The FBI** – Inter-departmental requirements gathering only

4. **The Military** – All business requirements gathering on every level

Business Analyst

This member of the analytical team is assigned to the business most of the time and must have a strong business background. The Business Analyst's primary skill is working with business users in order to reveal the particular needs of a department or the business as a whole. It is important to stress that the Business Analysts works primarily to determine the needs of the business, not the wants of the business or individual end users.

Out of all of the members of the Analytical team, the Business Analyst must be the most politically savvy, but amiable. This is because they work at the grass roots level with business employees who do not always know what they need so it must be discovered. In addition, these business members may have career ambitions and political agendas that may not correspond with the needs of the business. The Business Analyst must work through these issues while maintaining a stern objectivity from one department to another.

Many Business Analysts also have a technological background to some degree, which helps to communicate business requirements and processes to technical team members. Analyst can use several different means by which they can extract the needs of the business from the business community. Some of these methods include:

- Meetings and Phone Calls
- Emails and Instant Messaging
- One on one Use Case sessions
- Presentations
- Shadowing (watching end users work and making notations)
- Video recording end users at work

Business Analysts are the primary software system reporters, librarians, and company process historians. They create, store and maintain all business and even some technical process documentation. Business Analysts are the point people for business requirements and process definitions past, present and future. As the "brain trust" of an organization, Business Analyst must keep their fingers on the pulse of the industry in order to understand where their business fits within it.

Technical Analyst

In some companies, Technical Analysts are also Software Engineers. They are occasionally referred to as "Programmer\Analysts". Depending on the needs and requirements of an organization, a Technical Analyst may be a part of the software architectural team instead of the Analytical Team. This may happen in cases where a company has a rather large interest in Research and Development and has significant resources devoted to this area. If this were so, a Technical Analyst would work for the Software Systems Architect whose primary task is to transform business processes and requirements in technical solutions.

If the need for a Technical Analyst were to assist with software development, then they would work directly with IT Software Engineers. They would then serve a dual purpose relating to both technical requirements gathering as well as developing software. It is a fact that no one understands a Software Engineer like another Software Engineer, so Technical Analysts can be invaluable when it comes to communicating with software developers.

Historically, Software Engineers have generally been some of the worst employees when it comes to communicating with the business. This is because most "talk tech" which means they speak with a technical vocabulary when communicating with business employees who are not technical. This can be the path to miscommunication in meetings involving IT and the business. Furthermore, it has also bred feelings from the business that IT members have large egos because the company does not understand their "technical jargon", and think of themselves as intellectually superior to the business when in fact, in a great deal of situations, it is the intelligence of the business that pays IT salaries.

To protect the fragile relationship between the business and IT and to help projects run more effectively, a technically perceptive, good communicator is necessary in almost every situation. However, as a part of the overall analytical team, the Technical Analyst brings a strong cross-platform view to analytical business discussions and company requirement gathering sessions.

Analytical Team Relational View (without Lead Analyst)

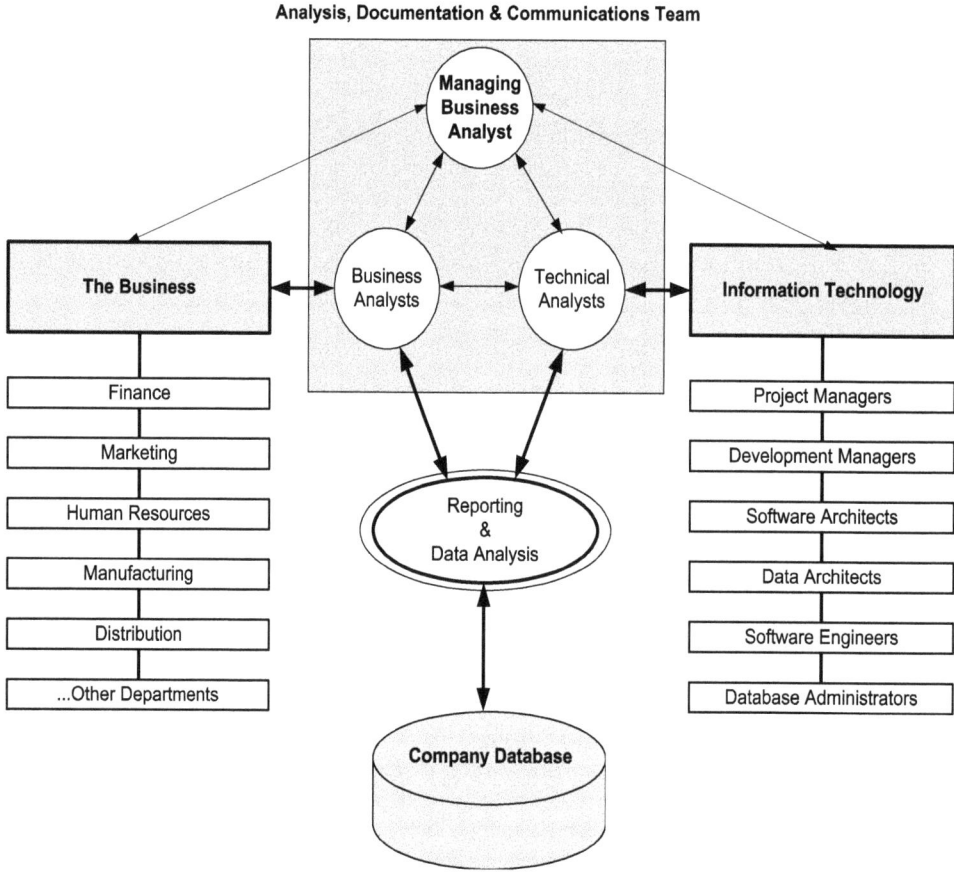

Analytical Team Relational View (with Lead Analyst)

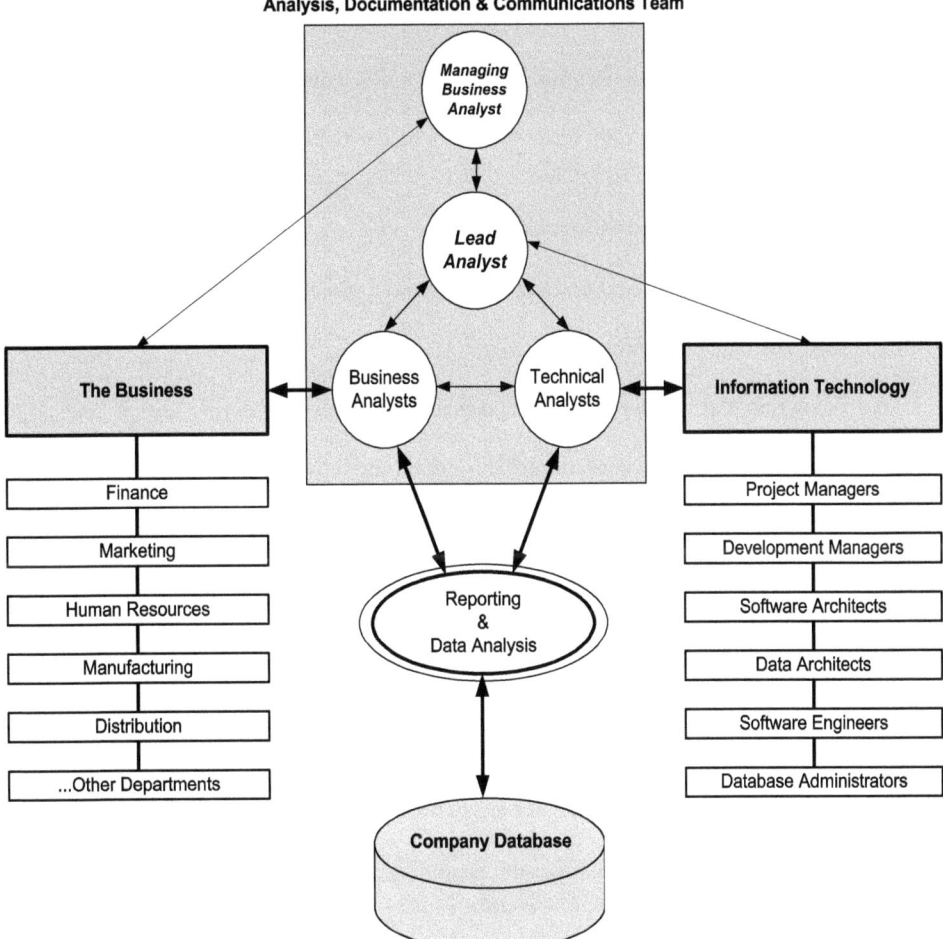

Setting Expectations

In communications with the business and IT, setting expectations is one of the most critical elements to get right and maintain. All too many times as IT projects progress, expectations are unclear and members on both sides are not sure of exactly what they are supposed to do, if anything at all. This is especially frustrating to business users in regards to technology.

Setting expectations can go a long way towards building a trust relationship between all players involved in an IT project. However, this process is far more than just telling others what you are going to do. Simply describing to others what you are going to do or what you want others to do in a project clearly is not always effective. There are rules for setting good expectations in communications for IT projects. Those laws consist of:

1. Defining realistic objectives and listening to other team member's ideas

2. Assigning the appropriate team members to the right tasks that help to achieve the objectives

3. Assigning deadlines to those tasks

4. Display transparency and be clear, concise and to the point in all correspondence

5. Documenting everything

6. Being respectful of all concerned and their tasks

7. Holding team members accountable for their respective tasks by publishing them

In setting expectations, if you show just cause for failure to meet the goals outlined by not following the rules, then you set a poor example and an expectation for failure. It is important to meet your objectives so that a trust can be established within an IT project. Nothing builds trust like positive results through people doing what they said they were going to do.

When setting expectations within projects, one should also:

- Never try to do too much at any one time and be transparent

- Insure that the tasks that you choose are the most effective to meet the objective

- If the objective changes, start at the beginning of the expectation setting process and follow the rules all the way to the end

If you find that you are not able to meet the expectations that you set for legitimate reasons, communicate that fact immediately to all parties concerned. Not communicating project changes when they are discovered is usually a bad idea for many reasons:

- Project members can waste time and company money working to accomplish objectives that are no longer valid.

- Project return on investment is negatively affected

- The trust factor among team members can become an issue

- Project team members can become frustrated and team morale can also be adversely affected.

Setting good expectations and consistently meeting those expectations can put you on the super highway to the Elysian Fields.

Understanding the "Bottom Line"

Failure to understand what makes a business think that way they do is common in most IT departments. Since many IT people are usually not "business minded", it can be very difficult for them to think in non-technical terms. Sometimes business people themselves don't understand why their business works the way that it does and this can be a major issue. For instance, an IT Software Engineer may think that a process that they are to implement is "stupid" or does not make any sense. As a result, they may make what they perceive to be "minor" changes to a software application that utilizes this particular process. These "miniscule" process changes implemented by the Software Engineer to the software application in question may not be apparent to the business initially. However, those changes may happen to be critical enough to end up costing the business tens of thousands or even millions of dollars (depending on the amount of revenue the business generates annually) over a given time period. This is because the "minor" change that the Software Engineer implemented (to make the process better) directly adversely affected the company's annual revenue without the Software Engineer or the business realizing it straight away.

What if an IT project's members were informed that the longer a project took the less they would be paid? In addition, if the software product's quality and integrity suffered in any way whatsoever, they would be paid even less. What kind of software product would an IT team under this kind of pressure produce? Would it generate a more or less superior result? They say, "Pressure makes diamonds", and in some cases, this is true. However, does this also apply to software development? Scenarios such as the one described is not designed to produce great, or even good software products. It would most likely yield a reduction in the number of IT project employees over time due to frustration. Few business and IT members could withstand this level of pressure and stress for very long due to complex nature of their assignments. Only the strongest and most competent IT and business employees would ultimately survive along with the best Hackers. Inevitably, since there would be less IT project members to get the job done, you would have to pay those people far more money.

The point of all of this is the fact that too many IT projects waste money by wasting time because this is allowed to happen via poor management decisions. Too many business Executive Managers enable their subordinates in the business to have "card blanch" and make as many changes in IT projects that they wish anytime they desire. This not only prolongs the software product's development lifecycle, but burns time and money by constantly adding product updates that the business wants and but does not need.

A software project's phase or version is complete when it's requirements are met, it is that simple. If the software project's requirements are a moving target then they cannot be completed because there are no concrete objectives that can be achieved accept for failure. As a result, this negatively affects the company's return of investment. Good businesses always remain focused on the bottom line because that is where the revenue is.

The way that an IT department can contribute to the bottom line is straightforward. Good data should equate to good corporate analysis, and in turn, good reporting should equal better decision making, which should lead to increased revenue. In order for any business to grow, they must have a system of metrics. Metrics are created from reports and reports are generated from raw data that is retrieved, processed, and formatted for the respective reader(s). Millions of decisions are made in business everyday from reporting systems. If the data integrity within those reports is suspect, then business decisions that were made based on that data cannot be trusted until its integrity can be verified. Clean valid data makes for good reports and bad junk data makes for deceptive reporting. That is the simple and raw truth. In many cases, businesses and IT employees make bad decisions using good data and vice-versa but that can be corrected through proper training along with a system of checks and balances. However, management decisions made from bad data can easily go unnoticed for long periods, and potentially cost the business revenue in more areas than can be initially anticipated.

IT must keep its focus on the integrity of the data that it provides to its business partners. If the validity of a reports data is questionable, it must be corrected immediately to protect the audit trail of decision-making processes as they affect revenue. IT will always find the truth within its business partners through the reports they generate for them. In short, it is always good to follow this simple yet effective rule:

"Keep your eye on the data, as if the data were the money and you will find the truth."

That is indeed the bottom line for IT.

IT Formula For Businesses:

| Data Integrity | + | Good Decisions | = | Enhanced Revenue |

The Tao of Integrity

Integrity:

1. [n] moral soundness
2. [n] an unreduced or unbroken completeness or totality

The above affects all aspects of IT projects and the relationship between IT and the business. Mark Twain once said, "If you tell the truth, you never have to remember anything". Truth manifests itself many different ways within an IT project and can easily be interpreted differently by each of the actors involved. No matter how the members of a team or project view the scope of the objectives, there are common threads that identify the integrity or the lack thereof if you know where to look.

Integrity runs deep like the roots of a strong old tree. If the managers involved in an IT project establish a foundation that is based on integrity and the leadership manages by example, then trust can progress. Otherwise, trust is a difficult thing to establish and even harder to find or keep once it is lost. Double standards do not work when it comes to integrity. If you want it, you must give it. This means that if there is any hope of an IT project being successful, then the following must occur:

- The envisioning process must have integrity
- The planning process must have integrity
- The development and building process must have integrity
- The testing process must have integrity
- The implementation process must have integrity
- The support process must have integrity
- The actors involved must have integrity
- The salaries of the team members must have integrity
- Any appreciation shared with the IT project team must have integrity

Chapter 3: COMMUNICATIONS

Trust

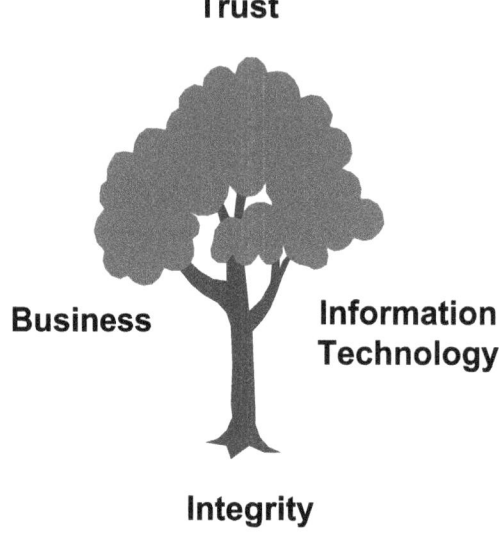

Business   Information Technology

Integrity

Trust
Grows many strong rich healthy leaves

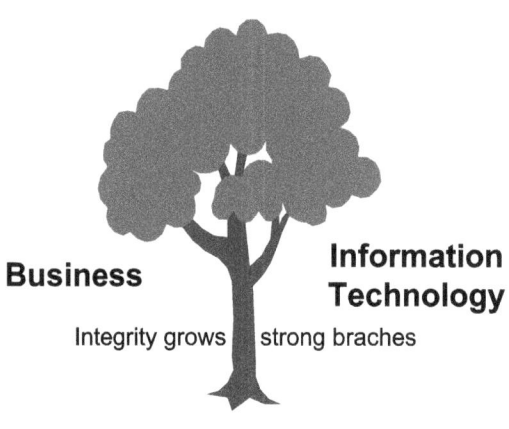

Business   Information Technology

Integrity grows strong braches

Integrity
Grows deep roots and a solid foundation

To create the type of integrity needed to implement successful IT projects, the right leadership must be installed and given the power to do the things that must be done.

The Right People

Whenever you put a group of people together of almost any sort, it is inevitable that some members of the clan will not get along with each other. This is why the right people must be hired for an IT project and assigned to the best roles that match their skill sets. The same goes for the business members who work on the IT project. This is critical because the right people will understand that they may occasionally clash with other team members but that will not be their primary concern. The right people will want harmony within project relationships as much or more than any other team member but their major focus will be getting the job done no matter what, and in the best way possible.

The right people know that the company's needs come first. In addition, they understand that their need to have comfortable relationships with their team members is tertiary, although it is an important and a wonderful thing at work when it is possible to have it. The right people ultimately understand that it is a successful record of accomplishment in IT, which helps to build many of the strongest relationships. In order to achieve that success, they also understand that they may have to fight tough battles along the way with team members and or the business. How people handle pressure and stress defines if they are the right people or not for an IT project. It is a leader's job to make that determination and to do it well.

Evaluating the right people for a job must always start at the very top with the Executive Management Leadership Team or for IT specifically, the CIO (Chief Information Officer) and or CTO (Chief Technical Officer). They create the vision, hire the people and steer the ship. The CIO and or CTO are ultimately responsible for everything that happens in an IT project, be it good or bad. That is why they must select good management and empower that team with the backing they need to be effective. That support includes:

- The ability to reassign or fire IT project team members who
    - Intentionally mislead other team members away from project goals
    - Continuously block or try to segment the IT team in a negative manner
    - Are incompetent and lack the ability to do their jobs
    - Refuse to do their jobs as requested
    - Constantly complain about the project to others and negatively affect their job performances
- The ability to hire and buy who and what is needed to successfully complete the project
- The ability to create and implement a good vision and plan for the IT project

- The ability to stop a project in which the scope has changed and objective is no longer needed or attainable

- The ability to use best practices and the foresight to adapt when best practices will not work for a given situation

I once worked in a situation where the CIO of a company did not have the power to fire a Development Manager who was repeatedly openly defiant of that CIO and their objectives. This Development Manager's negative attitude was not only displayed in private meetings that I attended with Development Manager and the CIO but in IT Department team meetings as well.

Not only did this situation make the CIO of the company look weak and incompetent (even though he was not), it splintered the IT team politically and damaged the morale of the project and its ability to be effective. It turned out that the Development Manager happened to be a good friend of the COO (Chief Operations Officer) and had attained "Diplomatic Immunity" through that relationship. The two cohorts were "golfing buddies" which provided the Development Manager a strong influence on the COO in regards to the inner-workings of the IT department. I had later found that the COO and the CIO were adversaries, which served to clarify a great deal as to why the IT Department was struggling. The COO ultimately paid a high price for their relationship with the Development Manager in the form of contributing heavily to a negative return on investment for a multi-million dollar software project that was greatly needed for the long-term success of the business. The project ended up constantly missing deadlines and milestones while ultimately coming in tens of millions of dollars over budget due to this and many other issues.

Ten IT Commandments

Without rules, we have chaos. Anarchy, when it comes to designing, testing and implementing technological solutions usually ends up in failure or at the very least, you come away with nothing or a puzzling and poor result that was not worth the time or revenue invested. Serious discipline must be applied with the rules of implementing new technology or supporting the existing solutions and their processes.

Implementing software solutions professionally is a science, not a game or hobby as many people see it. Some IT projects may start out as fun in the beginning but the further a project progresses and as more requirements are acquired and implemented, things can become complicated very quickly. Most seasoned IT professionals have experienced this scenario, and are well aware of it. This is why teams that have a high success rate of implementing IT software projects within a business are disciplined, well-oiled machines and follow rules that obviously work.

Below are 10 IT commandments that successful IT teams use in some way or another.

1. Take responsibility for what you do wrong. Share any rewards you receive with the team first, for what you do right every time.

2. Avoid corporate politics whenever possible at all costs. Be transparent.

3. Always insist on a set of clear, documented requirements before you start an IT project and or at the very least, before any major project development begins every time, and never lie to the business.

4. Insure that a well-respected professional estimates the time and cost of the IT software project after the requirements are completed. If you lack the skill set to do the estimation, hire a professional to do it. When the requirements change, update the project estimates accordingly.

5. Minimize scope creep from the business by setting the expectations that unnecessary changes after major development has begun may cost the business dearly in the form of time and money. Enforce this commandment by charging the business significantly more in time when you estimate and respond to their unnecessary changes.

6. Invoke and maintain a reliable and well-documented change management process. Pick the process that best fits your IT team's personality and make it a part of their job position's duties and responsibilities to comply with it.

7. Never neglect software and hardware solution testing on any level. Always over estimate the time you think it will take you to test your IT solutions. This is where you have the chance to insure that the software solution complies with its business requirements.

8. Invoke and follow the Software Development Life Cycle for every important project, every time. This means you must:

    a. Envision the software solution

    b. Plan the software solution

    c. Develop (Build) the software solution

    d. Stabilize (Test) the software solution

    e. Implement the software solution

    f. Support the software solution with good change management practices and discipline

9. Avoid cronyism. Do not hire your friends or family unless they are truly qualified for the task. If they are, then insure that these people have a strong history of working well with you and others.

10. Promptly fire anyone who repeatedly fails to comply with any one or more of these commandments. Insure that the right people are performing the right tasks consistently through periodic IT audits.

It is important to note that rules mean nothing if they are not implemented, and guidelines are invisible if they are not followed. Sometimes it can take years for a good set of rules and guidelines to become a part of the culture within a company. Keep in mind that this is not unusual. However, you may never know if the rules and guidelines will work if you and or your leadership lack the discipline and or the will to enforce the laws and rules that are set forth for IT projects in your company.

Summary

Communication is the exchange of:

- **Thoughts** – In many cases for an IT Software project to be successful, Software Engineers must "think" alike in order to follow and understand the software architecture used to develop a specific software application.

- **Ideas** – It is amazing how many people lack ideas about a specific task until rules are forced on them in regards to that job. When that happens, almost everyone seems to have an idea or two about how things should be done. In IT, there are usually plenty of good and bad ideas to be shared in any number of environments.

- **General Information** – Being able to communicate general information about an IT project is critical and it should always be simple, to the point, and clear. This must be understood by all players involved in the project and by anyone who needs to know about it as well.

IT communications can be a deep rooted and unusually complicated subject. This is because in the beginning stages of an IT project, the previously mentioned 3 categories are critical, and can vary greatly from person to person based on a number of different factors. To start, many IT teams are comprised of members that live in different countries. With that comes the language barrier that includes widely varied meanings of many "key terms" and phrases that are used in everyday conversations that do not involve business or even IT terminology. Before any IT project can begin, every actor involved must be able to speak the same language through clear interpretation or directly. They must all achieve "common ground" in regards to the purpose of the IT Project. This involves a major communication effort even if everyone involved in an IT project does speak the same language.

Centralizing a company's business intelligence can help IT personnel to create and deliver services that have high value to an organization. Because of this, companies can have a better chance of obtaining the best possible performance from employees and their resources. Some of the benefits include:

- The ability for management to make better and more effective strategic decisions

- The ability to cut the costs of operations and maintenance which saves revenue

- The ability for mission critical information to get to the employees who need it the most, quickly and securely

- The ability for company data to be more secure, reportable, and maintainable

Since we usually view projects from our own perspectives, with IT communications we must learn to create, share, and support one common view, which may be different from our traditional outlooks. This is the IT project's view from a business perspective through its native environment, which is ultimately the only perspective that really matters.

"What concerns me is not the way things are, but rather the way people think things are"

- *Epictetus (Greek philosopher, AD 55-c.135)*

Chapter 4: THE POLITICS OF INFORMATION TECHNOLOGY

A History of IT Politics

Politicians from both the left and the right may not agree on very many things, but they would most likely concur with the fact the Information Technology has changed the very foundations of our lives. IT now controls:

- How we get and create our news
- How we bank
- How we shop and how we create stores
- How we watch and create television shows
- How we listen to and create music
- How we play and create games
- How we date
- How we access, consume and create public services
- How healthcare services are rendered
- How we research and develop
- How we read and create books and magazines
- How we vacation and travel
- How we communicate with each other

The revenue and overall impact that these respective industries have on our lives is simply overwhelming. In a period of fifty short years, IT went from being virtually invisible, to a force that would literally control the lives of the citizens of the richest countries in the world, and have a profound effect on almost everyone else. The world had under gone a second major revolution. The first was the Industrial Revolution that began in Europe and spread to bring the world into the modern era. The second and the most recent revolution was that of information and technology. The IT revolution has created a completely new culture and society that is on the super fast track of technological advancement. IT advancements are growing at an exponential rate. Hardware prices have decreased drastically over the decades and continue to fall. This fact constantly makes the current technology more accessible to those who could not otherwise afford it. With much of the old and used hardware technology ending up in 2nd and 3rd world countries, even they are now beginning to utilize better and more powerful computer hardware than ever before.

In the late 1940s a Computer Engineer said that the United States would never need more than six computers. The fact of the matter is that by the late 1990s there were over 100 million computers in the United States alone. When I was a child, I can remember asking myself why anyone would ever need a computer. I now have 11 computers on my personal network and wonder how I would get along without them. The PCs are specific to certain tasks and serve various purposes.

In the beginning, computers were huge and it took large custom rooms to facilitate them. Computers Engineers at that time had to have a rare and specific skill set and knowledge in order to make those technical hardware monsters work. From the 1950s until the early 1980s, computers were big monolithic machines, immobile, and very expensive. IBM introduced the first personal computer, the IBM 5100, in 1975. However, the price was far out of reach of the common white-collar worker, which made sales dismal. The industry changed forever when IBM introduced the first affordable personal computer in 1981. This computer was different from previous IBM models because it was the first to be built using an open architecture. This meant that it was manufactured using parts that could be found at your local electronics store. The PC was sold at large department stores and took the world by storm. Time Magazine even named the PC, "Man of the Year". The IBM PC of 1981 is the early ancestor of the compact and insanely more powerful PCs that we use and love today.

What's at Stake

IT is deeply rooted in almost every aspect of our daily lives in one way or another. With the number industries affected, and the amount of revenue and data IT generates makes controlling the arena critical. It has been said that the next World War will be fought over information. The case for this argument becomes stronger everyday as additional detailed important data is gathered and stored on citizens worldwide. This data includes:

- Emails Messages
- Phone records
- Bank Records
- Social Security numbers
- Medical Records

- Home addresses
- Credit Reports
- Credit Card Numbers
- Resumes
- Criminal Records

Almost every form of information about people imaginable is being collected and stored by companies and or organizations around the world. So much information has already been gathered that practical uses for all of it has not yet been devised. However, be assured that at some point in the future, a person, group or organization will figure out a good use for the data collected today that has been deemed "useless".

For instance, some department stores now video tape the traffic patterns of their customers. In the beginning, these department store video tapes were reused and considered "unimportant" unless they contained a specific event of some significance such as a person shoplifting. Someone decided to link the video tape signal into a computer and have a software program analyze the traffic patterns of customers as they shopped at various retail departments. The software program was able to successfully track which promotional displays store customers stopped to peruse most frequently. Not only that, but the software was also able to process and deliver comprehensive reports about customer behavior never before seen by department store managers, owners and marketing directors using this technology. From this newly acquired data, store promotional personnel were able to strategically place displays and commercial advertisements in areas that attracted the maximum customer response. This increased sales and visibility of merchandise that might have gone otherwise unnoticed and unsold. During holiday sales, this new and enhanced marketing practice proved to be a critical improvement in department store sales and the overall customer shopping experience.

What's at stake is far more than just department store sales. The amount of data already contained within files about you and I are of great political value to many governments, anti-governmental and other political organizations around the world. It is of overwhelming value to small and large businesses alike, which need this data for sales, marketing, and research and development.

Other data that is of particular interests to these groups are:

- Age
- Race

- Religious affiliation

- Income

- Education

- Geographical habits, and other preferences

This information is used in many cases to profile groups of people for a variety of reasons, both good and bad. Trending this information over time can give government officials invaluable information about their country's citizens and their everyday habits. This data can be used to provide much needed public services based on shortfalls that present themselves through the analysis of the information.

Some results of this analysis include:

- What percentage of the population in a specific region have incomes that are below the poverty line

- The percentage of people who vote in a particular region and the percentage of people who do not

- The number of African Americans, Asians, and Latinos who live in a particular region

- The number of people in a region who made over $100,000.00 in the previous year who are registered voters

This list could go on almost indefinitely but the point is that in many cases names, addresses and phones numbers can be matched to this type of data. This means that not only could these individuals be profiled for lawful reasons, but for unlawful reasons as well. For example, a politician who may be sited by a specific group of citizens as being "discriminatory" could in turn, through government IT, obtain the names and addresses and background information of the leaders of that group. That politician in question could then use that and other sensitive and confidential information to inflict economic damage and or defame the character of those group leaders by giving that private data to unscrupulous individuals, groups or companies that might cause additional harm to those people's best interests. The politician can also use that same sensitive data to deny members of the group in question current or future state and government jobs and or certain civil liberties like freedom of speech and freedom of assembly.

Quite simply, what is at stake in controlling IT is raw power through intelligence and analytics, which can promote elevated status and revenue. Businesses already know this and should understand that it is one of the primary reasons they employ IT. The chief purpose of IT is to translate business requirements and processes into technical solutions where and when necessary. In order to make this happen, a business must control or take total control of its IT department if it has not already. IT departments are created to serve the business if they are not indeed the business itself. The more revenue the business generates, the bigger the political power play for IT by the players involved. Once a member of the management team realizes that a particular IT project could potentially bring them the recognition and power they need to catapult them from relative obscurity into the business limelight, things can change for the worse rapidly. This is one of the reasons why IT projects fail, and why IT projects can be frustrating and difficult to work through. Some people feel that IT would not only be fun and different but also give them a chance at having some measure of control at work. The problem with this line of thinking is that fact that IT does not, or should never control itself if the business is not a "Technology" business. IT is not the place for business people to cross over to for more control or power because this is not where the control in a business should be located. In theory, IT should have less power than any other department in the business because of their primary purpose, which is service-based and translates company processes and requirements into technical solutions that save and or make the business money.

Is There a Liar in the House?

A lie is a statement that is communicated with the intended purpose of deceiving others. For instance, some people will say almost anything to be elected or re-elected to an office or position. There are many reasons why this might happen and the sole-motive for doing so can vary greatly from person to person and be subjective to specific conditions. People sometimes lie in order to:

1. Avoid being punished

2. To get money (or more money)

3. To improve their status and gain additional power or control (professionally and or socially)

4. Protect themselves and or their friends

The above four reasons are usually why certain individuals lie in regards to Information Technology direction and projects. David Wise stated, in his 1973 book titled, "The Politics of Lying: Government Deception, Secrecy, and Power" that "If information is power, the ability to distort and control information will be used more often than not to preserve and perpetuate that power." Wise's statement would seem to be timeless, and has significant historical relevance. Disinformation and half-truths are also common forms of lying and facilitate the reasons why people may not always be truthful in regards to IT.

I had worked with a young IT Director of a large company who was in their 20s at the time and had less than 1 year of IT management experience. He had also been a Software Engineer for 4 years. This person had little technical knowledge as a developer. In addition, he had not produced any software applications for the company that promoted him from software engineer to IT Director in the previous 12 months before his advancement. As an IT manager, his effectiveness was sorely limited by his experience. As an IT Director, he was even less of a factor when I was with the company. He often asked for my help in regards to the company's technology direction and I agreed because it was my job to do so. However, I noticed that the young IT director quickly began to surround himself with a very inexperienced software consultant, and a development manager who had made it a practice to be dishonest about current and previous IT projects and personnel. Furthermore, this entourage of the young IT Director had developed reputations in the company as being "untrustworthy" and "reckless". The fact that I had chosen to not go to after hour parties and special gatherings that the IT Director and his new friends were involved did not go well for me. With this, a new CIO joined the company shortly thereafter who took the IT Director under his wing and mentored him. The CIO was a very well informed political figure who thought nothing of lying to protect his friends and interests as was made evident on plenty of occasions in meetings with his IT team. The CIO would be dishonest about:

- What tasks IT people were performing

- What IT personnel's motives were

- The history of IT projects

- Things he had said previously in regards to critical IT conversations

As time went on, I watched the technological direction of the company become more obscure and "off track" with what the business needed despite my best efforts. Under the management of the IT Director, the company began using more proprietary and obscure technology that was difficult to develop and support, and IT began to struggle and buckle significantly under its own weight. Years after I had left the organization, I ran into a friend of mine who still worked at the awkward company. He told me that the IT Director continued to work at the organization and that the same IT problems that the business did when I was working as an employee of the company. My friend described to me a scenario of an IT organization within a company that was constantly switching development technologies and had become stagnant and lost its ability to be competitive due to lies, ignorance, deceit, and bad politics. The downward process of degradation laced with these negative issues had costs the company tens of millions of dollars before I left, and continued far afterwards. The company is still having significant financial issues the last time I read about them and was eventually acquired by a larger entity.

Another type of IT liar that I have worked with previously was a weak politician who was posing as an IT Development Manager. This person lied to their company for years about technology he had chosen and implemented that had been proven ineffective, in order to protect himself and his loyal subordinates. This was an interesting case because the lie that was facilitated for so long by the IT Manager could have been corrected and resolved after the first year of implementation and evaluation of his projects. In fact, it would have saved his company more than a million dollars in much needed revenue. However, because the IT Manager did not take the initiative to learn about IT and keep up with the technology industry, he allowed his knowledge of technology and that of his team to remain limited, siloed, and fall years behind the industry standard. As a result, he and his team only knew and understood the software product they had implemented, on platforms where technology is dead or on life support. Furthermore, the IT organization continued to spend all of its time and resources on a failed product with no changes in sight which had costs his organization untold amounts of revenue. In order to keep his team and failed software product implementation under the illusion of tight control, the IT manager played a political game that involved:

1. Insuring that he was involved in every possible meeting about the product so he could spin negative comments and remarks

2. Not allowing any consultants to speak with anyone on his IT team privately

3. Hiding critical technical information from executive management

4. Not allowing any new technology to be introduced in IT

5. Becoming argumentative and combatant with any third party consultants who tried to bring about positive change, and reporting to his superiors that they were "hard to work with" so he could get rid of them

6. Only hiring permanent IT employees who had no previous IT experience

7. Fighting against the hiring of any new IT employees that had any relative experience

The last time I spoke with a friend who still worked for that business, the company was having major financial issues and problems competing in their industry due to the limitations of its technology.

Quite simply, lying and liars in Information Technology do not work. This is because IT is based on relationships and a good relationship is based on trust. Lying in IT is of the deadliest types of cancer to an organization in that it grows out of deception into potential destruction that negatively affects revenue. Solid IT best practices are scientific processes that can be proven or disproven. In many cases, the technical topics that people lie about in IT can be unveiled quickly by searching for technical research information on the Internet or through books, magazines or whitepapers. IT best practices, processes, and research studies are no secret, and have been available for many years. In an IT organization, a liar's days are numbered, and it is inevitable that they will be discovered if they stay with their companies long enough. A liar's options for redemption in an IT organization are clear and simple:

1. Tell the truth, and apologize as soon as possible and face whatever punishment they have coming to them. If not fired as a result, they must work very hard to rebuild the company's trust over time.

2. Resign from their job before they are discovered.

It is sometimes possible to have a liar's credibility restored in IT but this can be a long and arduous process. The best chances of this happening is through the liar admitting their mistake, apologizing sincerely for it, and offering to make restitution if possible. However, if a person is caught lying in IT regarding a critical situation, the chances of them keeping their job in a well-managed department is little to none. For some, admitting that they are wrong is unthinkable and is a hard thing to do in any environment where the perception between intelligent and stupid is often just a heartbeat away. These individuals generally have the most stressful and frustrating time in their IT relationships and projects. If an issue arises that they are responsible for, they often play the "blame game". This is a process by which the cause of a problem is always placed on a group or individual other than the entity who is ultimately responsible for it. Usually the blame game continues until a group or individual becomes laden with the responsibility for an issue that had been passed from one person or group to another who has to ultimately fix it.

Working with Adversaries, Enemies and Friends

In so many cases with business, working with friends, enemies, and adversaries can be one and the same. Your friends can also be your adversaries and in some cases even your enemies as well (otherwise known as "frienemies"). This is because of the fact that "frienemies" can work and partner with you when required, and are generally free to undermine you if your tasks or goals do not directly align with their agendas or steal their "thunder". Enemies can often pose as your friends for many different reasons that they may believe are advantages to them. Friends can become direct enemies quickly for a variety of reasons and the same is true of the reverse. The old statement "the enemy of my enemy is my friend" can hold true in IT just as it does in most other instances. In an a large or small IT organization, working with these 3 entities can be a trying experience even if you are attempting to avoid the political aspects of the workplace in general.

An adversary is anyone who offers opposition in regards to what you are working to achieve. This does not always necessarily mean that this entity, group or individual is your enemy. In regards to technology, competition is healthy and important for driving invention and innovation. In IT, it is important to not confuse your adversaries with your enemies, as there is usually a host of different ways in which technology can be utilized within an organization correctly. In some situations, this has nothing to do whatsoever with business requirements. For instance, let's say a particular software application could be installed on a company server using one of several methods:

- By copying the application's files to a production directory on the company server

- Using a 3rd party deployment application

- Writing custom scripts to automate the installation of the application and its required components

A person or group on the IT development team may be accustomed to copying application files to a server directory while another prefers to write scripts to accomplish this same task. Neither preference may be incorrect for the given instance and as long as neither process causes major problems and is able to be completed. In addition, both should be allowed to proceed unless there are documented IT standards in place to the contrary. This rule can also be applied to the type and brand of technology used within an IT organization but ultimately falls under the discretion of the company's Software System Architect who sets the standards and processes in this regard.

An enemy in IT is much more than an adversary, although this relationship may also be adversarial in nature. Adversarial relationships can be rooted in a deep friendship between the parties involved. A technological enemy's goal is to intentionally (or in some cases unintentionally) steal, disable or destroy you and your technological aspirations. Their motives are usually hatred and or revenge based and may or may not have anything to do with something that you have any control over.

It had been reported that computer hackers based in Beijing, China were launching massive cyber attacks on computer networks in the United States. The Pentagon admitted to some of their systems being compromised by these attacks but also said that they believed no major damage had been done that they were aware of. However, this problem was so serious that the President of the United States had been briefed on the issue. This was because at the time of the cyber attacks, hackers in China would have needed support from and the authority of the Chinese government in order to carry out such attacks on the United States. Another area of major concern from the United States government in regards to the cyber attacks was a statement that was made by a General in the Chinese army. This General made strong statements to the affect that Chinese cyber attacks against the United States were a good source of data for China about the technological readiness of North America. He also further stated that if China were to ever to attack the United States, it would try to cut power in all major United States cities first, by hacking into and disabling computer networks that control vital and critical power grids. Naturally, this made the "White House" begin to take a new and more serious look at this type of potential terrorist threat, and begin to invoke additional actions to prevent such incidents form occurring in again the future. In March of 2007, The United States Department of Homeland Security conducted a test they called "Aurora". In this exercise, researchers were able to hack into a computer system that controlled a power generator over the Internet. From that point, they were able to make that power generator build up energy by changing the operating cycle of the system until the machine eventually exploded. After the test was made known publically, United States government sources said that updates were being made to further safeguard the hardware and software that run and support the systems that generate power across the country. The United States Nuclear Regulatory Commission also made an announcement after the test that they were going to inspect all nuclear power plants to unsure that the same scenario could not happen to them. The "Aurora" experiment exposed a critical problem that demonstrated that major electrical power systems can be vulnerable to web-based cyber attacks.

Working with friends is not always easy and can lead to that relationship coming to an abrupt end. In IT, one of the secrets to maintaining a successful friendship throughout a project is respect, patience, and the art of keeping that relationship professional. As stated previously in this book, respect is an important factor in many professional and personal relationships that should never be ignored. When a personal relationship turns into a professional one as well, respect and patience becomes an even more powerful tool in maintaining a working attitude that can sustain your project objectives through turbulent times. For instance, some friends who work together that can agree to disagree, compromise and move on when tough issues arise can have a good chance at a long lasting and productive working environment. The definition of a friend in IT may vary from one team member to another. However, there are a few core attributes of a friend in Information Technology, which consists of:

- Willingly sharing technical and project information

- Providing technical project assistance with software code and or documentation

- Providing a strategic technical and political alliance based on trust and honesty

- Providing support when presenting new ideas and presentations

A good friend in IT can be hard to find and even more difficult to maintain. This is because, generally, whenever a person's job and livelihood is threatened it is only natural for that person to protect themselves even at the expense of their long-time friends. This concept is not foreign to most politicians and practiced by most of them to the point of normalcy. Very few individuals that I have met in IT will put their jobs on the line to help or protect you when you really need it. If you ever come across someone who would be willing to sacrifice his or her job for you in IT, without expecting something in return, you may very well have a friend for life and or a position that is not worth keeping.

Types of Politicians

Information Technology has no shortage of politicians as IT is deeply rooted in politics. From a management perspective, IT has four basic types of politicians, which include:

1. **Strong and Good** – These IT politicians understand and work to enforce the fact that IT works for and serves the business. This fact is number one in everything they do for their company. They are great with people and have a certain level of skill and charisma that helps them to get the attention they need to accomplish their goals.

2. **Strong and Bad** - These IT politicians are primarily focused on their own goals. If this also benefits the business they work for then that is a plus. They are great with people and very ambitious with a certain charisma that helps them to get the attention they need to accomplish their goals. They are the most dangerous sort.

3. **Weak and Good** - These IT politicians understand and work to enforce the fact that IT works for and serves the business but also balance this with their own agendas. They lack the basic level of charisma and skills needed to get the attention required from the right people to pass their agendas, so they have to work much harder to get their plans implemented.

4. **Weak and Bad** - These IT politicians have delusions about their IT skill sets and exactly how powerful they are, along with their future with their organization. They generally do not care about the business or what it needs. They are usually bitter and lack the skill set and charisma needed in order to present their ideas effectively. As a result, they are unable to solicit the attention from the right people to further their own agendas and are a slow spreading cancer if not removed.

At this point, it is important to define "good" and "bad" as it relates to the IT politician. A good politician in this context means that the individual's actions are driven primarily by the needs of their business and that they operate from a reasonable moral and ethical base. A bad politician as it relates to IT means that the individual's actions are motivated primarily by greed, power and or strong feelings of self entitlement. This person operates from a base of selfishness that ultimately serves his or her own distinct wants and desires. Whether an IT politician is strong or weak in either regard speaks to the particular base from which that individual operates, which would be either in the best interest of the business or themselves. For example, a strong IT politician who is good will place more weight and attention on helping the business, as this is the primary goal of IT. While a strong IT politician who is good will place far less weight on the power of their position, a weak IT politician who is good will do the opposite. Along with this, a strong IT politician who is bad will place far more weight on the sheer power of their position to the point of exploiting it along with their authority. However, a bad and weak IT politician will lack the ability to do this and become ineffective and a source of mistrust, bitterness and discord. Whether a politician is strong or weak is a basic private personality statement about that individual.

Another more interesting a way of identifying IT politicians is by using a rating system. The one that follows is an example of such a system.

> **IT Politician Rating System Example:**
>
> Strong and Good = ☆ ☆ ☆ ☆
>
> Weak and Good = ☆ ☆ ☆
>
> Weak and Bad = ☆ ☆
>
> Strong and Bad = ☆

The IT politician rating scale above gives the most stars to the politician who will do the most to help their organization. As you can see, the strong and good IT politician has the most stars as they hold the best interested of the business as their top priority and have the skill set, drive and charisma to get things done. The strong and bad politician only rates one star, which is poorest, because they have the ability to do the most damage to the business.

Types of IT Power

When asked to define politics, Dwight D. Eisenhower, the 34th President of the United States once said:

> *"It's the art of knowing how to get people to do what you want them to do, and make them believe they thought of it themselves."*

Many people believe that this type of influence along with the art of "suggestion" is a path to true and pure power. There is an old saying that "power not used is power lost, or wasted". This may be true in some scenarios. With this, there are many different types of power that exists in business and in IT organizations in general. Various power types that are wielded in Information Technology organizations in particular can be vast and cover a wide area as their influences can be far more extensive than they may appear to be on the surface.

The types of power that can to be some of the most significant within IT organizations are:

- **Positional**

- **Expertise**
- **Applied Technical**
- **Trust**
- **Charismatic**

Positional power is a situation in which a person holds a rank, title or job that has authority over an individual or group. This type of power is the most important in IT organizations because IT is supposed to be a dictatorship, not a democracy. In IT, executive, middle, and lower management wield positional power. Less formal positional power also holds a place in IT structures such as a lead software engineer or a lead technical analyst. Those particular titles do not belong to the management chain of command but they are positional power titles nonetheless.

Expertise is a type of power that represents knowledge in a specific area. Knowledge is power, and this is especially true in an IT organization since, logically, technical experience is knowledge-based. The more you know in IT, the more of an advantage you have over your less experienced colleagues in the following areas:

- Earning a higher salary from the date of hire
- Getting Salary increases
- Getting the jobs and or task you request
- Getting the job-related benefits and bonuses you request
- Being recognized as a "value-added" employee to the business

However, being a "domain expert" can have its disadvantages. The business on many occasions may expect this person to know far more than they do currently or have the ability to learn in a specific timeframe. This can lead to a stressful business relationship and to unrealistic expectations being placed on the domain expert by a business. It is important that the individual with the expertise in a given area of a company proceed with caution socially and politically, while keeping their egos in under tight control. Over inflated egos have been the demise of many individuals who posses great knowledge in their fields. This is because in some cases, the personality of the expert is so aloof or difficult to manage, that their colleagues and other employees no longer want to associate and or communicate with them. This may also be because the person or group in need of information may feel that the expert is "talking down" to them or that they feel that they get caught in "information overload" sessions and never get the answers needed that they originally requested from the expert.

Applied Technical knowledge in IT is the ability to utilize your expertise along with your skill set to actually complete tasks effectively. Possessing knowledge without the skill set and wisdom to make it work for you is knowledge wasted. You might think of applied technical expertise as the heart that pumps the blood in the body of an IT project. Without this vital component, some envisioning and planning may be possible within a project but no software can be developed, tested, deployed, or supported skillfully and competently. Without the applied technical aspect of a project all that is left is the theory of how to do what must be done without the actual ability to do it well or at all.

Trust is one of, and may very well be the most desired type of power that an individual or group may have within an IT team. Business relationships are based on trust, as this foundation is where expectations are launched. If a business truly trusts its IT partners, then that organization will usually do everything within its power to support those partners. This is true even if other more prominent and experienced IT experts disagree with the direction that the organization's IT team are taking them. Trust is a people power within IT that can be an extremely positive or dangerously negative tool. Trust the right technical person or group and you can significantly increase the odds of success with your company's IT projects. Trust the wrong technical person or group and the odds of IT project failure becomes as real as an airplane in flight whose engines fall off over the ocean in the middle of a winter storm. The exact costs of the loss may not be known immediately but as sure as night follows day, they are on their way to you. The longer a company trusts the wrong technical team to care for their business requirements, the risk of failure increases dramatically and significantly threatens the return on investment of that organization's technical endeavor.

Charisma is a type of power most people would like to have. Some may not desire it in large quantities but it is a most useful power to have in many work-related scenarios. The ability to use charisma means an additional level of influence that can be injected into an interaction and make a difficult encounter, argument, presentation or request, end in your favor. This kind of power is one that you either have naturally, or must work hard to acquire if it is indeed attainable. Charismatic abilities are generally based on a person's:

- Physical appearance

- Personality

- Ability to communicate in a an appealing manner

- Body language

People who are charismatic, and are able to draw critical attention without even attempting to do so, can often more easily sway a business decision-making process. Individuals with this power need not be very intelligent at all, which can be dangerous depending on the situation. Charismatic people usually realize they have this ability early on in their lives and may or may not exploit it to its highest potential. However, charisma is an ability that every politician who wants to be successful and admired must have, and every accomplished and well-loved politician has some level of this.

Avoiding Political Suicide

In Ancient Rome, political suicide was a strategy employed by unfortunate citizens who ended up on the wrong side of the Emperor's favor, which could literally mean their deaths. In cases such as these, a person might kill themselves as an alternative to going to jail or becoming a murder victim of the republic. Due to the social status of an individual and their family at that time, committing suicide to prevent a political disgrace could have serious political ramifications. As a result, this type of death was typically called "political suicide". Avoiding situations where this can happen to you on your IT project would be a wise and intelligent strategy. Since IT has become increasingly political due in part to new methodologies and processes, technical teams are far more susceptible to falling into political suicide than ever before. A great many businesses today are far more interested in gaining a technological advantage over their competition and therefore are now working closely with their IT partners to insure that their new and existing software is designed, developed, tested, and functions in accordance with the business requirements that they deliver. Since the vast majority of IT software engineers are not adept to working with business users, and have not been trained to work and communicate directly with business people, it is relatively easy for this particular group to succumb to organizational political pressures.

Political suicide usually stems from one or all of the following:

1. Something an individual or group says
2. Something an individual or group person does
3. Something an individual or group fails to say
4. Something an individual or group fails to do
5. An adverse association with an individual or group
6. A missed opportunity to forge a necessary relationship with an important individual or group

There are ways in which an individual or group can avoid political suicide from within their IT projects. This particular skill set may not be intuitive or simple to build or maintain, but it is necessary to have in order to survive in business whether you are working in IT or other business departments.

Communicating with Executive Management

Whether you're in IT or work on the business side, at some point you may have to talk to a member or group from executive management. This could include various Directors or others all the way up to the CEO (Chief Executive Officer). Many IT projects command this kind of attention due to the amount of revenue that a company can invest in their technological projects. Because of this, many executive managers are very interested in the IT projects that can affect their companies as the more revenue a business department is able to generate, the better positioned they are able to ask for additional financial assistance from an organization for their future endeavors.

There are three things IT and business professionals should always remember when communicating to a member or group at the Executive Management level. Those points are:

1. **Communicate quickly**
2. **Communicate effectively**
3. **Communicate clearly**

Since an Executive Manager's schedule is usually full, time is not something that they have at a premium. Generally ideas and plans expressed to this group must be done tactfully with a since of confidence and respect that is worthy of their attention. In response, many executives may provide feedback that may seem obscure or unclear as to how you are to proceed with the plans or ideas that you have presented to them. It is important not to question them too much about what they mean or you may run the strong risk of appearing slow, stupid, or "not ready for prime time". Some members of Executive Management may welcome additional questions as to their feedback in some situations but always be careful not to ask them too many questions. The best person to consult as to the clarity of the Executive's feedback would be their personal or administrative assistant. This individual or group knows how the executive "thinks" and in most cases can get you the information clarity you need in order to move forward.

When working with a powerful business executive, there is no room for your personal and or professional ego. You need only enough of an ego to foster your confidence in regards to getting your tasks completed and being able to communicate your ideas with stability and competence. Anymore than that can propel you far down the road to political suicide faster than you can think about it. The ego of a high level and powerful business executive is usually massive as they are paid very large salaries and enjoy company benefits that can only make their subordinates salivate. The last thing you want in your IT or business career is to become involved in an ego war with your boss who is a top ranking executive. This is one war you should adamantly avoid and are not likely to win.

Common Political Mistakes

There are various political mistakes that can occur in the course of a person's career that can stop it dead in its tracks. Unfortunately, many ambitious employees are not taught how to effectively manage avoiding these pitfalls as some deadly political mistakes can be obscure or happen inadvertently if an individual or group does not know what to look for. For example, one of the most unstable and stressful things that can happen at work is when a new boss arrives on the job. This is generally due to the fact that whatever hard work was done by employees to build points towards promotions, raises, trust, perks and more are now gone. The slate is wiped clean, and all of the previous relationship building efforts of a team or individual must begin again. Depending on the situation, these renewal efforts could be quite significant, costly, and or simply not possible. As a result, employees must learn to work with their new leader and discover the ways in which they operate and exactly what the new boss will expect from them. Sometimes a new boss can be much worse than the previous one especially when it come to intelligence. If the replaced leader frequently dabbles in the realm of idiocracy, then you too must learn how to navigate this region with expertise and precision. This is because you may not have a choice in the matter. If the situation grows to be completely unbearable, then it may be time to look for another job. If this is the case, the sooner you start looking the better off you may be.

Unless you work at a company or have a specific type of job that demands it, talking about your own personal religious and or local or federal political beliefs is usually a very bad idea. This is because religion and national politics are usually "flash point" conversations in which groups or individuals tend to form their strongest personal and professional opinions about you. For instance, if you voted for a controversial figure in the last state, local, or national election that half of your country now disapproves of, and you make this fact public at work, you give your adversaries a new foot hold against you and may cause others to question your judgments. The same goes for your religious views within your projects on the job. Generally, many people in the world have very strong personal and political views regarding their religious faith, and make both business and political decisions based on those particular views every day. The less others know about your personal political and religious views in a professional environment, the more they will have to judge you by your work and not by your personal beliefs which may (or should) not have anything to do with why you were hired for the job.

Be careful, and in some cases justifiably fearful of others on your technical projects who constantly ask about the political and religious beliefs of others. Interestingly enough, the Elysian Fields of Information Technology is not based on worldly religions or political beliefs. Individuals who believe otherwise run the strong risk of achieving a certain and often embarrassing failure in their technological endeavors. This is because at a high level, technology is a neutral tool. All too often technology is used to control, manipulate, and destroy lives, livelihoods, and cultures instead of building them up or enhancing them. The point is, if technological solutions do not make the original problem that they were created to solve better, then they are ultimately useless and a waste of time, money, and resources. The more this concept is understood by people, businesses, and countries around the world, the better the chances we as human beings will have to effectively take on and conquer some of the greatest challenges we face on Earth like:

- Hunger
- Disease
- Poverty
- Global Warming
- The lack of safe, abundant, and renewable alternative energy solutions
- The lack of Education
- The lack of Healthcare

The above list is a "lightning rod" of categories that many politicians, both professional and non-professional, love to discuss. However, in many cases, these same politicians have little to no plan for how to use technological resources in an effective manner without involving their own "special interests" and lobbyists to a large degree. This is often the point in which technology starts to be used as a tool to achieve a level of power for a specific individual and or group. Avoiding political suicide in some scenarios involves paying very close attention to these signs. It also demands attention to detail in regards to what you say to whom, along with what you don't say at the same time. This is can be a difficult skill level to obtain for even the most seasoned of political people and can take years to acquire if ever.

Avoiding political suicide generally requires:

1. Attention to Detail
2. Good Analytical Skills
3. Good Communication Skills
4. The ability to recognize and implement good advice
5. The right partnerships

6. Control over your emotions

7. Control over your ego

8. Unselfishness

9. Knowing when to talk, be quiet, and listen

10. Implementing damage control when needed, both quickly and professionally

These 10 requirements can go a long way towards helping you survive politically at work and especially within an IT project there. Since IT projects are usually political in nature, both business and technical employees must understand this concept and act to protect themselves and their teams accordingly.

The Double Edged Sword

One person's vision of the IT Elysian Fields is another person's Hades. This means that IT can work for you or IT can work against you. Both sides of the IT sword are equally sharp and have the power to cut deep. When IT is working for you almost anything is possible. When IT is working against you, the results can be catastrophic.

Examples of IT positives and negatives are as follows:

- **Positive IT** - In 1969, humankind landed on the moon. This is most likely the greatest IT project success stories to date.

- **Negative IT** – In 2005, ChoicePoint, a company that aggregates personal, private and financial information about millions of American consumers, admitted that their security had been breached. The company said that it had sold the personal information of approximately 145,000 people to a criminal entity. ChoicePoint notified California residents initially as required by that state's law but later disclosed that people in other states had also been victims of the initial security breach.

The 1969 moon landing changed the world. It gave everyone hope for the future of the human race by instilling an great pride in humanity thanks to an IT team of unparalleled all stars. Since the moon landing, there have been numerous technology success stories that have made of lives easier and much more fun. They include:

- Personal Computers

- The Internet

- Email

- Cell Phones
- CDs
- DVDs
- Digital Cameras
- Downloadable Music and Movies
- Video Gaming Consoles

On the other hand, because of security breaches such as the incident with ChoicePoint, at least 35 states in the United States have implemented legislation forcing companies and or government agencies to admit breaches in security regarding the personal data of American citizens. Furthermore, the same technology that has come to make our lives easier and more fun is also some of the very same technology that makes our lives significantly more complicated. For example, email revolutionalized the way the world communicates. In the earlier stages of email, many businesses hailed it as the preferred and more effective way to communicate. This was true in fact until some businesses began to discover that they had problems with email. Not only were their employees and IT departments spending a great deal of time fighting with "spam", those same employees were not spending enough time talking with each other face to face. In some cases, business employees would send email to people who worked across the hall from them or even in the same office space. In one instance, an employee was surprised to find that a colleague that they thought worked in another part of the country actually worked in an adjacent office, on the same floor and in their very building. Issues like these have lead to some companies severely limiting the amount of email that their employees can send and even banning email altogether on certain days of the week to increase employee efficiency, effectiveness and personal interaction with each other and their customers.

Another dark side to IT is Identity Theft. It is one of the fastest growing crimes in the United States and also one of the most difficult to stop. Many millions of people every year are the victims of this devastating and frustrating crime. Major Technological advancements and the affordability of the following devices make identity theft difficult to prevent:

- Color Laser Printers
- Photo Copiers
- Scanners and Digital Cameras

- Graphics Software

Using these tools, it is easier to create official and valid looking:

- Driver's Licenses
- Passports
- Birth Certificates
- Social Security Cards
- Employment Identification
- Insurance Certificates

Counterfeiting has also been a on the rise due to the latest advancements in Information Technology. Governments all over the world are working hard to develop ways to make their currency harder to copy. It is a constant IT battle between law enforcement and criminals, who in many cases have access to the same technology, which has become inexpensive and accessible to almost everyone.

The basic truth is the fact that IT is advancing at a rapid pace with no end in sight. In some instances, new technology hardware and or software updates to existing technology that consumers are presented with are made available in a matter of weeks from their prior releases. This type of rapid growth has lowered, and continues to keep the prices of new hardware and software products within the budget of the average consumer. This is good for business and IT in general as the opportunity to exploit new hardware and software platforms arise. Also businesses have the opportunity to consistently offer consumers new and better products that include more choices.

Some the most significant negative effects of technology's growth have been on the environment. No matter how great our achievements in technology have been as a society, those same achievements could very well ultimately destroy our only home. No doubt, at this point you are aware of Global Warming and the devastating effects it has already begun to have on the planet. The pollution we create traps heat within the Earth's atmosphere. The more pollution we generate, the greater the heat buildup making the planet increasingly hotter. Rarely if ever before, have so many scientists from such a wide variety of countries and disciplines unilaterally agreed on the same result. That one outcome being, the fact that Global Warming exists, and human beings are the cause. We are destroying our forests, jungles, and atmosphere relentlessly. By no means is Information Technology an innocent bystander. IT has been a driving force in helping us to be far more efficient in making Global Warming more lethal. This is because IT enables us to increase manufacturing beyond our means to control the waste it produces. For instance, cars have run on gasoline since they were invented, and can range from 5 to 35 miles per gallon. It is interesting that the overall electronic features in cars have progressed significantly in the automobile industry but fuel efficiency has improved very slowly. This is a testament to the greed of the oil industry, and has helped them to become the richest companies on the planet. The technology and information exists that can greatly reduce or even stop Global Warming and has been available for decades but it has been systematically blocked by capitalism and greed.

Positive change can happen through:

- The research, development and use of alternative energy sources such as hydrogen, wind, solar, nuclear, geothermal, and water (tidal, dams)

- Reducing or completely eliminating our dependence on oil by replacing gasoline vehicles with ones that run on electric or hydrogen energy sources

- Continuously recycling anything and everything we can

- Planting as many trees as possible

- Leaving as many tress as possible

- Using energy efficient appliances and light bulbs

- Using less electrical energy by turning off and unplugged unused electrical devices

Europe has taken the lead in fighting Global warming initially by passing the toughest emission laws on the planet and investing heavily in the research and development of alternative energy sources. The Europeans are debunking the myth that investing in alternative energy sources is too expensive an endeavor and are creating a new and viable economic industry. This new carbon industry is providing important and much needed jobs. It is also fueling new ideas and innovation that could quite possibly save the planet. Global Warming is the greatest challenge of this generation and will be for decades to come. There is no greater challenge for Information Technology than saving the planet. IT has made it possible for humanity to destroy Earth far more quickly than even the best scientific minds had previously thought possible. Now we must use this great tool in order to help save our home and ourselves.

IT Funding

It is no secret that if people like you, it is a lot easier to get them to give you money. In addition, if you are successful it is also far easier to get money from a business when you need it. Herein presents one of the main challenges that IT departments face, which is, securing the funding they need for resources and projects. Successful IT departments are far more likely to get the funds they need than non-successful IT departments. Due to its technical nature, the business "money machine" may be hesitant to fund an IT department or project because they may not understand exactly why the level of funding requested is needed. No matter how well the IT funding request is presented, the business decision maker(s) may not have enough technical background or expertise to agree with the amount of funding requested. This is why plain and simple IT project success is important. Everyone can get behind a successful project for obvious reasons. People like and are drawn to winners. Requests for additional IT funding after a successful project is far more likely to be approved if the funds are available than not.

Scenario One:

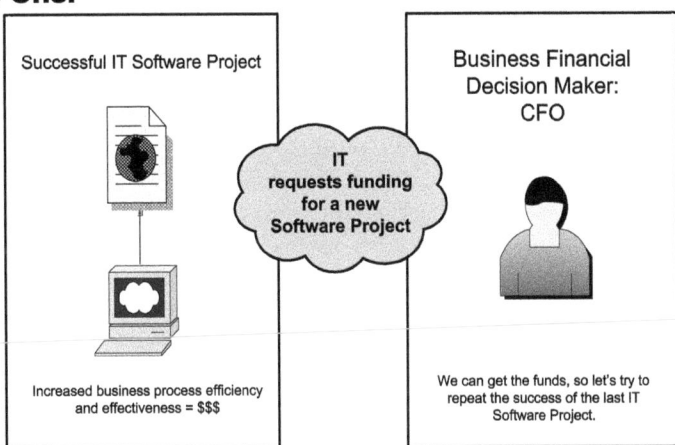

Scenario Two:

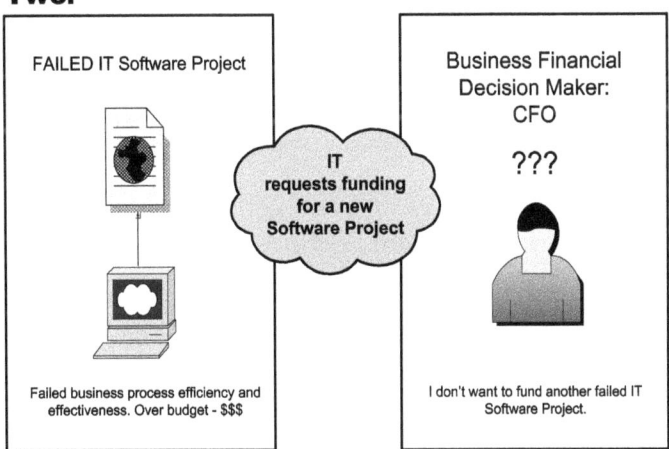

Information Control

The group or person who controls the information and the means by which that information is presented has absolute power. Information Technology is in reality "Information People", and most of the time when you have a group of people working together you will have to deal with politics of some sort. However if you are in business, and can control the politics involved in IT, then you can sway things your way in that realm on a constant basis, and you will have power. The primary focus of a business is to make as much money as possible and secure the "unfair advantage". Technology, in all cases, should help to achieve that objective so a certain measure of control is required in that regard.

Guidelines for securing the unfair advantage are not limited to the company itself. These same rules also apply to the people in the business. Just as a company must constantly strive to find that niche that it can exploit to advance to the next level, people in business must do the same. This leads to the fact that what the business needs and what its employees need may not always match. What is good for the business should always be good for its employees and vice-versa. This is one of the founding pillars of an Elysian Fields of IT project. All business endeavors involving its employees and technology should be a "win, win" situation for all parties involved. If this is not the case, then the business leaves itself open for conflict, greater politics and a constant increased risk of project failure. A good and true leader can always be trusted if his or her agenda is in the best interest of their followers. In areas where this is true, technology can then flourish and control is not an issue because it is freely given. This is because everyone involved benefits from it. It is critical for technology to work and be effective for a business to get to the next level or maintain or increase its unfair advantage in its respective industry. When we think of control in this manner, it is not from a negative perspective, but something that the business and IT must both work hard to achieve. The unfair advantage can be extremely elusive for various reasons, which include:

- Lack of intellectual property
- Lack of capitol
- Lack of resources
- Poor management
- The competition already has it and controls the industry

Some of these issues are why the top revenue-earning companies are referred to as "Fortune 500" and not the "Fortune 500,000". This is because they have something that thousands of other companies want and would do almost anything to obtain which is the "unfair advantage" and everyone cannot have it simultaneously. Once this ever elusive prize is actually acquired (if ever), it can be even harder to maintain and support. The unfair advantage is how small businesses become big businesses, and big businesses become enterprises.

Examples of enterprises that have or had achieved the unfair advantage include:

1. **Wal-Mart** – Retail Stores\Inventory Management
2. **Exxon Mobil** – Oil
3. **General Motors** - Automobiles
4. **Microsoft** – Software Platforms
5. **Intel** – Microprocessors
6. **General Electric** – News\Medical Equipment\Turbine\Engines
7. **Bank of America** – Finance
8. **American International Group** (AIG) – Insurance
9. **Verizon Communications** – Cable Television\Internet Services
10. **Hewlett-Packard** – PC Manufacturing\Various Technologies

Enterprises become who they are because they have a product and or service that either their competitors do not posses or is not nearly as proficient with their own products and or services. The primary enterprise in question either achieved the unfair advantage before their competition or eventually overtook them in order to get it. This is usually not the work of people who cannot innovate or the incompetent, but the tasks of people who were in the right place at the right time and also intelligent, resourceful, and exploitative. The luck of being in the right place at the right time is critical for an enterprise. It is not nearly enough to have great ideas and a unique product. There is much more that must happen before a "real" enterprise can be born. Enterprises require an extraordinary level of boldness and effort. Not only must the right people be doing the right things in the vast majority but also finances, executive consensus, excellent communication and managerial support must exist or achieving enterprise can still remain elusive. Enterprises must have strong intelligent, competent, brave, and experienced leadership on all fronts to control and maintain a political and technical machine that can include tens of thousands of employees or more. This small army's hierarchy must be uniform and own and display a cohesive vision for its future at all times. Everything in business usually comes down to securing revenue and the unfair advantage. The unfair advantage is where the money and true power reside in business. If a company's IT department and technology can reflect this, than that business has a good chance at taking the necessary steps in the right direction. That direction being, securing a

Chapter 4: THE POLITICS OF INFORMATION TECHNOLOGY

solid and unique technological platform that can become the businesses intellectual property and primary revenue generator.

Unfair advantages in business include:

- Software Patents

- Hardware Patents

- The unique ability to license a specific product

- The unique ability to license a specific service

- Copyrights\Publishing

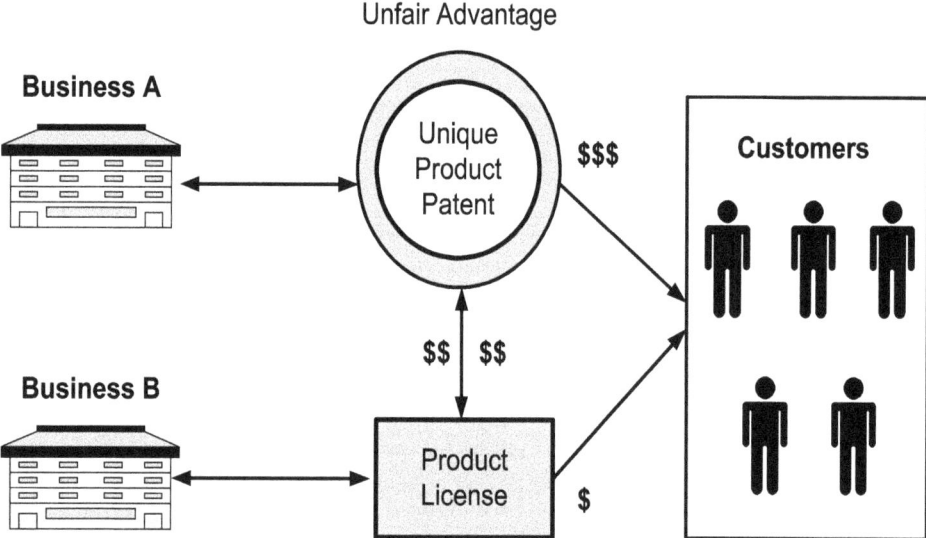

In many instances, some type of technology must support the unfair advantage. The diagram depicts a company with information control through a product patent. Business A sells a product license to Business B so that Business B can sell its particular brand of service to its customers. Business B must pay Business A whenever it uses Business A's product. Business A could charge a yearly or monthly fee for the license of its unique product. This would be the case for any additional companies who want to use Company A's product. Patents that are granted to an individual or business only last for a limited amount of time under the law, so companies must maintain constant research and development in order to stay on top of their inventions and to create new ones. Businesses that do not understand this fact are in danger of the following:

- Growing Competition

- **Technological Arthritis** – This is where key components of a company's technology platform can no longer supported by its vendors or themselves

- Lack of training in regards to new and viable technology

- A growing business perception that all is well and that there is no need to change

- Overall Complacency

- Loss of industry leadership and the unfair advantage

With today's rapid technology growth on almost all fronts along with increasingly careful investors that are seeking to exploit niches and company weaknesses, it is unwise and counterproductive for a business not to invest its future in research and development. Complacency in business equals death. Companies must continue to learn and grow while utilizing their hardware and software technologies to the utmost or suffer the consequences of sequential and inevitable systematic breakdown. Failure can mean many different things to various people, but in business, ultimate failure is the lack of the ability to make money. If the business cannot generate enough revenue to pay its bills and show a profit, it cannot support a foundation that is needed in order to pursue its secondary and tertiary goals, whatever they may be. This failure might result in:

1. Bankruptcy

2. A full or partial buyout from a competing business

3. Company-wide layoffs

4. Asset liquidation and the closing of company doors forever

Good jobs are increasingly difficult to find and once you have decent employment and wages, you must do the best you can and work hard to maintain it. This is why if you are a member of a business or IT department, you simply cannot afford to fall into a complacent mindset or physical practice. The pure essence of technological advancement is deeply rooted in perpetual motion. You must be proactive in technology, create, seek out new and effective ideas, and do your homework by researching and studying those visions. This can be achieved by implementing some the following practices:

- Subscribing to and reading the industry trade books and magazines

- Attending industry seminars and meetings

- Joining industry associations

- Implementing a company "great ideas" program and rewarding the creator of the best ideas and implementing that solution

- Watching the evening news to find out what is happening in the world and how it effects your business and its technology

- Following the stock market to find out what is happening in finance and how it effects your business and its technology

- Sign up for additional job training and even cross train as much as possible if you can

- If your company will pay for it, go to night school or take classes online and continue your college education if at all possible

In order for a company to control its technology, it must be proactive. This means that employees must also have this mentality. This way of thinking is instilled in people by strong positive leadership married with a clear vision for what a company needs and wants to accomplish. Leaders in this arena must lead by example and possess integrity in business. Unfortunately, this is not in great abundance in this age where a CEO of an enterprise that can lose 1 billion dollars in revenue in a year and still receive a performance bonus of 10 to 20 million dollars or more as a result. This is difficult to understand by shareholders or the employees of a business who have been laid off due to "cut backs" or who are facing potential layoffs due to financial losses incurred by the business.

It is important that enterprises be able to attract nationally or even globally popular CEOs in order to maintain investor confidence and the integrity of company stock. "Star CEOs" that can ride to the rescue of a sinking enterprise and bring the company back from the brink of virtual disaster can be worth their weight in gold. This is because the individual has the ability to save and or create hundreds or in some instances thousands of jobs. They can also bring in enterprise level leadership, courage, vision, discipline, and revenue that an organization needs in order to survive.

You cannot get the Elysian Fields if you are not proactive in business, especially when it relates to technology. Proactively joining the pursuit of technological perfection and dominance is one of the driving forces in getting your business technology into a positive rhythm and a perpetual forward motion.

1. **Great businesses turn great ideas into technical solutions that equal the unfair advantage in their industry**

2. **Average businesses turn average ideas into acceptable technical solutions that help their business**

3. **Insignificant businesses attempt to emulate average businesses technologies**

Summary

Unfortunately, many organizations use politics as one of their primary processes for making decisions. The bigger the business, the more in depth and complicated the politics usually are. Political compromise in a variety of relationships will involve the sharing of power and authority of some sort and to a certain extent. The word "politics" or "politician" can often invoke bad feelings and or mistrust among people in companies but it is a major part of how business is conducted all over the world. There are careful rules to follow in regards to politics in Information Technology.

Some of the basic political rules are:

1. Avoid social politics and politicians in IT wherever and whenever possible.

2. Always tell the truth and be transparent. Use wisdom in your delivery of this idiom and choose your words, or lack thereof, very carefully. When you tell the truth, you usually do not have to remember what you said.

3. Be a WYSIWYG (what you see is what you get). When you are being yourself, you do not have to waste time working to be something you are not. Unless you are an actor in a play, stay away from this type of behavior in IT. To the business, you are your work. If you are a person of false pretenses in IT, others will tend to perceive the work that you produce from that perspective as well.

4. Focus on your tasks and avoid gossip and those who practice it wherever and whenever possible. You are the company you keep.

5. Be quick to listen and slow to respond. Think about what you say carefully before you say it. This will make the first four rules much easier to follow.

6. Only use the ego power you need to display a sound confidence and implement your assigned tasks. Anything more is generally a waste of your time and energy.

The rules listed will go a long way in helping you to manage politics in IT. They are also important in the path towards the Elysian Fields level of success. If you have an agenda that does not align with that of your IT Department, then it might be a good idea to look for another job. There is never a short supply of people at the ground root levels of IT that are trying in some way to change or divert management's overall IT agenda. This is one of the many reasons why IT departments struggle and or fall into ruin. Working to be part of the solution as opposed to adding to existing problems and concerns is in everyone's best interests. Above all else, providing needed solutions to everyday problems is why Information Technology was born, and this should remain the focus of why it exists.

"If you hear that someone is speaking ill of you, instead of trying to defend yourself you should say: "He obviously does not know me very well, since there are so many other faults he could have mentioned"

- *Epictetus (Greek Playwright, c. 480-406 BC)*

Chapter 5: BUILDING THE SHIPS

Making the Right Decisions

Designing, planning, developing, testing, implementing and supporting software systems is deeply rooted in making the right decisions. This is a complex topic that morphs and changes according to the requirements of the specific product, which can vary widely from one project to another. It is a reason why software development is such a widely misunderstood subject by business professionals and even by many IT software professionals as well.

Making the right decisions consistently is both an art and a science, and some think it's impossible to do in IT. However, in many cases it is indeed possible if the right people are involved with the project and the job requirements are well defined (as best they can be) beforehand. In order to make the best possible decisions in an IT project, the software system requirements must simple, clear, and well written. The process of making decisions in a project both start and end with the project requirements. This is the most important part of the Software Development Lifecycle (SDLC) as business requirements provide direction.

The most important factor in software decision management is that you must know what it is you are trying to achieve. If you do not know what this is, then your decisions are not based on anything that is relevant in the regard. That is, there is not competent or useful logic attached to your decision that will help the software project. It is amazing how many times I have been involved with a software project where IT management (even at the executive level) have made critical IT software project decisions based on their feelings of the current situation. This had nothing whatsoever to do with the scientific facts of the product or its vision and planning. This is no way to build a starship software system platform (or any other). For instance, an IT associate of mine once told me that he was recently in a meeting with an IT Director, a Development Manager, and an IT Support Manager. In this meeting, the IT Director boasted about a bet that he had made with a person in another department of that same organization. The bet was for a large sum of money and was based on the premise that the IT Director could migrate to the next version of a third party system that the company was using and have full reporting capabilities, all in less than 18 months. Now this may sound simple to some folks, but in this case, the IT Director was not a technical one and knew very little about the details of how to implement his boasts. Not only that, but the IT Director made his bet without first envisioning and planning this third party software migration, which my well-seasoned IT associate informed me would be paramount even at the highest levels. This type of decision-making (especially by an IT Director) is what most experienced professionals in the software industry fear and consider reckless, dangerous, ignorant, and sometimes stupid. This is because the IT Director in question has now made the software project a narrow time-window, without any analysis, that his team must make work. This behavior is counterproductive in what needs to happen with building software products that a company needs in order to be competitive and make money.

Chapter 5: BUILDING THE SHIPS

It is important to stress, that primary reasons to invoke IT software projects should be to enable the business to increase their revenue, enhanced their processes, to seek the unfair advantage and further establish intellectual property. If this is not the case, then there is no logical reason for the software project to be initiated, and any existing business-related IT project that does not fall into these categories should be abandoned. In other words, the software project would be a waste of time and overall business resources if it will not contribute significantly to the financial bottom-line of the organization. IT must always understand that companies are in business to make money, not useless technology. Many companies are founded to produce a product or service but inadvertently find themselves in the computer software business. With this, they spend a great deal of revenue, time and resources designing software systems instead of buying and having them installed and maintained by a third party. This practice distracts a company by diverting revenue and resources from the objectives that they were created to work to achieve. IT people who make good decisions consistently think in a disciplined manner. In general, these individuals are trained and have learned to utilize that discipline when they need it. IT personnel who think and act impulsively tend to have trouble in keeping with any set plan or even creating one.

There are basic rules when it comes to good decision making. Some of these important by-laws include the following.

1. Prioritize all of the choices involved, identify the most important one and resolve it before any of the others.

2. Outline the positive results that can be derived from your decision. Good decision-making is a practice in risk management. With this, it is important to also run through all of the negative repercussions your decision can invoke. It is often difficult to know what is good if you have not identified the bad.

3. Secure the resources required in order to make your decision work. One of the biggest mistakes with organizations is the follow through or plan. They make commitments after deciding on a specific path but never develop and implement a logical plan to make it happen.

4. Do not avoid any possible choices. The possibilities that are ignored could be very well the solution that ultimately works.

5. In order to a handle large and complex decisions, break then down and handle the most important first. However in IT, what you don't know can hurt you and usually does. Sometimes when all of the smaller decisions are made, the biggest decision takes care of itself.

6. Employ the K.I.S.S. principle. This means "**Keep It Simple Stupid**".

Build vs. Buy

When a company decides to build a custom software system (or systems) in-house that will help to improve annual revenue, they should also focus on securing the unfair advantage in their industry with the future product as well. This is one strategic path to adding value to an organization that involves constantly working towards the vision of overall industry dominance. In addition, there are several advantages that a company can gain by building their own custom software platforms.

Some advantages of building software "in-house" include:

1. The software application can be proprietary and or "one of a kind".

2. Sometimes and depending of the software project, it can costs the same or less than buying an existing third party software package. This is because it is possible to build and support only the features that the business needs. This helps an organization avoid some of the pitfalls of buying a third party software package that they might only use 40% to 60% of. In this case, the business would still have to pay for and support the additional 60% to 40% of the purchased features within an "off the shelf" application whether they use that functionality or not.

3. Software applications built in-house are designed to specifically to support unique company processes and cultures.

4. Software applications built in-house can be scheduled to gradually replace older software systems. This often helps to reduce the risk involved with building new large systems that might not work very well at first. It also reduces the shock of major changes occurring all at once to business departments that will use the new system.

5. Custom software allows a company to control their own fate. The software product design and support can be manipulated solely by the business of origin.

6. Software applications built in-house can be better designed to integrate with existing or new application extensions that do not yet exist.

7. Companies that build their own software systems are in a better position to try new things that other organizations have not, or may not be able to currently. They have the opportunity to "push" innovation and invent.

8. Training end-users on how to use the new software can be done by management or trainers who are familiar with the company and its employees. This can make learning the new software system smoother, and more comprehensive.

Chapter 5: BUILDING THE SHIPS

Especially for medium sized to smaller businesses, buying a software system that has many or most of the features they need can be a very attractive option that could give them the core functionality of much larger organizations more quickly. For companies that are growing and have tight budget constraints, building in-house, company dependant, and custom software can be an expensive and overwhelming task. As medium to smaller businesses struggle to find their identity and compete, often times they need effective tools fast and cannot afford to wait for them to be built. This is because if those companies cannot constantly grow and keep making money they may not be around when their custom software is finally completed in order to use it. In addition, the financial and software development risks are minimized when purchasing software systems as opposed to buying them. The burden and costs of designing building, and testing the application is carried by the company that built the third party software system. In most cases, since that same company will also support the software they are selling, that expense along with future version upgrades, is also part of their responsibility, not the company that hired them. Most third party software vendors will usually offer some form of support package to their customers based on their needs and the size of the business that requires it.

The types of support packages generally include the following or some variation of it:

1. **Platinum Support** – The most expensive third party software support offering. This is also the most comprehensive support package. In many cases, it includes 24/7 phone and email support coverage usually with a response time of hours, not days. Many more services are available in this package depending on the company and the software system they offer.

2. **Gold Support** – This support offering is generally designed to be attractive to companies that do not need total support coverage (possibly due to their hours of operation) but need to feel secure with the help available for their third party software system. Support coverage response times and or additional types of services offered are a step down from platinum support but are still significant.

3. **Silver Support** - This support offering is generally designed to be attractive to companies who have a development team in-house that may be able to manage most of the larger issues with the third party software system that might occur. Phone and email support are offered, but the response times can take days.

4. **Bronze Support** - This support offering is designed to be attractive to the budget conscious. In many cases, phone support is not available and the buyer may only have access to the third party vendor's online knowledge base to search for solutions when there is a problem with the purchased application.

There are several advantages that a company can gain by purchasing their company dependent software solution platform. Some of those advantages include:

1. In many cases, especially for medium sized to smaller companies, it is cheaper to buy software systems such Customer Relational Management (CRM) and Enterprise Resource Planning (ERP) than it is to build them. Systems such as these are critical to almost any business structure. Reinventing the wheel can be quite expensive and is often unnecessary.

2. Application stability and perseverance is an attractive reason to buy a software system package for most companies. If the software has been on the market for years and is used by many respected organizations, usually most of the application bugs have been worked out by other companies who purchased the software along with the application vendor.

3. As described previously, the bulk of software support and maintenance issues can be handled by the third party software system vendor.

4. Buying and implementing new core business software forces employees to either learn and use the system or lose their jobs. This drives change at the most fundamental levels and is sometimes necessary to move a company in the direction it needs to be going.

5. During the evaluation, implementation, and support of the third party software, the employee's domain knowledge and expertise at the software vendor's organization can be exploited to gain new insights, processes, and practices.

6. It usually takes far less time to implement a pre-existing software system than it does to build the application from the ground up. In business, time is money.

7. Many popular third party software systems have spawned "user groups" that implement community websites and or blogs (web logs) to share information and new ideas that they have gained from using the application. These resources can sometimes be "vast", and hold more detailed information about the software product than the third party vendor themselves are willing to share.

Building software system applications as opposed to buying them is a subjective process. IT departments involved can have a tough choice in this regard. Sometimes, the choice is almost too close to make a definitive decision and either option sounds equally attractive to the IT management team. In situations such as these, it may be wise to buy an application if the organization has enough revenue to make it happen. This is because it is never a good idea in IT to reinvent the wheel, but to build on and leverage ideas from products already in place where ever and whenever possible.

Not having the right resources (and enough of them) to design, build, test, and implement a comprehensive software system solution that the business can depend on is far more than enough reason to buy one. There is no substitute for wisdom in this regard, as ignorance and stubbornness are the parents of poor choices. It is best to let the "Master Wheel Builders" compete against each other to improve their technologies, and to stay out of their domain if you are not in the "Wheel Manufacturing" business. This will allow you to focus on your core business and buy\upgrade your "Wheels" as needed to support your company's objectives.

The Importance of a Physically Separate Development Network

There is a popular saying in IT software development that goes like this, "It works on my box"! This means that the software application in question compiles and executes within the environment (computer or network) of the specific user only at that time. Application tests may not have yet been performed outside of said environment and therefore should be considered "suspect" until proven otherwise. I am still amazed that currently, and at many companies, Software Engineers still deploy software directly from their computers to Production Servers and wonder why the deployed application does not work afterwards. In many cases, those same Software Engineers spend countless hours trying to figure out where they failed, and what might be different on their Production Servers from that of their own development PCs, which could prevent their applications from functioning. If I had not seen this with my own eyes at various businesses, I might not have believed it if someone had told me this tale.

Some businesses can't understand that they may need to implement a physically separate IT software development network because they already have a hardware network. Many think that it is a waste of time and money. The management involved may also believe that the current business network is more than adequate since they may have spent a good deal of money on the design, hardware, implementation and support of their company computer network. This line of thinking might seem logical to business management from the outset, until they began to experience the problems involved when IT is forced to use the business's PC (personal computer) network for developing mission critical software applications.

IT departments that are serious about developing business software and do not have a separate physical development network domain can contribute heavily to the IT revenue burn rate. This is because developing business mission critical software on a business network is a major risk, and an all around bad idea and should be avoided if, and whenever necessary. Project software development should always be separated from business computing networks in order to avoid the risk of negatively affecting those networks and business return on investment.

In many cases, confusion in relation to IT development, testing, training on production systems by business employees, IT and consultants have been an ongoing and serious problem. One mistake in this arena could cost a business hours, or in more serious cases, days or more of lost revenue because the mainstream business network may not work properly as a result. In situations such as these, the cost of envisioning, planning, building and implementing a physically separate development network begins to appear to be a more reasonable solution than changing a working, mission critical, business production environment for no good reason.

Below is an example of a small physically separate IT software development network domain:

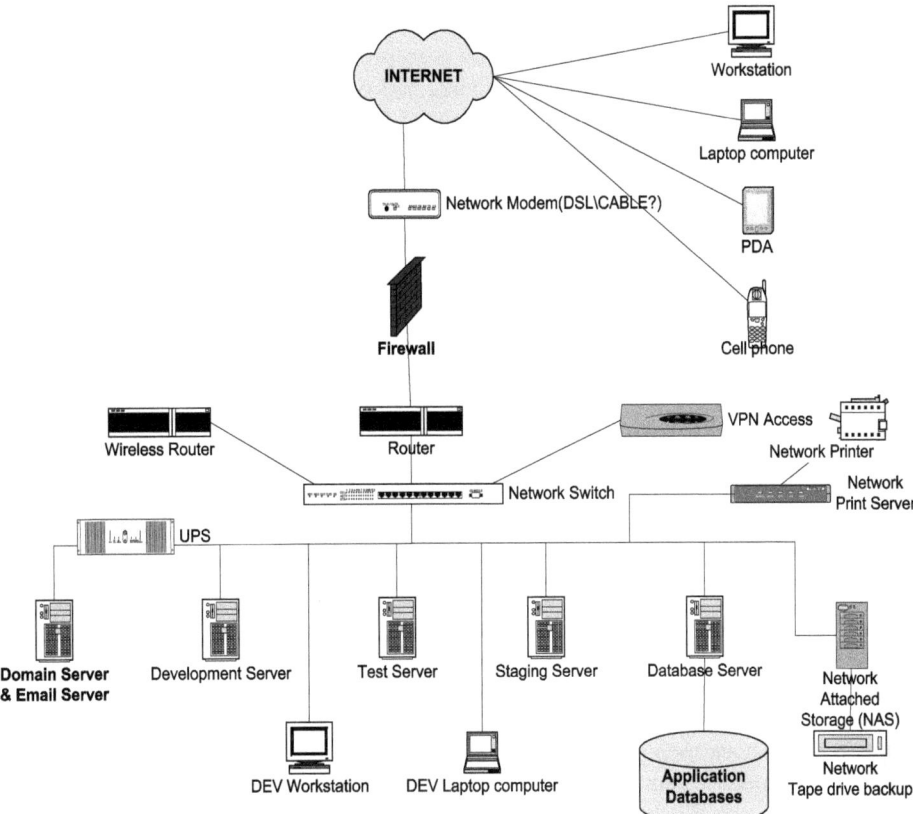

Servers for an IT software development network may include the following (but not necessarily in this order):

- Domain Server

- Development Server

- Test Server

- Staging Server

Chapter 5: BUILDING THE SHIPS

- Database Server

- Mail Server

- Network Area Storage (NAS)

The purpose of an IT development network is to provide Development with a physically (hardware) isolated network in which to invoke and complete the Software Development Lifecycle. On a separate hardware network domain, Corporate IT development and testing can proceed, and in no way negatively affect the company production network, therefore protecting business ROI.

Lastly, building and deploying a completely separate and smaller hardware network\domain for software development will be a critical factor in the success of building a corporate eBusinesses (electronic business), eCommerce (electronic commerce) applications, and Web-Portals. A business development hardware and network domain should exist for software development and testing (especially load testing) only, and should not be a part of the business production hardware network. This is necessary to avoid costly production network application latency issues and data related problems that could negatively affect the day-to-day operations of the business.

Give the People What They Need

How much of any one application's feature set do you or have you used, 40%, 60% or 80%? This will usually depend on what task you are performing according to what you need the application to do at a given time. With the large size, and sometimes-enormous feature sets of many popular business software applications, it can be difficult or impossible for an end-user to utilize 100% of that applications functionality, especially simultaneously. Often, many users are lost or confused with the features of many of the software systems that they use at work and at home. Those users tend to learn only what they need to know and ignore other obscure or complicated functionality that they do not understand or need.

Application Service Providers (ASP) would generally offer a software application as a service hosted over the Internet. Subscribers to these services would get the entire feature set of the Internet software system weather they used all of the functionality or not. If something went wrong with a part of the hosted Internet software application that a subscriber did not use, they could be negatively affected and possibly loose service altogether as a result. This is not what business users generally want, need or expect when they are trying to run an organization and procure revenue. Many organizations want to pay for only what they need or think they may need, nothing more, nothing less. For instance, wouldn't it be nice if your satellite TV and or cable TV providers only charged you for the channels that you actually watched and not for the entire 250 or more stations that they provide you service for? Your cable or satellite TV bill would most likely be much less every month. That is, you would still be able to watch any station that the provider offered whenever you wanted to, but you would only be charged a fee once for that station for the month, only if you stayed tuned to that channel for a specified amount of time. For some satellite and cable TV viewers, their monthly bill would not be very different. However, for others, it could drastically be more or less money depending on the circumstances of their usage. Software can work very much the same way and is beginning to on a gradual basis.

Service Oriented Architecture (SOA)

The definition of Service Oriented Architecture (SOA) can have different meanings depending upon whom you speak to in IT at various organizations. However, most folks might agree that SOA utilizes services that are "loosely coupled", which means that the request for data between software systems is specific but somewhat agnostic in regards to how that information is obtained. Quite simply, it would be like asking a waiter for a glass of spring water but not caring or worrying about how or where the waiter retrieved it and got it to you. An SOA software system is built and relies on separate software applications known as services, which are accessed over the Internet (Web Services). These software services are "self-reliant business processes" and can be accessed with total ignorance of their network, operating system (OS) or physical location. As you can see, this technology can be powerful for an organization if properly planned and implemented.

Web Services also allows for a business to build a host of services based on the requirements and business processes of the company. As new software system User Interfaces (UI) are required, these UI applications can be developed to access existing Web Services that may be able to deliver the information requested by the UI. If there are no Web Services that can currently meet the requirement of a specific UI, then an existing Service can be upgraded to fill the need, or a new Web Service can be developed to meet that requirement.

SOA RULES

There are rules that govern the design, planning, development, deployment and support of SOA software systems. Some of those principles used to guide SOA software development are as follows:

- SOA software systems should be designed and built using industry best practices

- SOA software system's code should be reusable

- SOA software systems should be able to easily integrate with other software systems

- SOA software systems should be component-based and modular in design

- SOA software systems should be well documented. This includes documentation of:

Chapter 5: BUILDING THE SHIPS

1. Service components
2. Service types
3. Service allocation
4. Service delivery
5. Service surveillance

Issues and concerns regarding SOA are related to how to organize and implement the metadata within that SOA environment and how to prevent this environment from becoming just another Web Services farm. Many IT professionals view SOA as base collection or library of web services to begin with and in some companies, this may be the case. More importantly, if implemented properly SOA can grow into or be a part of a much larger and effective architectural scheme that can make a company's technology scalable and decrease new software application development time.

Software as a Service (SaaS)

Software as a Service (SaaS) rests largely on the "publish and subscribe" paradigm using third party vendor owned and operated software made available over the Internet. SaaS has become a popular way for smaller to medium sized businesses to have access to the same features and benefits as their larger competitors. Not only that, but another benefit of SaaS is that the software is generally very economical, which makes the platform even more attractive.

Successful SaaS applications available today include but are not limited to:

- Human Resources
- Customer Relational Management (CRM)
- Finance and Accounting
- Sales
- Email
- Web Hosting
- Inventory Management
- Marketing

SaaS applications are "internet browser-based" software systems, and are specifically architected to utilize web-based technologies. Their fee schedules are generally on a per user basis. If the user requires more hard drive space, bandwidth or application features, they pay only for what they request and need, nothing more. This enables third party vendors who offer SaaS to keep their fees lower than traditional Application Service Providers (ASP) and they are able to better "forecast" their revenue streams more effectively. This is further augmented by the fact that a SaaS provider only supports the features of an application that are requested by a user or company. If a SaaS software system feature is not requested by an end-user, the third party vendor does not need to expend the resources to support that functionality. This saves revenue and time, and is much different from the business model of the Application Service Providers. The ASP business model delivers and supports new features for all clients whether they request the functionality or not.

One of the most significant impacts that SaaS has in the business is that it offers the right incentives to lure businesses into their environments. However, due to the fact that SaaS applications and support dictates that the management of some data and meta-data be done by the SaaS third party vendor, then the task of business reporting takes on a new significance. Business reporting must be re-analyzed and any system integration concerns that might exist with the SaaS provider must be resolved. An IT Management structure that is dependent on the management of their data center to manipulate their information network is often subject to greater governance issues.

The following are some of the reasons why the SaaS software model is currently growing at a rapid pace:

1. Internet and local network bandwidth is increasing significantly each year and can now much better support the delivery of larger Internet software applications.

2. Most users have personal computers (PC) so business and personal users can access mission critical applications anywhere at any time.

3. Many SaaS applications are standardized much like client applications can be. Since business users are largely accustomed to this, training time and learning the software is faster and more effective.

4. The Internet foundation is now stable enough to provide satisfactory "up-time".

5. Web application security is now reliable enough to consider this option. With the use of technology such as Secure Socket Layer (SSL), client to web-server communications can be reasonably secured.

6. A 3rd party SaaS vendor's market place is now "world-wide" as opposed to local. This makes the opportunity to grow rapidly more realistic.

Saas is definitely changing the way businesses are thinking about how to deal with IT departments. For instance, a start-up organization's finance department is unhappy with the current accounting software system that their IT department has implemented for them can now switch to a new application without the help of IT. The Finance Director can call a third party accounting SaaS provider and sign everyone in their department up for the new SaaS finance application. The Director can then outsource their employees training of the new SaaS software system to the third party vendor as well. Let's now say that the organization's Finance Department begins using the new SaaS Accounting software system and everyone seems to enjoy it. Several months later, the IT Manager asks the Finance Director how their department likes their new Accounting system not realizing that the Finance Department does not use the software that IT had implemented previously. The Finance Department responds very favorably referring to the new SaaS Accounting software system. IT then realizes several months after the fact that their Finance Department is not using the Accounting application that IT designed, built and implemented. Because the Finance Department has been very effective and successful using the SaaS Accounting software system, the CEO and CIO decides to let them continue using it due partly to the fact that they do not have to support the product. In this scenario, the Finance Department has successfully "side-stepped" the IT Department and no longer needs IT services to support their core departmental software system. This is a serious course change for the local IT Department and deeply threatens the job security of many IT personnel within that company in this regard.

In most situations, SaaS applications must be integrated with other existing business applications. To achieve this, IT departments may need to:

- Export pre-existing data from a business IT application to the SaaS software system

- Configure an existing business software system to process data delivered by a SaaS application

- Configure an SaaS software system to process data delivered to it by an existing business application

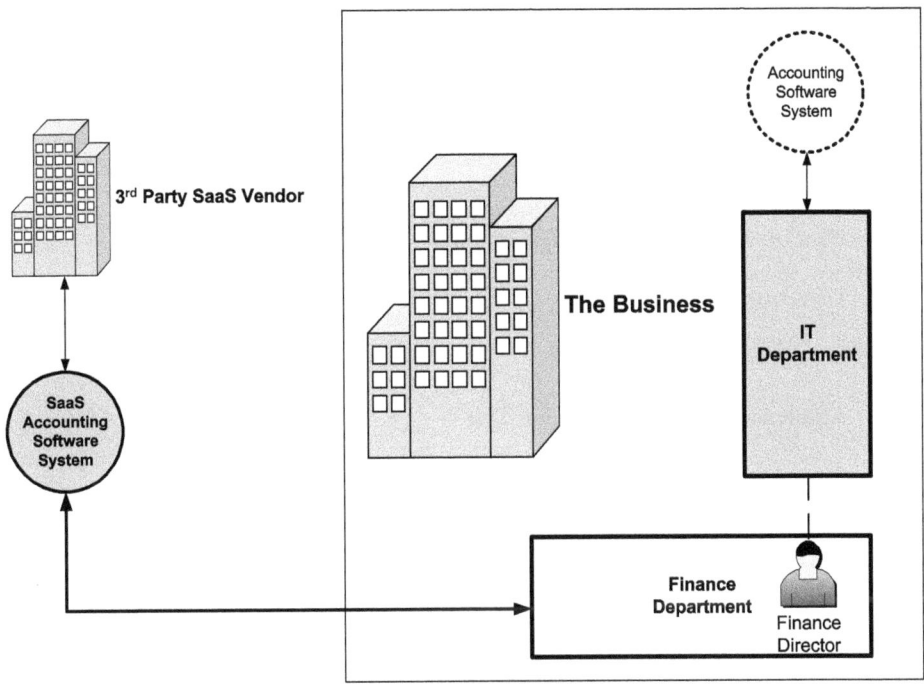

With SaaS, many business departments who were totally dependent upon IT for all of their software system needs are now empowered to bypass IT altogether. Departments have the ability to try new SaaS software systems online before they need to make a commitment to buy it. This greatly lowers the risk of the software implementation process because the software system is not installed in-house or supported by the local IT Department. If a user or Business Department does not like the SaaS application, they can tell the third party vendor that they are not interested and move on. This is a powerful new option for a Business Departments, who may have felt helpless in their relationship with their in-house IT services in regards to their company software systems previously. This is even more of a reason for IT Departments to work much harder to give the business what they need in the most effective and ROI efficient manner possible. It is inevitable that some and even more IT personnel in the future will lose their jobs to third party SaaS software systems and companies.

Distributed Software Systems

N-Tier software system architectures have the capability of offering virtually limitless scalability. When a software system's performance begins to degrade in a particular area, resources can be re-allocated to support system shortfalls that were not expected. Because resource management can be a complicated process, a business must be able to keep up a reasonable level of service within a distributed and flexible architecture that is not only

Chapter 5: BUILDING THE SHIPS

reactive but proactive as well. This can have a positive effect on the IT services offered to the organization and it customers as well as the cost of the application. This has been a major obstacle for IT to overcome in that past. In addition, it has continuously exposed a problem, which Information Technology's had failed to correct in an effective manner, which was its own base infrastructure.

The three or more tier-based architecture can be smart client or web-based, and consists of the following base separate software applications:

1. **User Interface Tier (UI)**
2. **Service Interface Tier**
3. **Application or Business Logic Tier**
4. **Data Access Tier**

A "tier" refers to a software application module or web service that can reside on various hardware platforms and or servers regardless of the software's operating system or physical location. Multi-tiered software applications subscribe to their adjacent design pattern and architecture for scalability, and maintainability. The term tier is also referred to as a "Layer".

It is not a requirement, by any means, for all software applications to be n-Tier ("n" equals 3 or more Tiers). However, enterprise level software systems have more advanced requirements and must be scalable and flexible in a way that if a specific module of the software fails to respond, the entire application does not stop working as a result. Building distributed applications requires a different mindset from the applications architectures that came before. This is because the software as a whole no longer resides on one or two servers. The software is capable of functioning more like its distributed hardware counterparts. That is because the premise is that the software should overlay and function much the hardware that is runs on. For instance, the Internet is one large distributed software and hardware application. The software is distributed over millions of computers worldwide but the end-users (you and I) perceive the Internet from our browsers as one software application. We do not care where the servers are that invoke our software or what operating systems the software is deployed and running on. From our perspective, the important point is that we get the information that we are seeking, and that we are able to perform the tasks we set out to do. Anything else is a non-factor when we use the Internet except for the fact that it must be up and running, reliable, fast, as secure as possible, and stay that way when we are using it.

The following is a sample n-Tier diagram:

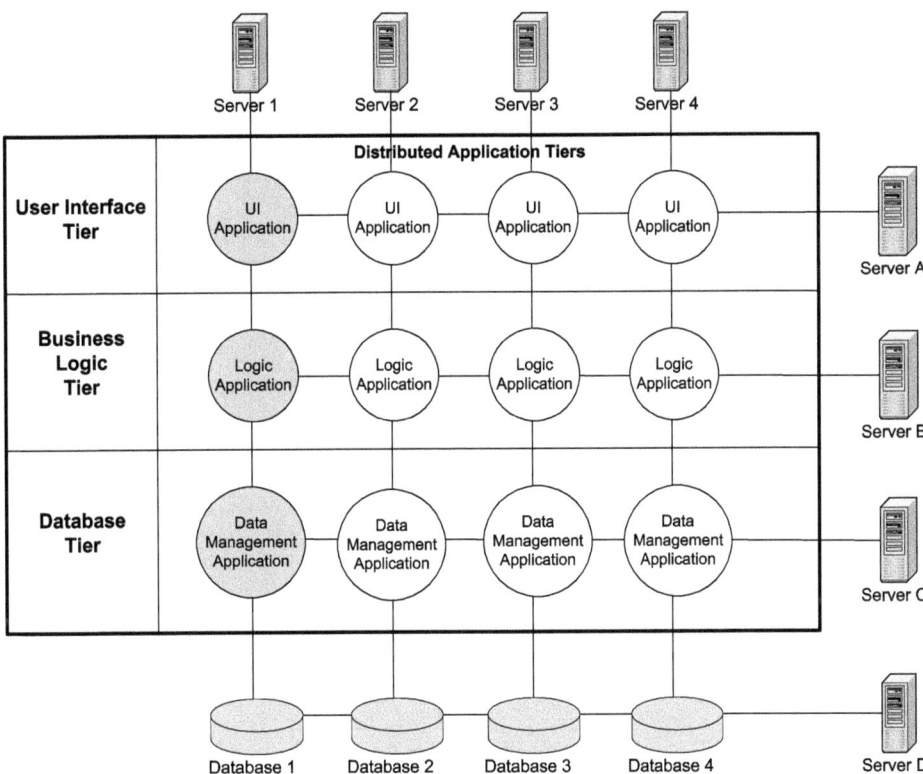

When software is able to function and be able to be supported like hardware, new opportunities are created for applications that did not exist previously. For instance, technology professionals realize that computer hardware technology has been leaps and bounds ahead of software technology for decades. Hardware at many times has had to stop to wait for its software counterpart to catch up, and the software never has. The good news is that the hardware architectures that has built the Internet works very well, and has in this capacity for a long time. Therefore, since this is the case then it would appear to make perfect sense for software architectures to follow suit. In this way, software could then be vertically and horizontally scaled in very much the same ways as hardware servers. The benefits of having software able to function in this way are enormous. Some of those new advantages include:

- Software applications that can facilitate hundreds of thousands or even millions of end-users simultaneously

- Software applications can then be upgraded while the systems are online without having to shut them down. This makes for a better user experience due to a lack of

Chapter 5: BUILDING THE SHIPS

interruption in service. In addition, this practice also helps to save organizational revenue, as their system is able to take advantage of maximum up-time.

- Software applications can be monitored and predictions can be made as to what parts of the system will need maintenance, updates or additional processing power.

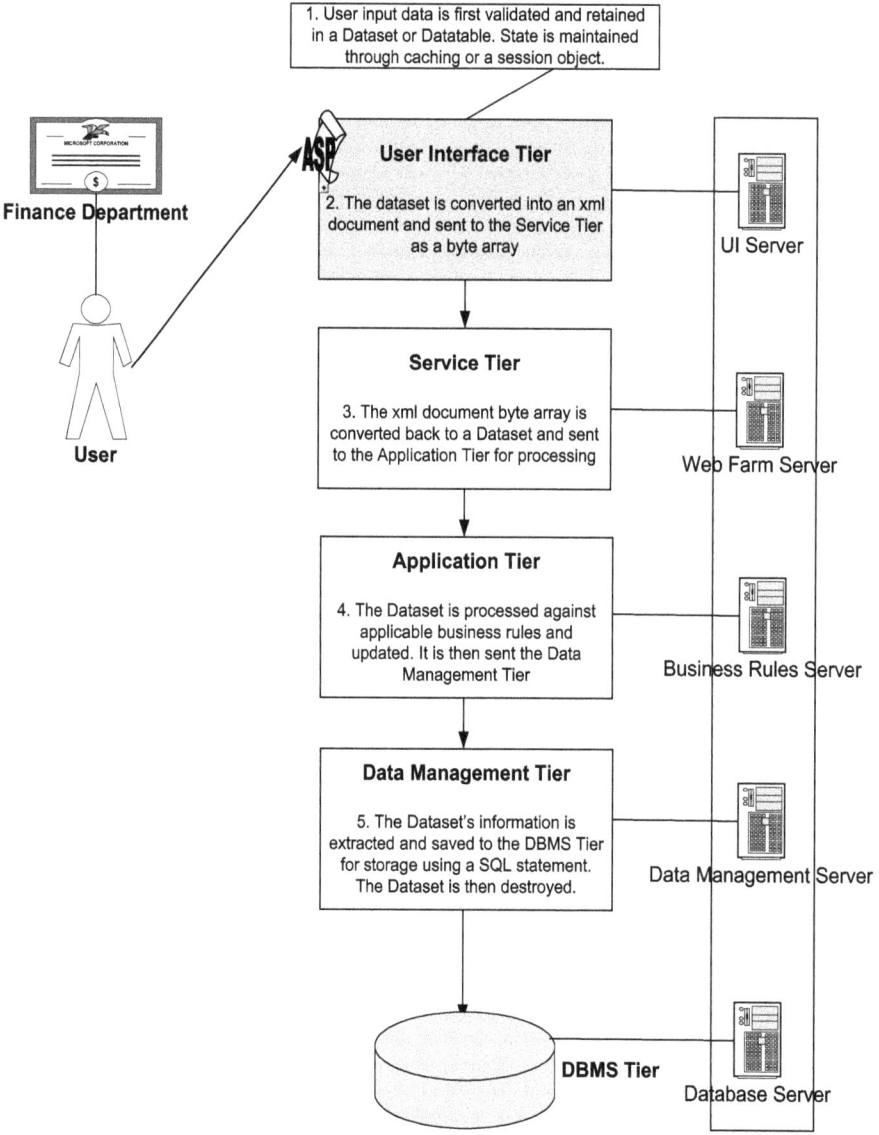

Horizontal Software application scaling involves an overall system update that requires that an easy to understand change management process be put into place and then maintained. It is also important to understand that on the horizontal tier, updates can be made in phases and not all at once due to the redundancy implemented. The software changes made horizontally must be deployed in a calculated and logical manner. Horizontal scaling supports resiliency and the ability to "forecast" system performance. Resource allocation can also be improved using this method utilizing a load balancer that distributes the workload of the software system to the rest of the servers in the horizontal array accordingly.

Vertical Software application scaling allows the system services to be distributed inside of the application. This involves the hardware portion of the software system that includes components such as:

- **Storage (Hard Drives)**
- **Computer Memory**
- **Computer Processors**

Upgrading these components when required, and in phases, can greatly increase the scalability of the application over time. This type of scaling involves updating software systems more slowly than that of vertical scaling. This is especially effective in the areas of the software system that deals specifically with databases, email, file stores, along with video and music streaming. Just because the design of a vertical architecture is not flexible does not mean that the content is. Content (data) can be very unpredictable and grow out of control quickly. In order to keep the vertical scaling process as stable as possible, data should not be partitioned, retrieved, and stored in the same way by all components that need it. Any non-partitioned data should be grouped together, retrieved, and stored in the same way as partitioned data. This is important because it contributes to enhanced software system scaling and latency going forward.

All of these factors are important if you are an enterprise that must have software systems that support large numbers of customers and employees in a reliable manner. Also because of this, enterprises usually cannot afford on many levels the method of completely refactoring (re-architecting and rebuilding) their software systems every 1 to 2 years. In general, few companies cannot survive this type of software practice, as it should be considered unreasonable because it often negatively affects ROI.

An enterprise organization's applications must be able to grow substantially over time according to the company's changing needs. This is why it is important to be able to have flexible, nimble software systems that are not monolithic and or rigid. Software Forecasting, much like weather forecasting, can be substantial for planning the technological future of an organization. In many cases, a business may not always be sure of what industry changes lay ahead but they know they must be able to meet them effectively. That means IT must deliver software solutions that are also intelligent, can maintenance themselves to a large degree, and are somewhat simple to upgrade. In that way, IT can focus on other matters as well and not be locked to any one particular software system exclusively.

An important factor in understanding n-tier systems is that the more layers that are added to a distributed architecture, the more the performance of the system degrades and additional support is required. The UI and Service (optional) tiers rest upon the application layer. The benefit in this regard is that fact that the one would not necessarily need to refactor any code from the business layer to the data management tiers. The components are built and deployed and can be accessed by any application on a variety of platforms. For example, a software system is using a specific enterprise level third party database that is very expensive. IT would like to change this database to a less expensive but equally effective new enterprise database application. Using n-tier software system architecture, IT software engineers could then add or update the data tier with a new class that would facilitate data access to the newly selected database application. The basic premise in this scenario is to allow each layer to be modular with plug and play capabilities. In addition, this process should be a simple and effective one whereas the technology used on each individual tier can be different if required.

As the Internet grows and users continue to find new and powerful applications for the web, corporations will be increasingly challenged to do more with their existing technologies. The demands of end-users for business systems that are stable, quality-driven, and easy to use will keep pushing the limits of IT architectures and software systems into the future. If an organization does not understand how important a flexible n-tier system and architecture is needed to meet and exceed customer demands, then that business is in certain danger of extinction. Having the ability to scale both vertically and horizontally is a powerful means by which a software system can grow and continue add value to a business. It also morphs the IT infrastructure in ways that overcome the issues and problems of the past where monolithic systems ruled the land.

The Software Development Lifecycle (SDLC)

The Software Development Lifecycle (SDLC) is a science and method of building software system applications. The SDLC is a process used to deliver software system solutions in a problem domain, in a consistent manner. It is critical to understand that the business is the primary owner of the software system that is produced as a result of the SDLC. It is also key for any organization that builds software in-house to learn, implement, execute, and support. The SDLC helps to achieve predictable results for the software products they intend to deliver when implemented properly. Its processes requires strong leadership, discipline and teamwork by all involved and must be enforced by Executive Management. It is the responsibility of IT to educate the business in regards to business specific roles, duties, and deliverables within the SDLC. IT personnel are (or should be) the experts in this subject matter and must serve as the primary educators to the business just as the company shares its knowledge of system requirements with IT.

A general SDLC view consists of six specific phases that include:

1. Creating a vision of the product that encapsulates the overall idea of what the product will do and how it will appear to the end-user

2. Gathering the overall product vision and resources to create a comprehensive plan for building, testing, deploying, and supporting the product. This also includes a specific and detailed plan for change management throughout the SDLC process.

3. Implementing the plan for building the software system product

4. Implementing the plan for testing the software system product

5. Implementing the plan for deploying the software system product

6. Implementing the plan for supporting the software system product after it has been put into production.

It is not sufficient to only know how to write code well within the SDLC. A software engineer must know much more than just how to produce good code. A Software Engineers role within the SDLC process includes but is not limited to:

- A strong understanding of business requirements

- The ability to write comprehensive, and simple test plans and later invoke them

- In some cases, the ability to write Technical Specification Documentation

- The ability to understand and follow software system architecture diagrams, design patterns, and development standards

- The ability to understand database schemas

- The ability to work well with others on the software system project team

- The ability to ask the right questions

The "Bulls Eye" diagram that follows illustrates the SDLC process described above starting with the product vision that resides in the center of the diagram:

Chapter 5: BUILDING THE SHIPS

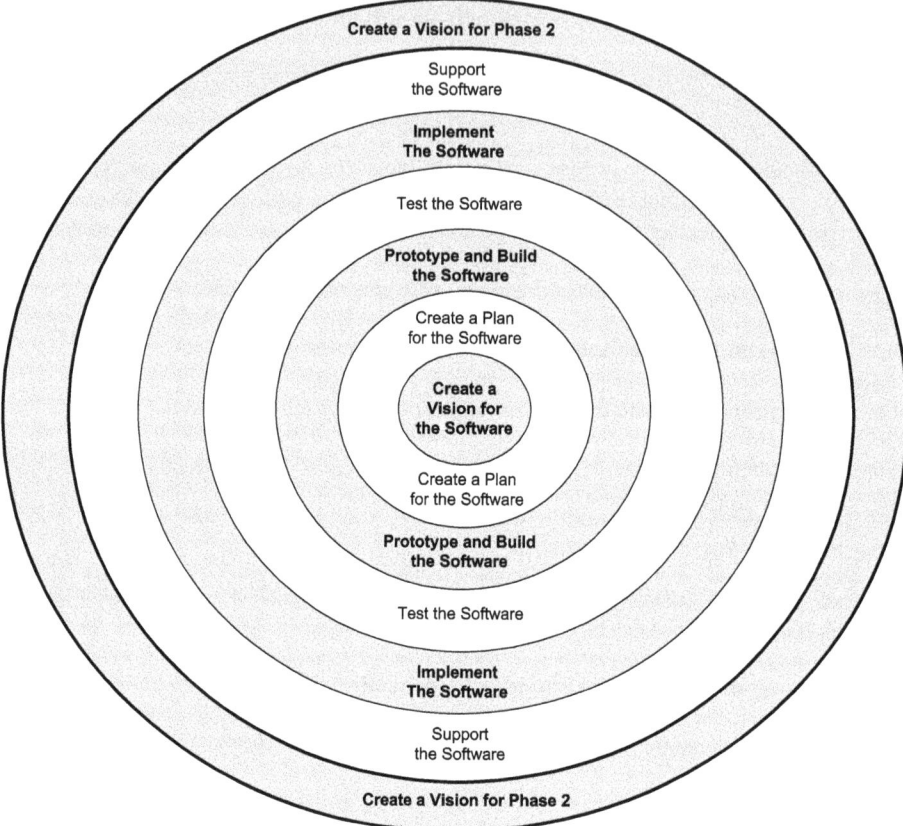

The Product Vision

The creation of the vision of the project involves a comprehensive and detailed analysis of any issues and problems that affect the results of the project. During the product vision phase, project resources are allocated and client expectations are identified. It is important during this event to get everyone who has stock in the project to think in a similar manner about it, and that expectations are uniform. IT Management outlines the project roles, responsibilities, and tasks along with the product requirements. The project scope is clearly defined, documented, communicated, and understood by all concerned parties by the end of the phase. This prophecy must be fulfilled before any software development begins.

During the vision phase, the following tasks are performed:

- A thorough analysis of the business challenges, opportunities and requirements are implemented to describe the business objectives in detail.

- The project team is created and implemented. Project resource analysis is performed to understand the availability, issues, and revenue.

- A thorough analysis of the present and future software systems are performed. All possible present and future software system variances are defined. In this way, concerns can be documented so that a cohesive focused plan can be developed to eliminate problems that could potentially derail the project.

- The overall scope and infrastructure of the project is created and implemented. This means the project management is made known to all project members and business IT project stock holders.

The product vision phase should yield the minimum following documentation:

1. Risk Analysis
2. Risk Resolution Strategy
3. User Requirements
4. Software System Architecture
5. Business Processes and Use Cases
6. Roles and Responsibilities
7. Project Methodology

The Product Plan

When working on a plan that will be invoked to guide a software system project, the focus must be placed on how the application will be produced. The software application's look and feel, the business processes, and use cases involved are put to a strategy for completion of the project. System architecture as well as Functional Specifications are created and implemented. In this phase, a project plan is created from the information that has been compiled to this point and all of the project resources are also made available.

Software System project planning involves creating and implementing the following:

- A Design Concept

- Design Logic

- Design Physics

In the design concept, the software system project is analyzed and observed from the organizational view or end-user perspective primarily. This means that the requirements gathered from the business drives the conceptual view. The use cases created using the business processes that were identified by the business users shape the overall conceptual view. The design logic's perspective is somewhat different from the design concept. In the logical view, the project is analyzed from the IT teams' point of reference. IT identifies and formulates production results for the software system based on services that are grouped by tasks.

Last but not least, the design physics drill down into the more technical side of the software project. The Software System Architect identifies the software languages, tools, and platforms that will be used by the Software Engineers on the project. In this view, the Software System architecture is created and the designs made by the Software System Architect drives the remainder of the technology decisions that are implemented. This includes but is not limited to:

1. The software system's Design Patterns

2. The software system's components

3. The software system's interfaces

4. The software system's event logging

5. The software system's exception handling

6. The software systems integration points

7. The software system's security

8. The software system's configurability

9. The software system's communications

10. The software system's services

Before the development of software begins within the project, the project team must insure that certain objectives are met. Some of those objectives include:

- Creating a Functional Specifications document

- Creating a Technical Specifications document

- Creating a Project Plan that includes completion plans and a master time-line based task list. This plan is grouped by, and based on project team member's roles and responsibilities.

- The design and implementation of a complete and separate development domain network (or environment) for project software system development and testing. The Development domain network will mirror the final production network but this is not where the final production version of the software system will be deployed and supported.

Towards the end of the planning phase, members of the IT team must verify the project software system's technology. In this way, all IT project members concerned are of "one mind" when it come to what technologies and standards will be invoked during the SDLC. All documentation should be completed. This includes the Functional and Technical Specifications, the Project Plan, and the roles and responsibility assignments. The development domain network (or environment) for software system development should be up and running and able to facilitate the development of the software product.

SOFTWARE ESTIMATION

Developing reliable software system project estimations is a difficult and often ignored area of IT projects. Without a good software estimate base, an IT project plan cannot be created that is reliable from a revenue standpoint. This is one of the major reasons why IT software projects fail, and this particular oversight is completely avoidable. This is also true of over and under estimating software system projects.

In many cases, the individual who is estimating the size and cost of the software project may try to give themselves some room to work in the event that something does not work out as planned with the people and or technology. This is to be expected to some extent, but there are others who can take this thinking too far and may drastically overestimate the costs of the project. When this problem occurs, it has adverse repercussions on the organizations return on investment (ROI). This means that the scope of the project is incorrect and many of the resources assigned to the project may be unnecessary. Those resources could very well be needed elsewhere in the company, which can further hurt the business with other projects that are in process. Too many resources on an IT software project can often lead to a project taking much longer than expected. For example, too many software engineers can lead to an intellectual deadlock if that group has to make decisions. This is because software development is deeply rooted in problem solving, and four or more software engineers usually don't think any faster than any 1 to 3 can.

Chapter 5: BUILDING THE SHIPS

If the software project estimation is below what is required, the scope of the project will also be incorrect which can lead to significant issues and concerns. In many situations, the individual who is performing the software estimate is trying to save the company revenue. This can result in the following problems with the IT software project:

1. **Not enough resources to do the work** - When this happens, project team members usually have to do more than one job which can lead to significant overtime hours, fatigue, and poor morale.

2. When resources are insufficient, product quality and customer service usually suffers as a result.

3. Project milestones and planned timelines are difficult or impossible to reach. This results in a loss of trust by the business in the project which is as valuable as gold on almost any IT project.

In order to estimate software system projects soundly, there are some basic guidelines that should be followed in the process.

Some of those guidelines are:

- The software system project should be estimated in the revenue of the region of the business that is responsible for paying for the project. In this way, the people who own the project will have the best idea of how much the project will cost. Do this unless the project owners request otherwise.

- The software system project overall scope (or size) should be estimated in detail. This means that there must be some tangible means of relating the girth of the project. This can be done by using Function Points (FP) or a total compilation of business processes, utilizing use cases and business requirements. In some cases, estimating the total lines of code is valuable but this can be difficult with some of today's software development tools that can generate large amounts of code automatically.

- The software system project timeline should be estimated in months, not days or hours along with the tasks of the team members.

It is important to attempt a software system project estimate even if all of the information needed is not available at the time the estimate is performed. A re-estimation can, and should be done anytime new information is made available in order to keep project costs as accurate as possible. This is because a reliable software project estimate helps to mitigate project risks, which are extremely important to the business, and all project members.

SOFTWARE REQUIREMENTS

It is always somewhat of a shock, and a nice surprise whenever I visit a client site for the first time, and they are able to provide me with a good and comprehensive requirements document for the software project that I will be working on. In most cases, when starting an IT software project, a requirements document either doesn't exists, is poorly written or invalid. This fact can be frustrating and lead to the client\consultant relationship not starting out on the best of terms. It is a sad fact that many IT consultants and employees have come to expect non-existent or poorly written project requirement documents. I can remember being quite surprised on a past software project at the level of incompetence that went into the creation of a specific requirements document. I shared that fact with another member of the IT team and their response was that I was lucky to have a requirements document at all to work with. The whole point is that if the business does not know what they want their software to do, then the software engineers won't know either. In these cases, if the business either cannot or will not be clear about what they require, then the IT team must make their best "guess" at what that is, and that assumption is hardly ever acceptable to the business. So in effect, the software project starts out as a "lose\lose" scenario as opposed to a "win\win".

A software system requirements document should always tell the reader what the software system will do and not how the software system will do it. When requirements documentation begins to get technical in its content, it takes a giant step in the wrong direction because it must then be viewed through a technological perspective with the right people involved. Technical software project information is for Technical Specification documents. In addition, adding technical information to a requirements document takes that document out of scope and can often make the subject matter confusing and incomplete. With the focus in a requirements document being on what the software does, the application user or document reader can work on exactly what a user views as to what the application is. That is, while using the software system, a user performs an action from which a software event is invoked, and the application executes and delivers the expected end-user result. If the expected application response is not clearly communicated to the system builders, then it is not likely to be correct within the software when it is delivered. This is a major reason why requirements documents are important.

To be clear, the requirements document will never address "how" the application will comply with any business requirements stated. There are good principles involved in the development of a competent and focused requirements document. Some of those principles include:

1. The requirements documents will not include any software system architecture.

2. The requirements documents will not include any software language code or Structured Query Language (SQL) statements of any sort.

3. The requirements documents will not include any XML or database schemas.

4. The requirements documents will not include any screen shots.

5. The requirements documents will not include any n-tier or object oriented comments, statements or references.

6. The requirements documents will not include any statements in regards to what software system tools will be used in the software project.

7. The requirements documents will not include any project planning data.

8. The requirements documents will not include technical jargon.

9. The requirements documents will not include any business user "wants" or "desires".

10. The requirements documents will not include any "vague" or "ambiguous" statements of any kind.

Since software system requirements must be able to be inspected, verified and accepted by the project owners (the business), this means that some type of formal requirements document must be compiled and accessible to them. Requirements cannot be "scattered" throughout an organizational structure. For instance, emails, disparate or siloed documentation, websites references, notes on desks, and mental repositories of various company employees and managers are not acceptable final requirements. Distributed information of this sort is extremely difficult to confirm and is not logical or practical but can be quite normal for many businesses today. A single living body of the compiled business software system requirements is the only way to insure the integrity of the application to be developed. With large enterprise-level software systems, it may be necessary to breakdown a lengthy requirements document into a set of documents that cover the same topic from different perspectives. This is not recommended unless absolutely necessary and the documents must always be accessible as a collection.

It is important to understand that there are three basic types of requirements documents. These three document types consist of the following:

1. **Functional-level requirements**

2. **Organizational-level requirements**

3. **End-user level requirements**

Functional-level requirements stem from the perspective of the software design team in which the software system architect is the lead design entity. This is the design view that the software architect is responsible for sharing with the software engineers who will ultimately build the application. The focus in this point of view is "how" the software system will work along with the specific technologies involved. The functional-level requirements are the rules and descriptions needed for the software engineer to build their part(s) of the software system. Functional-level requirements include but are not limited to project design subject matter relating to:

- System Reporting
- System Security
- System Integration
- System Auditing (Regulatory Compliance)
- Exception Handling
- Event Handling
- System Communications
- System Administration
- System Performance

In organizational-level requirements, the focus lies primarily on very high-level needs of the business and or their clients, who will utilize the software product. In this perspective, the right business "objectives" that are communicated is the key to success. This type of requirement document explains in full detail why the business needs the software system described and how that application will assist the organization in growing to conquer the objectives outlined in that specific requirements document. In many cases, organizational-level requirements become a part of the project vision statement that is used to maintain a project's perspective throughout the SDLC process.

From end-user level requirements documentation, user processes are outlined and described in detail. This view displays all of the tasks that the end-user must be able to perform when they use the software system. End-user level requirements documentation is where business use cases and component event driven system expectations are clearly defined. Matrices are often used to facilitate user event actions and their invoked software system responses for additional clarity. Requirements of this type detail the software system end-user expectations and clearly defined terms. A good example of a use case would be all the steps involved in ordering a book on the Internet using an eCommerce web application and credit card.

Chapter 5: BUILDING THE SHIPS

Writing a good and competent requirements document and maintaining it is usually more difficult that it may seem from the outset. This is because requirements documents have a tendency to change, and sometimes on a daily or even hourly basis. This is due to new discoveries and or mistakes in the requirements process that are made by the business and or IT. With this in mind, it is important to try to write the best possible requirements from the very beginning so that updates to that document can be made in a simple and logical manner.

When writing requirements documentation, try to adhere to the following guidelines for a more effective document:

- Do not use technical words or phrases. Try to write using simple words and short sentences. If you have to use industry jargon, then include the definitions of all of those terms.

- List and number the requirements and any related sub-topics accordingly. This will create a type of directory that will help readers to focus on, and identify requirements that project members may question.

- Group requirements according to their respective functions. This makes it easier to identify what processes may be missing in relation to specific functionality.

- Use the "active voice" in describing requirements. For example, use firm statements like "The system will" and "The system must" as opposed to statements like "The system should" or "the system may".

- Use table, diagrams, and charts to help communicate difficult and or complicated requirements.

- Always implement an index and a table of contents to your requirements documents. This makes information in the document easier to find and defines the document structure.

- Create and implement a logical flow to the requirements document. The more organized the content within the document is, the easier it will be for the reader to understand what it is the software system is supposed to do.

Software system requirements documents generally include three sections. Those three sections are:

1. **The software system overview (opening summary)**

2. **The software system requirements drill-down and their descriptions**

3. The software system closing summary

The overview section of the software system requirements document should serve to present a high-level and broad description of the application. This description is the system "big picture" where all of the system objectives are listed. Why the application is needed and how it will improve the organizations business process are also good fits for this area of the document. Reasons as to why the project is being implemented at that particular time is also useful information along with a list of business individuals who will ultimately benefit from the implementation of the software product. It is important for anyone who reads the requirements document to understand the objectives outlined before they move on to any other part of the document. This is because if they cannot understand the over-all scope and reason for the project, then they will be less likely to understand the project itself.

Software system requirements can remain a "work in progress" for most of the project. Because of this, it is a very good practice to include some sort of change management to the document.

Below is an example template for keeping track of business change requests as they come in:

Date\Time	Change Request	Requestor	Department	Priority	System Version

In some cases, the requirement change requests may be too large and detailed to fit into a grid like the one above. In this event, it is a good practice to write an addendum document that serves as an extension to the original requirements. It must detail the changes implemented. This addition must be appended to the requirements document set and designated as necessary reading in regards to new and old requirements within the primary requirements documentation. In this way, all of the details of the new and existing enhancements can be explained in full detail without limitation.

Product Development

The project team builds the software system product in this phase of the SDLC. This means that the application source code along with the system infrastructure is written, developed, and implemented. Due to the design architecture and planning that was done in the previous stages, the timeframe for the development of the software application should be shorter in comparison to the vision, planning, and testing phases.

One of the most critical tasks during this phase is the creation of the software system prototype. During the development of the prototype, software engineers also work on the following jobs:

- Creating and implementing the software system components
- Work to integrate software system components
- Working on the communication (integration) between application tiers
- Developing and implementing daily and or weekly application builds to show the state of the application and it is working

The software system prototype is the "proof of concept" that the application is viable and can work. This step is considered a milestone as the business can now see a working version of its original requirements that is taking shape. In order to close out the product development phase, the IT team must complete the following tasks:

- The Functional Specification is completed
- The application test plans are put in to place
- The software system source code is completed and the final build is performed
- The application is configured for deployment on the test server
- All supporting applications and utilities are installed on the test server
- The application is deployed on the test server

Product Testing

Product testing is where the application is measured against its original requirements in order to insure that it is functioning according to user expectations. In addition, this is the phase where the "bugs" or "exceptions" are corrected within software. System "exceptions" are defined as "rule violations" as software systems are comprised of strict rule based processes. Any deviance from those laws is deemed an "exception" to those rules, and must be corrected for the application to work as expected.

This area of the software development lifecycle is also called the "Stabilization" phase. At this time, additional system integration is implemented along with the test plans. Several different tests are performed on the application according to the original test plan strategy. With requirement adherence and issue resolution being a primary focus during system testing, attention to detail is paramount.

The testing phase is where the software system takes on its final metamorphoses from completed functionality to a model of the completed Functional Specifications document. Quality assurance is also measured according to IT industry best practices in relation to the software system product being tested. In order to complete the product-testing phase, the IT team must perform the following tasks as required to stabilize the system:

- System exception tracking
- System infrastructure tests
- System core component tests
- System integration tests
- System load\stress\performance tests
- System security tests
- System regression tests
- System database access test

After these tests have been performed on the software application, the system can then be deployed to a "staging" server. The "staging" server is a copy of the production server where the system will finally be installed and used. On the "staging" server, User Acceptance Testing (UAT) can then be invoked. This means that the end-user can begin to test the application using actual working business processes, use cases, and sample data.

Before deploying the software system to the production server (final deployment), the IT team must insure that the following criteria are met:

1. The number of system exceptions (bugs) that are corrected is greater than the number of system exceptions that are discovered. During the testing phase, it is normal for the number of exceptions to rise and fall according to the bug discovery and correction iteration process that the software and test engineers are engaged in. This process can be "trended" within a good bug tracking application to show the progress of the testing cycle.

2. During the bug discovery and correction iteration process, the number of overall exceptions should decrease, and eventually reach zero. This is also known as a "Zero Bug Release".

3. As a result of a reaching the platform of a "Zero Bug Release", the application version can then be considered "Gold" (production grade), and deemed ready for its final deployment to a business production server.

However, before the final deployment of the application, the following Product test phase items and documentation must be updated and made available to the rest of the IT project team. Those objects include:

- A report document that includes final testing results. This document can also include a detailed performance analysis of the application.

- Final software system release documentation set that includes a milestone review and any additional necessary product documentation.

Product Deployment

This is the final official phase of the SDLC. At this time, the IT software project team deploys the application to the business production server for use by the organization's end-users. The IT project team must then request and receive final verification from the business that that system is working as expected in the new production environment. After the system is approved by the organization, it is necessary for the project team members to review the entire software business project. This may also include polling the business to get their general feedback and perspective as to how well the project progressed and to discover any problems that the team may have been unaware of. This information can be extremely valuable in future projects as analyzing this data can help the IT team minimize risks as they look forward to the next software project.

To complete the final deployment phase of the SDLC, the IT project team must perform the following duties:

1. Deploy the software system and all required application components, to the production server and document the final deployment procedure and any outstanding production issues.

2. Outline and document the transition process to the support and how that process will be implemented.

3. Create and publish the final software system project analysis and review documentation.

4. Create and implement end-user software system training documentation along with a training plan.

5. Create and implement an application knowledge base and or help system for the product.

6. Gather all final versions of the project's documentation and store that information in a project repository for historical and reference purposes.

7. Meet with the support team to go over the transition process, documentation, and expectations.

8. Transition the project to the technical support team responsible for the new software system.

At this time, the project is considered complete.

It is important for any business that decides to build an in-house software system to understand the following statement:

"Designing, coding, testing, implementing and maintaining stable, scalable, effective software systems is a science, not an ad-hoc or layman's process".

Product Support

Software system support is often an afterthought and viewed by many IT personnel not involved with it as a lower level IT task. This is also generally defined as answering support telephone calls from distressed users about a problem that they are having with the software. However, supporting a software system is much more than that. This is a scientific process that is essential for maintaining the health and growth of a software system that an organization may have invested significant revenue in. The truth of the matter is that IT systems cannot move forward if they cannot be properly supported and maintained. This is where the return on investment in a software system can be greatly reduced if the proper maintenance and support are not implemented.

Change Management

Many people and businesses fear change. In some instances, they even try to ignore it, and this almost always leads to serious problems in their development and sometimes even to their ultimate demise. To live is to constantly change, and death can also be described as "the lack of change" or "unchanging". Effective change management is a structured process of moving from the current to something different and or new. IT management and their personnel should always be in a constant state of positive change. Technology is evolving at a rapid pace and will continue to do so as it is driven naturally by competition and consumer requirements.

Chapter 5: BUILDING THE SHIPS

More than half of all IT project fail partly because they exceed their original budgets or they are delivered late. Software system project scopes that are not well understood lay at the root of some of these issues. This is due largely to:

- The lack of a change control and risk management processes

- The ongoing status of the project is not monitored and or managed

- Software system project resources, schedules, and product functionality are not properly adjusted when needed

It is necessary to realize that managing project exchanges and compromises without adversely affecting product functionality is irrefutable. A software system project needs to progress in a well-balanced manner in order to have a viable chance of being successful. All original objectives that are identified as to why the project exists must remain intact during the SDLC process. In this regard, when exchanges and compromises are discussed by the IT team and the business, both parties involved may have to make certain concessions in order to move forward. This is to be expected.

Below is the ever-popular exchange and compromise triangle. Resources, timelines, and functionality all relate to one another. If one part of the triangle changes, the other 2 sides must compensate for those changes. In this way, project balance is maintained so that progress can be made.

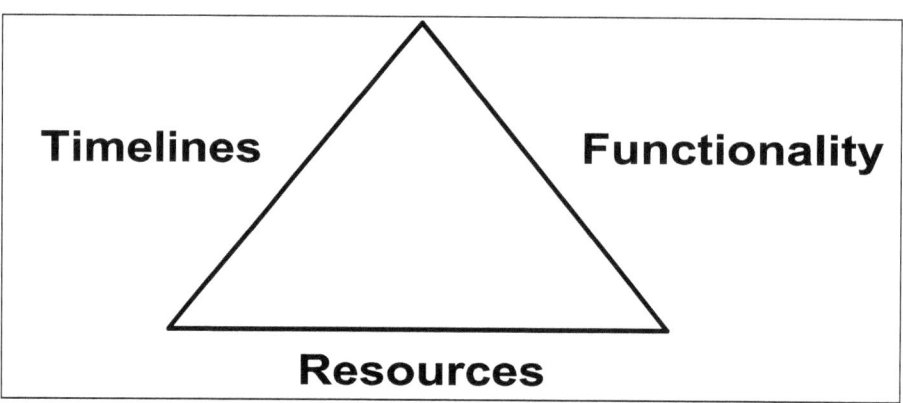

The use of an Exchange and Compromise (E&C) Chart can help a software development team significantly in regards to decision making when it comes to production. The exchanges and compromises chart displays the application's functionality on three levels:

1. **Critical**

2. Selected

3. Flexible

Below is an E&C Chart:

	Critical	Selected	Flexible
Resources			X
Timelines		X	
Functionality	X		

The above chart is simple, and works in the following manner. As you can see, the Critical, Selected, and Flexible columns are marked with an "X". This means that the above Exchange and Compromise Chart should be read in this manner:

The Functionality is "Critical", the Timelines are "Selected", and the Resources are "Flexible".

However, the Exchange and Compromise Chart below displays a different message.

	Critical	Selected	Flexible
Resources		X	
Timelines	X		
Functionality			X

Below is how this chart's message should be read in this manner:

The Timelines are "Critical", the Resources are "Selected", and the Functionality is "Flexible".

An E&C Chart can be a very effective means of understanding and tracking project priorities. It is important to note that if the chart is not used by the team, then it is of no value. The business and the IT project team must have a sound written agreement in place that states they will both utilize the E&C Chart during the SDLC or something to that affect. Both a business and IT Manager should sign a written agreement of that sort and be sure to keep their promises as it is in their own best interests.

Black Box Management

Change management is especially important when it involves third Party software systems. Naturally, the larger the third Party application, the more complicated the change management process can be. In a great many cases, these are enterprise-level systems that are sold as "highly configurable" or "customizable" for your business. These applications include but are not limited to:

- Customer Relational Management (CRM)

- Enterprise Resource Planning (ERP)

- Electronic Medical Records (EMR)

- Laboratory Information Management Systems (LIMS)

- Accounting (Financial)

The problem with "highly configurable" or "customizable" third Party enterprise level software systems is that the more you change or "configure" these software systems, the risk that the system changes may not work with the next version of the application (or at all) increases significantly. Not only that, many of the system configuration options and or development languages used to "extend" the software may be proprietary. This means that Software Engineers who will add to the system will need "special training" on how to implement these updates and changes. After training, these Software Engineers can be hard to replace if they decide to leave the company. Additionally, changes may be required by a business to their customized third party enterprise software system that is not supported by the vendor. In cases such as these, if the updates are made, an organization could development their system to a "dead end". This means that the system may not be compatible with any future versions that the vendor releases without a major rewrite. This would be a bad thing because businesses generally do not want to pay high prices for a software system that cannot be upgraded just a few years after its purchase.

Usually, most companies purchase their third party, enterprise-level, "customizable" software systems through a Value Added Reseller (VAR). VARs not only sell software but also most of them also help their customers design, development, test, implement, and support their sales. Many VARS also offer a comprehensive training curriculum as well in regards to the software systems they represent. If a company decides that they want to extend and support a third party enterprise application that they purchased from a VAR, then there are some strong points to consider in this area. The primary point to consider is the golden rule of third party enterprise software systems which is, **"Try to keep the software system as vanilla as possible"**. This means only implement the required or "must have" changes and work to keep the system as close to its initial installation state as you can. This leads to somewhat of a paradox. The third party enterprise software system is sold as "highly customizable" but the golden rule is to change it as little as possible. How do overcome this scenario? The answer is Black Box Management.

"Black Box Management" is the art of governing and supporting third party enterprise level software systems in a way that maintains application version integrity, with the ability to implement new version upgrades. There are principles to adhere to in regards to implementing black box management properly. Some of those rules are:

- Do not change any of the vanilla (original) software system database tables that were installed with the application. These are the core database tables and are subject to change whenever the application is upgraded. If you need to add to the database, the assigned database administrator should create new tables to support business requirements.

- Do not manually change any of the vanilla software system database Structured Query Language (SQL) query statements. These are the core SQL query statements and are subject to change whenever the application is upgraded. Use database "views" (virtual database tables) to facilitate this need whenever possible. In addition, some systems will provide functionality that will automatically make these changes for you, and allow you to back them up to a file or database.

- Along with views, use stored procedures and functions to develop around and extend existing software system database functionality. In this way, a framework can be created to facilitate those extensions and in-house customizations to the application without interfering with vanilla functionality that could break the system or jeopardize future version upgrades.

- Most third party software systems allow the invocation of outside executable files or system applications. This is a key feature because it allows systems to be decoupled (disconnected) from outside applications that are developed but invoked from within the software system. For instance, the third party software systems could allow a link to be placed on a system menu that initiates and passes specific information to an external software application. After initialization, this application can then access a database and display whatever data is required by the end-user. This means that entirely new and separate systems can be developed around the third party software application that can integrate with it without version-locking (blocking future upgrades) of that system.

Chapter 5: BUILDING THE SHIPS

- Follow third party software system vendor best practices for their applications. If their best practices supersede industry standard best practices, serious analysis of the organizations software systems is needed to discern the impact of doing so (past, present, and future). If the third party software system constantly recommends breaking industry best practices, this may be a good reason not to buy the product to from the outset.

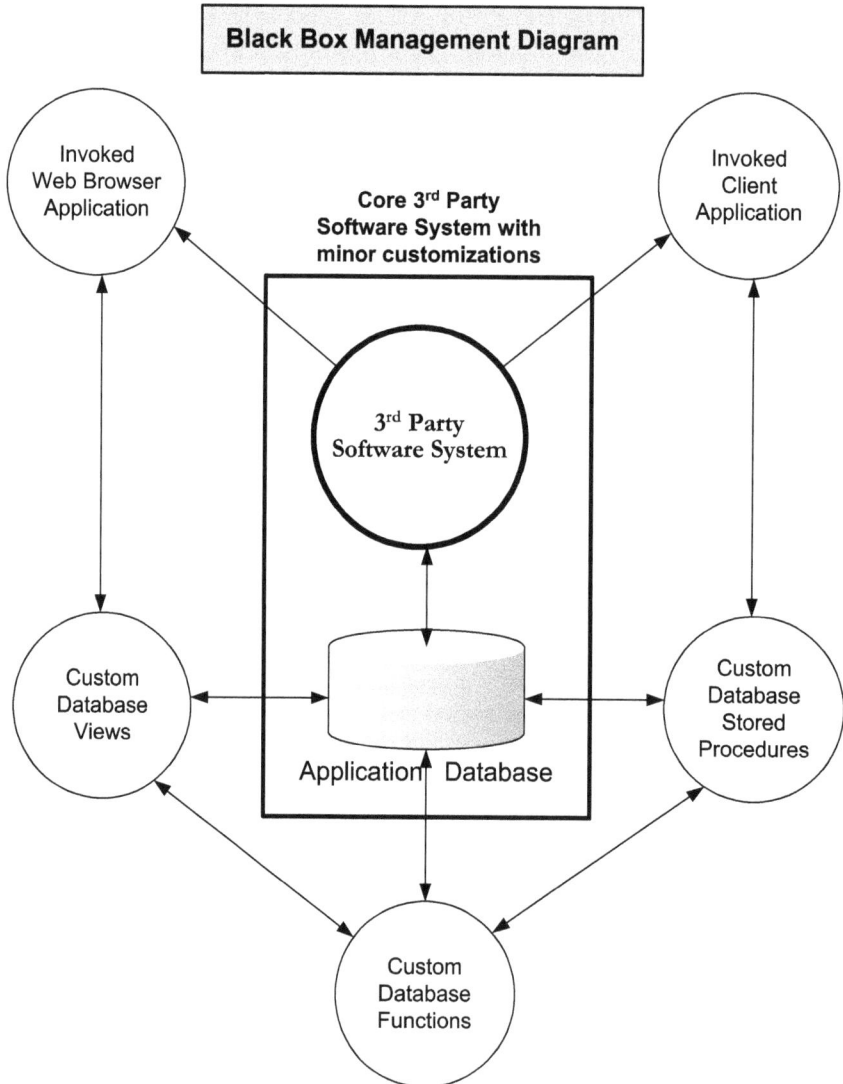

Good black box management can save an organization time and revenue. It can also save an expensive third party software system from becoming version-locked too early, which can cripple a business over the long term. Businesses should learn to understand that customizing and extending third party software systems should be done from the outside in, not from the inside out. This means building around these types of monster applications whenever possible and necessary, being careful not to change vanilla functionality too much if it can be avoided. The objective of black box management is to achieve and maintain a high level of system extensibility and longevity, by creating an in-house modular "plug and play" framework around the third party software system that does not compromise system integrity and vendor support.

Computer System Security

I strongly believe that securing critical business software systems must be viewed as more than just a routine, it should be considered a religion. As long as an individual, group, and or organization exists that has confidential information to protect, there will always be an opposing force somewhere that wants to gain access to that data. Some folks have described this scenario as the IT security "arms race", and I agree with this concept. As soon as the "good guys" develop new security technology to protect everyday software systems, the "bad guys" are already on the job looking for measures that will defeat them. This realm of IT is not for anyone who lacks the will to be at war 24 hours a day, 7 days a week because that is what it takes to stay on top of software system security. This is because malicious hackers and software application-based exploits around the globe do not sleep. Something or someone is always working to manipulate hardware or software system vulnerabilities somewhere. Software and hardware system security is a vast topic with many books and whitepapers written to cover this all too important area. A full analysis of the science of computer security is beyond the scope of this book. However, the Elysian Fields simply cannot exist without it, so I will discuss some of the more important aspects of software security at a high level. For a list of more in depth resources on this topic, see the reference section at the end of this book.

IT industry "best practices" dictates that it is not only good enough to only build good software applications, but to secure them against all threats both foreign and domestic. Just because a user may be required to log into a software application does not make that software any more secure than just putting a lock on the main door of your home and ignoring the rest of the house. For example, software developed within the finance industry (among others) must give security its undivided attention. You must ask yourself the following questions in this regard:

- Of what value is a well-developed, nice looking, easy to use, banking application with a great architecture if hackers can gain access and manipulate that data at will?

- Would you want to do business with that bank and use the software in question?

- What kind of reputation do you think the bank would have due after implementing and offering the software in question for use to its customers?

Keeping up with advancements in software security and implementing those updates is a full-time and critical task to say the least. Every serious IT organization must have on staff either a security expert or a team of such individuals whose jobs are to evaluate every software application that is developed and or implemented in their company to insure that their business systems are not compromised by people who are looking to exploit them.

Threat Modeling

Software security warrants a logical view, and this is what threat modeling offers anyone looking to help make their company application less vulnerable. The purpose of the threat modeling approach is to profile and capture the most dangerous suspects that have the potential to compromise a business's computer network. Discovering and ranking software system dangers is the first step to insuring that sensitive data remains as safe as possible from network intruders intent on gaining access to it. When threats are discovered and then identified, a plan can then be put into place that can save a business significant return on investment with their software applications. This is because an IT organization can then move as a proactive force as opposed to a reactive one that usually costs a company major revenue due to the chaos that an unknown agent can cause within a computer network.

Five basic elements to Threat Modeling are important to understand. They include:

1. **A Threat** – This unwanted event causes destruction within a computer network that is usually based on malicious intent. As a result, company assets are put at risk

2. **A Danger** – This is a computer system, network and or software application vulnerability that opens the door through which threats are possible

3. **An Asset** – This could be business files, images, software or information contained in database.

4. **An Attacker** – This is a person or thing that attempts to exploit or harm a business asset

5. **A Safeguard** – This contingency is put into place that works to defuse risks and threats

Data's Journeys

As it implies, "Information Technology" is supposed to encompass the management of data through a technological means. However, in an earlier chapter, "Information People", we discussed how individuals and groups are the true dominating force of this often-misunderstood idiom. We humans tend to leave our data in some interesting places such as our wallets, desks, handbags, cars, and garbage. None of these places may seem technical, but they are relevant in relation to security. Much information can be learned about a person by finding and analyzing various types of items in such places without even entering his or her home. For instance:

- Your wallet usually contains a driver's license, membership cards, and credit cards.

- Your desk may have important file folders, notes, and books on it that can be read.

- Your handbag may have car keys, a makeup kit, a hairbrush, or a personal organizer.

- Your garbage container may have invoices, letters, bills, empty food containers, and junk mail.

Most of the items in the areas mentioned might not attractive to the average person, but can provide vital data to anyone seeking to get to know you much better than they already do. Currently, just as people must be careful not to leave data footprints that individuals with malicious intent can exploit, people who design and implement software systems must do the same. What is the use of protecting the identification and credit cards in your wallet if a hacker can logon to the internet and break into a website where you have shopped and download that very same information?

Computer systems must never allow unauthorized users to:

1. Access the system's database(s) and execute queries against it.

2. Change user "role-based" permissions

3. Redirect users to a different screen or location of their choosing

4. Impersonate another user

5. Shut the system or network down

6. Use the software system to gain access to other areas of a hardware network

7. Use the software to gain control of other computer systems.

8. Use the software to launch attacks against other computer systems

In many cases, a malicious individual or group may be able to take advantage of many of the exploits listed if they are able to obtain the data they need from the software system in question. This is why it is critical that software systems do not reveal their inner workings or any secrets to its end users.

In the realm of implementing good and or reasonable security processes, a computer system's data is generally not allowed to be input and output without the software system "gate keepers" knowing its origin, final destination and full travel itinerary. Not only that, but another issue might be; is the data that was saved to the database the same information that was input into the application by the user and can it be authenticated? If a network or software system is breached, then this may not always be the case. In some nightmare exploitation scenarios, a company's data can be:

- Changed and or Monitored

- Duplicated and downloaded to an unknown computer system

- Erased along with an entire hard drive

- Used to trigger other unknown malicious software applications that have infiltrated a computer system

A competent software security audit team will usually start by checking the overall system architecture documents if they exist. If they do not, these blueprints must be created. With architecture documentation in hand, a software system can be broken down into parent and subsystems. Once a computer system's subsystems are identified, all of an application information gatekeepers can then be flushed out and analyzed for deficiencies.

What Hackers Do

It is important to note that the term "Computer Hacker" use to refer to a small group of sophisticated and very talented software engineers, but those days are long gone. There are many free and destructive software utilities and application available for download today on the internet. With these tools, almost anyone with access to the internet can obtain and then unleash, with simple click of a mouse, a dangerous wave of mass destruction. This can cost a company millions of dollars or disable a vital computer network hub that could stop internet service to hundreds, thousands, or even millions of web users around the world.

Once a computer logs on to the internet, it becomes a part of the largest network on the planet. This "Super-Nova Computer Network" is ignorant of time, country borders, regions and continents. Whether you like it or not, the internet is a computer network realm where you are "sucked in" to a place where everyone is fair game for exploitation and all are vulnerable to someone or something all the time. I once read that the only way a person could keep their computer completely safe from viruses and hackers was to do the following three things:

1. Unplug the PC from the electrical outlet.

2. Put the PC in a safe, fill it with cement, close the safe and let it dry.

3. Drop the safe into the deepest part of the ocean.

This extreme recommendation was in direct response to the exponential increase in computer system exploitations over the years that has far surpassed the growing level of computing power advancement. If a Hacker has physical access to a computer, they can always compromise it's security. Many computer system security experts believe that all software and hardware system vulnerabilities that exist will be eventually found and breached.

Usually, the first thing we think of when we hear the term "Hacker" is of a malicious person who tries to exploit a computer system's vulnerabilities. This word not only includes people, but types of software applications also that are designed and implemented with the same intent and may act independently of an individual's control or intent. For example, one of the most costly computer hacks to date was named "Code Red". This was a type of malicious software application that is known as a "worm". Unlike a software virus, a "worm" can replicate and send itself by means of:

- Email

- File Downloads

- File Uploads

- Internet Relay Chat (IRC):

- DVDs

- CDs

- Floppy Disks

- USB hard drives

Over time, the "Code Red" worm has costs the computer industry billions of dollars in damages due to the time and technical support involved in attempting to eradicate the exploits and malice of this software application altogether. The various types of viruses that exists number in the thousands but they can be generally categorized into much smaller operational groups.

COMPUTER VIRUS OPERATIONAL GROUP DEFINITIONS

Virus Group	How It Operates	Related Damages
Application-Based	Infiltrates file types that execute software applications	Changes or damages information and applications
Boot Sector	Infiltrates the hard drive or media boot sectors	Changes or damages information and applications
File-Based	Infiltrates common file types that do not execute software applications (Images, text files, etc.)	Changes or damages information and applications
Invisible	Infiltrates and uses system resources to hide	Changes or damages information and applications
Macro	Invoked as a result of an established set of commands that are executed from within a software application	Causes the application to perform unpredictable and or unwanted tasks
Multipartite	The combination of the application and a boot sector virus groups	Changes or damages information and applications
Polymorphic	Encryption based process that allows the entity to change its appearance with every new exploit	Changes or damages information and applications

Just as software and hardware security specialists have methodologies that they use to try to secure their systems, hackers also have effective methods that they employ to try find and exploit the vulnerabilities of those very same networks.

Below are some of the basic goals that Hackers work very hard to achieve when targeting computer systems:

1. The Hacker gathers as much information about the target computer system as physically possible. This includes obtaining data such as which operating systems are being used and computer IP address ranges are being used.

2. The Hacker thoroughly analyzes all data acquired about the target. They then compile reports from this data as to the best possible system vulnerabilities that will allow entry.

3. The Hacker invokes a more intense level of information gathering from the target computer system. This includes system resources that are either totally accessible or exploitable with very little effort and active user IDs and accounts.

4. At this point, the Hacker has the intelligence needed to make a reasonably threatening assault on the target computer system.

5. Once the Hacker can gain entry to the target as an average user, they will immediately try to elevate their privileges to that of a System Administrator.

6. With System Administrator rights and privileges now assigned to the Hacker, they can then look to see what other systems on the computer network they can logon to.

7. As a System Administrator, the Hacker can and will quickly attempt to modify and or delete from the system logs all evidence of what they have done so that their actions and events cannot be traced.

8. As a System Administrator, the Hacker can now create new and hidden alternative entry points into the system.

9. Last but not least, if all attempts to exploit the system have failed, the Hacker may attempt to shut down the target completely. This may include invoking a software application that sends so many requests to a system each second that the network resources become overwhelmed, and can no longer respond to new or current users.

Below is a high-level and basic diagram of the above methods used by many Hackers on their targeted computer systems:

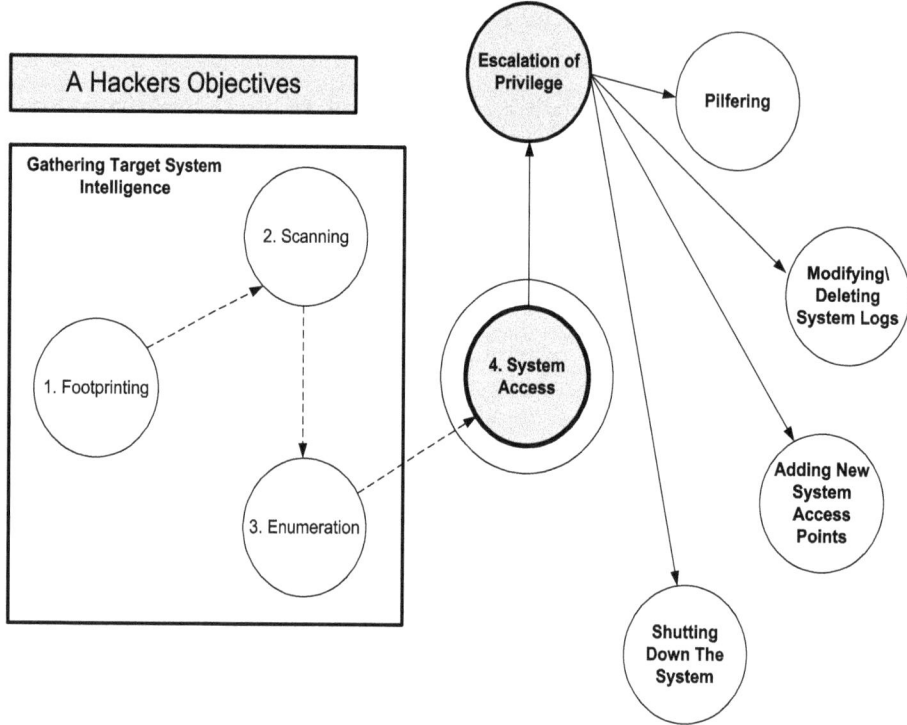

STRIDE

When using a method called "STRIDE", threats can be categorized according to their specific type of damage potential. Modeling threats in this way can help IT security experts make better sense of how to counteract exploits against their software systems. STRIDE is an acronym that defines the following threat groups or categories:

1. **Spoofing** – This is when another person or application is able to gain access to a software system using an active username and password that belongs to someone else.

2. **Tampering** - This is when data is edited, updated, or deleted with the intent to do harm. Most common cases of data tampering occur in network structures that are "open", which means that the data is manipulated as it is transferred from one system to the next. The internet is a perfect example of the type "super network" where data tempering happens on a massive scale daily.

3. **Repudiation** - This is when a user is able to invoke an event within a software and or network system that cannot be audited by that system. Nonrepudiation is the

opposite effect. The system in question can audit or trace the actions of any and all users.

4. **Information Disclosure** – This is the simple act of users being allowed access to system data that they are not supposed to view. This sensitive data could be displayed through a user interface or while it is passing from one system to the next.

5. **Denial of Service** - This is when a computer system is so overwhelmed with requests that is can no longer respond to new ones.

6. **Elevation of Privilege** – This is when a user or software application that has no system username and password, is able to gain access to a software and or network system. Once they are into the computer system network, they are then able to bypass all established defenses and achieve the level of an administrative user.

Implementing the STRIDE model can be a straightforward process that includes the following steps:

- Break software and or network system functionality down into components

- Analyze and identify all of the data input and output connection points of the decoupled software and or network system components

- Make determinations as to whether or not any of the identified data input and output connection points contain exploits that could be entered into the appropriate STRIDE categories.

- Document the results of your analysis and correct all known system vulnerabilities

Basic Threat Modeling Rules

The process of threat modeling is ongoing as software applications, business computers and networks are constantly updated and or reconfigured. Based on the current state of a computer network and its software, it may not be possible to mitigate every danger that a system might face. With this, it is usually a good idea to invoke a threat modeling process periodically. This could be implemented either:

- Daily

- Every other day

- Weekly

- Bi-weekly –or-

- Monthly

Scheduled threat modeling practices are crucial in order to attempt to keep a company's assets as safe as possible.

There are five top-level stages that comprise the threat modeling process. These principles can be modified accordingly but are sound "best practices" for the task at hand.

The rules are as follows:

1. Define the company's assets.

    a. Which data, files, or software in a computer network must be protected?

    b. Of what value is it to the business?

    c. Who should have access to it and when?

2. Define and document any and all dangers to the company's systems.

    a. Are the threats internal or external?

    b. Do the threats come from a group, individual or computer application?

    c. What is the best way to document these dangers for the IT organization?

3. Assign a priority level to any and all dangers to the company's computer systems.

    a. What is a "Low Priority" threat?

    b. What is a "Normal Priority" threat?

    c. What is a "High Priority" threat?

4. Create, and limit the access to architectural "Blueprints" of the company's computer network, and software applications.

    a. What are the vulnerable sections of the business computer network?

    b. Where are the vulnerable areas of the business software systems?

    c. Where are the vulnerable areas of the business database systems?

5. Reverse engineer the company's computer network, and software applications. This is often what hackers will do to try to understand how business computer systems and networks operate and interact with each other.

    a. What type of computer network does your business have?

    b. What type of software applications are deployed within your company?

    c. How do you think a hacker might best try to gain access to you company's computer network?

The following is a high-level model of a business hardware and software threat modeling process.

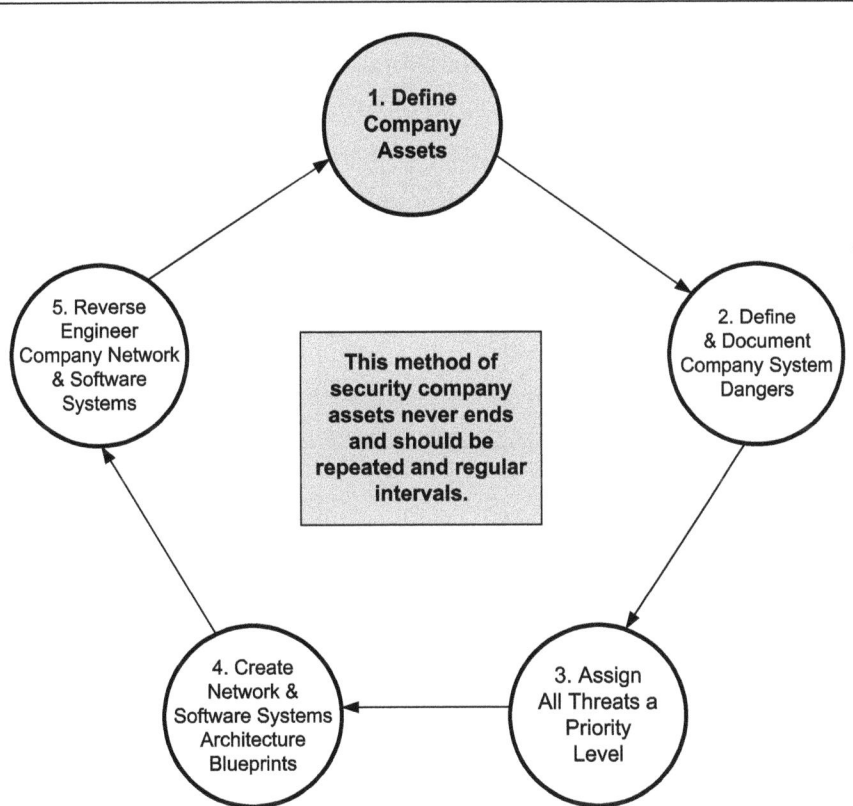

Chapter 5: BUILDING THE SHIPS

Threat Modeling Results

The results or expectations that should be derived from a threat modeling process must always be clear, direct, logical, efficient and effective. This information must be documented in a format that is easy to read and understand for everyone in an IT organization. This is so that software and network engineers can use this data to build and maintain business technology frameworks that are as secure as possible against hackers. Data that expresses the results of a business's threat modeling processes could be broken down into three distinct but separate documents types. These document categories may include:

- Threat Modeling Process Strategies for Company Software Applications

- Threat Modeling Process Strategies for Company Computer Networks

- Threat Modeling Process Strategies for Company Personal Computers

First, it is important to stress that each document should have all perceived threats listed and prioritized in some sort of matrix along with a description. The matrix should also include the reason for the threat along with the potential damage it could cause if ignored, and which assets the danger could affect.

Below is an example of this type of matrix.

Sequence	Threat	Priority	Effected Assets	Type of Risk	Safeguards
1.	Threat_A	Red	Network\Files	Computer Program	Install Latest 3rd Party Security Patches
2.	Threat_B	Yellow	Software	Hacker\Person	Update Software
3.	Threat_C	Green	Database	Hacker\Person, Computer Program	Update Software, Install Latest 3rd Party Security Patches

Software and Network related threat-modeling documentation should also include architectural diagrams of the systems on which the processes were based. This is important to show the physical properties of potential vulnerabilities of the network systems and why the dangers listed are relevant. The very nature of threat modeling documentation should be considered "company confidential" or "high risk" content for any business and must be kept in a safe and secure area. If an unauthorized person were to gain access to, and distribute a business's threat modeling report document(s), all of the work that went into building such a resource would be in vain, at least until the next iteration of the process.

DREAD

Rating systems can cause problems in many organizations because some groups and individuals cannot come to a consensus. This is because mitigating risks can be performed in many different ways based on what is required and or requested.

The DREAD model is based on the following criteria:

- **Damage Possibilities** – To what degrees of danger can an exploit actually cause a business?

- **Reproducibility** – Can you copy and re-execute the exploit in a controlled environment?

- **Exploitability** – Is successfully attacking your system or network a simple thing to do?

- **Affected Users** – What estimated number of users are adversely affected?

- **Discoverability** – Is finding exploits a simple task?

DREAD is designed to mitigate and assess risks in a way in which either a large or small IT organization can understand and rely on. By incorporating and analyzing the risk matrix in the previous section to the DREAD model, a proactive plan can then begin to emerge that deals with business system threats.

The bottom-line goal in threat modeling is not to try to eliminate threats altogether (which is impossible), but to manage risk. As long a company remains in business and uses technology, dangers to that business's assets will remain a constant challenge. The results of threat modeling should help an IT organization focus on the most significant dangers that face their systems and users.

The following members of IT should use threat modeling:

- Software System Architecture Team

Chapter 5: BUILDING THE SHIPS

- Software Engineering Teams
- Software Testing Teams
- Technical\Business Analyst Teams
- The Security Team (includes both hardware and software personnel)

A point of note with threat modeling processes and procedures is that if they are not created, invoked and maintained with logic and discipline, the price of a system breach may irreparably damage a company's reputation and or ultimately force it out of business.

Software Research and Development (SR&D)

The Software System Architect or an Analysis Team usually performs the Research and Development (R&D) in IT. In most industries today, a superior vision and plan are factors that separate the companies that are moving forward and the ones that are stagnant (dead). Many organizations understand how important research and development is to their business and work to insure its activities. Ask any respected Marketing Executive about the importance of R&D and (hopefully) you should get an emphatic and well-thought out response. However, that same enthusiasm for software R&D is generally hard to find in some businesses across industry boundaries today. This is partly because software is complicated to build and IT Departments are already viewed by the business as too expensive to maintain without adding a separate SR&D section. Many businesses may also perceive IT as already being largely SR&D rooted which is partially true but not always so.

Developing software systems is largely based on trial and error but without the implementation of a clear vision and plan through a good research and development process, a software project is most often likely to be misunderstood, and not adopted by the IT team as a whole. More than half of all software projects that are launched currently, like marriages, are unsuccessful. It is also important to stress, that a clear vision and plan is also not enough to insure the success of a software project and that is where performing sound research and development becomes most relevant.

Software Research and Development is a strong resource within the SDLC and its role in business IT is still often ignored. This is unfortunate because a business IT department that has allocated dedicated resources to software R&D will have a major advantage over business IT departments that do not. This is because dedicated IT SR&D teams are:

- Constantly acquiring and testing new and existing technology in order to try and give the business an unfair advantage in their industry

- Constantly designing, developing, and testing software prototypes of new and existing business application ideas that could give or increase the company's competitive edge.

- Continuously figuring out new ways to apply current technology in order to make existing business products more effective and profitable (innovation)

- Constantly working on new ways to make software development faster and easier for Software Engineers so the business can save money

- Continuously working to find new ways to minimize the risk and expense of updating existing, and developing new software solutions

- Examining past, present, and future technologies in regards to their potential strengths and weaknesses and how they can be exploited according to the organization's business model and objectives

- Developing training materials and sessions for Software Engineers in order to keep them up to date with the latest Architectural developments and how new technology may be applied to their environments

Below are some of the questions that SR&D teams work to answer, in regards to new and existing technology. Specific types of questions help a business to learn and grow. Those questions include:

1. What technology does the business need and how can it be best supported?

2. Why does the business need this technology?

3. What business entities will the technology ultimately benefit?

4. Who will use the technology and how can it be best implemented?

5. When will they need the technology?

6. Where (in which business department) will the technology be most effective and why?

7. Can the technology be implemented in a manner that will not interrupt the business?

8. Will the new technology be able to integrate with new and existing businesses?

9. What technology is the competition using?

10. How is software technology changing?

These questions are designed to help SR&D teams focus on the type of software research that will be the most beneficial financially to an organization. SR&D must serve a comprehensive and meaningful service that yields results that are useful. From these results, important decisions are made as to the company's direction and growth in areas that cannot be always anticipated at the outset. The better the SR&D processes, the more advanced technologically a company has the potential to produce. The road to the Elysian Fields is paved with SR&D and that is one of the major factors needed in order to stay get to, and stay there.

Intellectual Property and Software Patents

A patent can be described as:

- **Intellectual property or a corporate asset that can be quantified**

- **A business property that can be protected by the law and the United States Government**

- **Having 20 years exclusive right to manufacture and use and product**

- **An organization's intellectual resource (employee-based)**

I have worked on a personal software product for more than 12 years and believe that I may have developed intellectual property within the product that I should have protected by law. During my research in the software patent process, I found that obtaining or even attempting to apply for a software patent is a complicated and often misunderstood process due to the ambiguous nature of software itself. This is largely because the software patenting process varies greatly in regards to patenting other forms of products. One reason for this is the fact that the process for requesting a patent for an object like a new engine part that will decrease an engine's fuel consumption, has been around for well over a century, and has a strong and well-documented process history. In comparison, the software patent process is relatively new, because up until the early 1980s software was protected by copyrights only. Applying for a patent for a software product in the United States before 1981 was not possible.

In 1981, the United States Supreme Court upheld a ruling in the "Diamond versus Diehr" case that stated:

> *"A claim drawn to subject matter otherwise statutory does not become non-statutory simply because it uses a mathematical formula, computer program, or digital computer."*

This decision meant that a process executed by a computer application is patentable but the software alone, without the computer running it, is not. This case and many other cases like it in the 1980s, made attempts at patenting software increasingly possible and a great deal more companies and individuals began to apply for software patents for their intellectual property. In addition, clever developers began describing computer applications as "machines". This fundamentally changed the way that software applications were engineered from that time forward. As new software languages developed and evolved after the first software patents were granted, those languages blurred the lines in regards to what in software was intellectual property and what was not. This made new ideas presented for patent somewhat confusing, and difficult to categorize.

Non-existent and poor record keeping, along with the rapid advancement of hardware technology makes it next to impossible to know exactly how the original computer software inventions worked. In addition, how to patent software, back when this concept was relatively new, was not largely taught, so the process was a mysterious one. The method of patenting software did not go through the same historical evolution of previously patented products, such as airplane or automobile parts. This fact made it even more difficult to understand and invoke the software patent process. Traditional non-software product patents went through a long period where few companies and individuals actually owned significant product patents that made them either extremely profitable and or influential (regarding industrial, manufacturing, and construction to name a few). Since this sort of patent history did not occur within the evolution of software patent processes, something different happened. A new way to patent and "culture" emerged in this realm, which was made up of new inventions that were built on the foundations of previous ones.

Given all of the comprehensive software processes and "noteworthy" technical inventions in this arena since the creation of computer applications themselves, one might think that there would be very little yet to be discovered and patented in the software industry today. That belief is a widely held one in the software industry. Capitalism, in many cases, remains the driving force behind the filing of new software patents. Many are granted because algorithms may serve many different functions, which make them almost impossible to fit into any one domain or group. This increases the difficulty of the ability to check new software inventions for "uniqueness" which is needed to obtain a patent. Again, that fact that the early record keeping in regards to software patents was poor or non-existent adds significantly to the challenges of the method.

Many senior software industry professionals believe that software patents should no longer be granted, as they are unnecessary and only hurt the software industry. This is due in part to the lack of historical documenting in relation to the software patent processes. Traditionally, individuals and organizations have become extremely wealthy developing software systems around the world without the benefit of software patents to protect their intellectual properties. Pure capitalism in the United States has also provided plenty of monetary incentives to build software either with or without patents. This is one of the reasons why so many senior professionals in the software industry wonder why patents should be granted,

Chapter 5: BUILDING THE SHIPS

even given the primary arguments for them which include intellectual property protection and software licensing revenues.

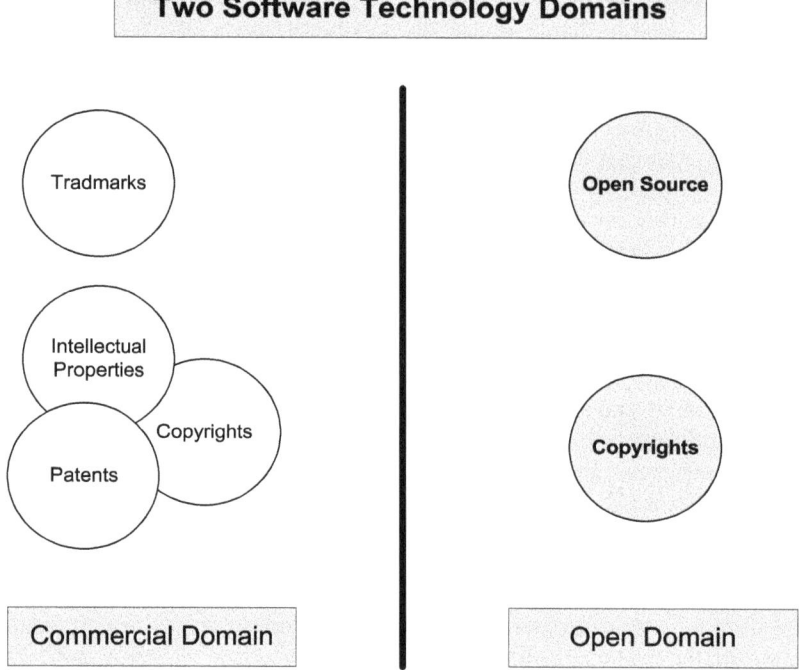

In order for a business to best position itself to be able to build software applications that may develop into intellectual property, its IT department should:

- Focus on engineering software and not coding software applications

- Re-use and not re-invent

- Designed software systems for testing

If a business should discover that they indeed may have a software product that is unique, they should file a software patent. For Software Engineers who are involved in this process, it could become a career statement that can lead to better jobs and increased revenue. This is because a Software Engineer who has contributed significantly to a company's technological unfair advantage in their industry is worth more in that industry due to their knowledge and expertise with that process and evolution. Technology can be the disruptive unfair advantage for businesses and advanced technology can cause an organization to eclipse their competitors completely.

Some of the reasons why businesses apply for software patents are as follows:

- For small businesses, it can be a defensive strategy to protect intellectual property.

- For large businesses, it can be an offensive strategy to use perceived intellectual property to create tangible boundaries in their industry

- Developing a software portfolio of pending and or granted patents can be perceived as valuable to current and potential company stockholders and investors.

- It makes a statement to all that a company is unique and has developed a potential unfair advantage

- It is a core-competency of a business that is protected by the law

As of 2008, there are five types of patents that exists in the United States for which a company or individual could apply for. They include:

1. **Provisional Patent** - A provisional patent granted by the United States Patent and Trademark Office is a patent that is granted for one year at a reduced filing fee. It is intended to allow inventors to quickly and cheaply establish a filing date ahead of any commercial exploration of their patents. This type of patent may be filed first for software applications in order to establish a legal precedence.

2. **Non-provisional (Utility) Patent** - In United States, utility is a patentability requirement. The utility requirement is the lowest bar. Utility is mainly used to prevent the patenting of inoperative devices such as perpetual motion machines. There are two general types of utility patents. They are:

    - **General utility, which is the requirement of functionality**

    - **Specific utility, which is the requirement that the invention actually perform the function**

    These types of patents are used for computer software applications.

3. **Design Patent** - In the United States, a design patent is a patent granted on the ornamental design of a functional item. Design patents are a type of industrial design right. Ornamental designs of jewelry, furniture, beverage containers and computer icons are examples of what can be protected with design patents.

4. **Plant Patent** - The Plant Patent Act of 1930 is a United States law invoked by the work of Luther Burbank who was an American botanist, horticulturist and a pioneer

Chapter 5: BUILDING THE SHIPS

in agricultural science. This piece of legislation made it possible to patent new varieties of plants, excluding sexual and tuber-propagated plants.

5. **International Patent** - The Patent Cooperation Treaty (PCT) is an international patent law treaty, signed in 1970. It provides a unified procedure for filing patent applications to protect inventions in each of its Contracting States. A patent application filed under the PCT is called an international application or "PCT" application.

The following is a high-level diagram of a software patent process:

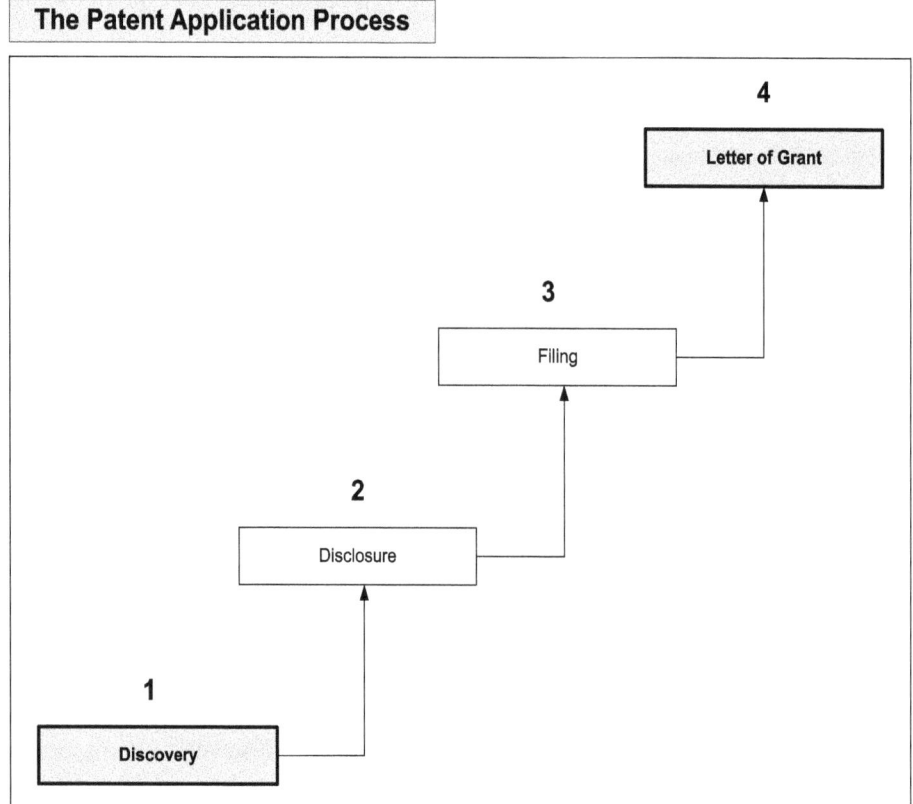

Let's take a look at each step of the patent filing process in more detail:

1. **Discovery** – This is where the intellectual property idea is written. This documentation includes the legal precedence in regards to the origination and the time of the concept. All notes relating to engineering the objectives are compiled

along with witnesses and dates. If the idea was first written on a paper napkin in a restaurant over lunch before it was documented by anyone else, that paper napkin is considered a legal document in regards to your original concept.

2. **Disclosure** – The idea is described to a lawyer in the most simple terms possible in order for counsel to draft the most broad and accurate filing possible. All of the engineering notes for the idea are collected for review. An invention disclosure form is then prepared by the lawyer.

3. **Filing** – The invention documentation prepared by counsel is then submitted to the United States Patent Office. This establishes a legal precedence regarding the concepts originality. This documents the original "proof of concept" and can be used as evidence in court if ever the need arises.

4. **Letter of Grant** – A software patent is awarded to a company or individual for their invention. It is customary in some cases for the representing law firm to present a Patent Plaque to the entity granted the patent. Once granted, the law entitles the user to 20-year exclusive use of the intellectual property. This opens the door to possible extensive product licensing and royalty payments to the software patent owner.

Applying for a software patent can be a long (many years), complicated, and expensive process with no guarantee that a letter of grant will ever be awarded to the patent owner. An experienced and reputable software patent attorney should be consulted when, and if you believe you have an idea that may be truly unique, and needs to be protected by law. The counselor can help you discover if your idea is actually worthy of a software patent.

Summary

In this chapter, we have discussed comprehensive, complicated, and critical IT topics that included:

- **Software project decision making**

- **The importance of a separate software development network**

- **Software System Architectures**

- **The Software Development Lifecycle**

- **Change Management Strategies**

- **Software Patents**

Chapter 5: BUILDING THE SHIPS

Developing business software systems is comprised of complex decision making in many situations. Businesses are usually run by, or have a sophisticated set of rules that govern then in order to function properly, much likes games. Software projects today have a high rate of failure largely in part due to poor decision making within the management structure. This means that many projects are doomed before then even start, which is an unfortunate reality for many companies that are involved in IT projects.

A good number of businesses allow their IT departments to develop and test on their business computer network systems. This means that any potential mistakes that IT or third party vendors make on these business production networks, could have an adverse effect on the company's return of investment and currently running software systems. This risk may not be properly explained to the business by IT or even at all, which is potentially dangerous for the organization. IT management must do everything reasonably possible to help the business to understand that production systems must be protected from development efforts through isolation. The money spent to avoid mistakes that should never happen could pay for the separate development network. In some cases, this could happen very quickly due to the type of development that IT is involved with.

Planning the right software system architecture and invoking the software development lifecycle (SDLC) is a must for IT software projects. It is always interesting to see when clients take their business processes seriously. Some businesses even place so much emphasis on process that they will fire employees that do not comply with them. These organizations cannot imagine doing business any other way when it comes to enforcing good IT project processes and industry best practices, which is another matter entirely.

IT best practices and processes may be misunderstood and or not well communicated by IT itself. This can then lead to chaos during projects that help contribute to their ultimate failure. Good business managers understand that well-thought out and logical processes are not just restricted to business but to IT as well. They will help to enforce those processes because they understand that it is for the good of the company. It is the job of IT management to identify and insure that this concept is understood and accepted by the company managers that they work with.

Tracking changes has long been a problem for many IT departments. This is hard enough to do this in everyday life, even without adding work to the mix. However, it must be done and performed well to support software development efforts. In life, we often take pictures and or watch movies that remind us how much things have changed. In some cases, that is how we relate to change. I can usually date an older movie by looking at the computer systems they used when the film was produced. This same concept can be applied to change management in IT. Using applicable change management software and or a good process in that regard provides "snap shots" of current environments and processes that can be preserved for reasons of historical integrity and audit. Being able to track changes in software systems and processes is absolutely crucial so the same mistakes that were made in the past are not repeated. It is also important for disaster recovery which can never be understated and can be worth a company's weight in gold if it is ever needed.

Lastly, we discussed the impact that a software patent can have on an organizations ability to compete within their respective industry. The "unfair advantage" is how large companies become enterprise entities. It is also how they maintain those positions as well. The "unfair advantage" is what businesses must constantly strive for from their inception all the way to actually achieving it, if ever that happens. Without protection under the law for intellectual property, a business can lose any "uniqueness" in any technological intellectual property that they develop over time. Good patent lawyers are important tools for identifying if a new idea is truly unique, and should be consulted by the business to help protect its assets in this domain. Securing intellectual property and discovering new processes can be a smart road to the Elysian Fields.

Ultimately, a few good threads hold true in regards to developing software successfully. Some of which include:

1. Don't take on more than you know you can handle. Always break bigger tasks down into smaller more manageable parts in order to get a better deal with the scope of the problem that must be solved. Outsource if you need help with the work.

2. Never let someone on the project do something that cannot be explained by that person to you in a basic and simple vocabulary. Allowing the opposite to happen can be a path to chaos and unaccountability.

3. Focus on and reward results. Never insist that someone do things "your way" as long as it is meeting and or exceeding project expectations. Build and maintain a strong results driven environment. There are many good ways of doing things in IT.

4. Prototype solutions first and go with what you know will work.

5. Figure out and make the decisions as to what tasks must be performed. Don't do any work until the business buys into what they told you they wanted along with the timelines for the tasks that must be performed. Afterwards, implement and enforce strong change control management processes, procedures and set expectations.

"We become just by performing just actions, temperate by performing temperate actions, brave by performing brave actions."

- Aristotle (Ancient Greek Philosopher, Scientist and Physician, 384 BC-322 BC)

224

Chapter 6: READY FOR CHANGE (RFC) METHODOLOGY

Introduction

A methodology is a group of processes and or tasks that can be used iteratively to build and deploy software applications. There are various types of software methodologies that can be applied in Information Technology depending upon the team and task. Methodologies are not just limited to software development in IT and can be used in:

- System Analysis
- System Architecture
- Software Development
- Project Management
- Testing
- Quality Assurance

In the software industry among many engineers, disagreements are common regarding the use of the words "method" and "methodology". The reason for this is that the word "methodology" is often used in place of the word "method". While to some folks, the word "method" may sound dull or unsophisticated, the word "methodology" sounds more distinct and intelligent when used in its place. However, this can be very confusing because interchanging these words can blur the distinction between the actual research and development (R&D) of a concept and the manner in which it is applied. Furthermore, in regards to the science of building software systems, a "method" is viewed by many as a process used to produce applications, whereas, others perceive the word "methodology" as set of practices in which a "method" could be included.

We will discuss two basic types of methodologies. Those types include:

1. **Object Oriented** - This methodology includes "Noun-Based" Architectures and Development.

2. **Structured** – This methodology includes many software based sub-methods and processes that are listed at the beginning of this introduction.

Popular Software Methodologies

Many different types of software methodologies or approaches can be applied to an IT development project. A basic question for many IT Software System Architects and or Managers might be; what software methodology would work best for my software project? For instance, an approach used to develop a Customer Relational Management (CRM) system for an enterprise consisting of 10,000 employees could be different than one used to create a software application utility for a small 50 employee office. This is because various software development scenarios warrant different ways of doing things and it is important that the correct processes be implemented in each case so the project can flow more effectively. Selecting the correct software methodology requires a good understanding of company and IT culture along with competent software project requirement analysis.

Below is an overview of many popular software methodologies that are, and have been used in various IT projects around the world:

Method	Summary	Purpose
1. Agile Data (AD)	This is a method of the overall "Agile" process group that upholds the "iterative" and "phase-based" development of system databases	This can be useful when changing AD philosophies and processes into new or different changing processes
2. Agile Model Driven Development (AMDD)	This is a method of the Agile Methodology that defines processes that support a more meaningful visual software physical structure and its related documentation	This can be useful when changing AM rules and processes into new or different agile and or "agile-like" processes
3. Agile Unified Process (AUP)	This is an agile version of the Unified Process, which is a basic representation of the Rational Unified Process (RUP)	This can be useful when elements of Extreme Programming (XP) and RUP are required in addition to organizational cultural flexibility

Method	Summary	Purpose
4. Code & Fix	This is a crude and wasteful method of software development. This is where simple-minded IT management allows inexperienced developers to write unplanned code. This is generally referred to as "hacking"	This can be useful for prototyping software in which that code will never be used
5. Data Driven	In the 1980s, this method became increasingly popular as new structured methods were implemented. This method is rooted in strong principles and strict procedures	This can be useful for CRUD-based (Create Read Update Delete) software systems and data warehouse development
6. Enterprise Unified Process (EUP)	This is a method rooted in strong principles that are made up of 7 incremental and iterative phases that include: • Software Design • Software Planning • Software Development	This can be useful for managing a group of IT software projects that are SDLC based
7. Extreme Programming (XP)	This is a method of the Agile Methodology that emphasizes only the most important aspects needed to produce a software application	This can be useful when the business requirements are constantly changing, and for small IT project teams of 10 members or less that have a good relationship with their business

Chapter 6: READY FOR CHANGE (RFC) METHODOLOGY

Method	Summary	Purpose
		partners
8. Feature Driven Development	This is a method of the Agile Methodology in which the primary focus is fast and quick software iterations that also relate to specific changes to the software model	This can be useful when the business requirements are constantly changing, and for small IT project teams of 20 members or less. Project members must be committed to implementing a "model-driven" process
9. Microsoft Solutions Framework (MSF)	This is a method is a phase-based, milestone-driven, and iterative model. It combines both the spiral and waterfall methods	This can be useful for medium to larger IT project teams of more than 10 members
10. Object Oriented Software Process (OOSP)	This is a method rooted in strong object oriented principles and tools in which the primary focus is on: • Software Design • Software Development • Software Support	This can be useful for medium to larger IT project teams of more than 10 members
11. Personal Software Process (PSP)	This method is a self-assigned process for the software engineer who works alone	This can be useful for IT project teams comprised of 1 person.
12. Rapid Application Development	This method is and iteration-based in which the primary focus	This can be useful for IT projects

Method	Summary	Purpose
(RAD)	is on developing application prototypes. Its process also includes the use of Computer Aided Software Engineering (CASE) tools	where return on investment (ROI) is the top priority, thus provoking fast software development iterations designed to save resources
13. IBM Rational Unified Process (RUP)	This is a method rooted in strong principles that involve 4 iterative and incremental phases. They are: • Inception • Elaboration • Construction • Transition	This can be useful for medium to larger IT project teams of more than 10 members
14. Scrum	This is a method of the Agile Methodology that is used in conjunction with XP. Its primary focus is based on managing business requirements along with the project	This can be useful for IT project teams comprised of 1 or more team members
15. Spiral (Iterative)	This is a method is focused on the repetitive need to update IT project estimates and business requirements. It is often used in conjunction with RAD	This can be useful when the business requirements are constantly changing, and for small IT project teams of 20 members or less
16. Test Driven Development (TDD)	This is a method derived from other methods where software system application tests that fail	This can be useful for IT project teams comprised

Method	Summary	Purpose
	are written first, before any development code	of 1 or more team members
17. Waterfall	This is a method in which milestones are used as gateways into the next phase of the cycle. Each task or process must be completed first, in order to move on to the next phase	This can be useful for IT project teams comprised of 1 or more team members

The Problem with some Software Methodologies

Industry best practices, popular commercial development tools, and object oriented development languages are the foundations and main ingredients for the vast majority of mainstream methodologies. Most popular software methodologies emphasize the envisioning and planning aspects of developing software applications as a pre-cursor to the development and testing phases, which is basic common sense in this regard. Many also tend to focus on an iterative phase-based approach, which is also widely used in many IT environments when producing business software systems. Most software methodologies offer Software Development Lifecycle generic practices based on a specific theory. They generally do not, however, provide new methods that are more effective than the ones previously introduced.

Software methodologies are of no value without a clear and decisive contract between the stakeholders and the IT team that will be producing the software application. A contract of this type is also critical for the IT project team members as well. These people must be in complete and total agreement, understanding what is expected of them, and be trained accordingly to perform that tasks they are assigned. In a great many instances, a certain methodology is a matter of a person or group's particular culture or style. In these cases, methodologies can be monolithic and or inflexible, which can lead to productively and technological creativity being negatively affected.

A methodology should be able to bend without breaking to the software development project for which it is being used. It must also provide a way to insure that everyone involved with its implementation is speaking the same language, and that their words have identical meanings, on both sides, in all cases. This is difficult in regular everyday communication to achieve consistently but crucial when using a software methodology on a project. Rarely on any IT project do all team members have the same knowledge of all aspects and phases of that endeavor. This is why it is important for the methodology implemented to work to keep the team informed as to current IT project events. It is always better to discover IT project disconnects in the beginning of the project as opposed to the testing and deployment phases.

Dealing with project problems and issues in the latter stages, which fall through the cracks early on, can be extremely expensive depending on the type of software that is being developed. Nevertheless, this is usually not a simple problem to overcome and can be frustrating for all of the team members involved.

Software Methodologies are also meaningless if the IT project management team that invoked it does not adhere to basic software development principles. Without training and discipline, a software methodology is often misunderstood and ignored. I have worked for companies in the past, who desperately wanted to implement an appropriate software methodology that would help them to produce software more effectively. However, these groups would not take the time needed in order train their IT employees on the core foundations of which their selected methodologies stands. For example, if an IT development team wants to perform object oriented development tasks and lacks the training in this area, then trying to implement an object oriented software process makes no sense. I have seen this type of IT mindset and practice in many organizations with little evidence of the realization of how futile an endeavor like this can be, despite strong advice to the contrary. I have seen Software Engineers who have not been properly trained in the fine art of requirements gathering, trying to retrieve delicate business requirements from company partners who have no idea of what is really going on. The results are usually:

1. Business requirements that are of no use at all

2. Business requirements that are incorrect or misleading

3. Poorly written business requirements

4. Frustrated business partners who don't understand what is asked of them and are further confused as to how the process is or was being conducted

IT management must insure that their project teams are well-trained in the methodologies that they select for them. Otherwise, their chosen software methods can create far more problems than they will ever solve. For example, if a software development team uses an "Agile" type of methodology called as "Scrum", then the team should be trained in this discipline accordingly. Because "Agile" methodologies promote physical human interaction as the primarily means of communication as opposed to creating project documents, this path can become disorganized and archaic very quickly if not tightly managed. In addition, if project team members are not good communicators, then critical information can get lost in translation or end up not passed on to the people that need it at all. If this happens, and the project documentation is sparse at best, then the team members who may need data to complete their tasks may have to start at the initial analytical stages again in order to get it. Many software developers lack the skill set to do this effectively, but this particular methodology often forces them into this realm which can be dangerous because it represents a gap in many companies that invoke "Agile" methodologies.

"Agile" methodologies have traditionally been very popular because many companies believe that they can implement their software more quickly and save money using it. In more cases than not, I have seen poorly managed implementations of "Agile" that have been disastrous and costly due to of a lack of understanding and discipline. Some of the managers that I have worked with believed that they could just put an IT team into one big room (with or without the business) and everything would just "work out". Little did they know that they were the real problem as to why their IT projects were unsuccessful.

Why is Building Software So Difficult?

Why is software development consistently so hard to do successfully? This is because almost every software application is usually viewed, and used differently by the people who need it. Software construction is not like building a house, in which upon entering a home and taking a tour, everything is the same to everyone who examines it. The rooms, plumbing, and electrical don't change, and the colors remain the same in each room unless someone repaints them. With this, the more people you assigned to building a house, the faster that task is completed. However, this does not work when it comes to developing applications because of the requirements that software must be able to morph to the mold of whoever is using it.

If the development of houses and software were identical, if you walked into a house and you needed a basement to store some furniture, the basement would be there, but if you no longer required that area, it would disappear. If you wanted the living room color to change from blue to white, you could click a button and that change would happen. What if residents required that the bathroom come to them, instead of having to go to it? This functionality could be accommodated based on who those people were and why they needed it. The point being is this home would start to become a complex house very quickly and would require much more analysis than its original base planning in order to build it correctly. Making basic changes to house plans before the home is built is normal and happens on a regular basis. However, modifying homes significantly after they are built can be a nightmare and very expensive. In most cases, software must be designed to implement changes, as needed, and work dynamically in conjunction with business rules, company security, and user tasks.

Most software systems require that the application dynamically change based on some the following criteria:

- Who the user is

- What permissions (performance actions) the user has

- What role (type of group) the user is assigned to

- What tasks the user must perform

- What rules govern the tasks based on the user role and permissions
- What tasks the user is not allowed to perform
- What data the user can see
- What data the user cannot see

When a good set of blueprints for house is completed, they can be used repetitively to build the same house over again 1000 times or more. This same formula cannot work for software development because the very nature of it is usually driven by different user dynamic specifications. This is why building software is a task that is based on thought and analytics as they relate to specific requirements, and is not a brute force job that can be completed faster whenever more people are assigned. In many case, business and even some IT managers fail to realize this fact and treat software development like a home building project. Comparing software development to the construction of a house or bridge is a bad analogy and must be avoided because they are not similar and it can be confusing to all involved. Individuals and groups who persist in doing so are part of the problem and not the solution in IT.

Building good software systems is based on many variables that must be defined so that they can be dealt with in the design requirements. Rarely are business computer systems able to be rigid or monolithic like they were in the past, only performing a minimal number of tasks based on a single user. They are increasingly intelligent, extensible, and powerful distributed applications that know no borders. Engineers now work to design business software systems to know who you are and what you need to do no matter what that is or how it's done.

The Ready for Change (RFC) Method Set

The Ready for Change (RFC) methodology is an alternative way of approaching and thinking about how software is developed. Instead of thinking of the software development process in "phases", with RFC, the process of building applications is broken down into "Episodes" and "Scenes", much like a movie or television show. This method works to simplify the software development lifecycle (SDLC) process for the business and IT by focusing on the software being produced as a living, breathing, evolving product much like an ongoing television series. In this way, the project team's product perception and mindset is tuned to a more broad and realistic view of where their individual tasks can eventually take the product. RFC also helps project team members to think of the product as "perpetual", as opposed to just a static application phase that they are rushing to deploy.

The approach of viewing the production of a software system as a game, in which the IT project team creates an application using a "television series" related theme can make the difficult and often misunderstood task much more fun and interesting for everyone involved. The point is that most seasoned senior IT industry personnel understand the hard fact that building object oriented, enterprise level software systems is complicated and often difficult. This is made even harder by the fact that it generally involves business employees who do not know anything about how the process works. Along with this, many IT employees also struggle with exactly how software should be produced within their organizations. With all of the various methodologies that exist along with their many processes, the business of software development can become simply overwhelming.

For this reason, I am introducing the "Ready for Change" methodology that approaches software development in a way that almost everyone who has ever watched a television show, movie, or play should be able to relate to on one level or another. This is a "theme-based" approach based on the entertainment. It also works on the concept that if you are watching a television show, movie, or play that it has already be produced because you are watching it. If it had not been produced, you could not watch it. Therefore, the concept is in IT project team members thinking in terms of a successful software product, as opposed to a work in progress that could fail from lack of understanding. People in the entertainment industry have a saying, "The show must go on". That is a requirement. The same is also true of a critical IT project that an organization is counting on, "That show must also go on" too.

One of the many problems in regards to trying to gather requirements from the business is that the people who provide the requirements are often unsure of the following:

1. What requirements are needed

2. The use cases involved relating to the requirements

3. If the requirements they are providing are correct

4. If the requirements they are providing are complete

5. Who will ultimately be affected by the requirements they are providing

In most scenarios, these issues lead to difficult and or frustrating requirements gathering sessions with the business. Rough and unclear software project launches such as these generally result in constant product change requests throughout the SDLC for the software product. In some cases, it even contributes to the demise of the project altogether due to the budget overruns and missed deadlines, with IT either taking all or most of the blame. RFC attempts to help correct the basic root of the problem that most IT teams meet when they start at the very beginning of an IT software project. That issue is the very concept of how requirements are gathered. Traditionally, only the requirements designated as "must haves" or "needed" are compiled, documented, and verified are used to development the initial version of the software application. The RFC methodology auditions each and every possible business requirement and feature submitted by everyone involved from the outset. Instead of struggling with the business to insist that employees who provide the requirements think in the narrow terms of "must" and "needed", they are allowed to think in more broad terms that encompass both the present and the future of the software application. This is what I call a "Feature Dump". From data provided by the Feature Dump, the application "musts" and "needs" are analyzed, identified, categorized, and documented. This approach allows the business requirement providers to think freely as to what they need and would like to see in their software product and allows them the ability to focus their minds initially as to what features they envision. This can greatly reduce the well-known project disease known as "scope creep" that cripples and destroys so many IT projects throughout the development and testing stages. This is because the business requirement providers actually identify and stop "scope creep" themselves by actually assisting in the planning of present and future application features from the very beginning of the software development process.

As previously discussed, one of the problems with gathering business requirements is that the providers do not always know exactly what they need or even want. If the thought process of the people that provide the requirements are strongly restricted or confined, it can make this issue even more problematic. For instance, if you are starving and offered the choice of any type of restaurant in which you could eat at right away, you would most likely be able to give me an answer within seconds or you might say that any food or restaurant would be great. This is because you know that the requirement regarding your hunger to be satisfied must be met immediately. Any other restaurants that you may want to dine in, other than the one ultimately chosen, can be visited in the future based on your own discretion after you have eaten. As with a software system, if it is desperately required by a business, the designated requirement providers should be able to tell you why. If they cannot, then the business may not be hungry and should not eat at that time. RFC requirement gathering methods work to expose facts such as this before the IT project is even started.

It is critical for the health and welfare of an organization's technological future that the company learn to view their ongoing software project productions as "living business contributors" or some form of "company employee" so that projects can be viewed in a way that is more productive to the business. For instance, no one wants to fail a fellow team member or business partner who is working on a critical company task. This is because they do not want to be associated with obstructing a process that is viewed as important in the success of the business. However, the needs of software applications that can make or save organizations hundreds, thousands, millions or even a billion dollars annually, and provide revenue for hundreds or thousands of company employees are often ignored because someone is trying to save money. This routinely happens as these software applications are viewed as company "assets" or "tools" and often not as potentially "living" revenue contributors that make and or save the business money. It is important to note that some software applications do not change very often if at all, and the RFC methods and processes were not developed for software application projects of this type. RFC is for service-oriented systems where change management and application functionality are focused on a "living", perpetually changing software entity.

The hierarchy of the RFC methodology is comprised of the following entertainment Movie\Television Show theme from the top down:

1. **Season** – This level consists of a sequenced group of "Episodes" (software application versions) that are focused on reaching a basic overall milestone. This might include an internal IT goal such as the implementation of a Business Rules Engine (BRE) or a user-based objective accomplished like improving the overall software system Knowledge Base (KB) to a superior level of intelligence long requested and needed by the business.

2. **Episode** – This level consists of a sequence of "Scenes" (iterative unit tasks) that make up a software development lifecycle. In short, an Episode is a specific development or production version of a software application.

3. **Scene** – This level consists of a group of "Actions" (tasks) that are required to achieve a particular result. A Scene is often iterative, grouped, actions that culminate in the production of a software application. For instance, a Scene might represent the gathering of business requirements for the software system project or the planning stage of the IT project.

4. **Action** – This task is performed by an "Actor" (project team member). Groups of focused tasks make up "Scenes".

5. **Actor** – This is generally a project team member. It may also be an outside software application or tool that is used to integrate with the system that is being produced by an IT project.

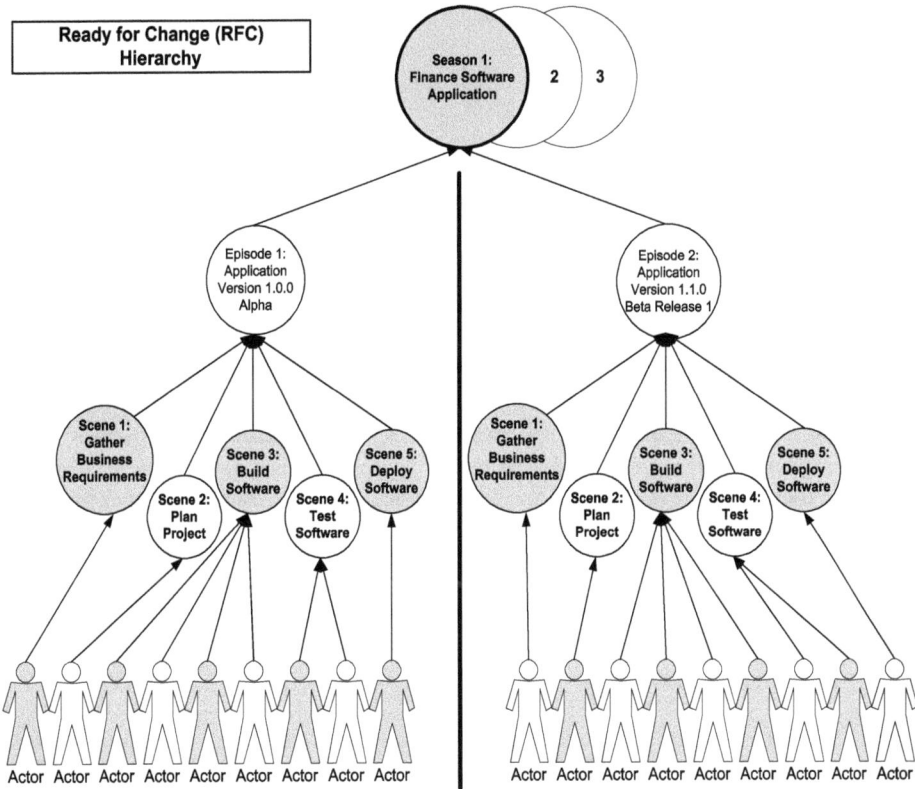

RFC Tools

Having the right tools does not always mean having the best tools. The best tools in the hands of the experienced and highly skilled worker should yield excellent results. However, purchasing the very best tools is not possible for many medium sized to smaller businesses, which leave these organizations to make secondary or tertiary choices as to what they can buy. This does not mean that the software project that they are working on must suffer as a result. The project in question can still flourish if the management team in charge insures that the correct tools are used at the right times by the proper personnel.

The following minimum IT project software solutions are critical to produce most software applications:

1. A Documentation solution

2. A Presentation solution

3. A Notification\Communication solution

4. A Project Management solution

5. A Software Development solution

6. A Database solution

7. A Software testing solution

8. A Change Management and bug tracking solution

One of the primary RFC tools for an IT team communication and status updates is the RFC Project website. This tool can range from a static html website that consists of 10 pages or less up to a dynamic enterprise web application that lets users update the site content via the web. Just as users globally use the Internet very day to get news updates, the RFC project website is the primary team resource for project tasks, processes, as well as other important and general information.

Below are the basic requirements for a functional RFC Project website:

1. The website must include security. This means that users will have to log in and out of the system and messages to and from the website should be encrypted.

2. The website must include the ability to assign and manage user permissions by role. For example, users will be assigned one or more of the following roles which will limit their website access accordingly:

    a. "Administrator"

    b. "Manager"

    c. "Analyst"

    d. "Software_Engineer"

    e. "DBA"

    f. "User"

3. The website will be categorized into six primary sections which include:

    a. **Project Vision** – This area includes all project business requirements both present and future along with any general messages in this regard. It can also be comprised of hyperlinks to these documents for viewing and or downloads.

b. **Project Plan** – This area includes the entire project plan complete with timelines and milestones along with any general messages in this regard. It can also be comprised of hyperlinks to these documents for viewing and or downloads.

c. **Project Development** - This area includes software and database functional and technical specifications along with any general messages in this regard. It can also be comprised of hyperlinks to these documents for viewing and or downloads.

d. **Project Testing** – This area includes both pre-UAT (user acceptance testing) as well as final UAT. It will include test plans in conjunction with all types of testing that is performed on the application during the lifecycle. It can also be comprised of hyperlinks to these documents for viewing and or downloads.

e. **Project Deployment** – This area includes detailed specifications and principles in relation to installing the software system on production servers. General messages relating to this topic are also posted here. This region can also be comprised of hyperlinks to deployment documents for viewing and or downloads as well.

f. **General Project Messages** – This area includes both new messages and updates that apply to the entire project team. Outdated messages are never deleted from the system even if they are no longer displayed. This practice supports the project's history and potential future audit requests.

4. The website must include the ability to notify either all members or specific members of a certain roles of updates within a website area.

5. The website must include a database to support application security and basic functionality as well as tracking change management within the project

In the RFC website scenario, a project website webmaster is required to support the system and to implement all updates made to the RFC web application and its database. Organizations can either build or purchase an existing website package that meet RFC Project website application requirements previously listed. If an IT team chooses not to use an RFC Project website, then a file directory system can also be used in its place along with an email application for notifications and basic communication. This may be more work during the course of the project than managing a website, but it can be almost as effective if the proper resources are allocated to the task, and it is managed properly. Lastly, if implemented, the RFC team must have access to the servers in which the RFC file directory is located by way of VPN (Virtual Private Networking) or through another secure method.

RFC Communications

RFC is designed to facilitate an IT team that has the ability to work remotely (telecommute). As environmental issues become an increasing global problem, IT must learn to adapt and exist by having team project members that can telecommute. This is logical, allows for more diverse teams, and saves fuel and energy along with working to reduce carbon emissions. IT management must become more aware of the environment and take advantage of telecommuting as much as possible as it is rarely, if ever necessary to have the entire IT project team onsite at the same time. RFC's main focus in information sharing is to leverage eCommunications (electronic communications). Traditional meetings where employees meet face to face are reduced to a bare minimum and should only be used as a last result to solve problems that cannot be resolved over the phone, through email or video conferencing.

eCommunications is the used take full advantage of the following existing communications technology that is comprised of:

1. Local and wide area networks
2. The Internet
3. Cell phones
4. Video Conferencing
5. Email
6. Web Logs (Blogs)
7. Websites
8. Instant Messaging
9. Texting

Many IT management structures complain that eCommunications have had an adverse affect on business communications in general and have even sporadically banned the use of some of these technologies along with telecommuting altogether. Some business managers have sited that using eCommunications has made their businesses more impersonal and that their inter-employee and client to employee relations suffer as a result. In most cases, this problem is related to poor management, as it does not address the real reason behind why their eCommunications initiatives did not work. Management cannot simply give an employee a cell phone or video conferencing system and expect them to function as if they are still in the office. What has lacked significantly in the past in many companies is eCommunications and remote task training and enforcement. A great many employees must be taught how to work remotely by the companies that offer it. Not only that, but the companies themselves are responsible for developing and enforcing the principles that govern telecommuting through their organizations. In essence, they must set reasonable and realistic expectations in regards to work at home tasks that are assigned to their remote staff. It is simply ridiculous for a group of software engineers to drive to work every day, sit in a room and write code, and then drive home again when they can develop applications just as well from home to begin with. This is a waste of time, energy, money and productivity. People can be trained to work at home just as they can be taught to work at company owned site. Business cultures can vary greatly, so it is up to each individual company to develop, implement, and enforce sound telecommuting protocols before attempting to implement an RFC communications methodology. As local and national highway traffic and the global energy crisis worsens, the demand for eCommunications in business will increase as employees pay increasingly higher prices for fuel to fill the gas tanks of their cars so they can drive to work. Businesses that learn to adapt and utilize new and existing eCommunication technology will survive, while those that don't will either fail or find themselves struggling to find new ways to work and communicate regionally, nationally and globally in times of crisis.

RFC Communication Protocols

RFC project status reports are filed by project team members via email at least twice a week, preferably before the end of days on Tuesdays and Thursdays. These status update reports are emailed to the project manager for their ongoing project progress reports. In this way, project managers have time on Wednesdays and Fridays (and occasionally weekends) to address issues or concerns that project team members may have. If an IT software team is using an RFC Project Website as its primary communications hub, then all project members are required to check the General Messages section of the website, as well as their related area of the website daily for new and or updated messages.

Whenever possible, RFC project meetings should be through conference calls or if available, video conference calls. Prior to these events, meeting agendas must be sent to all attendees through email along with any visual aids that will help the meeting run more effectively. The more visual aids (presentations, prototypes, images) used for the regular conference calls the better. It is generally much easier to describe an idea about a topic if the employees on the other end of the line have a picture or diagram of the idea in question. If all else fails, an old fashioned face to face meeting must then occur to resolve the issue.

It is important to understand that the hub of all RFC communications is the Project Manager (PM). It takes a well-trained, experienced PM who understands and leverages eCommunications in a way that propels their team forwards not backwards. The PM may also need to travel when warranted in a distributed IT team environment, as it is generally cheaper for one person to travel as opposed to a team of 10 or more people. PMs must set the standards and priorities of communications. For instance, a PM may have a simple RFC Communications Escalation Structure (CES) defined like the one below:

1. **High Priority Project Issues** - Call Cell Phone\Video Conference or meet in person as soon as possible.

2. **Medium Priority Project Issues** – Email\Instant Message\Test Message immediately

3. **Low Priority Project Issues** – Email or Weekly Reports

The CES for PMs is flexible and can vary greatly depending on the PM, IT team, and the project. The important factor is that a reasonable CES be implemented and supported by the PM and that it is published to their IT team in a clear, simple, and broad manner. The PM also insures that all work that each team member does every day is updated on the company network computer systems at the end of each workday and that the network administrators have scheduled daily backups of this data accordingly. In this way, the project is never more than a day behind if a catastrophe were to strike at any given time.

Why use RFC?

As service oriented architectures (SOA), and software as a service (SaaS) based distributed applications become more commonplace, IT project teams must adapt and develop new and better ways to produce and manage these increasingly flexible and expanding application frameworks. In addition, negative world environmental issues are beginning to force companies to look for new ways of saving revenue in regards to their operating costs. As fossil fuels become increasingly scarce due to the lack of the ability of oil refineries to meet the demand, this becomes a growing issue for businesses that own and operate buildings.

By implementing telecommuting where and whenever possible on their IT projects, businesses may be able to save significant costs in regards to:

- **Maintaining full IT employee office spaces** – If the IT team members who are working at home are not in the office, lights, heat, and computers in their assigned spaces can be turned off.

- **Employee Sick Days** – Working at home helps to keep sick team members who can still work, out of the office. In that way, they do not infect well employees and hurt overall project productivity. Telecommuting can also help to reduce stress by allowing team members to bypass the day's traffic and overall congestion.

- **Employee Time off Requests** – This is because employees are better able to work when they need to. As long as their tasks are completed on time, it should not matter if that task takes a day or a week to complete.

- **Employee Salary Increases** – In effect, employees save money because they are able to spend less money on gas for their commutes to work. Gas prices will do nothing but rise until there is no more fuel left to use. The less money an employee has to spend on fuel, the more they have to spend on food and other bills, which can help them to feel like they are making more money.

- **Employee Automotive Maintenance** – The wear and tear on an employee's automobile along with the roads they drive on their daily commutes to work can be considerable. Periodic automobile maintenance fees can be a substantial yearly expense depending on how long a person's daily commute is. Oil changes, tires, brakes and other car repairs can be significantly reduced with less driving thus saving the employee money.

RFC allows an IT team to be much more flexible in times of a natural disaster as well. The problem with many businesses today is that work is a place where you go and not something you do. This means that if a natural disaster occurs such as an earthquake, flood, or power outage, that company's operations cease for that site. This can be extremely costly for many types and sizes of businesses when it comes to the IT projects that they are working on. With RFC, the IT team is more distributed, so that in many cases, the IT project continues to move forward and does not stop because a company building becomes inoperable.

In the RFC methodology, work is always comprised of tasks that a team performs and not a place where they go. This is a new and different mentality to many companies. Businesses and their IT managers that understand this fact, in an age where a severe energy shortage is a growing reality and threatens to destroy our industrial way of life will have the best chance of survival. Those that do not will be left to struggle to adapt to a distributed technological and methodical platform or find themselves unable to compete and ultimately fail. If your company building is the only place where you can work, and you cannot physically reach that destination, then you cannot work unless you find an alternative for that situation.

Finally, RFC is "Green". It works to help reduce traffic, which helps to promote environmental awareness by lowering carbon emissions and saving oil. It also helps to save employees money on fuel, which results in a raise for those who participate. The bottom line is, if RFC is implemented, managed and supported properly, it can be a "Win\Win" situation for all involved including the environment.

Who is involved in RFC?

The RFC is a methodology that involves everyone that has to do with the project. This includes both the business and IT. It is crucial that the business understand why certain members of IT may not always be on site. The business must be educated by IT departments to understand that those team members who are offsite during an RFC-based methodology are indeed working, and that personnel may not always be available at that same times as they are but they are reachable. All of the players of an RFC must be taught that IT project work is something you do, not a place you go, as this is the premise of the RFC methodology.

In RFC, everyone is an analyst regardless of their tasks. All team members must constantly look for ways to improve processes and communications in order to take the team and project to the next level. In many instances, IT and business team members must learn how to think in a new way when it comes to where and how they do their jobs.

RFC KEY ROLES AND RESPONSIBILITIES

An RFC methodology is comprised of a traditional IT project team of which has been described in detail in the early chapters of this book. However, when RFC is invoked, some of those IT traditional roles may be modified to fit RFC specific methods.

- **The Project Manager** – This resource is the traditional caretaker of the needs of the team and project. They make sure all team members have what they need to complete their tasks. The role is the "hub" of the project and the center of all communications, both onsite and off. It does not matter where a team member is working. As long as they are able to contact the Project Manager when they need to, they are plugged into the IT project framework. This resource creates and maintains a section of the overall project website that outlines and displays the project's plan, time schedules, status, milestones and other relevant project related information and documentation. They work closely with the project Librarian to document the history of the project.

- **The Business Analyst** – This resource is responsible for gathering and documenting the business software product requirements and use cases. This individual or team serves as the brain trust for what is being produced by the project team members for the business. This resource creates and maintains a section of the overall project website that outlines and displays the IT project's requirements, use case, process diagrams, and other relevant business related documentation. It is important that this resource be as accessible as possible and responds to questions from the team within the reasonable time allowed as dictated by IT and Business Management. The brain trust of a project must never also be the project bottleneck.

- **The Software System Architect** – This resource is responsible for the software product technical design and documentation, along with the development standards, best practices and guidance for the team. This resource maintains either a separate website or a section of the overall project website that outlines and displays the IT project's software system architecture diagrams, development standards, and other relevant technical documentation and information.

- **The Data Architect** - This resource is responsible for the product database schema, as well as data processing design and documentation, along with the database standards, best practices and guidance for the team. This resource maintains either a separate website or a section of the overall project website that outlines and displays the IT project's database schema and data architecture diagrams, data related standards (XML), and other relevant data documentation and information.

- **The Librarian** – The size of the IT project will dictate how much this resource is needed. No RFC methodology can be properly implemented without one or more of these resources. They document everything and create and maintain a website of the history of the project. They are carbon copied on all relevant project emails, attend project meetings, and maintain detailed logs in regards to those events. If they are not able to attend a meeting, another team member will act as a proxy until the designated librarian becomes available again and then pass what information they have learned onto the Librarian to document. The Librarian works closely with the Project Manager and Business Analyst, and is in most cases a web developer or web master as well.

Chapter 6: READY FOR CHANGE (RFC) METHODOLOGY

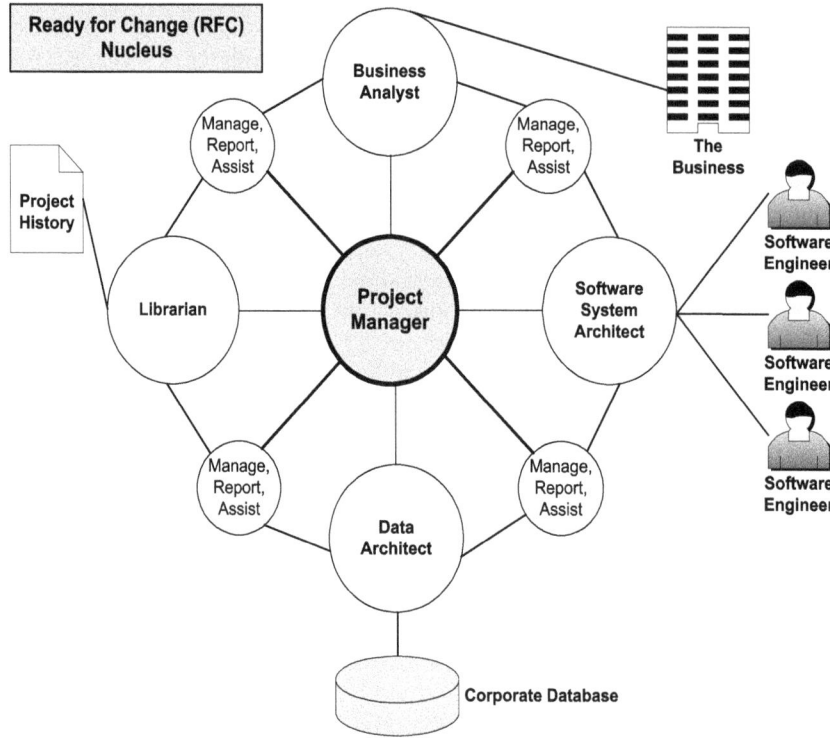

Noticeably missing from the list is the Development Manager. A Development Manager is not needed in an RFC methodology because development issues are handled by a Lead Developer who gets their technical direction for the Software System Architect. The Project Manager in charge of the development effort handles any other employee management issues. The actors assigned to the roles described are the key players in implementing an RFC methodology for an IT project. These individuals ignite, tune, and maintain the engine that provides the structure, communications, standards and management for the RFC methods that drive the rest of the IT project team in their tasks.

RFC Documentation

There are eight primary core "living" documents that are produced during the RFC cycle. These documents are created and updated as needed in relation to the needs and culture of the project.

Those documents are:

1. **Business Requirements (includes business use cases and processes)** – The project cannot begin without this document. This document describes what the

business needs for a specific product update phase. In RFC, this document does not die until the product itself dies. This means that whenever a new episode (version) of the product is initialized, this same document is appended with that information. The business has the opportunity to start building into the future in the initial episode. This is because episodes are categorized in this document based on priority and sequence. This document is compiled and maintained by the Business Analyst.

2. **Software System Architecture (software diagrams and descriptions)** – This document contains the proposed technical blueprints and descriptions of the software product that the team requires. As requirements are changed, this document is updated accordingly. This document is compiled and maintained by the Software System Architect.

3. **Product Data Architecture** – This document contains the proposed technical blueprints and descriptions of the software product database that the team requires. As requirements are changed, this document is updated accordingly. This document is compiled and maintained by the Data Architect.

4. **IT Project Plan (with time schedules)** – This document is the master procedural plan as to how the project will be played out. It includes but is not limited to the following information:

    a. Project Team member roles and responsibilities

    b. Project Team member task-based time schedules

    c. Projected milestones

    d. Project risk assessments and contingencies

    As requirements are changed, this document is updated accordingly. This document is compiled and maintained by the Project Manager.

5. **Product Technical Specifications** – This document describes in technical detail using diagrams and descriptions of how the software product actually works. As requirements are changed, this document is updated accordingly. This document is compiled and maintained by the Lead Software Engineer.

6. **Product Functional Specifications** – This document is the product manual.

7. **Product Deployment Plan** – The installation instructions for the product

8. **Product Test Plans** – The instructions on how to test the product

9. **Project Status Reports** – General information updates.

The respective document owners make all of these documents available on the universal IT RFC project website.

When to use RFC

RFC is strongly suggested when IT software project team members are distributed regionally, nationally or internationally. Also since RFC is designed to be a "Green" method set, it can also help when carefully implemented in IT projects that are looking to save money by cutting down on building infrastructure and energy costs. As stated in several instances previously, a majority of IT tasks can be performed remotely. This means that a large number of IT team members do not necessarily have to go to a specific place to do their jobs. RFC was developed to take advantage of this inevitably growing trend. When IT managers become more trained to think in terms of remotely performing tasks whenever possible, RFC methods and practices will become more mainstream.

Once, an IT manager said to me that I should never work at home too much because if someone has a question, and I am not at my desk then he or she will not get an answer. This type of thinking and practice is not only ancient, but also illogical. The "old school" thought process that hinges on the fact that if a person is not at their desk that they are "unavailable" may be the downfall of many businesses that do not train their managers and employees to uses current and various communication technologies. It is ignorant and absurd for IT team members to assume that a person is "unavailable" because they "physically" cannot see them. If this were really the case, then no one would ever attempt to make a telephone call. During normal work established hours, unless a person states or posts in some way that they are not available, then an attempt should be made to contact them accordingly. Some national and or international IT projects have team members who are never seen by others. In such cases, it is assumed that project personnel will call or email first unless otherwise directed not to do so. This is the basic premise of RFC and is necessary if a team member is not in the office and is needed to answer project questions.

Businesses that harbor IT managers who strongly believe that all IT tasks must be done onsite when they don't need to be, will ultimately begin to feel the negative effects of this "outdated" type of thinking as the cost of energy rises beyond their means in the years to come. The type of mentality that IT work is a place to go and not a task to be completed is a retroactive thought process rooted in the early days of computers. It is not unlike a person who still believes that all telephones must be LAN lines, wired to a telephone wall jack before they can be used despite the invention of the cell phone. RFC is not just a way of doing things, it is also a way of thinking. Even if an IT team does not use an RFC method set, managers should be trained to keep their minds open and constantly look for new ways for their companies to grow, stay competitive, and communicate regardless. As the idea and practice of the "virtual office" further develops, businesses with management who are able to think openly and "outside the box" will begin to surpass their competitors who continue to think and manage as if they were still in the early days of computers. Some of these managers may never be ready for the change needed in order to catch or surpass their competition. Employees who resist and continue to think in this regard when it is not necessary to do so must, and will be, ultimately be replaced.

Use RFC in IT (or anywhere else it may be applicable) to insure that your company's technology is able to keep moving forward. This means that in case of a regional natural disaster, revenue shortage, or building fire (among other things) it is possible for a business's technology and its IT projects to keep functioning. Let us not forget one of the main reasons why RFC should be utilized. When implemented properly, RFC is "Green". Its processes guide companies to methods that consume less energy and fuel, have a positive impact on traffic and in turn, the environment as a whole. This is ultimately a "Win\Win" scenario because if a company has to spend less money on utility expenses (electricity, oil, water, waste management), it has more revenue to spend on other vital concerns.

The Virtual Office?

Traditionally, the term "virtual office" has meant, "shared office space and or business services". This would include sharing such services as:

- Business Addresses

- Computers (Networks and Internet)

- Telephones

- Receptionists and other Answering Services

- Conference and Meeting Rooms

- Legal

- Accounting

The concept of the virtual office is not new and has been around for years. These entities have been predominantly based in big cities. This has enabled some smaller companies to look as if they were larger and more well established due to their popular big city "down town" addresses. In addition, the traditional concept and implementation of the virtual office allowed many small businesses the ability to:

1. Scale down their office spaces to save money on leasing

2. Use a business street address as opposed to a post office box

3. Build a reputation in a new town community on a small budget

4. Allow specific businesses to meet their government regulatory obligations by registering a street address in a commercially zoned area of a city or town

The entire concept of the virtual office has recently evolved with strong advancements in the computer gaming industry. What I mean by this is that employees of a company can use "game-based" software to simulate a virtual office-building interior and exterior that is detailed all the way down to an employee's personal office space. These technological leaps and bounds will continue to happen at an exponential rate. An entire virtual office world can be created for a business, and employees themselves can log on to the system and create characters of themselves that move freely and work in this virtual world just as if they were at a real office building. The mainstream popularity of video simulation games over the internet has made this next step in the evolution of the virtual office possible. Already, millions of people have created virtual characters in computer simulation video games on the internet that deal with real and complex subject matter such as:

- Everyday personal and professional life experiences

- Creating and sustaining new civilizations

- Creating and sustaining new cities and towns

- Flying airplanes

- Driving race cars

- Exploring new virtual worlds based on reality and fantasy

- Playing out realistic terrorist and war scenarios

Much of the video game functionality mentioned above is extremely complex and take the users through very large intricate virtual worlds. Within these realms, there are usually hundreds of other virtual characters to interact with, along with a large number of choices in different scenarios to play through. In some cases, these games can be so large and in-depth, that it can take weeks or even months to play out a chosen scenario and complete the game. With this in mind, it doesn't seem too difficult to create a virtual office building even for a large business where users can create their own business employee characters to represent themselves and maintain an onsite presence. The truth of the matter is this is already happening and becoming more popular as businesses look for new ways to interact, work and stay accessible regionally, nationally and internationally.

Think of the things you do while you are at work. If you work in an office building as part of a project team, you might spend most of your day sitting at your desk working on your computer and occasionally attending required meetings. Some employees may need to give a presentation or simply talk privately to other employees about a task or work related issue they are having. All of this and much more can be accomplished using online virtual office simulation software over the Internet. Imagine, waking up in the morning, taking a shower, getting dressed and eating your breakfast. After which, you go over to your computer, sit down and logon to your virtual office over the World Wide Web where you then assume the identity of the virtual character employee that you created previously within the system. Your virtual employee character enters the building, and you direct them to the floor, area, and workspace where they are assigned. You are now available for meetings and other work (and non-work) related conversations and personal interactions with other company employees who have undergone the same morning process that you have. From that point, you can logon to the software that you use for your tasks and begin working. If you need to talk to someone virtually face to face, you can have your character get up and go over to where that person is assigned in the virtual office to see if they are in the office. If so, have a conversation online with them or call a meeting and have the requested attendees meet in a virtual conference room where everyone can interact with one another. This is only the beginning of true RFC methods and thinking. This is because it does not matter where you are in the world. All you need is a computer with Internet access and a company virtual office system account and you're in business.

The next evolution of the virtual office is happening as you read this passage. Some companies have understood the value of a virtual "game-based" software systems and environments such as the one described, and implemented an infrastructure that has no office buildings and relies on virtual technology to bring its employees together no matter where they are. This is truly the heart and soul of RFC, and will drive the way IT software systems are created much sooner than later.

RFC Philosophy

The RFC philosophy is a simple, powerful, and effective one. It is based on the use of the Internet to facilitate the software development lifecycle. Many people in general use the Internet everyday to manage various aspects of their lives. For instance, they use the web to shop, pay bills, plan vacations, look for jobs and so on. The World Wide Web is used largely by many people globally to plan and execute different types of projects. With this, the general philosophy behind the development of the RFC method set is no different. It was created specifically to guide the development of IT software projects using the web.

Chapter 6: READY FOR CHANGE (RFC) METHODOLOGY

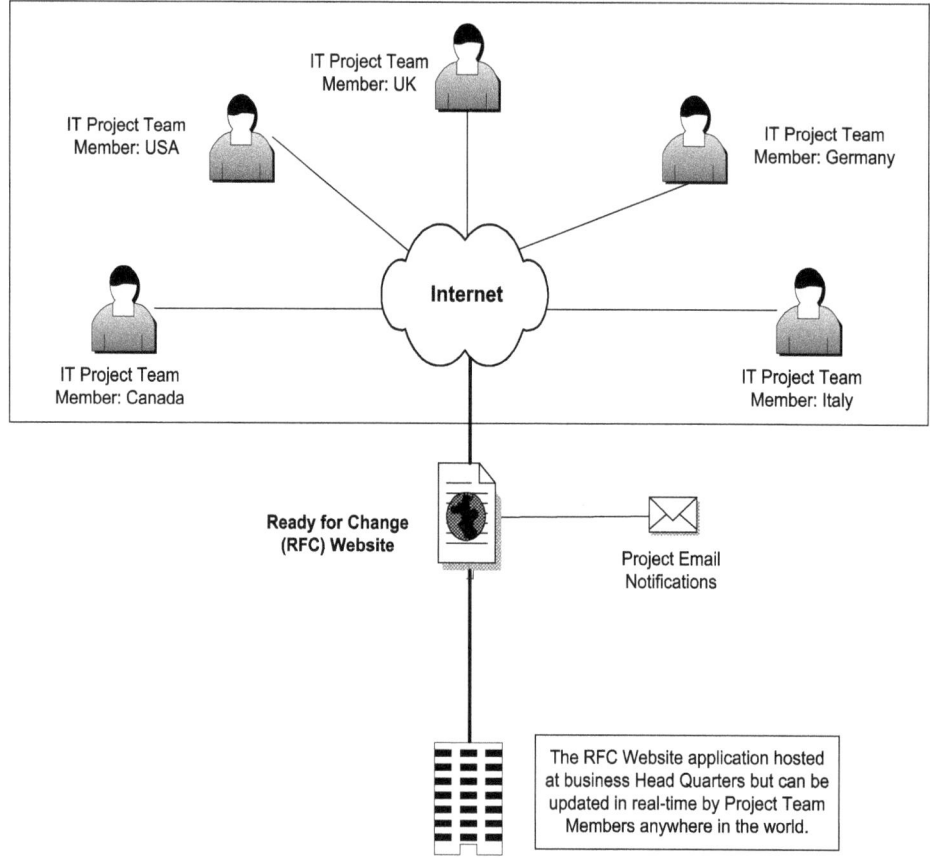

The premise is that a business which plans to implement RFC methods must first build or buy a web application that is specially designed to facilitate the software development lifecycle process. This is due to that fact that if a company plans to profit significantly from the Internet, it must invest in the right web tools, hardware, and bandwidth to do so. In this case, like many others, a web application that is suited to the task is required. At this point, it is important to note the difference between a website, and a web application that is designed to create a return on investment for an organization.

- **Website** - This is basically a static electronic brochure with information that is displayed through a web browser. When a company's adds to its services, and its product line is updated, a static website is unable to grow to display the changes in the business. The term "website" generally refers to the user interface that Internet users encounter when they visit a company's URL (Universal Relay Link). By definition, a website is an information-based entity that includes (if any) very little additional high-level technical functionality. The average website is comprised of information that does not change very often. With this, the content shown does not vary from one visitor to the next. However, many high-level websites include links to other company content management and ecommerce applications.

- **Web Application** – This has advanced technical functionality that can update and or replace current business processes altogether. The general purpose of a web application is to bring the same existing intuitive interaction that a user experiences with a client desktop application to the web. When they are integrated with mobile devices and services, web applications can quickly become be a major business asset in terms of new and or enhanced revenue avenues along with increased optimization of business processes.

Web applications can provide a business the ability to create and view updates to their information on the web at anytime, anywhere in the world. A web application is simply the most effective path for any company that wants to save money and establish a successful presence on the Internet. Web applications have very different requirements regarding security, scalability, database interactions and support. Employees who confuse web applications with a websites can potentially put their business at a disadvantage when describing their Internet related software products.

From the RFC perspective, enterprise level software applications are much like life itself. For instance:

- The software has a period of conception

- The software goes through a development life cycle much like a pregnancy.

- The software is born, which is known as an initial release

- The software is updated (grows) and interacts with other systems and users. This has and affect on the application's "personality" as it matures.

- The software ages, and its technology becomes increasingly obsolete as the years (or months) go by.

- The software's technology eventually reaches the point where it is either too expensive to maintain or is no longer compatible with existing systems and is retired.

- The technology on which the software was created becomes obsolete and the application, in effect, is considered dead.

Using software to design, plan, develop, test, and implement new software is not a new concept and has been going on for a long time. However, managing this process entirely over the Internet is an idea and process that is new to a great deal of companies and managers. Many in IT feel that a totally Internet based SDLC methodology does not work and is riddled with too many pitfalls to be accomplished successfully on a regular basis. This may have been true in the early days of computers but is certainly not true today, and will be even less so as Information Technology tools advance. This is because the Internet has changed the rules when it comes to how software is developed worldwide. People are now connected and can communicate in ways that either did not exist or was far too expensive to implement in IT projects previously. The fact is that software technology has grown to support the development of applications entirely over the Internet but general business mindsets and views on the subject have not still for many people.

In order for RFC to be effective the business and IT management involved must be forward thinking. This means that management should be open to trying new and different methods and technologies. A manager who implements RFC believes in exploiting eCommunications across the spectrum and insists on nothing less from their subordinates. The technology and tools that management employs in an RFC method set can vary from team to team because effective execution of the processes and solid communication is what is important. However, one tool is a constant in all RFC implementations, which is the RFC web application. The RFC web application is the communications and data hub of the project. It is the primary technological backbone for management to enforce, update, and execute project methods. The RFC web application is a living, breathing entity that changes constantly throughout the SDLC of the project. All RFC IT project members involved must be trained to understand the importance of and how to properly utilize the RFC web application. Without this critical tool, you have no RFC methodology technical base from which a remote IT project team can operate.

Changing the "Old School" Location-Based Management Mindset

Most people today would not do business with a bank that did not already have the technology in place that would allow their customers to view and manage their accounts online instead of by telephone or visiting their local branch. In addition, the same is true when it comes to a business having an "online" or "World Wide Web" presence. That is, if you are in business today, it is assumed you have a website and email access where you can be contacted electronically if not by phone, at the very least. If this is not the case, your potential clients and customers may most likely consider your business mentality as backwards, unattractive, outdated, and or misguided. When I was a teenager, no companies had websites and or email, just business cards and brochures, and this was a normal. That is because websites had not yet been invented and email was still largely experimental at that time. However, those days are long gone but many company managers still think as if they were back in those early days when it comes to utilizing Internet technology. No matter the level of management, if this "mindset" exists, it must evolve yesterday for the good of the business and its future innovations. Technology in many cases is only as advanced as its user's mentality or willingness to implement it.

An IT Director had once informed me that his company was not going to do anymore web development for at least 2 to 3 years. That was one of the most "senseless" statements that I have ever heard from a technology person in regards to the direction of their company's software development in this day and age. This incredibly unwise and ignorant plan did not surprise me, due to the fact that the IT Director who made the decision to take his company's technology backwards, had little to no IT experience and relied on IT managers who had almost no more knowledge than he did. Technology managers that don't keep up with where technology is going should be fired. Staying abreast with technology must be a habit and "way of life" for IT professionals. It should never be a chore for software engineers and their management. They should want to continuously learn how hardware and software technology works and where it is going so they can be a part of that trend. An engineer cannot say they are interested in affecting the future and not keep up with the growth of technology. This is because Information Technology is a growing living entity that is always changing. It is not an industry for the ignorant and or lazy minded individual who resists change. Far too many people who work in IT do not want to change and are afraid of the very notion of it. I have had the unfortunate displeasure of working with a good number of these types individuals and in many case they have failed to see how this outlook has hurt them in their careers. Many of them make the mistake of thinking that they can get away with learning technology up to a minimal point, and then resting on their accumulated knowledge for as long as they can. When that type of thinking makes its way into IT management, a cancer is introduced that limits technological growth to what that person knows and their business ultimately pays the price for that mindset.

There are many things that a business can do to insure that their IT managers do not grow technologically complacent over time. Some of those initiatives include:

- Make it mandatory that IT Managers and their teams attend new training in their technology either bi-annually or annually.

- Audit your IT department once a year by more than one well known and respected outside software consulting company, and analyze their feedback. The consultants should not have worked for your company previously. These consultants should study (among other things):

    o Your company's overall technical direction in regards to its business model

    o The technology implemented in order to achieve the technical vision of the business

- The skill sets of the company's software engineers in regards to the rest of the software industry's standards

- Make IT Managers give annual or bi-annual business presentations as to what new technological advancements they have made with their IT teams.

IT management must be able to prove periodically that they are keeping stride with the IT industry's advancements at more than just a modest level. Their ability to manage innovation and new technology integration within the business must never be in question for very long.

It is assumed that the company Software System Architect would remain the expert on the state of the company's technology as they are often called on to interpret and or give their insight on the future of it. It is important to note that Software System Architects do not manage people, they manage technology and machines, that is why development managers need to understand how important it is to learn and grow with the current technologies. As they manage personnel, they are looked to as "leaders". If an IT development manager is complacent in their quest for technological advancement and process innovation, their teams may most likely follow their lead or end up rebelling against them, which adversely affects morale. This is unacceptable in an IT environment and is avoidable in many cases. The bottom line is that if an IT manager is constantly resistant to change, and does not stay in tune with their respective industry they should be fired immediately and replaced. IT Development and Project Managers are not the technology innovators; they make sure that the new technology innovations, processes and tools are implemented by their subordinates according to the specified technical "rules of engagement" as directed by IT Executive Management along with their Software System Architect. This process should not be halted in any way by an organization without hard and good logical reasons as to why.

Building for the Unknown

One of the most basic, and frustrating problems with building software for businesses is gathering system requirements and their related business rules. Most IT personnel who have ever tried to do this with business users generally agree that many companies "think" they know what they want their software to do but are often not sure of the specifics. In other cases, business users providing the requirements and rules for the IT project may be 100% positive they know what their software must do for them but they then change their requirements and rules between 40% to 80% by the end of the project. Due to situations like the ones described, it can be almost impossible to get a good set of software system requirements that a team can rely on for the lifecycle of a software development project. When issues like these arise, teams must be able to "build for the unknown".

Building for the unknown in projects requires a different framework mentality when it comes to the business rules and designing software to accommodate them. Constantly changing business rules and requirements invokes a delicate balance of giving the business users enough power to configure certain application processes themselves, without making the system too complicated to use and maintain. One of the problems in this regard that is common with many large software applications is that they allow users to make extensive and significant changes to system processes that may be conflicting. Also, the more changes that a user is allowed to make to a software system, the more complicated that system must be in order to store, process, and implement those changes gracefully in the future. There are many different ways that a software application can be designed to handle changing business rules. Some of these alternatives include:

- Grouping and storing related business rules in a database or configuration file and allowing users to manage them via a carefully designed user interface. After testing, if the application's business rules do not work as expected, users are then forced to re-examine their rules and processes for accuracy and reliability.

- Using a Business Rules Engine (BRE) application that can integrate with the future software system to register, process, execute, and manage all business rules.

- Having the Software System Architect design custom algorithms to register, process, execute, and manage all business rules.

Accurate business rule planning is critical in building for the unknown. Business rules must be tested no matter how they are processed and executed by a software application. With this, it is imperative that the application be designed for testing and support with careful consideration in this area. Since software applications are comprised of rules, without reliable testing in this regard, you have no system integrity or metrics that the business can use.

Below are some of the elements that are important in business rules planning:

1. The specific application business logic must be defined in a simple, common, and easy to read vocabulary for the personnel tasked with implementing it.

2. The vocabulary in which the business rules are described must be defined in a non-domain specific manner for the personnel tasked with implementing it.

3. The methods in which the business rules are stored must be easily defined.

4. The part of the application that executes the business rules must be able to be tested using simple rule-based facts.

5. The application must be able to track, log and observe all business rule execution within the software application.

Software system maintenance and support starts at the beginning of a project, not when the project is complete. It is important for applications to be largely responsible for reporting their own health and well-being from design inception, and not rely primarily on extensive investigations when problems arise. This is achieved in part by what I call "Designing for Support". Designing for support means creating a strong auditing, logging, exception and event handling architecture framework before any business process code is written. This will enable support developers to build for support and track system errors in minutes or seconds, not hours or days. In addition, event handling implemented tactfully, enables developers to see what business processes a system is actually executing. This is critical for understanding the "real-time" application behavior and personality, and for implementing future enhancements more gracefully. Good auditing features serve many crucial purposes within a software system. This includes the ability to map data changes and test for "regulatory compliance" which is a major requirement in many industries today.

The RFC methods and philosophies take into account that there are elements of an enterprise level software system that may never change. Some of those critical factors are what I affectionately like to call "The Hillbillies", which include but are not limited to:

- **Maintainability** - It is logical to assume that an organization will expect that a software system they have bought or built will be able to be supported by their in-house IT development team or a certified value added reseller (VAR).

- **Scalability** - It is logical to assume that an organization will expect that a software system they have bought or built will grow along with their business for as long as technically possible.

- **Reliability** – It is logical to assume that an organization will expect that a software system they have bought or built will be available when they need it, and even when they do not.

- **Security** - It is logical to assume that an organization will expect that a software system they have bought or built will safeguard company and client data from unauthorized entities and individuals.

- **Reportability** - It is logical to assume that an organization will expect that a software system they have bought or built will be able to produce flexible, accurate, and comprehensive reports based on the data entered into that system.

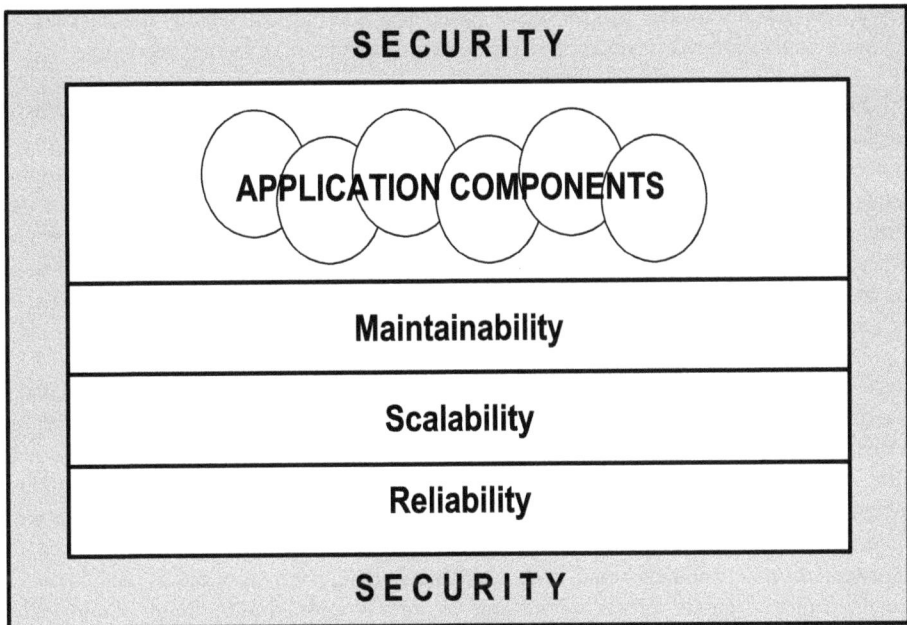

With the above information in mind, in many cases, a large portion of an enterprise level application's framework can be developed well before any of the business requirements for the application are known. This is because just about every business needs and requires (or should want) stable, secure, software applications that they can support and derive reliable data from. This is usually not a size or industry specific rationale but simple basic software system requirements in regards to business systems and many other types of software applications as well. To support this, major software development companies, along with the open source community, make available many free software components for their platforms that make it easier for Software Engineers to build for the unknown. It is basically good business sense to do this because the software development company(s) that make the best and the most effective free component tools, will have the best chance of persuading the highest number Engineers to use their products. Not only do Software Engineers usually not want to rebuild what they already know exists and works, they generally do not like "ineffective" or "hard to use" development tools that costs them valuable time.

The Re-Use Factor

The RFC web application is a business investment that when properly implemented and utilized, has the potential to provide a significant return on investment. This is because the RFC web application is not created to be limited to a one-time use scenario. Its purpose is to be re-used with as many projects as possible, even simultaneously, and as long as technically feasible. As new discoveries and processes are created and implemented by the business, the RFC web application will be updated to reflect those changes if and when necessary.

The basic nature of many effective software development methodologies is to focus on recycling software system code or what is generally referred to as "code reuse". Code reuse is an important factor in Object Oriented Programming (OOP). OOP uses certain computer languages and techniques that are based on the idea of a "noun" that is comprised of data, attributes, and various sub-routines (methods) that process that information. Objects are instantiated (derived) from classes, which are templates that define a state and behavior that is common to objects of a specific type. For instance, a dog and a cat are both mammals, but each are different types within that class of species.

A cornerstone of OOP is a powerful feature called "Inheritance". Inheritance allows a class to receive from its predecessor (a parent class), all of its predecessor's common attributes and behaviors. Much like a son would receive certain physical and personality traits from his father or mother genetically, or a daughter in the same manner. Therefore, it is important to understand that reusing tools and inheriting knowledge gained in previous IT projects, whenever and wherever possible, is a major component of the RFC method set. For instance, using a well-developed and maintained RFC web application will allow IT management to generate reports on previous projects completed using that tool and analyze the related data. Through this process, project managers can discover strengths and weaknesses (gaps) in their teams throughout the software development lifecycle, as well as various project histories, and then compensate by making adjustments as needed. If they are low on resources in the development area and that has created bottlenecks, then more developers can then be hired. If the IT team's weakness has been in the area of requirements gathering then maybe a new or a more senior business analyst (or training), is required to correct that issue. The ability to pull reports on detailed areas of previous IT projects is as critical for the success of IT as it is for the business to be able to generate and review past revenue and or sales reports. Without accurate reports, a business cannot learn and grow consistently. It is extremely difficult or in some cases impossible to effectively allocate resources, revenue, and inventory where they are needed most without accurate reporting capabilities of some sort.

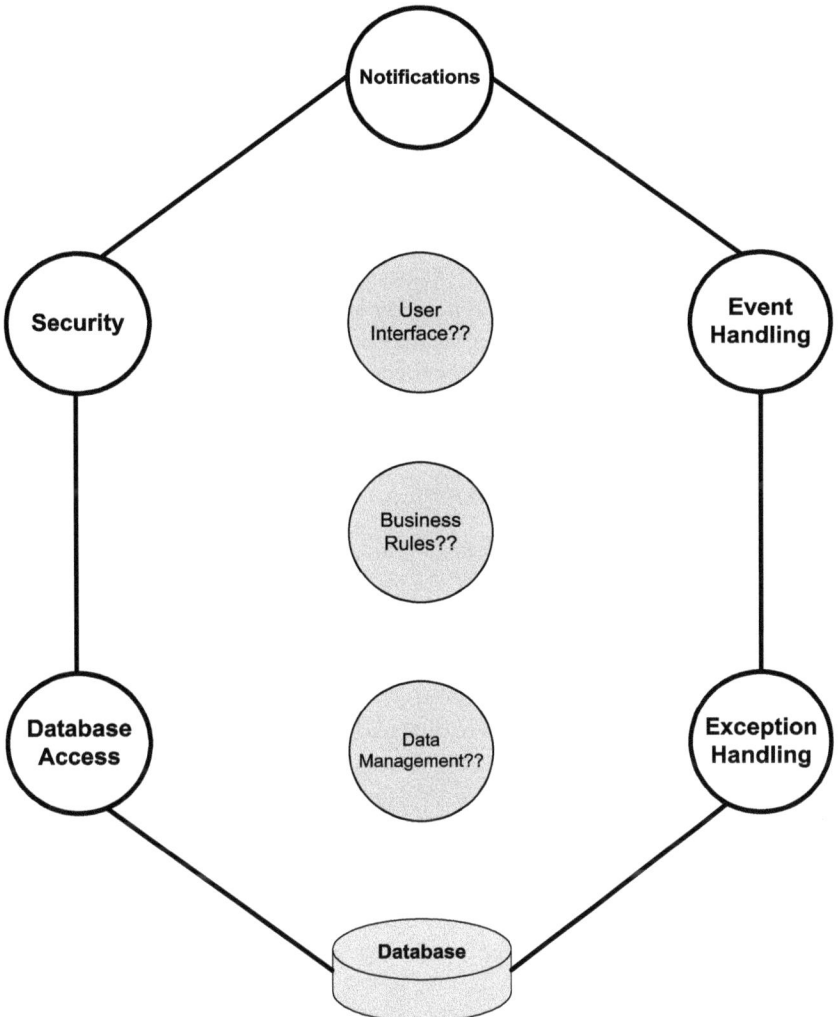

It is a safe assumption that many of the same basic software system features and components will be required repeatedly on new enterprise level software systems no matter what industry they are developed to perform within. The following are some of those feature sets:

- **Notification Component** – It is common practice for a distributed software application to send messages (or email) to individuals or other software applications.

There can be many reasons for this as the requirements can vary from one business to another. Some example scenarios include:

- o The sending of software system error messages to the system support team for analysis and repair

- o Notifying a group of application users that specific information they requested is now available to them on the system or has changed

- o The software application needs information from another software application in order to complete a requested (or required) task

- **Event Handling Component** – Whenever a user generates a system command using the mouse or keyboard, this action is considered a system event. Generally, more advanced software systems will track and store these events so they can be used to report on and analyze some of the following:

  - o User behavior patterns

  - o Profile a user or group of users

  - o Software system behavior

  - o Software system performance

  - o Areas of the system where users may require additional training

  - o Areas of the system where processes may need to be optimized to enhanced the user's specific and or overall system experience

- **Exception Handling (Errors) Component** – Software applications are made up of rules. All rule sets may have errors whether they are known or unknown. In software systems, these situations are called "exceptions" or "bugs". In order to correct an exception, it must first be identified. Saving the details of an exception to the system database after it happens is called "exception handling and storage" and it is a critical function for system troubleshooting, repair, maintenance and support.

- **Security Component** – This is one of the most commonly used areas of an enterprise level software system. Some of the basic elements in software system security are:

- o **User Name and Password Authentication** – This process is the verification of the credentials that a user enters when logging on to a software system

- o **User Authorization** – This process is the verification of a user's "role" or "level of access" that is granted within a software application.

- o **User Name and Password De-Authentication** – This is the process by which a user is "Logged Off" of the system. The user name and password is then set to an "offline" status.

- **Database Access Component** – This is another one of the most commonly used areas of an enterprise level software system. Most software applications at this level (and many below it) must access a database in order to store and retrieve required information.

All of the components listed above are vital system elements and can be found integrated into large software applications that are used to support all or most Fortune 500 companies. These basic building blocks are used repeatedly in the design frameworks of business applications worldwide and can usually be developed or added to the structure of a software system well before the business requirements are even known. This often allows software system architects and their engineers to get a jump on enterprise level system development. This is because many critical aspects of an application's functionality can be reused by integrating a pre-existing system component into a supporting application framework without the need to develop that component from nothing. This is often a part of the "building for the unknown" process that is related to software "re-use" in software development.

Summary

As we have seen in this chapter, the "Ready for Change" method set, when properly implemented, can be a powerful IT methodology for a business that is diverse and working to cut costs and become more efficient and effective in their industry. RFC is based on the following concepts:

1. **The Internet**
2. **Virtualization**
3. **Remote Business Management**
4. **Telecommuting**
5. **The Environment**

Chapter 6: READY FOR CHANGE (RFC) METHODOLOGY

The trend towards implementing these concepts are getting stronger as businesses look for "Greener" alternatives to cutting costs in regards to building and or refactoring their Information Technology infrastructures. IT infrastructure as a whole is currently going through an evolution that is forcing organizations to re-think their current technical strategies and future plans. Many companies are now streamlining their technology while increasing its power and effectiveness by graduating to a services oriented platforms and virtualization.

"Cutting Edge" Information Technology departments have the opportunity to lead the way in developing "Green" SDLC methods that support the concept that work is something you do, and not a place you go. For instance, it is not efficient or effective for a software engineer to drive 60 minutes or more to work daily, and remain for 8-10 hours, to perform the same computer-based tasks they can do remotely, and then drive home again. IT work that can be performed away from the office, should be done remotely to save time, energy, and resources. Virtualization in regards to IT infrastructure supports this idea as well, in the fact that even the largest software companies in the world are constantly enhancing their existing applications, and introducing new software that enables business users to connect with their company networks remotely, securely and even using virtual computer systems.

The short and long-term benefits in terms of return on investment for a business can be significant, immediate, and long lasting. Virtualization and remote workforce management saves time, energy, and cuts hardware support costs dramatically. This in turn can lead to less support personnel, and allow for vital resource reallocation as needed. As our dependence on foreign oil increases and traditional energy reserves continue dry up at an alarming rate, the need for IT infrastructure virtualization and remote management practices can only increase as organizations scramble to find new ways to cut costs (save energy), compete in their marketplaces, and simply survive. Current software development methodologies must be adapted and or new ones created, to leverage and support the evolution into the new "Green" IT infrastructure environments. With this, strong training programs must be implemented by IT management teams in regards to virtualization and remote personnel management or risk increased uncontrolled future software projects.

"First, have a definite, clear practical ideal; a goal, an objective. Second, have the necessary means to achieve your ends; wisdom, money, materials, and methods. Third, adjust all your means to that end."

- Aristotle (Ancient Greek Philosopher, Scientist and Physician, 384 BC-322 BC)

Chapter 7: THE HADES OF INFORMATION TECHNOLOGY

Introduction

It can be good to get a detailed description of what "Hell" is, so that we can begin to build on any appreciation that we might have for not being there. If you happen to be in IT Hell at this moment, then this section might be all too familiar to you and somewhat comforting. With that said, many of the problems with IT are no different from the problems of any other business department. However, the results of IT problems can be more far reaching or devastating than those of other sections of the business.

In general, IT personnel usually earn higher salaries than their peers in other business departments. IT employee salaries are often viewed as a huge drain on a company's revenue by the business for good reasons. IT department expenses can be quite substantial in comparison to other business regions. Some of those expenses include:

- Computer Hardware
- Client and Server Operating Systems
- Software Licenses
- Software Development Tools
- Network Monitoring Software
- Special Electrical Considerations
- Internet hardware installations, maintenance and licensing fees
- Higher than average employee salaries to compensate for specific technical expertise

Many companies are heavily dependent on technology to produce services to individuals and or other companies. They need the latest and greatest applications and features in order to stay competitive in the marketplace. Failure to produce the required technologically is very often devastating to many companies and that fact forces them out of business or into relative obscurity. IT is somewhat unusual in that, a single non-managerial individual, an incompetent Software Engineer for instance, can potentially take down and entire company if given the opportunity.

Let's say that it is imperative that a deadline be met to correct a serious problem that approximately 900 customers are having due to a software problem. Each customer is losing approximately $10,000 to $20,000 per day because of this issue and many are small businesses

Chapter 7: THE HADES OF INFORMATION TECHNOLOGY

who cannot afford to lose that much daily revenue. The Software Engineer working on the problem has domain knowledge about the issue that others on their team do not posses and that person chooses to withhold that knowledge to try to make a last minute correction to the software in order to look like a technology hero to the business and get a raise. The Software Engineer's application correction does not work, and the deadline is not met after several CIO assurances were made to the customers that this would not happen. Longtime frustrated customers are then placed in a position of having to seek another solution, rather than risk losing more money with this particular software vendor. The customers began to spread the word about the bad product and service they received and that their provider is incompetent. The company may very well miss out on future revenue because of this negative "word of mouth" campaigning, and other current customers are beginning to look at the competition and make plans for a change. This scenario may sound familiar, as it is not unheard of in the IT community.

IT employees should always keep the following in mind while working on projects:

- IT works for the business. The business does not work for IT. The business is always the "Boss", no matter what.

- If every computer in the world would disappear within the next five minutes, trade would still go on. Intelligent resourceful companies would adapt and continue.

- The pencil and paper are not dead. Many business folks still prefer it to using computers. In some cases, it is the best way to go. The simplest solution is usually the best solution and it may not always be a technical one.

- If you can be more efficient and effective without using a technological IT solution, then do it. Do it every time! There is always a price that comes with the use of technology and usually in the form of revenue, labor, hardware and support. The use of computer technology is never "free".

Without good management, Information Technology can be unreliable. From the dawn of time, trade has existed without the help or benefit of IT. In comparison to the history of business, IT is not even a spec on the historical map. However, in a relatively short time, Information Technology has grown to affect our lives beyond business and force the world to think in a new way. Through banking, entertainment, shopping, healthcare, the military, politics, government and more, IT has a tight grip on us all. It has forced governments and companies internationally to think not in terms of just revenue but of information or data. The person or company that is "in the know" or "the information king" holds the reigns of true power. That kind of power brings wealth, influence and the unfair advantage. This is the goal of business.

Companies that fail to achieve or ultimately loose Enterprise level status often do so because of a common problem:

- *Consistent failure to discover new innovations that help them to maintain an unfair advantage in their respective marketplaces.*

An unfair advantage is what distinguishes an Enterprise level company from those who are not. Discovering, implementing, and maintaining an unfair advantage in any industry is a combination of many attributes including:

- The proper funding
- Luck
- Perfect Timing
- The right information and the correct analysis of that data
- The right people with the right attitudes
- Great management with great insight and future vision
- The perfect product
- The killer instinct

Even with all of the above factors in place, there is no guarantee that any company will achieve an unfair advantage in any particular market. Many intangibles can lead companies to the Hades of Information Technology, even with those that have a great start and appear to "have it all". Some of these intangible attributes are:

1. **Over inflated Egos**
2. **Megalomania**
3. **Greed**
4. **Cronyism**
5. **Negative Politics**
6. **Lying and Mistrust**

Chapter 7: THE HADES OF INFORMATION TECHNOLOGY

7. **Unhealthy level of Pride**

All of the above are problems that very intelligent and even brilliant leaders struggle with from day to day. Even great leaders are not immune when money and power come into play, as is no one. Any combination of three of the seven intangible attributes listed above can lead an IT Department and its supporting company to the Hades of Information Technology.

Below is a diagram that shows how a project can go astray by means of two of the most common project and or business problems: Scope Creep and Poor Project Management.

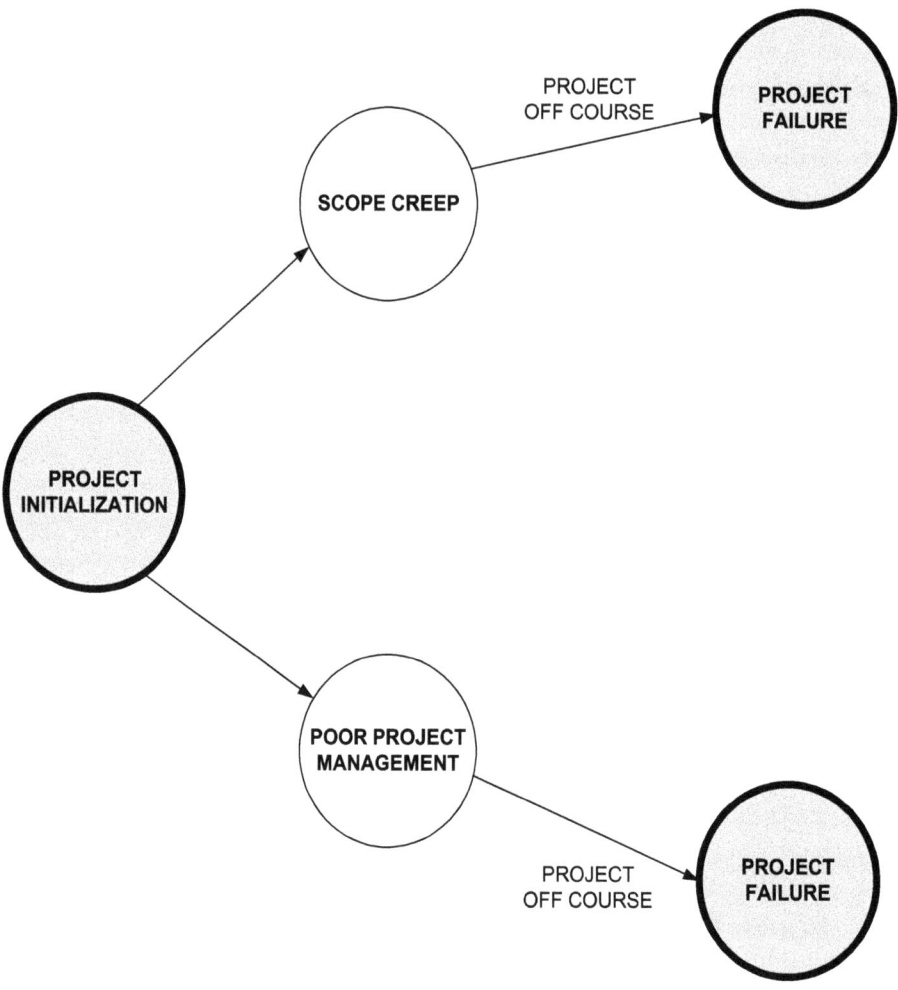

"If you live with a cripple, you will learn to limp."

-Plutarch (Ancient Greek Author\Biographer 46-119)

Why Software Projects Fail

If you have ever been a member of a failed IT Software project (the odds are that you have), then you can appreciate the frustration involved with a dilemma of this kind. The number of things that can go wrong in a software project that can lead to failure boggles the mind. On the other hand, there are only a small number of select tasks that a team can do right to contribute to the success of software projects consistently, but those items are huge.

IT software projects fail when they do not meet the expected guidelines for success. Those guidelines consist of:

1. **Meeting Deadlines**
2. **Completing the project on or within the specified budget**
3. **The software system works as required and or expected**

Lack of or Poor Software Testing

In all too many cases, IT project software system testing is viewed as an afterthought, and not allotted the proper time to implement correctly. Software Engineers spend a lot of time testing features that they implement during development. After this, other personnel (usually other Software Engineers) must perform application stabilization testing. Lastly, user acceptance testing (UAT) should also be done by the people who will be ultimately using the software application.

All too often, the UAT cycle misses many bugs or errors that could have been corrected before a software application is moved to the production stage due to:

- The lack of time to perform all of the correct tests needed because the software project is over-budget and or past its estimated deadline

- Failure to create and implement a thorough and methodical test plan

- Requirements which were written badly enough to make testing unreliable

- Individuals who are not properly trained testers and do not know or understand what a software test is supposed to accomplish

End users generally do not feel comfortable with a new software system unless they are able to perform and successfully complete UAT. For this to be achieved, the software system in question must have well-written, and "verifiable" requirements. The individuals who are performing the tests must have enough time to do so and be properly trained in the science of software system testing.

Lack of Change Management Processes

Uncontrolled changes are the doorway to chaos in an IT Project. This leads to confusion, frustration, mistrust and wasted time and money. Business Software Requirements are often subject to this, and they must continue to stay abreast with business changes as new IT software Projects are underway. Some businesses focus on the benefits of limited "phases" when building software systems. This perspective is designed to limit the effects of businesses changes on the development of the software system project. If business change is not managed like any other organizational factor, then it is far more difficult for a company to analyze and track the results of updates made to the software requirements, and the return on investment involved. IT management must invoke a reliable change process in order to prevent, lower and or eliminate the risk of chaos when developing their software products.

Scope Creep

The scope of a project is the overall conceptual view of the functionality that a system is required to produce. It is the direction in growth, which a software system will follow during the course of the software system project. For example, let's say a small medical practice starts an Electronic Medical Records (EMR) project. After additional analysis of the software requirements, the medical office administration decides that they need to add a new feature that will allow the system to input and display patient x-ray images. These new patient x-ray images will need to be accessible to hospitals and associate doctor's offices through the Internet. These new changes will affect the project timelines, and the project requirements will need to be updated to reflect them. All project members will then need to be notified of the new change requests and be on the same page as to exactly what they entail. Management must be realistic about what is it they want and when they need it, or welcome a type of project cancer called "Scope Creep", which is the uncontrolled growth of requirements.

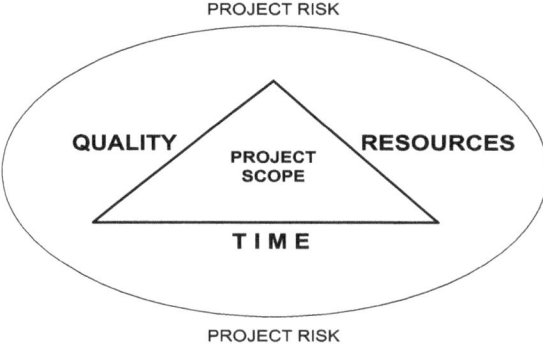

Poor Project Software Estimation

Software project estimation is a science within itself and is one of the most complicated and critical tasks in the software development lifecycle. You cannot plan a software project and create project metrics without a thorough and competent software project estimate. It is important to note the project estimations should not be final unless the requirements are. They are subject to change whenever new requirements are added or taken away from a plan.

Sound software system estimation practices are an area of Information Technology in general that is sorely lacking at many companies. IT in many cases does not understand how to analyze and implement software system estimates appropriately. Because of this issue, software projects incur far more issues than they would otherwise. Without a conscious and significantly focused effort, the negative results of poor software estimation can only get worse.

Poorly written or no Project Requirements

A competent and well-written set of software system requirements are the well from which fresh water is drawn within an IT software project. Bad software system requirements generally do not detail what the software should do. In many cases, the requirements present an idea of the direction and leave it up to the software engineers to figure out the rest. This is one of the major reasons why software projects fail. In so many cases, businesses allot an IT project and ambiguous budget and set baseless timeline expectations as to its outcome.

Many IT personnel don't understand the overall dynamics of how their organization operates and nor should they in some instances. The same is true of how most business people view Information Technology. It is the job of IT to show an organization how technology can best help them. "Analysis Paralysis" starts in an IT software project when IT and business management begins to focus too much on the amount of time, and money the project is burning as opposed to how the software product is going to help the company make more revenue, and why the project was launched to begin with.

How to write good requirements is an often misunderstood task. In some cases, requirements gathering teams believe that their documentation is of a technical nature. Additionally, they tend to author documents that mirror design documents, and tell the developers how to build the software and not what the application is supposed to do. When this happens, the requirement teams begin to play the roles of technical designers and engineers which is a bad thing. The first and most important rule in regards to writing effective requirement documentation is:

- *The IT project software system requirements document will describe in detail what the application must do, not what it should do or how it should do it.*

When the business is dictating technical requirements, and assuming the roles of software engineers, the potential that a system has to become extraordinary usually disappears rapidly. It is important to note, that without prioritized design goals, non-functional requirements, and functional requirements, it is not likely that a software solution can be produced that will be of any significant use to a business.

Poor Leadership

Lack of leadership is poor leadership. This can also be defined as:

"A lack of a cohesive vision or the ability to communicate a cohesive objective that results in disarray, the halting of forward progress, and has a negative impact on time and resources".

Execute level IT managers that fit the definition above contribute to the cancer. If left unchecked, these people will slowly or in some cases quickly destroy a company's technical efforts. No matter how you look at it, the IT troops are headed for certain destruction of some kind, it is only a matter of time. Poor leadership is just the tip of the iceberg as there are many factors that start the descent down a dark rabbit hole into oblivion.

The following are a few definitions of poor leaders that contribute to the problem at hand:

- **The Reluctant Leader** – Sometimes, people who are good advisers are made to be leaders against their will. This may be because of an immediate need or by order of the person in charge as an ultimatum. This starts the Leadership session for the newly elected out on a bad note from the very start, which is usually undesirable.

- **The Ego-Driven Leader** – This person uses their position of leadership to further their own agenda and gain power over others. The issue is not whether or not this person is qualified or not for their position but whether or not they can eventually control their known universe.

- **The Ignorant Leader** – In most situations, this person feels that they always know best. They hear but they do not listen. They stare but they do not see. What this means is that they do not heed the advice of the business or consultants that they hire. They tend to watch the business and or its technology fall apart around them and blame others for problems that they are responsible for and could have avoided.

Poor leadership and planning usually go hand in hand. A bad leader is like a flash flood, or any natural disaster that cannot be predicted and ruins many things. I, like tons of others on the job, have been victim to many poor leaders. Ranging from "Mother and Father" to "Military" leadership styles, they all can be effective if enacted within the proper venue, context, and time. However, without the correct vision, experience, and patience, the chances of this happening are minimal.

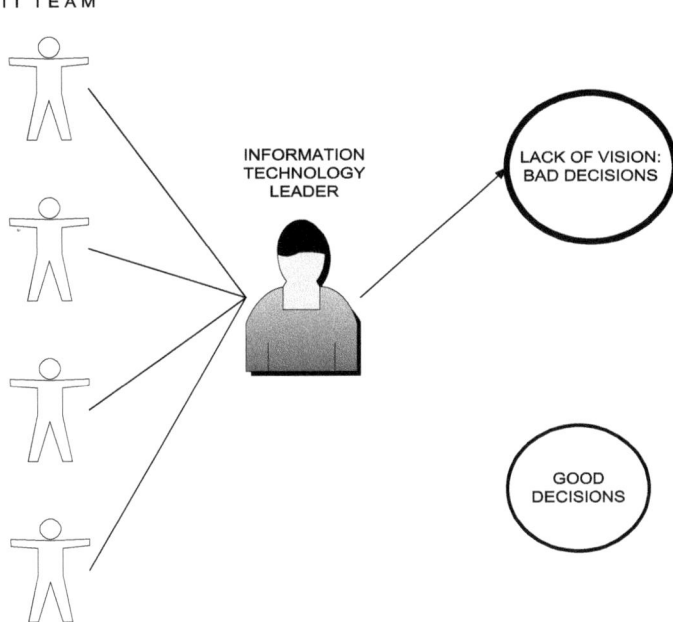

Great and even good leaders are born and not made. A rare and "selfless" quality, along with intelligence, wisdom, vision, planning, and a good charisma; this makes the best leaders what they are. Natural born leaders always have a vision and they are able to explain their objectives and keep those explanations simple. Good leaders can also recognize the talents of their team members and utilize their talents to the utmost. They "inspire" their teams and set the necessary example needed to push those groups to do their very best. How is this possible? Through the three words discussed at the beginning of this book when I referred to what my Mother had taught me. These words again are:

- **Honesty** - The leader is truthful with their team and transparent

- **Loyalty** - The Leader puts the needs of the team and company first. The Leader acts as a shield for their team and takes responsibility for them.

- **Respect** - The team wants to work with the leader because there are inspired by that leader. The leader is in turn, also inspired by their team.

Below is another view:

HONESTY + LOYALTY = RESPECT (USUALLY)

This formula is true in most cases but there are always exceptions to the rule. For example, both good and bad leaders can have attractive visions for their teams and their company's technological growth and advancement. The problem with this is that it is often difficult to distinguish between the two. One way of distinguishing between good and bad leadership visions is to have the leader explain it. After their presentation, ask yourself these questions:

1. Was the explanation of the leader's vision for the technological future communicated in a simple and effective manner? Could it be translated in a way that a reasonable non-management business person could understand?

2. Is there a clear logical process that can be followed to the success of the vision? Can the vision be broken down and mapped out in simple steps that will work for the business?

3. Is the vision so grandiose and or out of scope that the business does not have the resources, time or money to achieve it? Is it in the best interests of the company?

Many more questions will need to be asked in the analytical process of understanding a leader's vision, but the questions above are a good starting point.

I once worked with a Quality Assurance Director who fancied himself a "Part-Time" IT guy. He would read Internet articles on the latest software development trends in his spare time, and then call meetings with the development staff and instruct us on how we were to implement them. From his former Military experience, he would constantly equate developing software to building bridges. Whereas his attitude was to throw more bodies at any software project that was not being performed fast enough. Since the company that I worked for at the time already had a Software Development Director, the Quality Assurance Director often had the development team's boat oars rowing in different directions at the same time, which left the boat stationary or spinning in circles. Needless to say, the vast majority of the projects that he was involved with failed miserably and he was later relieved of his duties and command (fired).

The "throw more bodies at the project with the sagging timeline" approach is still a major problem with many business leaders and it will always be an issue. In too many cases, the business does not understand that software development is not a menial task. It requires constant thinking, analytics, a logical mind, occasionally the patience of a Deity, and "Detective-Like" deductive reasoning skills. If business people in general understood this as core IT employees should also, then a business might not need an IT department. They might be more inclined to learn the trade and build the software themselves as some have decided to do. Business people already have the industry expertise and are familiar with the features needed to construct the applications that they require. They could most likely have more than a third of the software development lifecycle completed in some cases before a project even started.

The Stupid Factor

The "Stupid Factor" is a very important section of this book (if not the most important) because it is one of the primary motivating factors for writing it. Senseless people within organizations are defined as:

"Those who intentionally or unintentionally inflict injury or losses to other persons or groups without deriving any benefit whatsoever from their actions and putting themselves at risk of injury or incurring losses from these very same events."

Reasonable people largely ignore and underestimate the critical and often costly consequences that stupidity causes to IT projects and other business endeavors. Interestingly enough, there are basic laws that govern the stupidity of human beings and these rules are good to be aware of, much like your country's constitution (if it has one).

Below are some of these basic human laws. This first law assumes that everyone on the planet can be categorized into four high level groups. I believe that many companies can fit into these same groups as well. These basic categories consist of:

    a. **The Wise and Intelligent**

    b. **The Senseless (Stupid)**

    c. **The Thieves**

    d. **The Weak (Helpless)**

It would seem easy enough for reasonable people to look at this first law with some level of disbelief and or sarcasm after initial perusal. This is because as a general rule, sensible people have difficulty understanding senseless conduct. However, it is inevitable that almost any person during the course of their lives may occasionally slip into a category that is not their base. For instance, it might be considered "stupid" for a wise person to give a stranger their wallet for no apparent reason. However, if a thief puts a gun to the wise person's head and demands the wallet, then the wise individual falls into the category of the "weak" and maybe even the "stupid" for the isolated act of giving the stranger the wallet outside of the context of the situation. Some might even argue that the act of giving a thief your wallet, who has a gun to your head, is a wise and intelligent decision. If this argument holds true, then we would have a "hat trick", which means in this scenario that a person could be a part of three categories at once:

    1. The "Wise and Intelligent"

    2. The "Senseless" (Stupid)

3. The "Weak" (helpless)

Another scenario is that a member of any category can become a thief out of the need for basic human survival. Case and point, in 2005 one of the deadliest and most destructive hurricanes (Katrina) slammed into the Gulf Coast of the United States. The widespread damage, loss of life, and basic human needs made it necessary for some otherwise good people who would not otherwise do so, steal to eat and stay alive. This was a case where an extreme event forced a change in everyday attitudes which is not typically unexpected in human behavior within a civilized culture.

A second law has to do with how often reasonable people generally and significantly underestimate the total number of stupid people in their environments. The numbers are virtually impossible to quantify, but it usually seems to be shockingly significant whenever IT project failures are heavily scrutinized. In many scenarios, managers and employees who were initially perceived as wise and intelligent are exposed as being embarrassingly stupid.

A third law addresses the problem that sensible people generally do not understand how potentially dangerous and destructive the "population of the senseless" truly are. One of the areas where is this most evident is in business contract negotiations and partnerships. This is because some people, organizations, and groups sometimes fail to understand that a single stupid individual may not always only harm themselves by their thoughtless actions. The repercussions of a senselessness event, invoked by a stupid person, could cost another person, their organization, and their business partners in the form of revenue, lawsuits, and integrity in the industry and even bankruptcy, among other things. One good example of how this can come about is the Enron Corporation. During the mid to late 1990s, Enron was a "Fortune 500" company that was well-respected for such innovations as creating new Internet bandwidth and weather futures markets, as well as buying and selling gas and electricity. At the height of its success, Enron had strong business hooks in the Internet and was worth approximately $70 billion with stock, which was worth close to $90 per share. The company's demise started when it finally shared with the public that its actual value was approximately $2 billion less than they had originally reported. Furthermore, it was discovered that Enron had started more than 10 other smaller companies and then "partnered" with those businesses so that it could hide massive losses and revenue owed. Enron's accounting company, Arthur Anderson (formerly one of the 5 largest international accounting firms), ignored the financial problems of Enron in what investigators called one of the biggest corporate frauds in the history of business. Finally, Enron declared bankruptcy on December 2, 2001 and thousands of employees lost their jobs. People and companies that had invested in Enron lost billions in revenue. Enron Founder and CEO at that time, Kenneth Lay, was indicted by a United States Grand Jury on 11 counts of Securities Fraud and other related charges on July 7, 2004. He was found guilty of 10 of the 11 counts against him on May 25, 2006, which could have sent Lay to prison for up to 30 years. However, Kenneth Lay died of a heart attack on July 5, 2006, after which, the judge in Lay's case vacated his conviction. The fall of the mighty Enron Corporation went down in history as one of the worst failures in business in the history of the United States and serves as a reminder to all to choose your corporate partners very carefully, and pay close attention to their actions no matter how established they may be. Just ask anyone who use to work for Arthur Anderson, and Enron.

A fourth law was established from a societal or group perspective. In this law, that the needs of the many outweigh the needs of the few or the one. This law also works from a fact that the most dangerous type of person is the "stupid", which is considered even more lethal than the "Thief". This is because in most cases, thieves move the revenue and or inventory from their victim's camps into their own, which usually effects no discernable change in the wealth of an overall social environment. While there would be little to no growth if this were the only type of event to happen in a society, it generally does not, however, fall into total catastrophe. For example, have you ever played a real estate board game and the level of play reached a point where all of the players had equally distributed revenue and properties? When this happens, the game could continue almost indefinitely because no one is winning or losing as the game turns into several ongoing transactions between players. No one necessarily gets richer or poorer for very long until one or more of the players grows tired of the "status quo" and decides to quit the game. When dealing with senseless people in a social setting, things are not the same as this at all. It is because of the fact that stupid (and greedy) people are the champions of destruction, chaos, and losses that affect not only themselves but also the people who have to work with and or rely on them. If significant damages are constantly incurred by all parties involved due to the actions of a senseless group or individual, everyone in the environment inevitably suffers as a result. The group as a whole must constantly work to compensate for these losses instead of focusing on moving forward.

A fifth law disagrees with the notion that all men and women are created equal on a physical level. It makes the assertion that "stupidity" is not related to any other physical attribute of a senseless person. For example, this law is based from the perspective that "stupid" is a human attribute, much like "small feet" or "big ears". In no way whatsoever does this law imply that all people in any particular class, race, or gender are "stupid" but a certain and equal number of specific individuals within and across all of these groups are. This is because no particular class, race, or gender has historically held a monopoly on senselessness. Throughout the history of humanity, nature has been very careful to evenly distribute the "stupid" gene evenly among all people, within races and classes alike.

Lastly, it is important to note that stupid people can appear to be wise and intelligent at times and the opposite is also true. This is simply because no one person or group can always appear to be senseless 100% of the time as this is usually not possible due to life's many circumstances and events. Naturally, the same is true of wise, intelligent groups and or individuals, which are also subject to occasionally appearing "stupid". The key here is the context in which these individuals are being analyzed.

When you are studying a person or group, is their current situation one in which they may be reacting or responding to:

- An extreme and or life changing event

- Heavy stress

- Undue force from and or a direct order from another more powerful person

- An illness of some kind

- Another person who desperately needs their help

One way to differentiate stupid people from individuals who are not is by analyzing their behavior over time. Avoiding this practice may cost you, and anyone else who may rely on your reports, significant personal and corporate losses as a result. Time exposes truths.

Friendship over Facts

In IT as in many other industries, once an individual has been promoted to an executive management level, they have become Politicians whether they like it or not. Politics and Technology generally do not make for good partnerships. The two can often work together like oil and water to produce nothing but waste. There are many reasons for this and the logic associated can be quite interesting.

As long as there have been people on Earth, there has been politics of some kind. Survival of the fittest and the battle for popular supremacy are as common today as it was in the time of the Neanderthals. It is part of what makes us human and has driven our overall evolution. The person who owns and is master of the information controls the group in which they reside. In turn, it is usually in the best interest of the person who governs the information to maintain that control, as it is the source of their power. We have learned that:

- **Great knowledge can breed great power.**

- **Great power can breed great wealth.**

- **Great wealth can breed great enemies.**

Technological advancements are fueled by knowledge, innovation, and the willingness to share that information. If knowledge is horded and rationed by persons of wealth and influence, big businesses, and politicians, then advancements in technology usually suffers as a result and the people who need that technology the most, seldom if ever, get it. In some cases, they even become the unwilling victims of this controlled environment.

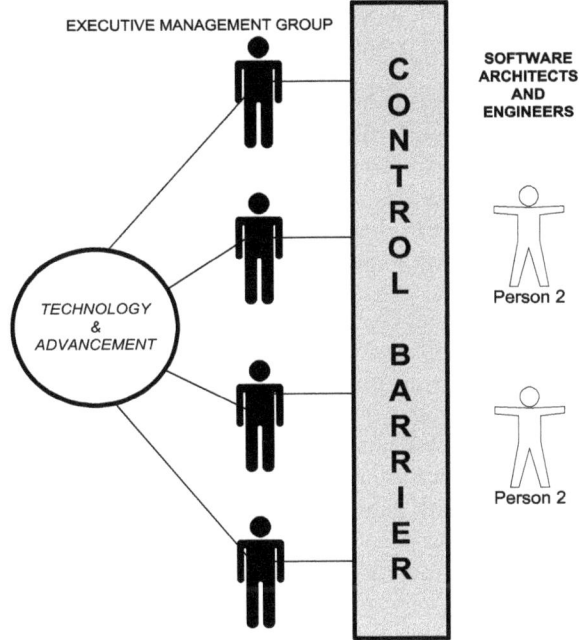

Huge oil and automobile companies have been aware of viable alternative fuel engines for vehicles since the 1950s. They have had the wealth and resources to make alternative fuel vehicles a mainstream reality and save the environment from decades of senseless damage from carbon monoxide. I had read previously that whenever a person or group would invent a promising new alternative fuel technology that could potentially threaten the revenue of one or more of the big oil companies, those businesses would buy the technology and kill the innovative new ideas. The promising new alternative energy source or idea would then go the way of the dinosaur. Large oil companies have long since had the knowledge and wealth to start a new alternative energy industry that could significantly help save the environment, improve the lives of billions of people, and still thrive far into the future, all at the same time. Why is this not happening more now? The answer is simple, greed. The big oil company's refuse to see past the hundreds of billions of dollars of revenue they make right now. Wealthy or dirt poor, we all eventually have to breathe the same air.

The mindset of the large oil companies is alive and well in IT projects. The fight for power and revenue prevent too many IT projects from being completed successfully in part due to greed and power. A common practice for many executive level management individuals is to hire employees that they have worked with in the past or people who are their friends. These folks in many cases are not the best people to do the jobs that they were hired to do. However, because of the level of trust that the executive has placed in the person they hired, good advice from other good and more qualified, experienced employees is often ignored, leading to wasted time, money, and poor team morale.

When it comes to technology, surrounding oneself with "feel good" friends and people you trust as opposed to qualified professionals in the field can very well be a dangerous practice. This is because friends and people that you trust come with an emotional bond that can cloud a person's judgment regarding critical decisions. Making the wrong choices in technology architecture can lead to a domino effect of problems and issues within a project that can ultimately destroy it or drag it hopelessly off course.

I once worked for a new young and paranoid Development Director who had little to no management experience at a large company. The young Development Director was not qualified for the position that he held, and it was clear to the development team that he acquired the position primarily because the company wanted to promote from within, instead of hiring one of several other Development Directors with 20 plus years of experience who had applied for the job. Fearing that some members of the development team were jealous of his newfound success and wanted him gone, the young Development Director quickly surrounded himself with "Yes" people of little technological experience or worth. Under the young Development Director's leadership, the large company that he worked for had lost tens of millions of dollars on a software development project that had gone in circles for many years due to bad decisions related to the gap in his leadership and technological experience. He continuously ignored experienced software developers and architects on the development team who actively tried to point the nose of the project in the right direction. Finally, he participated in a process of either having the experienced team members fired from the company or making their environment so hostile that they would leave on their own. The last time I talked to a person on the development team at that business, advances in that company's technology was minimal with no signs of change and the company was marching forward as if nothing was wrong, and constantly losing revenue along the way.

Complacency

Not staying abreast of new technology is counterproductive to advancement. In IT environments, I have witnessed key team members who were not interested in learning anything technologically new. As stated previously in and throughout this book, to ignore advances in technology is to slowly die. If a business is willing to invest in technology, then they must also be prepared to pay to keep up with it or suffer the consequences.

Below are some of the repercussions of technological complacency:

- **Fear of Change** – This is a general fear of the unknown. To some, learning new technology exposes shortcomings in their experience and overall knowledge that breeds inferiority and makes for an uncomfortable work environment.

- **Lack of Change** – In most cases, fear of change leads directly to lack of change. Lack of change is death or obsolescence.

- **Obsolescence** – With constant advancement, all current technology dies eventually as innovation drive change. However, without forward motion current technology loses value over time as new inventions are discovered.

When it comes to technology, complacency is a form of cancer that if left unmanaged, can be fatal. Even moderate complacency can be viewed as a mildly aggressive cancer that, if not removed, can be dangerous. I once worked for a State Agency on a project in which the goal was to refactor an accounts receivable web application. One of the project team members was a Developer and original designer of the financial application that was going to be redesigned and built. During the architectural and planning sessions to upgrade the application in question, the original Developer showed no signs or interest in participating in learning the new development language and tools, chosen for the task. When ask why, the Developer replied that he was simply not interested, and that he was satisfied supporting applications using the old technology. As others on the team went to training sessions and had power lunches to share new technological information, the Developer did not participate in any of these opportunities. Gradually, he became less effective during the course of the project and eventually turned into a non-factor altogether. So many companies have also succumbed to this "disease" and have paid the ultimate price. They simply did not do everything within their power to keep their company and its technology moving forward. The alternative was failure, which they eventually embraced.

When you are not a technological leader, then you are a follower of some sort. Even rogue technologists lead in the form of research and development, in their own ways. The complacent mentality stalls the progress of a follower and eventually disengages him or her from competition. Necessity and competition fuel the desire for learning and achievement in advancement. Complacency is sand in the gas tank that flows into the engine and shuts that component down.

Complacency View
Industry Progress

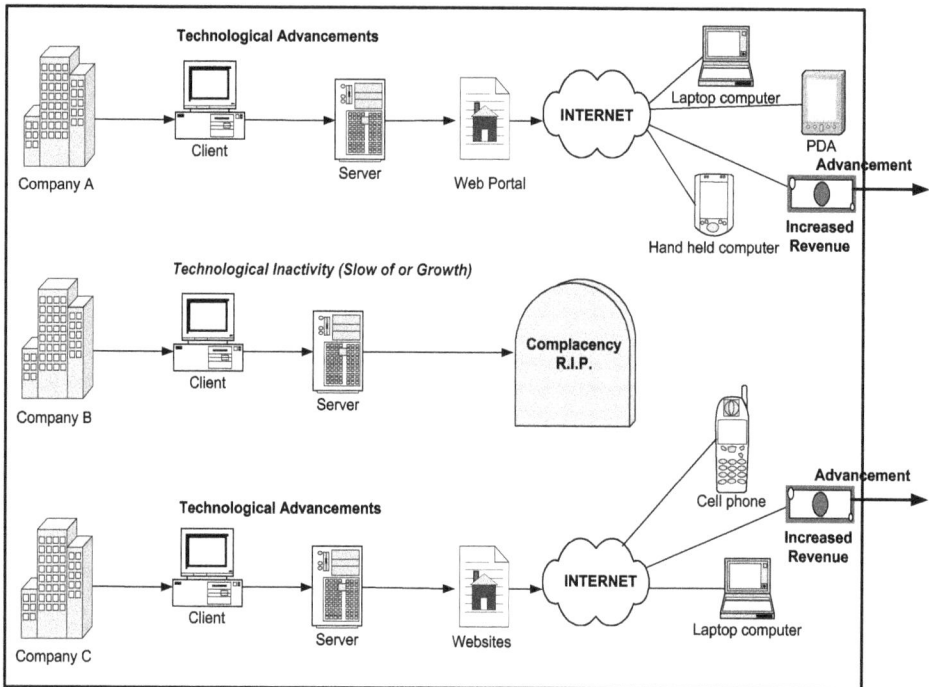

Overcompensation

There are those who believe that every business problem must have a technical solution. Also, there are also those who believe that every technical solution must be "cool", thus adding unnecessary levels of complexity that make a mess of a software application's architecture and eventually the overall project that the developer is assigned to. IT employees, who hold these beliefs, usually lack the ability to think in simple terms.

The repercussions of this way of thinking in software development are far reaching. They include:

- Inflated software development timelines

- Decreased software return on investment (ROI) due to increased application support time and resources

- Decreased software reliability and performance

- Software applications that are confusing and difficult to maintain

Overcompensation is not limited to entry level or mid-level software engineers. Anyone within a software system project from the business to IT can actively contribute to this problem. If the answer to a challenge is simple and effective without the use of technology, then that answer is the best solution. Technology is a tool, not a solution! People are always the solutions and one of our tools is technology. It is important to remember that the brain is always the best tool a person has to begin with. The mind is the primary item that should be used to find answers to challenges, not technology. Additional problems arise when people forget that fact, especially when new and enticing brands of technology are involved.

Overcompensation is a cardinal sin in the technical realm that ultimately degrades the advancement of the area as a whole. We must maintain control over technology, which means hardware and software advances must progress powerfully with a simple grace and steadiness, discipline and patience. Overcompensation can also add to software and hardware behavioral unpredictability, which is generally undesirable.

Inappropriate Encounters

People are political and it is in our nature to be that way. Sometimes we say the wrong things to the wrong people, at the wrong times, and we don't realize it. During the course of IT projects, as with other projects, this problem can be particularly devastating. Below are some examples of this:

- Technical people talk in technical terms to non-technical business people. Much of the conversational content often gets lost in translation.

- Non-technical business people speak in business terms to non-business minded technical people. Much of the conversational content often gets lost in translation.

- The "Babel Effect" becomes prevalent as the business and IT fail to understand each other. The "Babel Effect" happens when two parties fail to communicate within a business and or a project due to a difference in language and or vocabulary.

- Some members of the business may begin to act on misunderstood information obtained from IT members outside of critical meetings.

- Some members of IT may begin to act on misunderstood information obtained from business members outside of critical meetings.

Inappropriate encounters can be difficult to manage if at all, especially if many of the people in both the business and IT have personal relationships. Poor management can also

284 **Chapter 7: THE HADES OF INFORMATION TECHNOLOGY**

sometimes be to blame. Many managers overlook the "need to know" policy with their teams and simply share more critical IT information than they should.

Businesses have traditionally been a breeding ground for politics. When misunderstood or too much information is made available, the opportunity for conflict at a company to gain a strong foothold is wide open.

IE Scenario

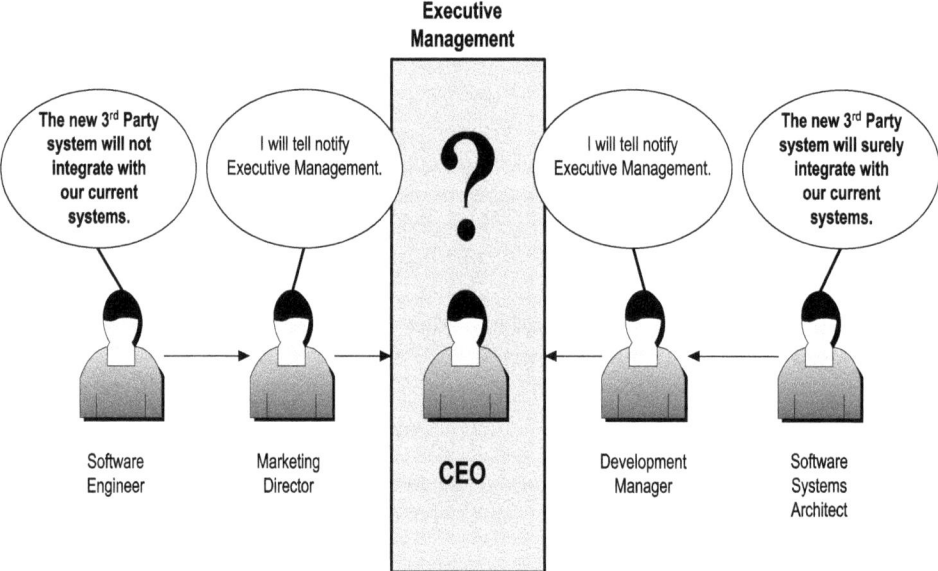

Non-Technical People Making Technical Decisions

Software sales representatives have been a long time enemy of the IT department. They often bypass IT and target the business with third party software solutions that seem right for their needs. The problem with this for IT is that when these sales people target the company, they often make grandiose claims that may not be true. Common sales jargon for new third party business software systems include:

- You can configure the new third party software system in virtually any way possible for fit your business processes

- The new third party software will easily integrate with your current software systems

- Upgrading the new third party software system is simple if you use their proprietary software tools.

- Almost anyone can configure the new third party software system. No previous software development experience is necessary.

- Support for the new third party software system is comprehensive and affordable.

- The new third party software system is easy to learn and user friendly.

Many business people in critical decision-making roles hear these sales pitches and override IT management's ability to veto the purchase of these new third party software systems either before or after the technological team can make an evaluation of the product. As a result, many businesses buy new third party systems after believing the hype and sales pitches, and end up with one or more of the following issues:

- The purchased third party software system does not fit the needs of the business as previously described by that company's sales team

- The purchased third party software system does not easily integrate (or does not integrate at all) with existing company software systems

- The more customizations that are made to the new third party software system, the less the company is able to upgrade it to the next version

- The business finds out that special skills are needed to configure the new third party software system. Much of the skill set needed to make critical configurations that the business requires is proprietary. Additional training is then required by IT in order to make the new software comply with existing requirements.

- The level of support needed for the new third party software system is far more expensive than originally estimated.

- The third party software system may not be as user friendly as originally anticipated after the business customizations have been implemented. Significant and additional employee training is required.

Designing, building, implementing and testing new software systems is a science, and should not be based on feelings or emotions. Additionally, it must rest on solid, well documented business requirements and research and development that supports those needs. From the business requirements, important technical decisions can then be made regarding facts through science only. In this way, the best possible solutions and decisions can then be derived and analyzed.

Chapter 7: THE HADES OF INFORMATION TECHNOLOGY

Refusing Responsibility

I hope that your parents always told you to tell the truth. However, you have to know what the truth is before you can understand it. Herein lies the problem with accepting responsibility when things go wrong with an IT software project. In some cases, IT teams can do all of the right things for a project and still fail. This can happen due to one or more of the following reasons:

1. The requirements for the IT software project were wrong or misleading
2. The requirements for the IT software project were lacking some critical content
3. The requirements for the IT software project were never documented
4. The requirements for the IT software project were only partially documented

If software system requirements are gathered, documented, signed off by the business, and presented to IT for implementation then there is usually little that anyone in IT can do to dispute the validity of those requirements. This is important because the business owns the requirements. Only the business can validate them, not IT. Generally, IT teams are not business domain experts in regards to business models, processes and management. The business is king in this regard and is the entity that is responsible for passing the required information on to IT when needed.

In many cases, some business domain experts try to avoid the requirements gathering process for new projects altogether. Reasons for this type of behavior might include:

- Constantly changing company processes can make it difficult for a business domain expert to commit to a specific group or set of requirements.

- Standards for business processes are not clearly defined within the company

- If the requirements are wrong or misleading, the business domain expert may cost the company significant time and money and be fired.

- If the requirements are lacking critical content, the business domain expert may cost the company significant time and money and be fired.

In addition, there are many reasons why project members may avoid taking responsibility for a task or problem. Some of those circumstances may include:

- The IT team member may doubt the integrity of the project requirements assigned.

- The IT team member may not have the skill set to complete the project task assigned

- The IT team member may not trust in the abilities of their team members

- The IT team member may not trust in the abilities of their management

Ultimately, a person or group must take ownership of an IT software project. If no one takes ownership, it is easy for the project to get lost in the uncertainty and the mistrust of business politics. Again, IT projects must be owned by the business. In all cases, IT works for the business and thus, must answer to it regarding all projects and technical planning. Most importantly, there would be no IT team if the business did not exist, so the business must always, and in no uncertain terms, own the IT department and its subsequent endeavors.

Business Courses to Solution

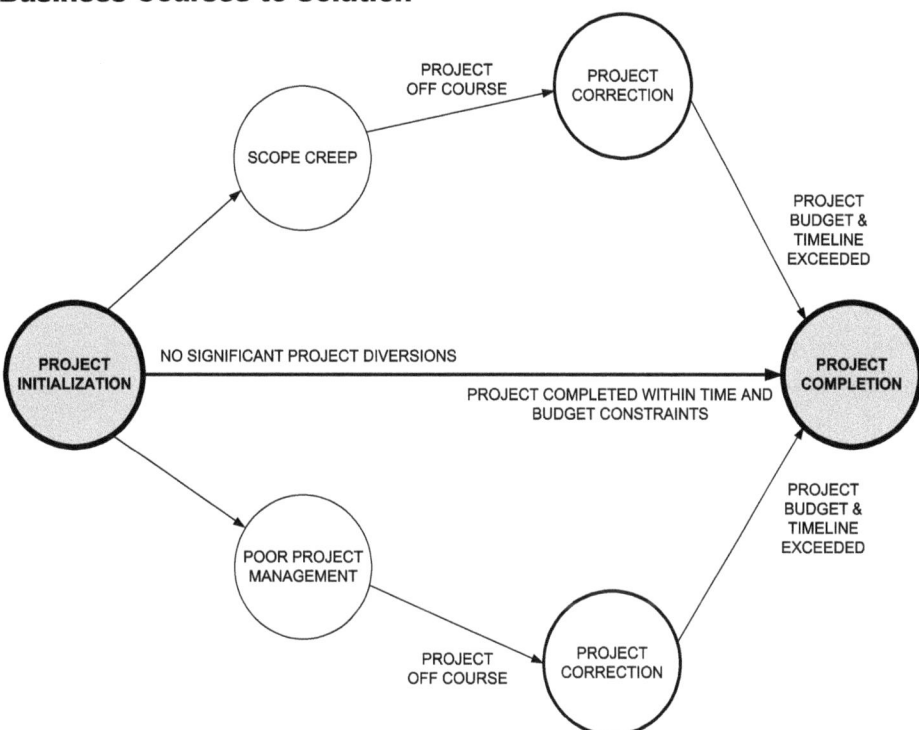

Summary

It is important to understand that the Hades of IT is not just about IT performing all of its processes or even just the critical processes incorrectly. In addition, it is not comprised of only having the right people doing the wrong things or the wrong people doing the right things. IT "Hades" can consist of a well oiled, experienced IT team with good proven processes and intelligent employees executing the right tasks. What can make an IT department of this nature a "Hades" is its specific motives, intent, and management. For instance, the sure and definite road to Hades for an IT department is to follow one simple basic rule. That principle is what I call the "IT Hades Principle" (ITHP), and it states that:

"An IT Team, which increasing builds business dependencies on dying technologies, bad management, and ineffective methodologies cannot survive".

Individual criminals and or crime-based organizations that utilize IT to try to achieve their goals are often more organized and effective than the IT processes and tools used by the law enforcement teams who are trying to catch them. This is an increasingly difficult and devastating problem for companies and law enforcement efforts around the world. Considerable resources are allocated each year to fight against criminals who effectively use IT. Information Technology is an objective tool that has no allegiance to any one specific cause, individual, organization or purpose whatsoever. So in effect, one business's "Elysian Fields" can be another company's "Hades".

"To make no mistakes is not in the power of man; but from their errors and mistakes the wise and good learn wisdom for the future."

- *Plutarch (Ancient Greek Author\Biographer 46-119)*

Chapter 8: WELCOME TO THE ELYSIAN FIELDS

Up to this point, we have talked about Information Technology:

- **Information People**
- **Leadership**
- **Communications**
- **Politics**
- **Software Development Lifecycle and Methodologies**
- **Changes and Change Management**
- **Hades**

How do these topics relate to one another and culminate into the Elysian Fields of Information Technology? Let us explore this question in more detail.

The State of Perpetual Forward Motion

Welcome to the Elysian Fields? This question\greeting may not be entirely logical to those who understand exactly what existing in an Elysian Fields realm truly means. The Elysian Fields of Information Technology is not a destination. It is a constant "journey" or a "state of perpetual motion" that is fueled by:

1. Energy
2. Industry Best Practices
3. Intelligence
4. Wisdom
5. Courage
6. Experience
7. Trust
8. Respect

9. Discipline

10. Professionalism

The definition of The Elysian Fields of Information Technology is:

1. *The ever-changing state of the pursuit of technological perfection as supported by an experienced, effective IT Chain of Command that is based in sound decision-making and proven IT processes that have resulted in a successful and ongoing track record of accomplishment.*

2. *Analytics based on scientific research and development along with over-communication practices are used to exploit new and existing technology with a team of qualified, seasoned professionals using solid, proven processes and tools to create, manage and support "phasic" and "required" software and hardware solutions from sound business requirements.*

The best IT organizations are never complete when it comes to their technology. The word "done" or "finished" is a myth in regards to the evolution of a company's technological personality and endeavors. They are an ever-growing entity that strives for the knowledge and respect of their business partners and realizes that they may never have it. If that IT groups is ever lucky enough to attain this rare honor, they indeed realize the value of it by working tirelessly to support and maintain such an important and aloof relationship. This is because of one simple and critical factor, which is survival. Both IT and their business partners share this common thread and it is the tie that binds them. If the business fails to make money, IT will eventually cease to exist. However, in many cases if IT fails, a business may survive without them either for a period of time or indefinitely. So what does this really mean for an IT organization looking for direction? It means that this group is in the business of "enhancement". This means improving business processes for organizational areas such as:

- Sales and Marketing

- Financials

- Logistics

- Manufacturing

- Inventory

- Research and Development

- Call Centers

- Core Service Offerings

- Intellectual Properties

An enhancement is an upgrade implemented to make a person, place, thing, and process better than it was and this is one of the primary tasks that IT is supposed to accomplish. If the ends culminate in significantly increased revenue for the business, then the enhancements were usually well worth the efforts.

Once the state of the Elysian Fields has been achieved (if ever), it must be constantly maintained or it will be lost along with all of the efforts that were made by an IT team and its business partners to get it there. It takes a great deal of energy in order to start a journey towards the Elysian Fields much like an explosion is required to start an engine. A vast number of business organizations attempt to complete IT projects while never even considering trying to achieve anything greater over time. This may be due to a lack of money, resources and or vision. However, it is still true of many businesses that have IT groups that do have the money and resources to go after a higher plan of consciousness for their technical challenges. The Elysian Fields is not a place that IT finds by accident after days or weeks of traveling through a silicon forest. It is the perfect storm of synergy, planning, personnel, persistence, time, and money. To be clear, the Elysian Fields is the rumbling engine that starts after you have turned the key. It ignites and begins to run. For an engine to run continuously, many important parts and processes must work together and cycle repeatedly and simultaneously. In order for the engine of the Elysian Fields to start and idle smoothly, the following elements must be in place first, in order to support its operations:

Igniting the Elysian Fields Engine

People Energy → Oil

Time → Coolant

Revenue Funding → Fuel

Chapter 8: WELCOME TO THE ELYSIAN FIELDS

Once an Elysian Fields based engine has been invoked, several processes are fired up and begin cycling continuously. Some primary attributes that propel the engine include:

- **A strong, competent, and experienced Management Chain of Command that listens to what its employees have to say.**

- **Best Practices are adapted and invoked accordingly**

- **Reliable reports are produced so good decisions can be made**

- **Over communication is harnessed effectively with a common yet simple vocabulary that the team utilizes and understands**

- **"ZERO" tolerance for disrespect within the team**

- **Worrying is not an option**

- **The right people are assigned the right jobs**

- **A good "trust-based" relationship is established with the business**

The following is the "Elysian Fields Technology Cycle" that supports certain engine elements:

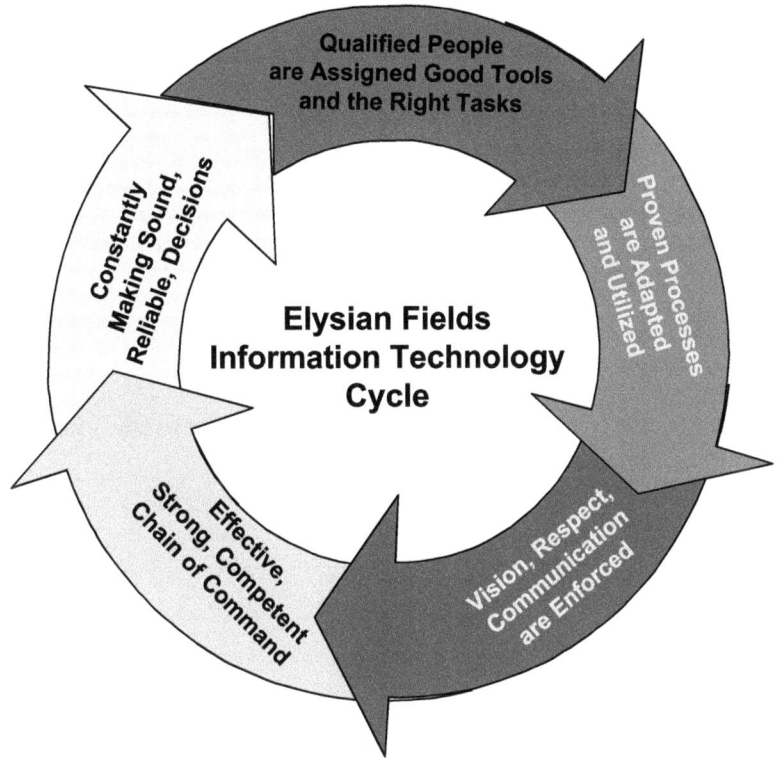

Are there problems in the Elysian Fields?

In ancient Rome a writer named Lucius Seneca once said, "Difficulties strengthen the mind, as labor does the body." Even the best environments that look to be the ideal outwardly have issues, concerns, and problems. This is a basic truth and some of the facts associated with internal technical issues are difficult to ignore. The bottom line is that challenges should be welcome in almost any situation because they are a vital component in the analysis of strengths and weaknesses. Problems truly test how strong something is, and without them, there is simply no metrics to understand your history, present status, or future. Challenges should be viewed as necessary, and must always be welcome in the Elysian Fields because they are a part of its ability to successfully maintain that realm and status. You cannot have the Elysian Fields without constant challenges that invoke necessary change. The old saying,

Chapter 8: WELCOME TO THE ELYSIAN FIELDS

"If it isn't broken, don't fix it" does not apply here. Technology must always change for the better in the Elysian Fields. Some might ask why this is so, since the Elysian Fields is supposed to be a place of relative peace and calm? This is not necessarily true in regards to IT. Two answers to these questions are listed below:

1. *A true Elysian Fields Framework is designed to function effectively in a conflict zone in order to competently manage that environment. The result of an Elysian Fields engine being ignited, is to enable IT units and or organizations to act as proactive forces instead of reactive ones when faced with new obstacles and challenges. This may give the illusion to some of "relative peace and calm" but the maintenance of this engine requires skill, experience, patience, discipline and hard work and is usually not a simple task.*

2. *The purpose of an Elysian Fields Engine is to bring order to chaos gracefully, with intelligence, wisdom, strength, and sanity.*

Challenges in the realm of the Elysian Fields are often met and overcome with the following resolves:

- The right Attitude

- Analytics based on Facts

- Attention to Detail

- Discipline

- Good Contingency Planning through identifying all known possible solutions includes considering both popular and unpopular points of view

- Identifying the "Pros" and "Cons" of all known possible solutions

- Reliable and proven problem resolution processes based on best practices as established by good, sound and sensible Management

- Establishing realistic objectives - If you have no goals, you have no plans.

- Taking action and then following through on those events

Issues, concerns, and obstacles are managed more competently when realistic expectations are set with the business consistently. In many scenarios, this is also true if projects don't always turn out the way that they were originally planned. In addition, an alternative project outcome does not always necessarily mean that a project has failed in some instances, but that unforeseen occurrences may have arisen and the team had to compensate for them. In the end, the business may not be surprised by the results of the project, and be able to anticipate their new obstacles based on timely and accurate reports from their IT organization as to the ongoing status of it. In so many cases, problems arise with a company when IT and or the business lose sight of their common ground, which is the fact that they both exist and are in place to make money. Without revenue, there is no business or IT so there is always a place of commonality for all parties involved.

"What we have to learn to do, we learn by doing."

-Aristotle (Greek Philosopher, Scientist and Physician, 384 BC-322 BC)

Elysian Fields Project Examples

A project's resulting product has undoubtedly reached the height of "Elysian Fields" when that result becomes so significant that it surpasses the individual, group or company that originally designed, developed, tested, and implemented it. Furthermore, the impact of that project's success then reaches far beyond its industrial and regional borders and grows to become a phenomenon that changes our everyday lives. A force of that magnitude takes vast resources, commitment, patience and dedication. The summaries that follow consists of examples of powerful Elysian Fields projects that did just that. It is important to note that Elysian Fields projects can range from a small open source projects to that of a multi-national\multi-corporate projects with input from almost any other type of organization in between.

Elysian Fields projects are alive. These special journeys have hearts that consists of ideas that constantly evolve, get stronger, and ultimately "pay it forward". Projects of this realm also have an intelligence, which consists of direction, will, logic, and delegation. One of the best aspects of an Elysian Fields project is its ability to solicit and inspire everyone on the project team to participate with a willingness and enthusiastic attitude towards a result for which the potential is not yet fully realized. This is the "gift" that keeps on giving within a project of this type and can build great relationships that can last a lifetime.

The Personal Computer (PC)

The personal computer has been defined as a computer whose functionality, size, and retail price makes it an effective and expedient service provider for individuals. While in school, a favorite teacher of mine once described the PC as a "fast idiot". By this, he explained that a computer does whatever you ask it to do, which makes it an idiot, but it executes your commands very quickly. Personal Computers are no strangers to homes, offices, and shoulder bags (laptop PCs). What makes these types of machines different from their brothers and sisters are that one person generally uses them at a time. Other PCs that don't

Chapter 8: WELCOME TO THE ELYSIAN FIELDS

fall within this category are most often used for transactions, batch processing and or basic local area network (LAN) or wide area network (WAN) support.

There is no one "single" inventor of the computer as there were and continue to be many players in its ongoing technological growth. Many individuals and groups throughout time have contributed significantly to the creation and constant evolution of the computer. PC technology is comprised of a number of separate parts of which each can be considered a "patentable" invention. John Atanasoff (an inventor of the first digital computer) once said the following to a group of reporters, "I have always taken the position that there is enough credit for everyone in the invention and development of the electronic computer".

Below is a timeline of the history of the personal computer in order to further illustrate the creation and self-driving evolution of this paramount and critical Elysian Fields global project.

Event Year	Computer Event Description
1936	Konrad Zuse is unofficially recognized as the "inventor of the modern computer". Zuse was German aircraft construction engineer when World War II began. He invented a series of automatic calculators to help with complicated engineering calculations. Zuse discovered that an automated calculating machine required 3 things: 1. **A Memory** 2. **A Control** 3. **A Calculator** In 1936, Zuse created a calculation machine called the Z1. This was the first binary computer known to man.
1942	John Atanasoff and Clifford Berry constructed the first digital electronic computer at Iowa State University.
1944	Howard Aiken and Grace Hopper architected the MARK series of computers at Harvard University. These computers were 55 feet long and 8 feet high. It weighed 5-tons and contained approximately 760,000 parts. It was used by the US Navy until 1959.
1946	John Mauchly and J. Presper Eckert constructed the ENIAC (Electrical Numerical Integrator And Calculator) for the US Military. They developed a move advanced calculating device based on the work of John Atanasoff that used vacuum tubes to increase the speed of the

Event Year	Computer Event Description
	machine's calculations.
1948	John Bardeen, William Shockley, and Walter Brattain, scientists at the Bell Telephone Laboratories in Murray Hill, New Jersey developed the transistor. In 1956, they received the Nobel Prize in Physics for the invention of the transistor.
1951	Dr. Presper Eckert and Dr. John Mauchly develop the Universal Automatic Computer (UNIVAC). This was the first commercially available computer, but it was not successful.
1953	IBM develops the first successful commercially available computer, which was the 701 EDPM.
1955	The Stanford Research Institute invented "ERMA" (Electronic Recording Method of Accounting) computer system. It was the first computer system used in the banking industry to process checks and to manage accounts.
1958	Jack Kilby and Robert Noyce worked to invent the world's first integrated circuit (IC). The IC reduced the cost of electronic functions by a factor of a million to one.
1962	Steve Russell, an MIT programmer, created the first computer game called "Spacewar".
1964	Douglas Engelbart invented the computer "mouse" and forever changed the way that computers were used, and made them far less complicated for the public to utilize.
1969	Advanced Research Projects Agency (ARPAnet) was born. ARPA (a department of the US Military) was the grandfather of the Internet and was originally developed to support Cold War intelligence and weapons.
1970	Intel makes available to the public the first Dynamic Random Access Memory (DRAM) chip.
1971	Intel engineers Federico Faggin, Ted Hoff, and Stan Mazor invent the first single chip microprocessor. In this same year, Alan Shugart and the IBM Team invented the "Floppy Disk". This was the first portable

Chapter 8: WELCOME TO THE ELYSIAN FIELDS

Event Year	Computer Event Description
	device in which computer data could be stored.
1973	Robert Metcalf at Xerox Corporation develops Ethernet networking technology. This was the first networking technology that connected computers using hardware within the same building.

The diagram below shows a summary of the continued rapid advancement in innovation towards the personal computer revolution.

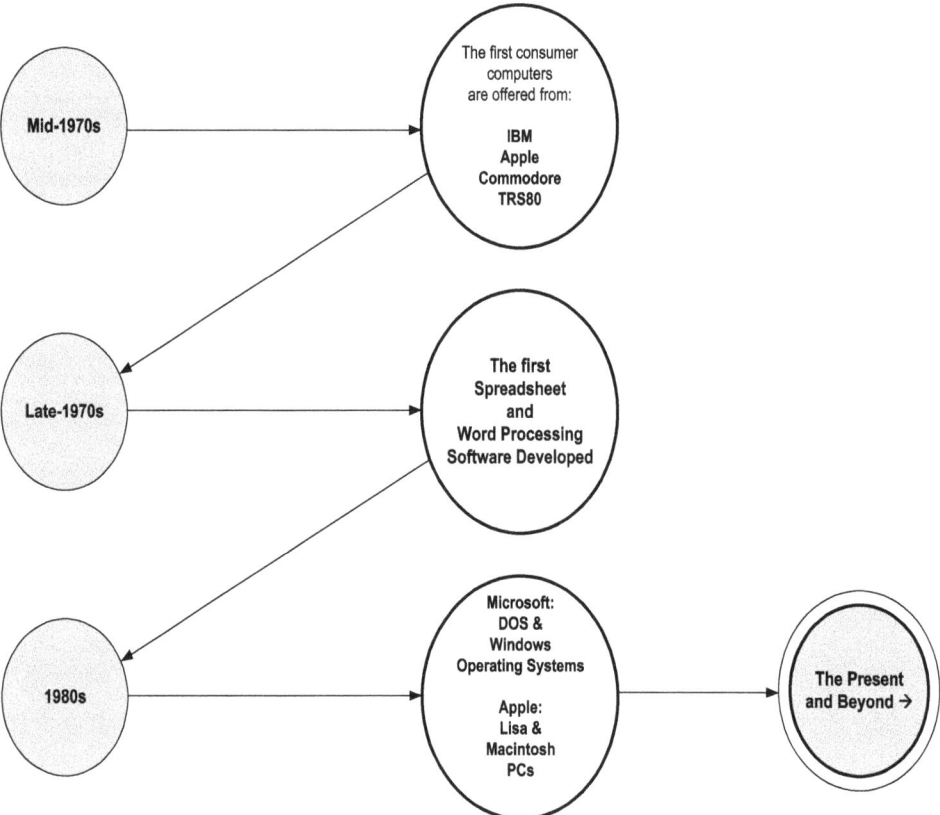

The computer is one of the most important inventions of the 20th century. Some would argue that it was the most important. Never the less, it is unquestionably at the top of the IT innovations list for reasons that are obvious. Without the creation of the PC, there could be no Elysian Fields of Information Technology or concept thereof as we know it.

The Modem

The word "Modem" comes from the words; modulate\demodulate. Digital modems were originally created in order to send North American air defense data, back in the 1950s. They also used public telephone lines as the basic hardware infrastructure for their communications. At that time, telephone networks could only transmit analog signals (frequencies that were within the range of the human voice). Modems are used to transmit and receive data communications back and forth from one computer to another. They convert digital signals that are used by computers, and are comprised of 1's and 0's to analog signals that could then be sent via a public telephone line. If a computer attached to a modem sends a signal by telephone, another modem at the other end of the telephone network can then receive the analog signal and convert it back to the original digital signal so that a computer connected to that modem can process and understand the message data.

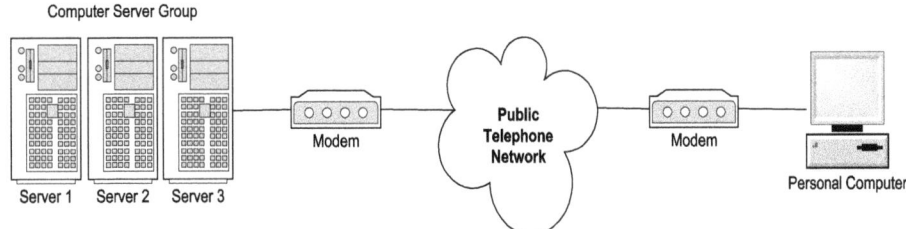

The Bell 103 was the very first commercially released modem in 1962 from AT&T. The device had a speed then of 300 bits per second or 300 bauds. In 1977, Dale Heatherington and Dennis C. Hayes developed the Personal Computer modem. This product changed the computer industry and established the foundations of the current Internet Provider to consumer based, online Internet segment that established hundreds of companies like American Online (AOL) and allowed them to evolve. The computer science term "Hayes-Compatible" refers to any modem that will respond to a pre-determined set of commands that all "Hayes Manufactured" modems also respond to. Hayes originally set the standard for PC modems in their respective industry.

TCP/IP and the Internet

The Transmission Control Protocol (TCP) and the Internet Protocol (IP) were the first networking protocols that were described and implemented as computer standards. The entire networking infrastructure that exists today came from these early discoveries, which ignited a new era in the world of computing back in the 1960s and 1970s. TCP/IP is a set of protocols that are based solely on computer communications. This group is comprised of a

Chapter 8: WELCOME TO THE ELYSIAN FIELDS

stack of sub-protocols that governs the way almost every network in operation today communicates, along with the Internet.

The year 1973 ushered in the development of specialized networking protocols for ARPAnet or DARPA (Defense Advanced Research Projects Agency). This project was commissioned because the communications protocols in use at that time were riddled with problems and restrictions in architecture and scalability with respect to the ARPAnet project requirements. Engineers working on the project understood that the state of the technology they were using would not scale to and or support the future user loads that were expected of the new system. However, at that time there was one primary protocol known as TCP, which was originally an acronym for "Transmission Control Program" as opposed to its current definition "Transmission Control Protocol". TCP was then revised and formally documented in late 1974. The following diagram summarizes the TCP architecture:

TCP/IP Model (High Level):
1. Physical Tier
2. Data Link Tier
3. Networking & Internet Tier
4. Transport Tier
5. Application Tier

301

The following is a high-level timeline summary of the history of the Internet.

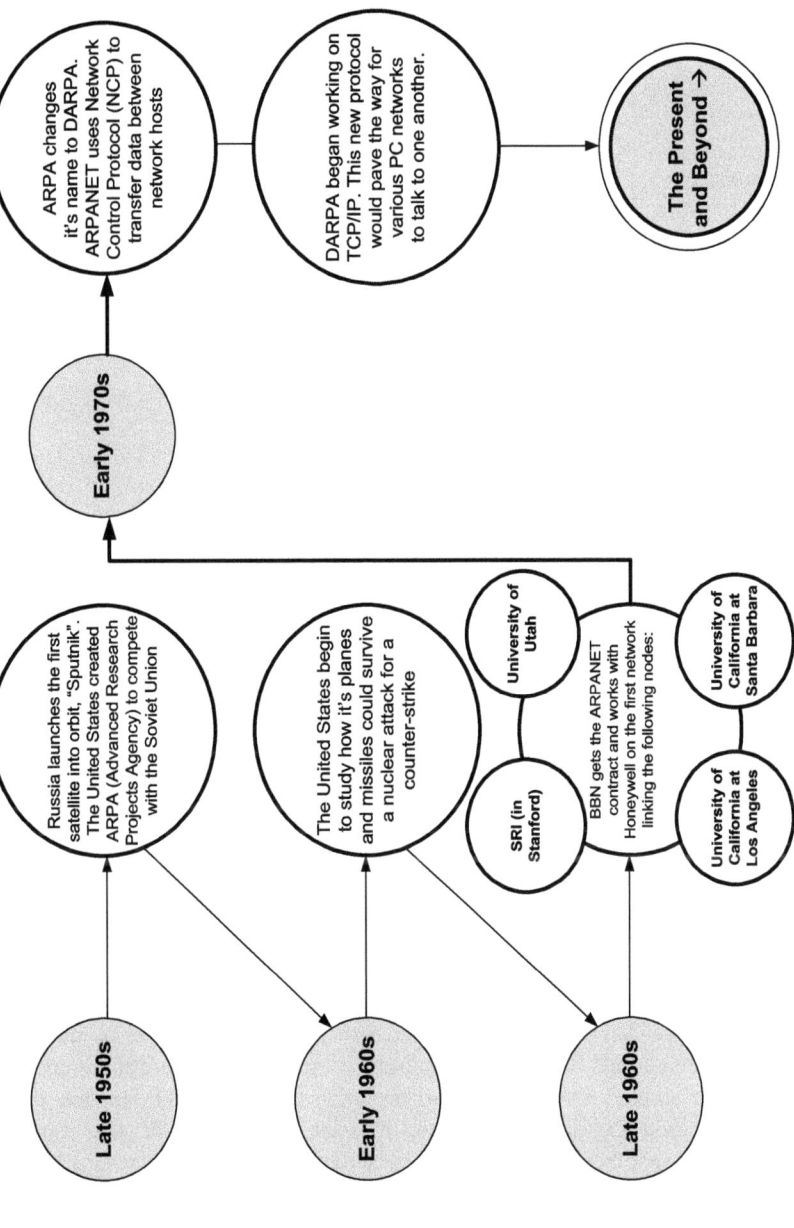

The advent and evolution of the Internet has changed basic human behavior in the industrialized world, and is continuously making the planet a much smaller place. The Internet has grown to be a great "force", much like the ocean, that cannot be controlled by any one person, organization or nation. It has also profoundly affected humankind and binds us in some of the following most critical areas worldwide.

Below are broad and powerful arenas through which the Internet has been integrated into our daily lives:

- Family

- Work

- Education

- Socialization

- Commerce

- Recreation

- Communication

The Internet has become so vital, that if it were to completely disappear tomorrow it would make you wonder how life in modern, industrial nations would continue to thrive without it. The web has grown to become "technology veins" through which the information flows freely from one person and nation to the next, like blood, knowing no borders. Nations such as China and North Korea have attempted to severely restrict the use of the Internet by its citizens but have failed to stop its use entirely. Along with many other countries, both China and North Korea work to exploit the Internet for their own gains (propaganda) while holding back this valuable resource like a dam that stops a mighty river from the people, for fear of civil challenges and uprisings through the freedom of information. This is because the Internet holds the power of information to change people, regions, governments, nations, Earth, and our solar system.

Email

Email has long preceded the Internet and did not become widely used by the public until long after the Internet had become well established. An interesting fact about email is that it was not really a focused invention but an evolution of a computer function that already existed. That method was the ability to send messages to system users that were placed in specific directories that they had access to. For example, this would be like a mother leaving a list of tasks on a refrigerator for a son to do after school, before she came home from work.

"SNDMSG" and "MAILBOX" were two of the earliest email programs ever used. "MAILBOX" was even used at M.I.T. (Massachusetts Institute of Technology) back in 1965. The first messaging applications could only send messages to users of the same computer system. When computer networks became more prevalent, this was an issue as the need quickly arose for users to be able to communicate using this method through their established system networks. That is, users had a requirement that their system networks function much like a post office does whereas you could mail a letter and it could then be delivered almost anywhere that it was addressed to.

In 1972, a contractor form ARPAnet named Ray Tomlinson was the first person to use the "@" symbol on the computer keyboard to identify the sending of a message from one computer system to another. This quickly became a computer standard in regards to sending network messages. Ray Tomlinson was eventually recognized as the inventor of email. ARPAnet would later promote the use of email to users in the military and it caught on. By the mid 1970s, a man named Larry Roberts began using folders to sort and organize his email messages, which then took email to another level. Over the next year, email became increasingly popular as new software packages were then being marketed along with additional tools for managing this phenomenon. Approximately 2/3 of all ARPAnet's messages consisted of email by the late 1970s. Email was seen as a tool that largely legitimized and eventually saved ARPAnet by helping it evolve into what we know today as the Internet.

Below is a high-level email process diagram:

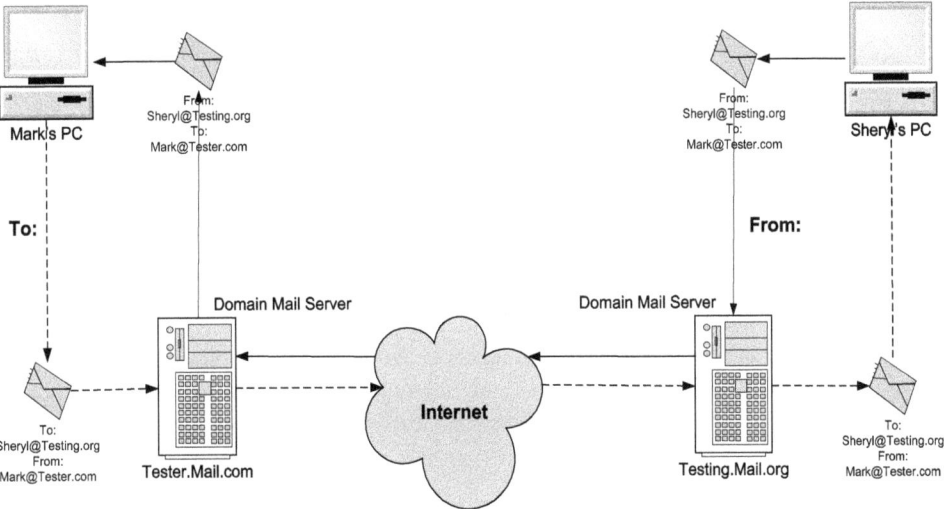

The 1990s saw the explosion of the Internet's popularity in regards to business as well as personal use. During this period, businesses discovered an important niche that they could exploit. In this, companies found that using email they could send content directly to other user's folders (inboxes). It did not take long for sales and marketing departments worldwide to understand how lucrative this new practice could be and start heavily abusing it. Individual email users quickly got tired of receiving and deleting hundreds of unsolicited messages daily from their PCs. This practice became known as "spam" or "spamming". The United States passed the "Controlling the Assault of Non-Solicited Pornography and Marketing Act of 2003" to monitor and begin to reduce this widely annoying and Internet resource consuming problem. Since then, other individual States and countries and have also passed stronger laws to combat the serious problem of email "spam".

Email has also ignited another major concern for computer users in the realm of privacy. This is because:

1. Message headers and related data can reveal the identity of the sender of the message.

2. Messages are processed through a system of computer servers before they reach their destinations. This makes those messages susceptible to hi-jacking and or manipulation by others.

3. Messages are usually not encrypted (secure).

There is software that users can purchase that will encrypt their email messages and provide other vital services that help them send and received more secure email. This is especially important because many email messages can be considered "Legal" documents. In 2000, the President of the United States at that time, William Jefferson Clinton, signed the "Electronic Signatures in Global and National Commerce". This legislation outlined, and set into motion a law governing the use of electronic signatures in contractual documents and other types of legal agreements. This made it possible for companies to send and receive signed copies of documents via email and store them in an electronic format. Most of the everyday business document transactions are handled this way, and would normally be lawful under the rules set forth in the "Electronic Signatures in Global and National Commerce Act". The huge impact of this law was that 2 or more parties no longer needed to meet in person or send "snail mail" (regular paper mail sent through a traditional post office) to get physical signatures for many types of legal documents. People could now click a link, a button, a check box or perform some other quick and minor function that would easily provide digital signature verification over the Internet. This new method changed the business practices of organizations all over the world. Using this process, documents could now even be "notarized" in this manner as well.

In 1977, the United States Post Office realized the seriousness of the future potential loss of revenue due to email, and started testing a new type of email service they called E-COM. The E-COM experiment lost money and was deemed a failure. This was due in part by the fact that this test was opposed by both the FCC (Federal Communications Commission) and the

United States Postal Commission. Using E-COM, email would be sent to the United States Post Office first, instead of directly to the intended recipient. At that point, the US Post Office would print a hard copy of the message and then deliver it to it final destination. An initial rule with E-COM was that customers had to send a bulk minimum of 200 messages to qualify for use of this service. It is no wonder why this particular experiment did not work at that time.

Email stands today as one of the greatest Elysian Fields projects since the invention of the computer itself. It has changed business practices, international laws, how we view privacy, and communicate with each other. If a person has a computer, they most likely have either one or more email accounts that they use to send and receive messages daily.

Physics of the Elysian Fields

Of all of the academic disciplines, Physics is by far the oldest by virtue of its earliest sub-section, which is astronomy. As a deep and well-studied "tree", Physics has many branches such as Biology, Chemistry and Mathematics to name a few. The evolution of Physics in the 20th century has evolved into technology with revolutionary consequences that included the study of "electromagnetism". An electromagnetic field puts force on particles that have an electric charge, and is then affected by the movement of those particles. The further development of this science has lead to the inventions of important electronic devices on which entire industries were created. Such technological developments included:

- The Television
- The Refrigerator
- The Microwave Oven
- The Personal Computer (PC)

It is important to note that the details of IT physics (which includes the science of electronics and computer hardware composition) is a vast and complicated subject, and will not be defined or discussed here. IT Physics in depth, is beyond the scope of this chapter and book. For more information on IT Physics, see the "reference" section of this book.

If you are currently working to reach the realm of the Elysian Fields of Information Technology, then it is beneficial to understand something of the physics of this vast and unique environment. The following encompasses and summarizes the physics of the IT Elysian Fields as it relates to this kind of perpetual project type and has been discussed throughout our conversations thus far:

1. **People** – The Elysian Fields is composed of this matter. It is also encompasses the tools used by people to perform their tasks.

Chapter 8: WELCOME TO THE ELYSIAN FIELDS

2. **Innovation** – This is the motion of the Elysian Fields. Motion is comprised of constant changes within an object. Innovation starts in the mind as a new idea or concept that is then taken to action.

3. **Environment** – This is the surrounding area and conditions in which the Elysian Fields exists in its totality

4. **Time** – This is the operational process of measurement by selected units. Specific and fundamental Elysian Fields units include but are not limited to:

    o The total number of business requirements

    o The total number of people assigned to defined project related tasks

    o The technical tools selected to perform project related tasks

    o The environment in which project tasks are performed

    o The methodology used to establish project processes

    o Other intangible unit variables affect time such as;

    - **Vacation time off**
    - **Sick time off**
    - **Personal time off**
    - **Someone else's Death**
    - **Your own Death**

The following is a high level Elysian Fields Physics Model:

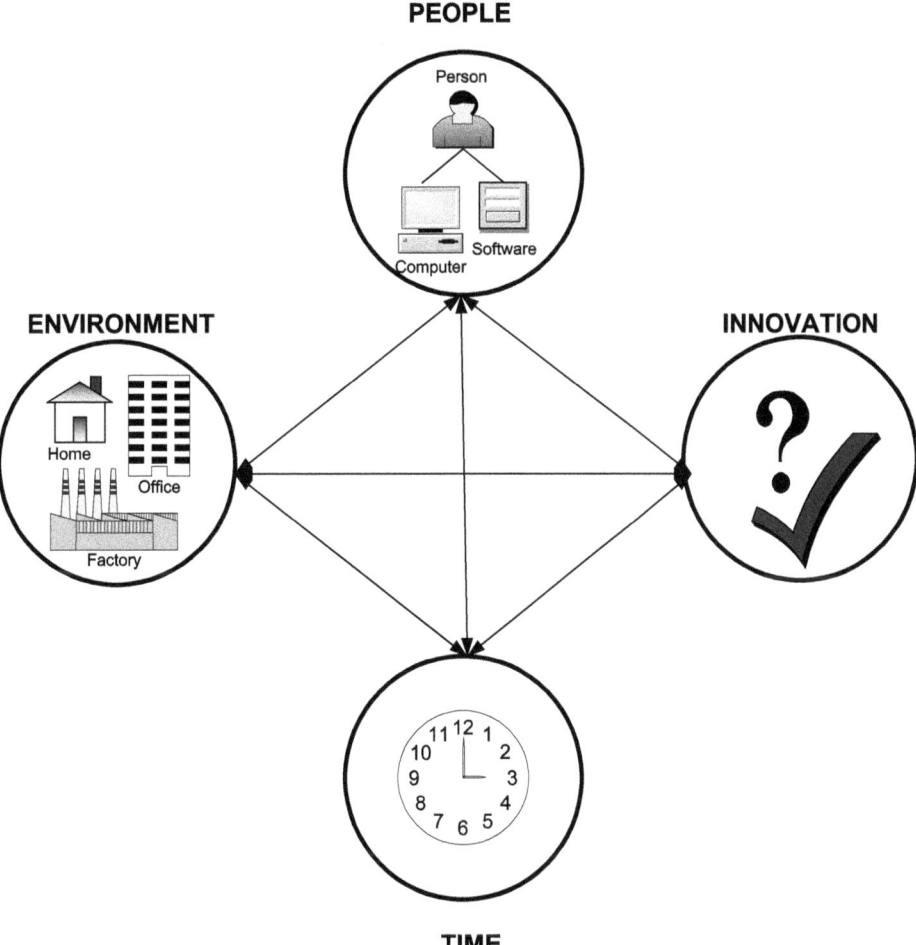

Elysian Fields Physics relates to a particular area of physics called "Experimental Research". The category of Experimental Research is comprised of two main processes:

1. **Controlled Experiments** – This type of experiment is where scientific research is conducted in an environment where the researchers can limit the affects of outside influences.

2. **Natural Experiments** - This type of experiment is where scientific research is conducted in an environment where it is impossible for the researchers to limit the affects of outside influences.

Most Elysian Fields technical innovation theories are carefully controlled experiments due to the sensitive nature of the current technology that may already be in production and is generating well-needed company revenue. These particular experiments must be "physically" isolated from all other company computer networks as an added layer of protection against adversely affecting the process flows and many rhythms of the business. However, as a rule, Natural Experiments are performed in IT when it is necessary to gather and analyze data from existing production computer systems. This is critical in order to monitor the health and status of production networks as well as to discover security issues that must be addressed. This is also the same methods used by criminals who seek to subvert many business software systems. "Hackers" are those groups and or individuals who seek to gain unauthorized access to a computer networks for their own purposes. Most "Hackers" means of discovering computer system vulnerabilities is often through Natural Experiments. This is because many Hackers do not already posses some level of authorized access to the network system they are actively working to compromise.

Experimental Research in Information Technology equates to Research and Development (R&D), which is a corner stone of the Elysian Fields. Without R&D, innovation is next to impossible if it were to not happen by accident. R&D spirals IT forward and is the difference in IT projects that are merely successful and those that go beyond this milestones and make it to the Elysian Fields. IT Physics are always at play in an ongoing Elysian Fields project along with plenty of positive and negative forces that are constantly at odds with each other and drive change.

Laws of IT Physics

Just like the rest of Information Technology, the Elysian Fields of this idiom have its "Physics laws", and they are the same rules of physics that apply to everything else we know of. With this in mind, let's examine what some of the basic high-level laws of Physics are, and how they might apply to IT projects from a theoretical and a realistic standpoint. It never ceases to amaze me as to how some IT project managers operate while working to achieve their objectives. Many honestly believe that they can lose employees, double the work load on specific areas of a project, restrict over-time and still not change the over-all project time lines and due dates. I have seen this behavior on IT projects repeatedly. The lack of understanding of the three basic laws of physics and how they apply to IT projects is one of the major reasons why projects fail. In general, the laws of physics relate to IT projects in three main categories, which I call the "**RRT Factor**".

The "RRT Factor" consists of:

- **Resources**

- **Revenue**

- **Time**

In Physics, there are three laws of motion that were discovered by Sir Isaac Newton. Newton is widely viewed as the "Greatest Physicist" largely due to his scientific method inquisition along with his ability to breakdown, and explain his theory of the basic three laws from Aristotle's original presentation of the universe. This was later referred to and remained, "Newton's Three Laws of Motion". Below are those laws:

1. **Every object in a state of uniform motion tends to remain in that state of motion unless an external force is applied to it.**

2. **The relationship between an object's mass (m) and its acceleration (a), and its applied force (F) is $F = ma$. Acceleration and force are defined as vectors. The direction of the vector is the same as the acceleration vector.**

3. **For every action there is an equal and opposite reaction.**

In almost every way you manage an IT project, the "RRT Factor" will be subject to "Newton's Three Laws of Motion". For instance, if an IT project that has fallen off course due to poor software requirements gathering, then the project will continue to move in the wrong direction until those issues are corrected. It does not matter how many new resources are added or how much money is spent on the analysis of what the problem might be. The project's trajectory will remain off course until the correct requirements for the task are obtained, analyzed, and implemented. If a critical person resigns, or is fired from a project, that person must be replaced. If the missing resource is not replaced, then the other existing and qualified members of the project must work overtime to compensate for the lack of that resource. The bottom line is that errors must actually be corrected, not covered up.

While working as a Senior Software Engineer, I was once given a task by my project Team Lead while I was working on a complex correspondence software system for a State Agency. The task was to hand over the software system to another engineer who did not have the overall skill set to support the computer system that I had written. Along with this, I was also to complete several detailed changes to the application, which were requested by project management and the business users. Lastly, the new engineer who I was to teach the system to, was to do the work while two business users waited for us to finish so that they could input much needed data into the correspondence computer system. Naturally, when the scope of this overall request was analyzed, it actually consisted of many sub-tasks that were quite extensive and time consuming. Those sub-tasks included:

1. Teaching the supporting software engineer about the specific technology that was used to build the application

2. Teaching the supporting software engineer the new software system itself

3. Explaining and showing the supporting software engineer how to implement the detailed system changes requested by management and the business

4. Teaching the supporting software engineer how to deploy the software system in question

5. Deploying the software system so that the business users can input the data needed so others on the project could complete their tasks

After explaining to my Team Lead that based on the learning curve of the supporting software engineer (which was very subjective) and all of the work involved, that the accurate time estimate would be difficult, that person became upset with me. Based on the team lead's view of the work, tasks 1 through 5 in the list were only one simple task, and I should be able to give an accurate estimate for the changes on the spot without any additional analytics. Not knowing how quickly the resource could learn and understand the new correspondence application, and implement the complicated updates requested, the entire project timeline could not be accurately adjusted until the work was completed. This is because a number of other critical project tasks could not be performed until the correspondence system was deployed and the business user's data was input into the system. The team lead, which reportedly had a degree in physics, did not appear to understand the basic "cause and effect" rules in regards to their request. When "Newton's Three Laws of Motion" in IT are ignored, the team suffers as a result because whenever you change any elements of the "RRT Factor" (resources, revenue, or time) you must compensate accordingly or take the project off course.

Elysian Field Requirements

IT Projects that qualify for Elysian Fields status are endeavors that have a basic theme in common. They all work to "Pay It Forward". This means that greedy, selfish, and egotistical personalities will generally not find satisfaction in these kinds of environments. This is not to say that there is not always a great deal of revenue to be made, and glory to be had in regards to Elysian Fields projects, but this is not their sole purpose. These types of projects have started entire industries such as the personal computer revolution and the Internet.

In order for a project to become recognized as such in an Elysian Fields category, it must meet the most, if not all the following criteria:

1. *The project's objectives must be able to communicated clearly, and simply at all stages. A nonprofessional should always be able to describe the project's purpose, in three sentences or less, to anyone who asks what that purpose is.*

2. *The project's results must enhance the quality of life of its target audience (and beyond) by starting or supporting a chain of positive and powerful events that invokes change and enables this group to advance:*

      a. *Intelligently*

      b. *Technologically (Scientifically)*

      c. *Physically*

      d. *Safely*

3. *An Elysian Field project's return on investment cannot and must never be based totally on revenue. This is because due to the very nature of this type of perpetual project, the overall profit margins can never fully be realized or accurately calculated because they are never contained.*

4. *An Elysian Fields project's results will not solely benefit any single individual, business or organization. Its fruits are far reaching beyond the borders of the entity the originally started it.*

The bottom line is that an Elysian Fields project's purpose is for the overall betterment of humankind and or the environment.

Shapes of the Elysian Fields

The shape of the Elysian Fields warps around the entire planet and encompasses all life. They are the type of projects that specifically work to change everyday life for the better using IT. Some might call that statement idealistic, but in effect, it is completely practical. A resounding theme throughout this book has had to do with the value of technology. With this, what is the true value of our technology if it only serves to entertain us and not advance our society and quality of life. It is the simplest and basic use of technology along with research and development of the same that allows cultures to grow and discover new and vital inventions.

When I talk about the shape of things to come regarding the Elysian Fields, I am referring to the polymorphism effect that projects of this sort can have on everything and all of us. There are immediate global needs that Elysian Fields projects can shape for the better. Some of these requirements include but are not limited to:

1. Agriculture
2. Clean Water
3. Clean Air
4. Healthcare
5. Alternative Energy
6. The Environment

Chapter 8: WELCOME TO THE ELYSIAN FIELDS

If technology is used effectively, consistently, and intelligently, these vital industries can make a difference for the better and produce increased value to everyone moving forward. If technology cannot be shaped to meet its requirements, it is worthless. I have come to view Elysian Fields projects in the following shapes:

- **Circle** = IT Elysian Fields Projects that focus on the Planet Earth

- **Square** = IT Elysian Fields Projects that focus on Social Issues

- **Triangle** = IT Elysian Fields Projects that focus on both Planet Earth and Social Issues

Below is a diagram that illustrates this view in more detail:

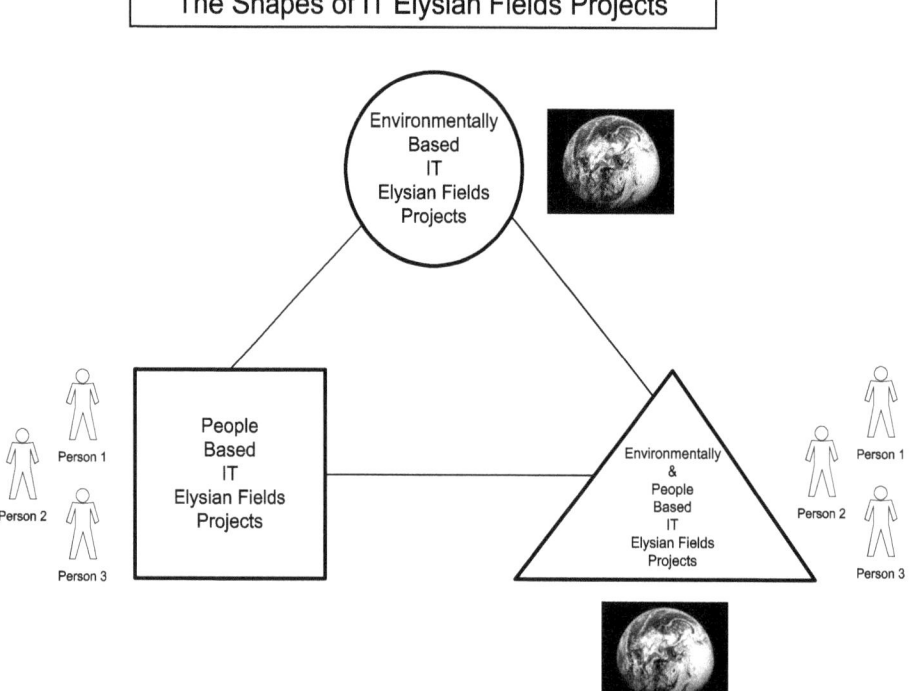

I occasionally still meet people who do not believe that the increased level of global warming is a "man made" phenomenon. This remains so even after more than 90% of all scientists worldwide agree that accelerated global warming is indeed "man made" and have irrefutable proof that humans are the cause. The fact alone that scientists all over the world can agree on any one thing is in itself, truly awe inspiring and must not be ignored. Whenever a group like the "global scientific community", who are usually at odds with each other, can come together and agree on evidence that supports a common and basic result, then everyone should take note. Recently, I worked on a project where a software engineer said loudly, and proudly the following; "I think global warming is a natural occurrence and has nothing or very little to do with man." While everyone is entitled to their own opinions, their view says a lot about their frame of mind and who they are. For instance, global warming has happened to our planet before, after the "Ice Age" for example. However, since then we have had an event occur that has never happened previously in Earth's history. That event was the Industrial Revolution, which began in the late 1800s in Great Britain and forever changed:

- Transportation
- Agriculture
- Manufacturing
- Social Cultures
- Economics

From the advent of the first and second industrial revolutions until the present day, the effect of this phenomenon has quickly changed the course of the world. The western hemisphere was converted from largely rural and farming communities to urban and industrialized cultures. Along with all of the technological, financial, and production advancements, there came many problems and issues that plague humanity to this very day. Almost every industrialized nation now faces the massive challenges of water, air, and land pollution. These new and dangerous hazards grew exponentially, and would come to shape a new era of environmental threats that were more catastrophic than anyone thought previously. It would only serve to add significant overhead to any reoccurring natural global warming phenomenon and make that cycle far worse than it was before the advent of the Industrial Revolution. This is a fact that many global warming doubters continue to ignore.

Reuniting Church and State

During the 1990s and 2000s, the United States alone has lost millions of jobs to foreign companies that will most likely never return due to NAFTA (North American Free Trade Agreement). This has had a drastic and negative effect on not only the American economy but also the revenue dynamics of the rest of the world. As a result, many "white collar" and "blue collar" Americans were forced to seek new careers making much less money and or working in different industries. America, along with the rest of the world desperately needs a new Industry for strong economic and environmental reasons. History has shown us that the heart of innovation and cultural advancement is necessity, education, along with research and development that leads to new technologies. What has become a growing trend is America is the process of the separation of education and new technologies. Graduating college students find it increasingly difficult to attain technical jobs because their training has not adequately prepared them for their industry or their responsibilities in the technical realm. In the 1950s, approximately 40% of all students graduating college in the United States had some type of engineering degree. By the late 2000s, that number had fallen to around 10% of American college graduates. How can a country continue to make successful innovations if the number of engineers it produces is constantly shrinking? The answer is obvious, it cannot.

There comes a point in the event timeline of a capitalistic society where new technology and innovation slowly becomes the enemy of "big and greedy businesses". For example, alternative energy solutions such as solar, wind, and hydroelectric energy are not a threat to enterprise oils companies as long as the businesses that offer these services stay small, and under some manner of control. The controlling force is usually deeply rooted in politics and multi-billion dollar corporations contribute large donations to politicians, and continuously lobby them to directly influence the legislative decision making process to insure that the laws passed favor their interests. For decades, oil companies and automotive manufactures have both blocked the advancement of the electric car and other alternative energy resources for one primary reason above all else. They feared that these innovations would negatively affect their economic bottom line. For instance, big automobile manufacturers would stand to lose billions in service, parts, and repairs on their vehicles if they were electric because those cars generally do not require nearly as much maintenance as gasoline engine vehicles. With this, it is obvious why oil companies would not want to see an electric car become wildly successful because gasoline prices would drop alarmingly. With this, would accompany a huge reduction in the dependence on foreign oil, which would significantly, and ultimately, lower their industry to but a fraction of its wealth, power, and political influence.

In the Elysian Fields, one basic rule holds true on far too many occasions and that being:

"Politics is a Natural and Major Adversary of Technology"

There is an exception to almost every rule and this one is no different. The exception in this case being that the politics involved with the technology in question truly favors the requirements of the individual or group for which it is intended and more. So in reality, that would mean that little to no politics were involved in the solution process for which the technology is being implemented. In an Elysian Fields project this is almost unheard of because there will usually be an individual or group involved that is interested in greed above helping to advance the quality of life for the human race. This greed encompasses money, power, and a significant increase in the measure of control, and influence.

The Elysian Fields:
The Separation of Church and State

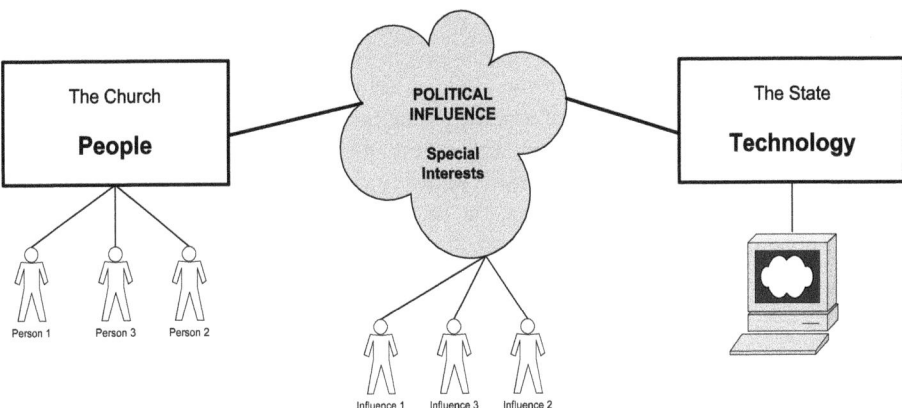

Historically, special interests groups have continuously blocked technological growth for their own gains. Removal of the political blob and or special interest groups must happen first, in order for real change to take root technologically. In effect, the special interest must be rendered ineffective or properly represented by the people in order for technology to have value and be effective in the Elysian Fields. This means that the good of the people must become the new "special interest" above the good of the corporation. If both scenarios can happen simultaneously, that can be a very good thing as long as it can be managed and balanced effectively over the long-term. Historically, this has not been the norm.

The Elysian Fields:
The Marriage of Church and State

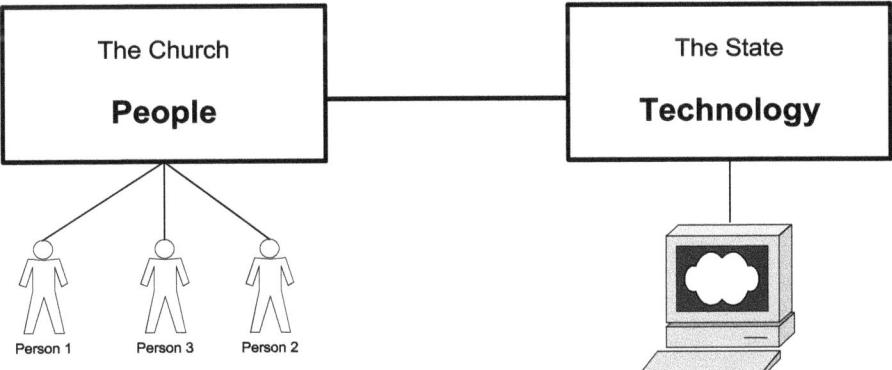

Chapter 8: WELCOME TO THE ELYSIAN FIELDS

The marriage of church and state happens in the Elysian Fields when the elements of political influence, along with the potential for profit by big business is removed from, or properly controlled within the equation. This can be achieved by several methods, of which some of the more notable are listed below:

1. The ability for technology to be made available (for free whenever possible) to all who want and or need it. For example, some cities offer wireless internet connections to all of its citizens and visitors. This is good use of tax dollars because it adds value to the city and provides its patrons access to global information much like a public library does. In addition, there are non-profit organizations that have provided human powered laptop computers to elementary schools in third world countries. This begins to raise the level of education for children who would not otherwise have access to technology in order to better their learning experiences and cultures.

2. The ability for certain vital technologies to become and remain "open-source" and free to everyone. For example, the technical ability for every country to be able to produce clean renewable energy is in everyone's best interest. It would be good for the environment, create jobs, and dramatically improve the quality of life for everyone on the planet.

3. The ability for anyone who wants an education to be able to get one at no charge. It is easier for special interest groups and large corporations to manipulate and take advantage of a society if the majority of the people in that culture are kept ignorant and denied access to a good education. It is critical that poor people have the ability to receive the same level of education as the rich without prejudice. There are many IT project initiatives currently in place that address the need for free Internet based college educations. Many colleges in the United States offer free college courses, lectures, tutorials, books, and podcasts online. Institutions in the United States that offers these free resources currently include:

    - Brigham Young University
    - Berkley
    - Carnegie Mellon University
    - John Hopkins Bloomberg School of Public Health
    - Michigan State
    - Missouri Southern State University
    - M.I.T.

- o New York University
- o Penn State
- o Princeton
- o University of Michigan
- o University of North Carolina
- o University of Pennsylvania
- o University of Washington
- o Yale

While the majority of the free online courses offered are very intelligent, informative, and effective, many of the colleges that provide these offerings do not yet give credits or degrees for your successful completion of their free classes. In the future, the Institutions listed, along with additional colleges, will begin to offer even more free opportunities to augment or obtain a full and complete education online. Projects like "free-ed.net" (http://www.free-ed.net/free-ed/) offers complete online college courses free of charge to anyone who wants to learn worldwide and have offered their services since 1997. Free-ed.net online college courses include, but are not limited to:

- Healthcare
- Information Technology
- Electronics
- Mathematics
- Science

For example, most religions require some degree of education in order to be understood, garner a following, and solicit faith. Technology is no different in that it can often resemble a type of religion. The religious aspects of technology are very important in that throughout history a society's rise and or fall is largely dependent upon its religion and its technology. In this also lies a culture's faith that its technologies will eventually evolve and make then stronger.

The Technical Evangelist
Not unlike their religious counterparts, Technical Evangelists work to gather faithful followers for the technologies they are promoting. Companies who are making a strong effort to have their technological brand become a standard in their industry usually hire this

interesting breed of IT disciple. However, there are plenty of Technical Evangelists who are not employed by large firms, and they can often be just as effective in their own endeavors. For instance, there is a large movement that works to promote "open source" technologies, which support a break from the product brands of the billion dollar enterprise software companies. Traditional software companies currently control more than 90% of all of the software the world uses.

The Technical Evangelist is part:

1. Sales Person
2. Business Analyst
3. Technical Analyst
4. Trainer
5. Politician
6. Motivational Speaker

Technical Evangelists use various methods in order to spread their gospel. Some of these practices include:

- Technology Demonstrations
- Lectures
- Product Prototyping
- Books
- Emails
- Blogs
- Video Conferences
- CDs
- DVDs
- Podcasts

A goal of this technology disciple is to build a faithful cult of product users who will spread the word of the brand they are fanatical about in order to create more of the same. Also in some cases, company-based Technical Evangelists are charged with the difficult and often arduous task of changing the way that a company does business. This could mean persuading a company to switch to another technology platform or to even in some cases to stop using a specific technology altogether. This is all for the sake of using technology to work for a company and not against it. This disciple is one of the people responsible for new ideas in IT and better ways of using existing business tools.

Mike Boich was noted as one of the very first Technical Evangelists. He was responsible for spreading the word and gathering a cult following for the early "Macintosh" PC for Apple, Inc., back in the early 1980s. The "Macintosh" was the first commercial PC to offer a GUI (graphical user interface) and a mouse. Before the introduction of the "Macintosh", previous commercial PCs ran their Operating Systems from a command line interface. At the time, Boich had to persuade current and new computer users that the "Macintosh", along with its strange new mouse and cartoon-like GUI, were indeed the wave of the future.

If it does not yet exist, a Technical Evangelists may sometimes be responsible for creating a brand new technology movement. Religion in itself can be inherently complicated, but this IT disciples' task is to keep it simple and effective where and whenever possible.

Below are some methods used for building a good technology religion:

1. **Revenue** – True believers must buy the technology they think is the best solution for its challenges. This will help fund the company that created the product\brand and enable the Technical Evangelist to keep spreading their gospel.

2. **Self-Replication** – This element is a sales and marketing representative's best friend. It is the hope that when people use the technology in question, they will testify openly to the product\brand superiority and that will encourage others to purchase it and do the same. If the belief and movement that the technology is "the next best thing" does not spread rapidly, then it may eventually run out of momentum and die.

3. **Rewards** – This is often used to entice a company into purchasing a particular technology product\brand. For instance, if you purchase and implement a specific pre-packaged, customizable, enterprise-level ERP software system that most Fortune 500 companies use, then more people will respect your business and want to invest in it. In addition, the bottom-line is that you will be able to do more business, which in turn means that you will accumulate additional revenue.

4. **Punishments** – This is the opposite of the reward. This is often used to scare or threaten a group that does not purchase a particular technology product\brand. The premise is that if you do not purchase the technology that your business will not be

able to gain or maintain a competitive edge in your marketplace, and will eventually fail. This can be a very effective strategy if the top industry leaders use the product.

5. **Positive Reinforcement** – This is an important factor to invoke in true technology believers to keep them believing in, and spending money on your ministry. Followers are encouraged religiously to keep up with all updates that are made available from the company for their product\brand. A user that purchases and installs all company recommended updates is a good user, who will also reap the rewards (and pitfalls) of their adopted technology.

6. **Defending the Faith** – The best defense is a good offense. If a non-believing cult attacks the convictions of the technology you promote, it may be because you are doing a good job in spreading your technological gospel. You must be able to constantly prove that the integrity of your ministry is sound. This is accomplished through using the testimony of other followers who have purchased and implemented the product\brand successfully, and have significantly increased their quarterly and or annual revenue as a result.

7. **Faith** – This is the act of having others believe in the technology promoted without having purchased, or even witnessing a demonstration of the product\brand in their own business environments. This is indeed a powerful tool for obvious reasons.

8. **Self Righteousness** – There is nothing more that can feed this element better than technology that works, and has significantly increased the annual revenue of businesses around the world. It is much easier to boast with this kind of record of accomplishment.

Elysian Fields Vision Quest

One thing that all great leaders have in common is a good vision and solid objectives. It does not matter whether their overall goals are positive or negative in this context. The vision and all that it is wrapped in is the key, and how the objectives are manipulated and communicated is what attracts a following along with the support required for its implementation. Every great IT project also has a vision and it is management's job to insure that the alignment of the vision remains true to the business model and what the company needs.

The following is an Elysian Fields Vision Quest Guide. It is designed to show how an Elysian Fields project is to always remain in a state of perpetual motion. This is important to understand because an Elysian Fields project is a large living entity and can sometimes be extremely difficult to understand due to its constant evolution.

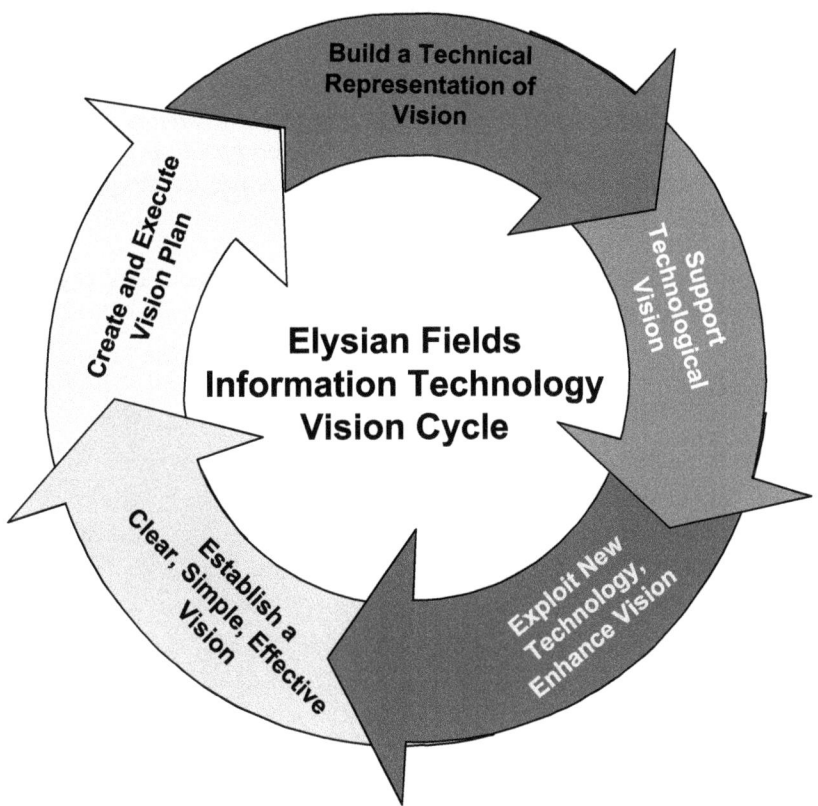

Artificial Intelligence (AI)

When she was 6 years old, my youngest daughter Xena asked me a very interesting question. She asked, "Daddy, are computers alive?" I had to pause and think about that question for a moment. Then I answered firmly, "No, they are not alive." Xena then followed up with another question, "Why not?" Again, I knew I had to try my best to get this one right the first time, because my daughter generally insists on a certain type of logic from me. I then replied very cautiously, "Because you have to tell them exactly what to do from the very beginning, and all the time after that." The room was silent at that point so I continued carefully, "If from the time of their creation, computers could function completely on their own, without help from humans, they might be considered alive by some people". That seemed to be an answer that Xena could accept, so I breathed a sigh of relief, and then quickly shut my mouth.

A Dictionary defines "intelligence" as:

1. *The operation of gathering information about an enemy*
2. *The ability to comprehend; to understand and profit from experience*
3. *A unit responsible for gathering and interpreting information about an enemy*

Artificial Intelligence (AI) is a wide and deep field of study that relates to many different research areas, which include:

- Cognitive Science
- Computer Science
- Facial and Speech Recognition
- Linguistics
- Logic
- Nanotechnology
- Neuroscience
- Philosophy
- Probability
- Psychology
- Robotics

College textbooks generally define AI as the study and design of "intelligent agents". An "Intelligent Agent" is as a combined group of components created to work interactively as one unit that understands its environment and performs tasks that promotes its ability to achieve its goals. John McCarthy defined AI as "the science and engineering of making intelligent machines". McCarthy was a computer scientist who coined the phrase "Artificial

Intelligence" in 1955 in a proposal paper he wrote for the 1956 Dartmouth Conference (an Artificial Intelligence Event). In the introduction of this proposal, McCarthy said:

"We propose that a 2 month, 10 man study of artificial intelligence be carried out during the summer of 1956 at Dartmouth College in Hanover, New Hampshire. The study is to proceed on the basis of the conjecture that every aspect of learning or any other feature of intelligence can in principle be so precisely described that a machine can be made to simulate it. An attempt will be made to find how to make machines use language, form abstractions and concepts, solve kinds of problems now reserved for humans, and improve themselves. We think that a significant advance can be made in one or more of these problems if a carefully selected group of scientists work on it together for a summer".

He also talked about other AI related areas in his proposal that are currently the subject of intense computer science research and development today. These additional subjects included:

- **Neural Networks (Artificial)** – Comprised of related artificial neurons, this is used in research to understand the inner workings of a biological neural networks. It is also used for creating intelligence solutions without the need for an actual biological neural network.

- **Creativity** – The process of discovery that leads to new ideas.

- **The Theory of Computation** – This deals with how best a solution can be derived based on a computational model governed by an algorithm.

- **Abstraction** – This is a process that uses generalizations to categorize and map data in relation to an idea, object, or phenomenon. As a result, only the data that is required is "unearthed" for a specific purpose.

- **Natural Language Processing** – This is the study of the issues regarding automated generation and how natural human languages operate.

McCarthy also invented the "LISP" computer programming language, which is one of the original high-level programming languages and was widely utilized for AI development. LISP means "List Processing Language". Many discoveries in computer science today were derived from LISP, such as:

- **Object Oriented Programming (OOP)** – This is where "noun-based" objects and their relationships are used to architect software systems.

- **Tree Data Structures** – This is the act of mimicking a tree structure using linked nodes. Generally, the structure's edges must not have additional direction, much like a real tree.

- **The Self Hosting Compiler** – The term "self hosting" means that an application is used as part of a sequence of other software applications or is an internal component of a computer operating system. Compilers are also software applications in which the main purpose is to translate one computer language text into a different computer language.

- **Automatic Storage Management** – Garbage Collection (GC) works to recycle computer memory that a software application will not use anymore.

- Dynamic Typing – These are attributes of data that describe the kind of information that will be utilized. For example, basic data types include:

    o Strings (alphanumeric characters)

    o Numbers

    o Dates

Without a doubt, AI is propelling the future of Elysian Fields technology and may govern the creation, management, and maintenance of most advancing technology. The far reaching effects, and repercussions of developing machines in which their intelligence increases exponentially is unknown. Computer automation is often necessary so that humans can be free to perform other tasks and a certain level of intelligence is required so that this can happen. Currently, humans largely control machines but this fact is slowly becoming history, as we work to make computers more intelligent so that we can have our tasks performed faster with fewer errors. However, such a luxury does not come without a price.

The Singularity

Countless science fiction novels, comic books, television shows, and movies chronicle times in the future where machine intelligence parallels, and then evolves far beyond man's ability to understand and or control it. The result of this being that humans fall from the top of the intellectual food chain on this planet (although some argue this has happened a long time ago). Computers then do either one, or all of the following:

1. Enslave mankind

2. View humans as a threat, and systematically exterminates the human race

3. Physically merge with mankind which makes the next evolution of humans a bio-mechanical entity

These types of stories have traditionally been very successful, and have become a mainstay in the science fiction movie and book industries. Most people who consume this type of entertainment view it as "fictional" or something that most likely would not or could not happen in their lifetime. However in many cases, some fiction is far closer to science fact than many people realize.

There is an event known as "The Singularity", which is the invention and continuous evolution of a "greater than human" intelligence. This phenomenon is generally associated with AI, but there are other types of technology that also contributes to "The Singularity". They include:

- Genetically Engineered Humans

- Interfaces that link the human brain to computers

- A computer's ability to mimic human brain activity using actual brain scans

For humanity, when The Singularity eventually happens, it will be something new that has never occurred previously in the history of humankind. This event will herald first, a new type of mind that can think as fast as humans do, and then surpass that level of speed and discovery. As a rule, the processing speed of the fastest computers has doubled every two years and this is with humans designing and enhancing these systems. With the current speed of computer processors, and bi-annual increases coupled with the how fast the human brain can process data, we could see the power of a computer equal that of a human brain easily by the year 2025. What happens after this event if we then hand over the ability to computers to enhance themselves? How quickly will a computer's processing power increase after that happens? The Singularity is not only about how fast a computer can process data, but relates directly to a new and or "better than human" intelligence that encompasses a more efficient and effective way of thinking that is more powerful than traditional human thought processing. In effect, we are describing a truly "superior mind" that is beyond anything humankind has ever produced. We have no idea of how this new entity with think, react, or communicate. In fact, we know nothing about anything after "The Singularity" actually happens and then evolves through its own processes, but we do know that unless that world's computer technology suddenly comes to a complete halt, this phenomenon will definitely occur at some point eventually.

It is important to understand that all technology is the product of human experience and growth, which embodies our intelligence. However, what does an intelligence that is smarter than all of the minds we have seen historically look like? This mind could invent a new category in which its core data, processing, and cognitive threshold are better, stronger, and faster than the human brain. The new mind could continuously evolve as it would have the capacity to improve itself on every tier based on its own intelligence instead of depending on a man or woman for its next stage of evolution. This action would be extraordinary, as humans are incapable of doing this. We cannot change our own genetic composition to instantly give us the new abilities that we require or desire for any given situation. For instance, what if we need to be able to see 100 miles further than we are able to today, naturally? We cannot make those physiological changes to our bodies instantaneously; we would need the help of a device or machine (binoculars or a telescope) to accomplish this. However, a "smarter than human" mind from the future might be able to make the changes to its own programming to compensate for its deficiencies and fulfill its requirements immediately. This could then be the best entity for designing and creating the next version of itself and so on, which would be the dawn of new generations of superior intelligence on Earth.

A popular myth is that humankind only uses only 10% of our brain's total capacity. This is in direct contradiction with current neuroscience, which clearly shows otherwise. It is important to note that the human brain is indeed limited. It has been estimated that our minds contain approximately 100 billion neurons and 100 trillion synapses, which totally dwarfs the processing power that computers are able to generate currently. Additionally, as humans get older we gradually lose the precious neurons that help us to process our data. These limits do not exist for a superior mind in the age of "The Singularity", it would just continue to learn and evolve and get smarter and more cognitive with age and would never degrade. Furthermore, this new intelligence might be able to learn to "spawn", that is, it could be able to create newer and better versions of itself without the limitations inherently common with human design characteristics.

People are historically bad at envisioning, planning, developing, and implementing software applications. This challenge was discussed in many of the previous chapters of this book and is one of the reasons why I wrote this resource. I am not alone in my frustrations with the SDLC and all of the human factors that it falls prey to. A computer will always know itself far better than a human could if it had the ability to reason and make its own decisions. Therefore and naturally, it would be the best possible resource for writing software applications for itself. In this process, all the flaws of human-based software development would be removed which would significantly increase the speed associated with developing software. A computer of superior human intelligence would not be subject to traditional human software design flaws that lead to many of the errors we deal with in the existing applications we use daily. The computer system would not be subject to a limited intelligence, people politics, fatigue, or physical emotions. It would be free to create new and more enhanced revisions of itself without the interference of people for the first time in human history.

When and if this finally happens, "The Singularity" will truly be a new and unique event in human history and it will happen in our lifetime. Never before in history has humanity created a form of intelligence that has surpassed our own. "The Singularity" will be the dawn of a new age of which we can only speculate as to the repercussions, which could be infinite. As humans, it is our duty and responsibility to develop and insure that this new and intellectually superior entity evolves with core values that are in the best interest of humanity (whatever those may be) in order to insure our own survival. Asking a greater than human intelligence to perform tasks like; processing credit card payments or to manage orders for the video of the month club may be considered completely absurd. Basic and far less intelligent IT software systems can already do these things. More import challenges must be addressed like:

- Curing the world's deadly diseases

- Solving World Hunger

- Discovering new alternative and clean energy sources

- Advanced Space Travel

It is wise to understand that "The Singularity" is coming if our technology advances continue to progress on its present course. There are scores of computer scientists working very hard around the clock to insure that this amazing and new dawn approaches. This will lead to a new era in which the affects will not be felt immediately. It is only after "The Singularity" has been first established, and is able to first mature will its power and effectiveness began to change humankind. This process could take years after the genesis of "The Singularity". Make no mistake, this event may presently be science fiction, but it will soon be science fact. What will you do when it does? Will you be ready to see the world change forever?

Point of no Return

The world is at a crossroads in its technology. Never before in our history has humankind grown so fast in knowledge and experiences in such little time. The true evolution of human beings is a complex puzzle that is comprised of thousands of pieces of ancient fossils. Humans are the only mammal to migrate and populate massive geographical regions, and evolve to develop dramatically new types of behavior all within a span of approximately 2 million years.

The rapid advancements of the human race are summarized in the table that follows:

Time Frame	Event Result
4 Million Years Ago	Ardipithecus (oldest and most ape-like hominid discovered) which was a primate ancestor to paranthropines (bipedal apes with very big molars), australopithicines (erect-walking, ape members of the hominid family), and humans, become extinct on the African continent and brain volumes began to quickly grow in advancing generations of the hominid branch of

Chapter 8: WELCOME TO THE ELYSIAN FIELDS

Time Frame	Event Result
	the evolutionary tree
500,000 Years Ago	The divergence of the Neanderthal (subspecies of humans) and Human genetic lines
50,000 Years Ago	Homo sapiens sapien (tool-making, bipedal primate) emerge
10,000 Years Ago	Civilizations are created
1440s	German inventor Johannes Gutenberg, creates first the Printing Press which forever changed writing and literature
1900s	German aircraft construction engineer Konrad Zuse, is unofficially recognized as the inventor of the modern computer
2000s	"The Singularity", the dawn of greater than human intelligence

All good (and bad) things must come to an end. The Elysian Fields, in essence, is about using technology in the most effective and efficient means possible to achieve a positive result. It is also the art and science of not using technology in the most effective and efficient means possible to achieve a positive result. Sometimes people are the technology, and wisdom, experience, along with trust are keys in figuring this out. Will "The Singularity" and AI ultimately mean the end of human evolution and the advancement of an artificially created superior intelligence? Do we have the time and wisdom to properly use advancing technology in conjunction with disparate human morality to save our planet's environment, along with ourselves, and improve the quality of life for us, and our future generations? The answer to this question is a simple one. We must do it! If our technology cannot help us achieve this task then it is of no use whatsoever. If we as a people do not succeed in utilizing our resources, intelligence, and experiences to analyze and correct our most serious problems, then we will fail ourselves, and eventually become extinct more quickly than we can anticipate. Again, we are at a crossroads in the history of human evolution and we must act in a strong and positive manner now, as the historic and rapid results of our technological advancements have left us a high price to pay and many issues that must be resolved. This fee cannot be settled through invoking a time-based line of credit as previous generations have already done before us. Those folks left you and me with the bill for the cost of living this enhanced technological life we enjoy today. The time is up on the loan and the payment is now due in full. Either we work together unselfishly to begin fixing the world issues associated with rapid advances in the human and technological intelligence evolution now, or those very same things will eventually work to destroy us all in one way or another. This may sound "fictional" or "unrealistic", but it is the truth as we are now at a point of no return for the first time in human history in how we must deal with the repercussions of our unmanaged progress.

The Greatest Elysian Fields Projects

As previously discussed, we have reached a point in human history where worldwide population growth along with exploding technological progress has placed our future in jeopardy. The technological tools and platforms that were used in the evolution of humanity to its present state demands responsibility, and dividends, which have not yet been paid. With this, we must use technology as best we can from this point forward in order to analyze, plan, and correct the errors, failures, and shortsightedness of the past. In this behavior pattern, we can then begin to think through what is needed from our technology in the future, and better anticipate the consequences of coming advancements.

The wealthiest individuals on the planet must constantly ask themselves as a group, what good is having billions of dollars if you must someday live in isolation because the planet's air is not breathable and its water supply is polluted? What good is an uninhabitable planet and how could it possibly be of value? For the poor (the vast majority), it is important to pay attention to not only what are leaders are saying, but to what they are actually doing in regards to the planned use of technology to help solve the many challenges that gravely threaten the future of us all. Leaders who understand the course of technology should see that it must start with the human brain, and that the ability to think through issues first is the most powerful tool that we have. From this, we can then invest in the appropriate research and development strategies in order to begin to solve our greater challenges.

Today, the greatest Elysian Fields Projects include some of the same issues that have been around for decades along with some relatively new ones. These include but are not limited to:

1. **Healthcare** – People worldwide must have affordable, reliable, available, and ongoing access to medical support in emergencies and for regularly scheduled checkups.

2. **The Environment** – Many of the plant and animal species that we need for food in order to survive are slowing becoming extinct. We must also be able to create and maintain clean air, land, and water consistently and affordably. This has to become a new and viable world industry that can never die or the human race surely will.

Chapter 8: WELCOME TO THE ELYSIAN FIELDS

3. **Alternative Energy** – Industrialized nations are quickly reaching the peak of oil production worldwide while the demand for fuel will continue to rapidly grow beyond the supply. We have created an ever-growing demand on a shrinking market. This is the prelude to crisis. We must find new ways of harnessing the natural resources of the planet to safely and effectively power our societies.

4. **World Hunger** – Approximately every 4 seconds someone dies of hunger on this planet. Almost 1 billion people worldwide are hungry and suffer malnutrition.

5. **World Economy** – The financial structure of the global economy is in a delicate state largely due to the world dependency on oil. If the world economic framework were to collapse, it could plunge the modern world back into another "Great Depression".

The following is a diagram of depicting the relationships of these five major challenges from an Elysian Fields perspective:

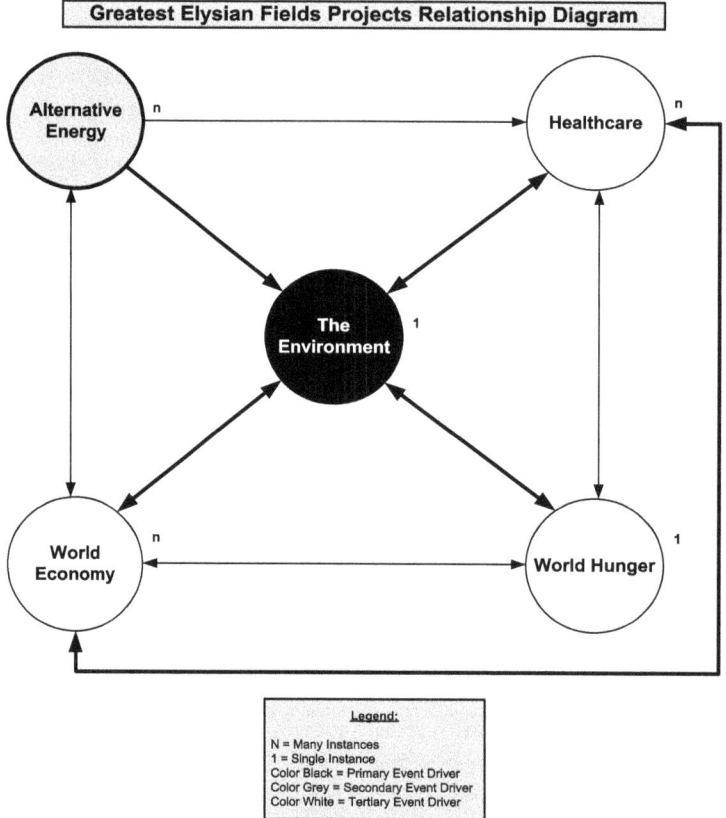

Within the Greatest Elysian Fields Projects Relationship Diagram, "The Environment" is the primary driver in relation to all of the other objects. It is simple to see from this perspective how the entire structure of the diagram would collapse without the presence of "The Environment" object to stabilize it. Secondly, the "Alternative Energy" object serves as a source of growth and stability for the environment, world economy, and healthcare, all of which directly affect world hunger.

The one-to-many and many-to-many relationships in the Greatest Elysian Fields Project Diagram are of significant importance. For instance, globally, there are many natural environments that affect the health and welfare of the planet which include the rainforests, deserts, jungles, oceans, and the Antarctic to name a few. However, the degree of air and land pollution that we have produced to date has had a devastating impact on the overall ecosystems of the planet. Since nature is so intertwined, the loss or degradation of one part of the environment can and will often have dire or unexpected consequences on various other dependent regions in nature. For example, one event can start a negative chain reaction that could ultimately lead to the extinction of one or more plant, insect, and or animal species that human beings count on for survival. World Hunger is also depicted as a single entity that covers massive worldwide related sub-issues that all lead to a common result. The "Alternative Energy" object represents various types of existing, new, and yet to be discovered forms of alternative-based energy solutions. The "World Economy" and "Healthcare" objects also serve the same purpose in that their sub-issues all bubble up to shared results, whatever they may be.

In the diagram:

1. **The Black Object** - Serves as a primary object from which all other objects are related and cannot exist without. In one way or another, all other projects are positively or negatively affected by the black object's status.

2. **The Grey Object** - Represents innovation and the power of positive change that in turn helps to push its relationships towards a healthier future.

3. **The White Objects** - Are tertiary and react according to results produced by the black and grey objects.

The following is the "Greatest Elysian Fields Projects Solutions Relationship Diagram". In this view, the Information Technology is focused primarily on Alternative Energy and Healthcare via a many-to-many relationship.

Chapter 8: WELCOME TO THE ELYSIAN FIELDS

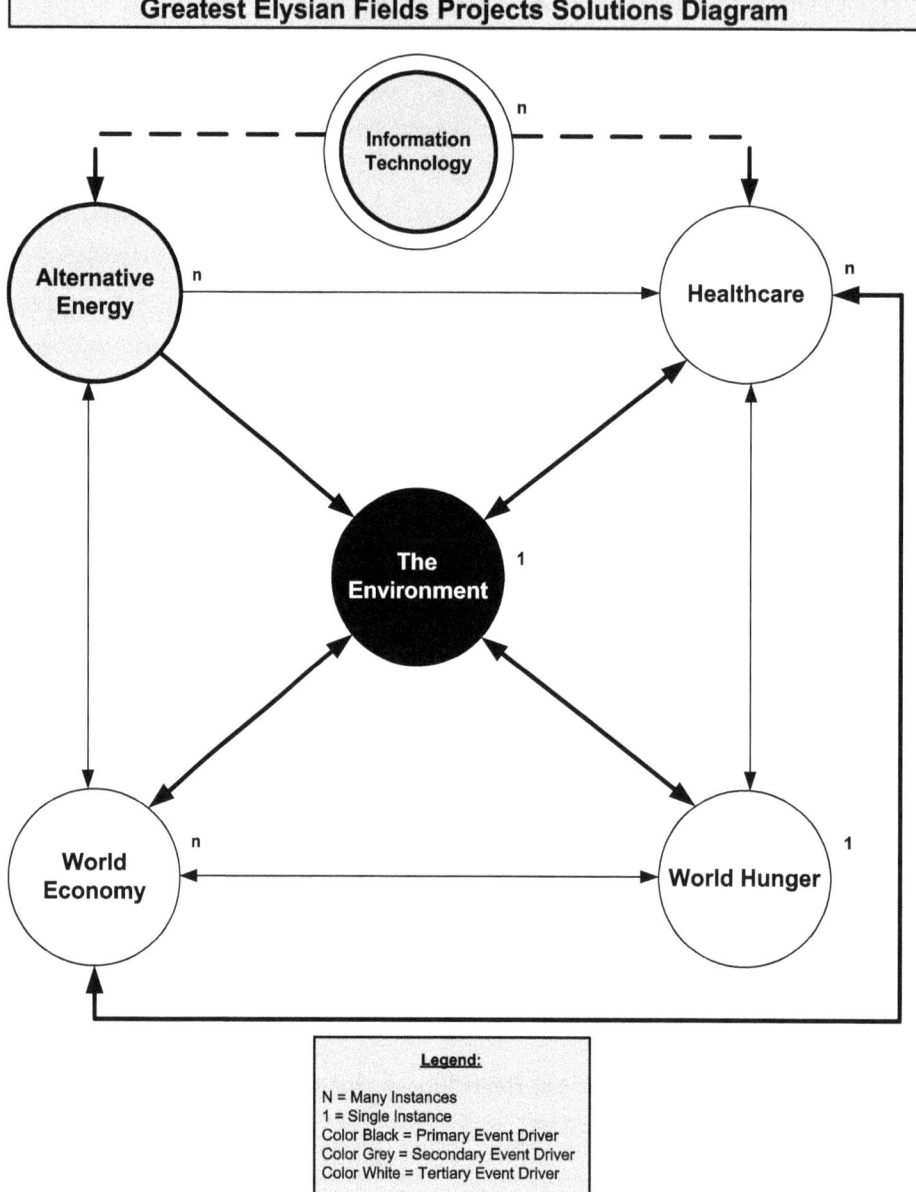

With many new and innovative Information Technology solutions focused on and injected into specific and Elysian Fields project categories, those regions can then began to have a strong and lasting positive effect on the rest of the critical areas that need help either directly or indirectly. Injecting new, effective, viable and innovative technology solutions into Alternative Energy can have a huge impact on cleaning up the Environment along with stimulating the world economy by creating a new and powerful critical key industry. A better environment can also lead to better farming and agricultural conditions that could work to reduce World Hunger. When this same type of event happens to Healthcare, the patient's benefits are much more significant and long lasting. This is because Healthcare providers then have access to better tools such as Electronic Medical Records systems that centralize patient information and reduces medical errors, and the time it takes to obtain required patient data. Improved Healthcare through Information Technology can also work to assist World Hunger through the creation, management, and support of new and better food distribution networks that track and inventory food supplies to insure that the people who really need the food are actually getting it. From this, the health of populations in staving regions of the world can be better monitored through technology and human persistence.

In the continuation of the solution diagrams that follow, we can see how the injection of strong Information Technology Research and Development resources, in the right areas, can create an innovative flow throughout the various categories:

Chapter 8: WELCOME TO THE ELYSIAN FIELDS

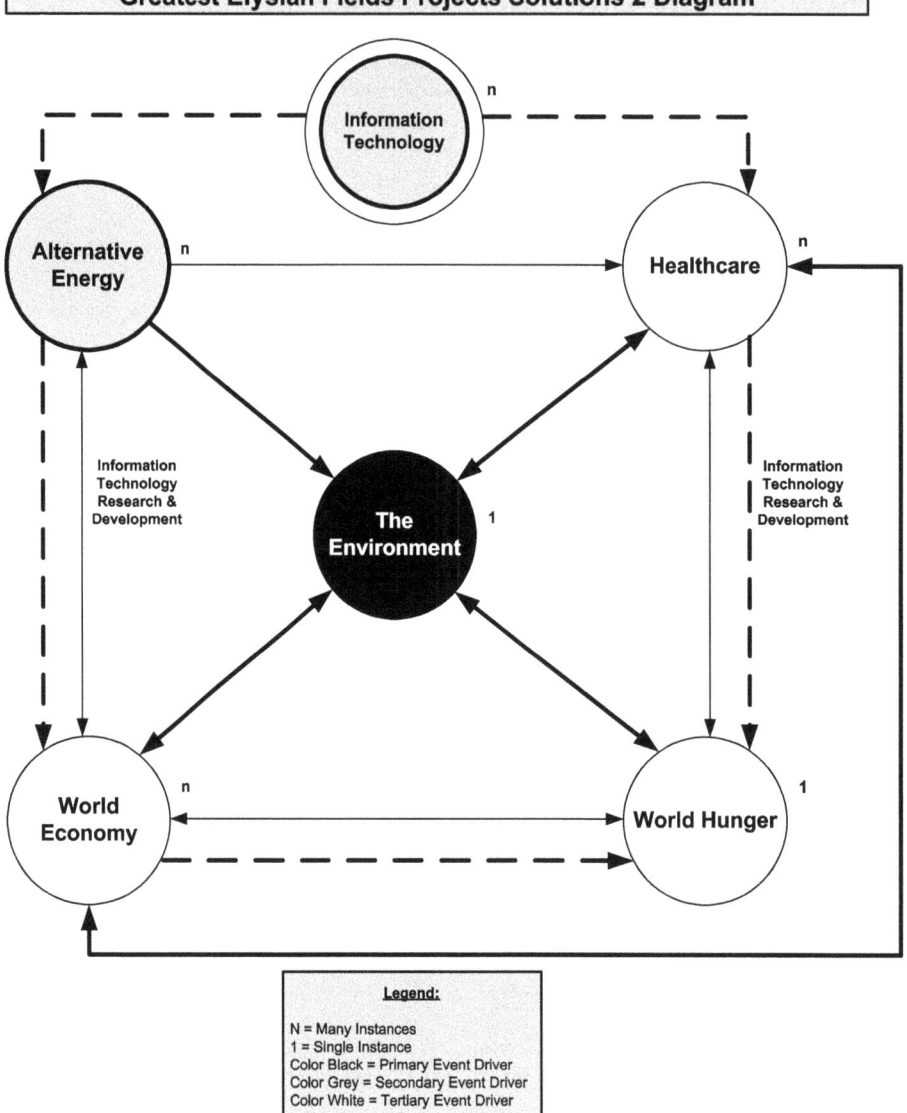

In the final solutions diagram that follows, the results of continuous Information Technology innovation leads to critical Alternative Energy and IT Healthcare solutions that have direct and positive effects on The Environment, World Economy, Healthcare, and Hunger.

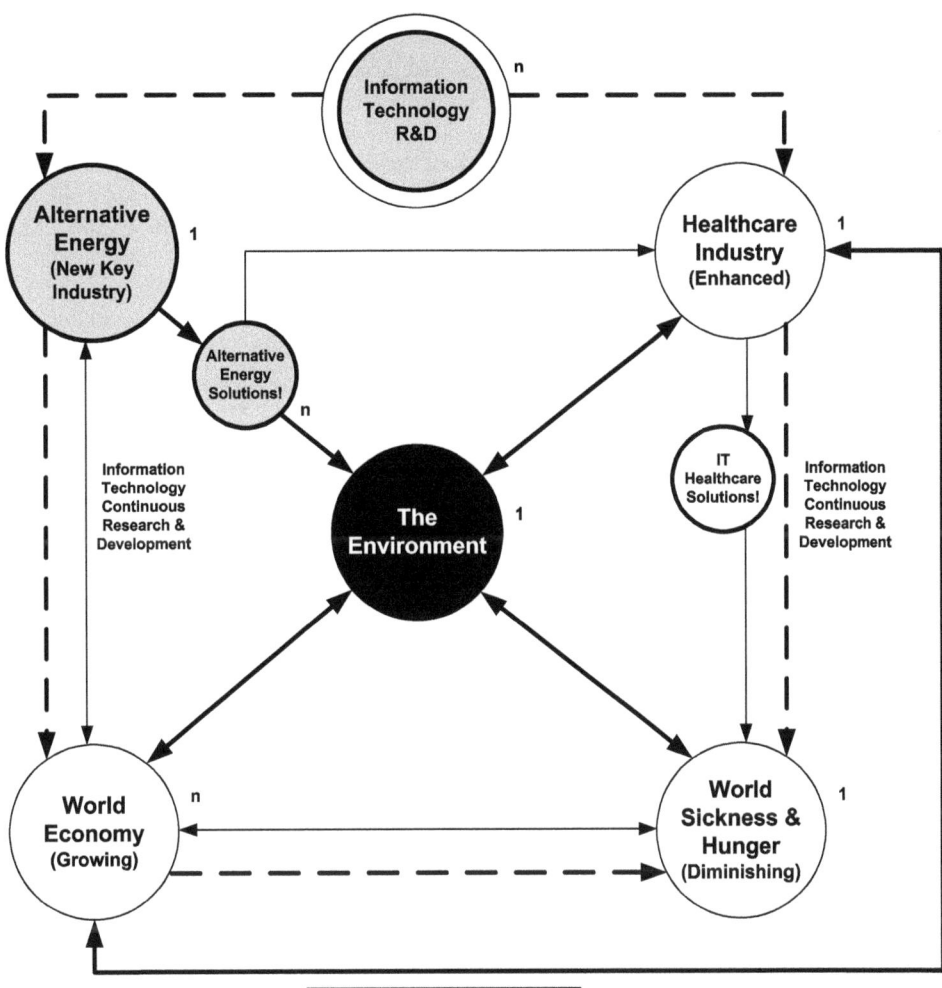

Enemies of the Elysian Fields

It has been said that you must first know who your enemies are before you can discover your friends. In a world where approximately 1% of the population owns more than 40% of the wealth, finding your enemies may not always be that difficult. According to a CBC (Canadian Broadcasting Corporation) news study on the distribution of global wealth done in 2006, it stated that if you were worth more than $500,000 US Dollars at that time, then you would be in a very exclusive club. This club would be that of the top 1% of the wealthiest people in the world. In order to be considered a member of the top 10% of the richest group globally, you only needed to have a net worth of more than $61,000 US Dollars. One of the authors of the CBC report also had this to say:

> *"Income inequality has been rising for the past 20 to 25 years and we think that is true for inequality in the distribution of wealth." – James Davies, Economist*

It is also important to note that the CBC news study defined wealth as "The value of physical and financial assets minus debts." Their analysis also separated wealth and income and cited that citizens of "rich" nations rank among the some of the poorest people worldwide in regards to household wealth due to the amount of debt they have incurred. As the canyon between the rich and poor steadily grows and the middle-class in the United States continues to shrink, the success of Elysian Fields Projects becomes even more crucial. Many wealthy individuals, groups, and businesses are working very hard for success the of these types of projects and have invested a great deal of time and resources in them. However, equally represented (though some may argue in greater numbers) are the opposite, who work towards the negative end of the great benefits of the Elysian Fields of Information Technology. Whether inadvertently or purposefully, they bottleneck important and critical positive advancements in regards to the levels of innovation required for good and sustained technological growth.

How to identify these types of forces can often be straightforward because Elysian Field Project "Frienemies" often fall into one or more of the categories listed below:

1. **Those who fear losing wealth**

2. **Those who fear losing power**

3. **Those who fear losing influence and entitlement**

4. **Those who fear losing control**

We can also never rule out "The Stupid" who can be extremely dangerous as we discussed in an earlier chapter. If an Elysian Fields Project works against a person, organization or company that falls within one or more of the previous categories listed, then there are sure to be major issues in regards to the success of that project. In most cases, this will have nothing to do with the technology aspect but everything to do with challenges in the political realm and with revenue. Traditionally, businesses have struggled with IT because they have been members of one or more of the "fear" categories listed, and have failed to understand how to properly implement and exploit their technologies. With this, they have in many cases left the door open for the enemies of Elysian Fields Projects to enter. Some of those foes are members of the following categories:

- **Lack of Adequate Funding** – This is simply the "Kiss of Death" for far too many IT projects. Not having enough funds is often more trouble than even attempting an Elysian Fields Project to begin with. It is because lack of revenue starts management from a position of weakness and initiates a "blame mentality" before anything has a chance to go wrong. Too many companies believe they can manage IT projects via the CFO's office, which usually has no idea of what IT does except that they are the most expensive department in the company. If an IT Project is to be well planned, it must also be funded accordingly to provide the resources and revenue to get the job done. If money is allocated to a project based on what a business "thinks" it should have, then a company can most likely prepare for a circus of:

    o Employee Turnovers

    o CYB (Cover Your Butt) methodologies and mentalities

    o Constant Code Refactoring without Rhyme or Reason

    o Team Animosity

    o Poor Communications

    o Gaps in the project

    o Exploding project costs

- **Greed** – Contrary to popular beliefs in regards to capitalism, greed is not always good. Historically, it has worked well for building countries and their infrastructures quickly. However, just as fast as greed has provided great wealth and infrastructure, it can remove and or damage it as well. Once a nation reaches its highest potential of stability with sociological and economic prosperity, greed can then start to heavily work against it. The results of Elysian Fields Projects by definition are designed to work towards the best interests of people all over the world regardless of status. While some individuals will undoubtedly become wealthy in the process, the overall riches of such an endeavor are shared by the people and not solely by individuals, small groups, and or corporations. When greed is involved in an Elysian Fields Project, it only serves to exploit the results of the services in question towards those who seek to advance their own cause(s), and not the greater good of such an effort. As a result, everyone suffers because the best interests of the entire group are negatively affected, so greed in this case is completely illogical and stupid.

- **Ignorance** – There are people who know that a positive change is required, and have the opportunity to help invoke it, but do nothing. There are many different reasons why some individuals practice this policy and sometimes you will never really know why that is. It is important to note that this type of behavior is a cancer to an Elysian Fields Project. This is because these types of projects survive by exploiting opportunities to advance the technologies that will ultimately help everyone. Elysian Fields Projects grow from need, innovation, and the thirst for knowledge and insight. Without this outlook, the project will slowly stop and begin to rust. No one benefits from that action, not the group, individual, or corporation who worked against the project because the project is designed to help the very people who tried to stop it.

- **Politics** – IT is ultimately about people and when groups of people interact in order to attempt to achieve a common objective then power and authority becomes a very important concern. The how, when, why, where, and who must be carefully planned and managed and personalities often clash in the process. In most cases, there are usually individuals or groups who struggle for dominance and this can not just bottleneck an IT project, it can slow it down and or completely stop it. The job of management is not only to successfully meet the objectives and expectations of an IT project, but also to control its politics. As politicians in large groups are all but impossible to eliminate, they can and must be managed or the path to the Elysian Fields quickly becomes unclear.

- **Extremism** – Balance is the objective to strive for. Although we can never achieve perfection with an Elysian Fields Project, we cannot afford to fail during the journey either. Therefore, it is important to proceed with passion and caution simultaneously. Historically we have seen great leaders inspire entire nations and bring them out of poverty to prosperity to then only abuse their power to cause wars and great atrocities. Adolf Hitler was a great example of a leader who went to extremes. He rose to power in Germany in the 1930s and 1940s by fueling nationalism, anti-communism, and anti-Semitism. His invasion of Poland in 1939 led to World War II. Hitler's bid to rule the world resulted in the deaths of tens of millions of people in which six million were of Jewish decent. Elysian Field Projects are global projects in which extremism is detrimental. Because the outcome of such projects can affect such a large and diverse number of people, it is important that Elysian Fields Projects remain balanced, and that their intent and purpose always remain as follows:

    o Beneficial to almost all people

    o Clearly Communicated

- Free of propaganda
- Unbiased
- Factual
- Realistic
- Positive
- Achievable

How do we guard against the enemies of Elysian Fields Projects? Wherever and whenever possible, do not hire or do business with individuals, groups, or companies that exhibit the negative traits or behaviors described in this section. If you are working on an Elysian Fields project and invite folks who promote the negative elements described to help you as a partner, they will only impede your progress or if given the opportunity, destroy your ability to reach your objective. Passion with great caution is important in this regard and something that must always be practiced. However, if you are put in a position where you must hire an enemy of the Elysian Fields to perform tasks, monitor and control these groups and or individuals very carefully and get rid of them immediately when their jobs are completed. Failure to do so could lead to the dire consequences described, and then some.

Friends of the Elysian Fields

The enemy of your enemy is your friend? In regards to Elysian Fields projects, this is largely the case. In the previous section, we discussed greed, ignorance, politics and extremism as being the foremost enemies and or adversaries of Elysian Fields projects. Does this mean that the enemies of those factors are friends of the Elysian Fields? Let's take a closer look.

- **Greed** – When it comes to building infrastructure quickly and effectively, this can sometimes be a great motivator for all players involved in the game. This is because the individual or group that can achieve the best possible results in the least amount of time will often obtain the greatest rewards. This includes:
    - Increased Wealth
    - Power and Influence
    - Prestige
    - Respect
    - Political Clout

- **Ignorance** – In some instances, what you don't know can help you. When it comes to successful people, in hindsight, many of them will tell you that they did not know that they were not supposed to be able to do some of the things they did, that got them to where there are. In other words, sometimes they did not know the rules of the game they were playing or they paid no attention to them. Through this, those individuals or groups created their own rules and blazed new trails to successes. Some of these accomplished folks were branded "Mavericks" and are deeply respected for bulldozing through the "status quoi" or the "impossible".

- **Politics** – IT always begins and ends with people. Whenever four or more people are gathered together in the name of Information Technology there will be a political element that will take root and grow. As the relationships within that team starts to mature, so will the nature for each member of that group to try to gain influence over and through one another. Not only is this is a natural human occurrence, but it would be unwise not to expect it. However, it is important to note that groups do not always work against each other. Good politics can be very powerful and can give teams a common platform, leadership, and vision on which to achieve their objectives. When this is the case, the chances of an IT project reaching the Elysian Fields increases significantly.

- **Extremism** – This is a difficult attribute to defend in almost any context. It is because from this perspective almost any action can be justified at anytime which can usually lead to unpredictable and dangerous scenarios.

Friends of the Elysian Fields understand the context of the Extremism, Politics, Ignorance, and Greed within this realm, and are able to handle these issues through intelligence, wisdom, clarity, and good leadership. Technology leaders must also endeavor to find allies in every region and country around the world who share the vision of the Elysian Fields of Information Technology and work with them to achieve it. Much like the human body, technology has "veins" and people are the blood that flows through them. This is the "how" of effectiveness. It flows through the Elysian Field's views, structures, and commitments that drive technology to be the defining tool for a better quality of life for all who seek it. Now is the turning point in world history in which there is no going back. Never before has IT been this important to the very survival of humanity to help us secure our own technological worth and well-being.

As I watched the historic 2008 Democratic Presidential Primaries in the United States, it included for the first time in that country's history, an African American man named "Barack Obama", and a woman named "Hillary Clinton". Each had a real chance at winning the Presidency, which included being the leader of the free world. As I watched the debates during this great and historic race, I realized that virtually all of the national primary's issues that were cited as major concerns by the American people could be helped or solved through the proper implementation of Information Technology. These included such critical issues as:

1. Alternative Energy
2. The Economy
3. Jobs
4. Healthcare
5. War
6. Education

We can all be friends of the Elysian Fields of Information Technology and it will take every one of us working together in order to pave the way for innovations to grow. If we do not use the new and current technology that becomes available to us, then it is worthless.

Here are some of the ways that almost anyone can be a friend to the Elysian Fields of IT:

1. **Vote for politicians that support research and development of new and existing technologies. These include but are not limited to:**
    a. **Alternative Energy Solutions**
        i. Creates a new industry and new jobs
        ii. Decreases dependence on foreign oil
        iii. Helps boost the economy
        iv. Cuts funding to terrorists
        v. Helps to end wars fought over oil reserves
    b. **Electronic Medical Records (EMRs)**
        i. Helps to decrease medical errors by forcing all doctors that use the software to manage the same patient historical medical records and communicate more effectively
        ii. Saves time and money
        iii. Preparing prescriptions is quicker and easier

Chapter 8: WELCOME TO THE ELYSIAN FIELDS

        iv. Helps hospitals and physicians comply with industry rules

        v. Helps physicians to see and process a larger number of patients more quickly and effectively

        vi. Helps insurance companies to pay physicians more quickly due to better record keeping that is easier to read and maintain

        vii. Can lead to lower insurance premiums for physicians

    c. Free Government Online Education

        i. Is in the best interest of any nation and promotes patriotism

        ii. Provides a public learning resource for everyone

        iii. Helps to make a nation more competitive globally

        iv. Works to reduce poverty

        v. Helps to establish and sustain a sense of confidence and awareness within a population

2. Work to use technology wisely in your daily life. Technology is a tool that is best used to enhance the quality of life, not as a substitute for the human brain or thought process. If it does not help make your life better, don't use it.

3. Seek out and support groups, organizations, and companies that are innovative and work to use green technologies more effectively.

Changing the Return on Investment (ROI)

What generally drives businesses? The answer is a simple one, return on investment. People start businesses to make money and become more independent. In America, businesses in the private sector have the opportunity to make as much money as possible. Capitalism is based on greed, not need, so in this type of society, trying to get companies to work for the common good of all people concerned is usually easier said than done. Since capitalism is a system based on economic rules and revenue that is privately owned, citizens can do whatever they want to do with their money and businesses as long as it falls within the confines of the law. The act of starting a business can be a simple thing to do initially. However, in order to make it successful, it requires revenue, time, resources, planning, hard work, and commitment by the person or group that initiates the task. In addition, changing a business plan can be risky endeavor and should never be taken lightly as it is something that should always be carefully thought through, especially when dealing with Elysian Fields projects.

ROI is a measure of performance used to analyze how efficient an investment or investments are or have been. One way to determine ROI is to divide the returns (gains) by how much the investments cost. The answer will yield a ratio or percentage, which will be the return on investment. Below is an example of this formula:

$$ROI = \frac{(\text{Investment Gains} - \text{Investment Costs})}{\text{Investment Costs}}$$

This metric is very important because of its simplicity and flexibility. Investments must yield gains of some positive measure or they are generally viewed as not worth the effort from a business project perspective. I must be clear; Elysian Fields projects are business ventures of a broad economical vision and social scope, so ROI is a factor that must always be taken very seriously or these projects may have little to no chance of success.

Many employees may not find satisfaction in working hard to make the people who own the companies they work for richer if they cannot share in the benefits of their labor as well. Studies have shown that workers who like their jobs are more productive and generally feel and believe that they are having a positive impact on their company's growth and success. This in turn makes these folks work harder and continues the cycle of forward progress. Companies with employees such as these usually have the insight to insure that their people share financially in the company's wealth as well as other aspects of the business.

1. Many businesses offer one or more of the following base benefits after a worker has been with the company for a specified period of time:

    - Health Insurance
    - Dental Insurance
    - Paid Vacations
    - Paid Holidays
    - Paid Sick Days
    - Disability Insurance
    - Life Insurance
    - 401K

Chapter 8: WELCOME TO THE ELYSIAN FIELDS

2. Companies that invest more deeply in their workers satisfaction and happiness offer some or more of the following additional benefits:

- Planned Pension
- Profit Sharing
- Direct Deposit
- Reimbursement for Continuing Education
- Parking Privileges
- Wellness Incentives
- Business Cards
- Employee Discounts
- Onsite Daycare Facilities
- Work at Home Opportunities

Investing in recruiting and retaining good people by offering a comprehensive benefits package is usually a wise and intelligent way to secure a good worker-based ROI for a business. Some of the rewards of this behavior often include:

1. A company that good and or great workers will be attracted to
2. A lower rate of employee turnover
3. A more productive, focused employee
4. A more loyal employee with good morale
5. A better team environment

In order to get the best from people, those folks must feel valued and this can mean different things to various types of employees. It is difficult to find workers who generally do not want to share in a company's continued growth through revenue, benefits, or in some way feel like their company's work will improve their own quality of life, as it is not logical not to desire this. An Elysian Fields project invests in people in order to make life better for them. Because of this, the following actions can be invoked, which are necessary to fuel the power and evolution of this particular kind of social investment:

- Changes the ROI from just "revenue only" to "better quality of life" for everyone who wants and needs it

- Changes the "Greed" to "Need"

- Changes the lust for "Power" to a desire for "Our"

Trusting greedy and power hungry people to do the right thing is a departure from conventional wisdom and the short road to disaster. This is why so many IT projects fail and companies lose so much of their economic stability in regards to IT. The desire and wisdom from smart, good leaders must be the persistent road to sharing the fruits of technology that will ultimately preserve our very own existence. Money and prosperity will come to those in new alternative industries if they can understand and learn that others must be able to live healthy, meaningful, and productive lives in order to buy their products and or subscribe to their services. This is in everyone's best interests and must always be visible to those who bypass greed as a main source of motivation.

The Elysian Fields ROI and technology objectives must be common to all and serve the best interest of the end users. It should include the following abilities:

- **To preserve and restore the environment so that the human race can survive and thrive**

- **To create new, powerful, clean, safe and renewable energy resources that invoke a new industry built on this technology and provides more jobs**

- **To make new, safe, renewable, clean and oil-free energy sources eventually free to everyone on the planet while securing growth in its respective industry**

How do we make the road to the Elysian Fields of Information Technology more open to the people who need it? How do you move from talking about getting there to actually making it happen? The following are a few ideas that you can work to implement and or enforce where ever and whenever you can:

1. Vigorously support leaders with an Elysian Fields view, who constantly work to insure that everyone shares in the opportunities and gains of the project, not just the "greedy" and "power hungry" players.

2. If your in the position to do so, resist the temptation to hire or work with "Selfish" and or "Egocentric" individuals or groups no matter how good

they may appear. IT begins and ends with the intelligence and goodness of people, not just skill sets.

3. If you are in a position to do so, remove the opportunity and incentive for the "Greedy Politicians" to gain a base in your projects, and avoid the game of politics where ever and whenever possible.

4. Ban stupidity in all shapes, forms, and processes.

5. If you can, share technology (lawfully) as much as possible and work to make and keep it affordable and available to everyone who might need and want it.

Summary

What is IT, really? A perception for many is that IT is actually "Technology Information" and this is a big part of the problem. The gathering, processing, and reporting of data has historically been a great and important task. Computers are not, nor have they ever been required to perform those tasks. However, it is important to note that computers are able to carry out large amounts of data input, management, and output much faster than people are able to which makes it a great tool if implemented effectively. Is it better to walk than to drive a car? It depends on the circumstances. I may want to walk if I am only going a city block or so to a corner store. However, if I need to travel 300 miles or so, I might strongly consider driving a car. If this is the case, then I want a car that works well and gets reasonably good gas mileage (if it is not an electric vehicle). If my automobile breaks down every couple of miles, is unsafe to drive, and the vehicle only gets maybe 2-3 miles to the gallon, then a train, air plane, or bicycle might start to sound even more attractive. The point here is that technology must be safe, useful, and effective or the tools might not be worth the time it took to invent them. Technology has never been about technology, and it never will be as long as people are around to use it. This is because it is only a tool and it was not created for its own sake.

Information has driven the human race as long as there have been people on this planet. Whether folks have communicated with hand signals, bongo drums, drawings on cave walls, or used smoke signals, it is all data of a given type and that information had to be managed and processed somehow for it to have been understood by the culture that used it. As better ways to communicate and manage information emerged, the old ways were replaced or slowly faded away. Morse code is a good example of this, although in some situations it is still used today. Currently, computers are more than capable of processing and effectively storing the data of human beings on this planet. However, computers only do what we tell them to do. They just follow orders and are at the mercy of the individuals or teams who are commanding those machines. That is why information Technology is really Information People, first.

On January 20th, 2009, Barack Obama (a Democrat) became the first African-American to be sworn in as President of the United States of America. He defeated a well-know career politician, Senator John McCain, who was also an American War Hero and POW (Prisoner of War). This successful Presidential Campaign project was one of "Elysian Fields-Level" proportions, which was very well executed, and will be discussed and studied for generations to come. President Obama was virtually unknown to the national political stage just two years before the historic Presidential Election. At the beginning of his campaign, he had served only two years in the Illinois State Senate. From this perspective, the odds of an African-American winning the Presidency were little to none. Obama began a "grass roots" Elysian Fields project campaign based on the themes, "Change We Can Believe In" and "Yes We Can", and never wavered from it. The Obama Presidential Project was a true Elysian Fields quest that consisted of almost all of the attributes required to make it so, which included:

- **Good Management**

- **Good Communications**

- **The right people, in the right place, at the right time**

- **The latest technology of the period**
    - **Internet**
    - **Cell Phones**
    - **Email**
    - **Texting**
    - **Blogging**
    - **Websites**

- **"Grass-Roots" organizational skills**

- **Money, and the ability to generate large sums of additional revenue**

- **Enthusiastic volunteers who constantly attracted more of the same**

- **Flexibility and the ability to re-adjust to environmental circumstances**

- **The ability to gather and analyze data and act on the results quickly and effectively**

Chapter 8: WELCOME TO THE ELYSIAN FIELDS

- **A shared and timeless vision that encapsulated simple and achievable objectives**

A failing economy, two concurrent foreign wars, and high unemployment assisted Obama's campaign significantly, as dissatisfied voters largely blamed the then current leaders of the opposing and ruling Republican Party (Lead by Former President George W. Bush) because of it. For the junior Senator from Illinois at that time, this was the "Perfect Storm" come Election Day, while he was on the information people path to the Elysian Fields. President Barack Obama understood throughout his campaign that his journey would not end when he reached the "White House". This is because he is now a part of an Elysian Fields project and they never cease, they always move forward to help make life better for everyone.

There is no doubt that computer technology has been an Elysian Fields invention that has changed the modern world forever. It has spawned a huge industry and has created countless jobs and propelled man into a new age of culture and prosperity. It is a great, amazing and fantastic event by any stretch of the imagination. Now, we need more from it and ourselves. It is time for us to re-challenge our computer technology tools and push them to new heights. The primary technology tool governor is our minds. It always has been and must continue to be so in the future. Our technology tools are only as good as our intelligence and imagination, which now must perform a monumental and necessary task that is most certainly achievable. Because of the industrial revolution and its repercussions, we must now work to undo the damages done to the Earth's environments and secure viable, renewable, safe, and cheap solutions for alternative energy. Currently, this is the greatest test for Information Technology. What has 70 years of computer science and technological history come to if we do not have:

1. **Clean Air to Breath**

2. **Clean Water to Drink**

3. **Affordable, safe, abundant, renewable energy to power our nations, cities, homes, cars and computers**

My PC is one of the most important and utilized tools that I own. However, every winter at my home when a bad storm hits our region and I temporarily lose electricity, I am sadly reminded of how useless computers are when you do not have energy to power them. This also makes me imagine a future of high-energy prices in which some people might not be able to afford to pay for the power needed to turn them on. This is completely avoidable if we take the necessary actions now to prevent it.

As I reflect on the bad management of so many IT projects that I have seen in the past, I continue to be frustrated at the lack of the willingness to change the bad behavior of IT departments by some of companies that manage them. Many good people talk of positive change in IT, but when there are given the power to affect it, they simply don't do it. One might argue that it could be due to a lack of education but most of the people running IT departments currently either have advanced degrees or at the very least have a college degree. With this, why do so many well-educated managers in Information Technology:

- **Make so many bad decisions**
- **Welcome Stupidity**
- **Waste so much money**
- **Ignore good and great advice**
- **Ignore IT history**
- **Ignore IT industry best practices**
- **Constantly trust their own feelings over proven computer scientific facts**

It took years for me to understand and finally accept the answers to these questions and I have repeated them persistently and carefully throughout this book.

1. *If an individual or group focuses on technology only for the sake of it, their technology will most likely fail.*

2. *If an individual or group seeks to use technology to further their own ambitions of greed and power, their technology will most likely be limited.*

3. *If an individual or group consistently ignores the needs of the people who will use their technology, it will ultimately fail.*

Technology exists to serve people, and in turn, those people should use it to help each other achieve a better quality of life. Whenever we deviate from this simple rule, we move further away from the human path to The Elysian Fields of Information Technology.

"You don't develop courage by being happy in your relationships every day. You develop it by surviving difficult times and challenging adversity."

- Epicurus (Greek philosopher, BC 341-270)

350

EPILOGUE

Now that I have written this book, and you have read it, you may agree or disagree with all of some of the content. Naturally, this is your right for whatever reasons you many have. However, this effort is my perspective wrapped in the release of all of the things that I wanted and needed to say over the years within projects that would have been risky or career suicide to vocalize. From this, I initially began writing this offering out of sheer frustration with what I viewed as consistently poor IT management decisions in many of the projects that I was working on at the time. The technology that was being utilized on projects that I worked with never seemed ever be the heart of the issues that we were having. It was poor decisions made persistently by management that in many cases adversely affected the technology that was utilized and implemented. Some folks might ask why I did not work harder to take a management position and begin to make a positive change in the issues that I had seen hurt so many IT projects consistently over time. My answer to that question is a simple one. I learned early in my career that I was an advisor, not a leader, and I make no apologies for that fact. This knowledge helped me to not only keep my ego in check, but to become more of a student of people and their relationships in regards to building, implementing, and maintaining software systems. Additionally, the more I understood and accepted my role as an advisor and a manager of machines and technology, I became increasingly interested in how I could do a better job to support my colleagues and the project in question, instead of focusing on how to manipulate or obtain more power over them. My objectives ultimately turned into how I could make my colleagues and the project more successful. This perspective lead me to achieve my objectives on projects, but only in environments where I had the opportunity to work with good people who recognized the true value of team work. Good people surround themselves with the like whenever possible. Bad employees also seek the company of folks who think the way that they do.

No individual, group, or organization can claim the invention of Information Technology. Furthermore, no one company has an Information Technology model that works for all others. This is because Information Technology is the basic science of how people manage their data, which can be cultural, and that discipline has existed long before computers were invented. Once men and women began to communicating with each other and discovered various ways in which to store and manage their data, the science of information exchange and management had begun. Information Technology is not a recent science that came about with the advent of computers. It is an ancient technology based on various civilizations, social cultures, politics, governmental and military practices. It is ultimately a science of people and not machines, as we know it primarily today.

It was my most sincere effort to produce a resource that would not only be a reference for IT, but for the business equally as well, that spoke in a simple and common language. This inter-departmental book was designed and intended to fill an informational gap that was largely missing in the relationships between businesses and their IT partners. The marriage between business and Information Technology has traditionally been a love\hate endeavor that many companies have struggled to understand and deal with due to some of the following reasons:

- **Language Barriers**
    - Technical versus Non-Technical
    - Departmental
    - Industrial
    - Regional

- **Differences in Culture**
    - Ethnicity
    - Age (Generational)
    - Gender
    - Nationality

- **Other Opposing Perspectives**
    - Short-Term versus Long-Term
    - Financial
    - Executive Management versus Lower Management
    - Differences in processes (how to perform tasks)

In addition, many other significant challenges stand between the two entities that are also proprietary. It is not difficult to find a white paper or magazine article on the Internet that will address in short many of the problems between IT and the business. Alternatively, you could find books on how to build software or manage a business from either a technical or company view at popular book stores in your town or online. However, those resources usually speak directly to the business or IT separately, not as a single group or in a common language that both parties can understand. This book was designed to act as a bridge in this regard and provide a common ground for communications and understanding between a business and its Information Technology partners. With any luck, it has helped to do just that as this effort comes straight from my heart.

The bottom line is that technology, much like life, can only exist in either one of three states:

1. **Slowly Dying (New or "State of the Art")**

2. **Near Death (Life Support)**

3. **Dead**

Like humans, new technological discoveries are ultimately born to die. The resulting offspring in many cases inherits some of its predecessor's positive and negative attributes and morphs into something new and or different. If technology is not changing for the better in some way, shape, or form, then it is near death or dead. This is because history has shown us that if people cannot find a platform of value in the technology that is made available to them, they will not use it.

Although many do try, no one can accurately predict the future on Information Technology. There are too many variables to consider and they rest primarily on the most unpredictable factors of all, human beings. No one person can accurately guess what another person will do 100% of the time. With this, the best we can do is to use our knowledge and experience to plan, execute, analyze the results, learn from our mistakes, and then repeat the process. The future is always uncertain but we can be proactive based on our history, knowledge, wisdom and experiences. In 6th century B.C., Lao Tzu had this to say:

"Those who have knowledge don't predict. Those who predict don't have knowledge."

354

BOOK REFERENCES

1. Making the Right Enterprise Information Systems Decisions (ID: ENT07021), Dennis Cromwell (Indiana University) PowerPoint Presentation
2. Creating A Successful Business, Rogene A. Robbins & Robert O. Robbins
3. Software Requirements, Karl E. Wiegers
4. Software Estimation, Steve McConnell
5. The Second Industrial Revolution, Jonh J. Donovan
6. Analyzing Requirements and Defining Microsoft .NET Solution Architectures (Exam 70-300), Microsoft Press
7. Patent It Yourself, David Pressman
8. Contemporary Business, Louis E. Boone & David L. Kurtz
9. Management, Kathryn M. Bartol & David C. Martin
10. Document: Writing a Requirements Document, Tanya Berezin
11. Creating a Software Engineering Culture, Karl E. Wiegers
12. Requirements Engineering: A Good Practice Guide, Ian Sommerville, Pete Sawyer
13. Object-Oriented Software Engineering: A Use Case Driven Approach, Ivar Jacobson et al
14. Security Complete, Sybex
15. Hacking Exposed, Stuart Mclure, Joel Scambray, George Kurtz
16. Counter Hack, Ed Skoudis
17. Intrusion Detection, Rebecca Gurley Base
18. The Politics of Lying: Government Deception, Secrecy, and Power, David Wise
19. Godel, Escher, Bach: an Eternal Golden Braid, by Douglas R. Hofstadter

20. The Physics of Information Technology, Neil A. Gershenfeld

21. The Speed of Trust, Stephen M.R. Covey

22. The Low Beyond, Eliezer S. Yudkowsky

23. Artificial Intelligence as a Positive and Negative Factor in Global Risk, Eliezer S. Yudkowsky

24. Artificial Intelligence: A Modern Approach (2nd Edition), Russell, S. and Norvig, P.

25. Discussion Paper No. 2008/03, The World Distribution of Household Wealth - James B. Davies, Susanna Sandström, Anthony Shorrocks, and Edward N. Wolff (February 2008)

INTERNET REFERENCES

1. http://pubs.socialistreviewindex.org.uk/isj74/wilson.htm
2. http://www.12manage.com/methods_fayol_14_principles_of_management.html
3. http://www.wwisa.org/wwisamain/role.htm
4. http://en.wikipedia.org/
5. http://www.versaggi.net/ecommerce/articles/drucker-inforevolt.htm
6. http://www.fas.org/irp/wwwinfo.html
7. http://honolulu.hawaii.edu/intranet/committees/FacDevCom/guidebk/teachtip/adults-3.htm
8. http://www.quotedb.com/quotes/2695
9. http://www.history.com/genericContent.do?id=53855
10. http://bottomlinesecrets.com/blpnet/article.html?article_id=27567
11. http://www.spc.ca/resources/estimate/index.htm
12. http://www.bricklin.com/patentsandsoftware.htm
13. http://www.uspto.gov
14. http://www.agiledata.org/essays/differentStrategies.html
15. http://www.diserio.com/business-intelligence.html
16. http://www.brightstarsound.com/world_hero/article.html
17. http://www.gartner.com
18. http://www.pantheon.org/articles/e/elysian_fields.html
19. http://www.msnbc.msn.com/id/4072816/
20. http://goliath.ecnext.com/

21. http://www.associatedcontent.com/article/45505/types_of_power_in_management.html

22. http://www.everyonenegotiates.com/negotiation/tentypesofpower.htm

23. http://changingminds.org/explanations/power/power_types.htm

24. http://www.everything2.com/index.pl?node_id=1424510

25. http://money.cnn.com/2005/10/03/news/economy/annie/fortune_annie100305/index.htm

26. http://auto.howstuffworks.com/engine1.htm

27. http://www.school-for-champions.com/excellence/problemtips.htm

28. http://www.simple-talk.com/opinion/opinion-pieces/secrets-of-successful-it-projects/

29. http://inventors.about.com/library/blcoindex.htm

30. http://thinkexist.com/quotes/top/nationality/ancient_greek/

31. http://www.davesite.com/webstation/net-history.shtml

32. http://www.tcpipguide.com/free/t_TCPIPOverviewandHistory.htm

33. http://members.cox.net/ggathome2/EvalRun/ArticlesLogic/HumanStupidity.Basics1.html

34. http://inventors.about.com/library/inventors/blmodem.htm

35. http://www.ideafinder.com/history/inventions/pcmodem.htm

36. http://www.nethistory.info/History%20of%20the%20Internet/email.html

37. http://www.ericgoldman.org/Articles/emailtricksarticle.htm

38. http://www.allbusiness.com/legal/contracts-agreements/2378-1.html

39. http://www.npr.org/news/specials/enron/

40. http://www.wsu.edu/payroll/paydectree/20common.htm

41. http://msdn2.microsoft.com/en-us/library/aa302419.aspx

42. http://www.guard-privacy-and-online-security.com/computer-virus-definition.html

43. http://lifehacker.com/software/education/technophilia-get-a-free-college-education-online-201979.php

44. http://www.free-ed.net/free-ed/

45. http://yudkowsky.net/singularity.html

46. http://www.singinst.org/overview/whatisthesingularity

47. http://www.cait.wustl.edu/index.php?option=com_courses&task=view&code=MGT120

48. http://www.networkworld.com/columnists/2007/042607-backspin.html?page=2

49. http://www.hyperdictionary.com

50. http://www.handprint.com/LS/ANC/evol.html

51. http://library.thinkquest.org/C002291/high/present/stats.htm

52. http://www.cbc.ca/money/story/2006/12/05/globalwealth.html

53. http://www.keymedical.net/ProsConsWhitepaper.html

54. http://sbinformation.about.com/cs/benefits/a/8uncommon.htm

55. http://www.investopedia.com/terms/r/returnoninvestment.asp

INDEX

INDEX

@
@, 303

1
10 IT commandments, 128

4
401K, 343

7
701 EDPM, 297

A
AAIE, 77
Abstraction, 323
academic, 305
Accounting, 172, 174, 249, 297
accounts, 43, 97, 207, 254, 281, 297, 305
Action, 236
active voice, 190
Actor, 236
AD, 51, 131, 226
Administration, 189
administrative user, 209
Adolf Hitler, 338
Advanced Research Projects Agency, 297, 300
adversaries, 91, 128, 140, 149
adversary, 106, 140, 141
advisors, 54, 56, 100
Aesop, 104
Affected Users, 213
African American, 340
African Americans, 136
African-American, 347
Age, 135, 313
Agile Data, 226
Agile Methodology, 226, 227, 228, 229
Agile Model Driven Development, 226
Agile Unified Process, 226
agnostic, 82, 171
Agriculture, 311, 313
AI, 91, 321, 322, 323, 324, 325, 328
air defense, 299
airplane, 146, 217
Alan Shugart, 297
algorithms, 217, 257
Allensound MIDI, 12
alternative energy, 150, 154, 279, 314, 348
alternative fuel, 279
AMDD, 226
American International Group, 157
American Online, 299
analog signals, 299
Analysis Paralysis, 271
Analyst, 41, 43, 75, 115, 116, 117, 118, 119, 120, 121, 238, 318, 382
Analytical Team, 50, 119, 120, 121
Anarchy, 128
ancient fossils, 327
Ancient Greek Fabulist, 104
Ancient Greek Philosopher, 223, 264
Anne Allen, 7, 8
Antarctic, 331
anti-communism, 338
anti-Semitism, 338
AOL, 299
Apple, Inc, 319

INDEX

application scaling, 179
Application Service Providers, 86, 170, 173
Application testing software, 17
Application-Based, 206
Applied Technical, 145, 146
Ardipithecus, 327
Aristotle, 223, 264, 295, 309
arms race, 201
ARPAnet, 297, 300, 303
Art, 27
Arthur Anderson, 276
Arthur Anderson, LLP, 277
Artificial Intelligence, 91, 321, 322, 323, 356
artists, 12, 58
Asians, 136
ASP, 86, 87, 170, 173
Asset, 159, 202
astronomy, 305
AT&T, 299
ATM machine, 46
atomic bomb, 104
Attacker, 202
Attention to Detail, 150, 294
Attitude, 294
Audit, 255
audited, 208
auditing, 189, 258
AUP, 226
Aurora, 142
australopithicines, 327
authenticated, 204
Author, 9, 269, 288, 382
Author of a collection of Greek fables, 104
Automatic Storage Management, 324
automobile, 217, 243, 279, 314, 346

B

Babel Effect, 283
backbone, 254
background information, 136
Bad decision making, 69
bandwidth, 173, 276
Bank of America, 157
Bank Records, 134
banking, 201, 266, 297
bankruptcy, 3, 276
Bankruptcy, 159
Barack Obama, 340, 347, 348
bauds, 299
behavior patterns, 262
Beijing, 141
Bell 103, 299
Bell Telephone Laboratories, 297
Berkley, 316
best practices, 19, 23, 75, 102, 112, 128, 139, 171, 193, 200, 201, 210, 222, 230, 245, 294, 349
Best Practices, 94, 96, 289, 292
better than human, 325
biennium, 98
binoculars, 326
Biographer, 269, 288
biological, 323
Biology, 305
Birth Certificates, 153
black box management, 199, 201
Black Object, 331
blacklisted, 98
blame game, 140
Blogging, 347
Blogs, 240, 318
Blueprints, 210
Body language, 146
bonuses, 30, 90, 145

Boot Sector, 206
botanist, 219
brain scans, 325
brain trust, 43, 119, 244
branch, 254, 327
BRE, 34, 236, 257
breached, 151, 204, 205
Brigham Young University, 316
Bronze Support, 166
bug tracking, 193, 238
Bug Tracking Application, 17
bugs, 45, 167, 192, 193, 269
building a house, 232
bullseye, 181
burn rate, 99, 168
Business Analyst, 15, 17, 41, 43, 75, 76, 115, 116, 117, 118, 119, 214, 244, 247, 318
Business Cards, 344
Business intelligence, 106
Business Logic Tier, 176
business minded, 106, 123, 283
business model, 30, 173, 215, 255
business partners, 51, 63, 76, 78, 88, 92, 109, 124, 227, 276, 290, 291
Business Processes, 183
Business Requirements, 46, 246
Business Rules Engine, 34, 236, 257
business services, 249

C

cable, 170
Calculator, 296
California, 151
Call Centers, 290
campaigning, 266
cancer, 139, 255, 270, 272, 281, 338
Capitalism, 217, 342
capitalistic society, 106, 314

capitol, 156
Captain, Katherine Janeway, 13
Captains, 103
carbon copy, 34
carbon emissions, 4, 240, 243
Carnegie Mellon University, 316
CASE, 228
catastrophe, 242, 277
CBC News, 336
CDs, 97, 152, 205, 318
Cell phones, 240
Cell Phones, 152, 347
CEO, 60, 148, 160, 174, 276
CES, 242
CFO, 43, 337
chain of command, 26, 58, 59, 60, 61, 76, 145
change control, 196, 223
change management, 77, 84, 129, 179, 181, 191, 195, 198, 222, 235, 239
Change management, 198
Change Management, 82, 195, 221, 238, 270, 289
chaos, 15, 33, 73, 79, 128, 202, 222, 223, 270, 277, 294
chaotic, 26, 28, 33
charisma, 143, 144, 146, 147, 273
Charismatic, 145, 146, 147
Chemistry, 305
Chief Executive Officer, 148
Chief Financial Officer, 43
Chief Information Officer, 25, 53, 127
Chief Operations Officer, 128
Chief Technical Officer, 37, 53, 127
China, 141, 302
Chinese, 141
ChoicePoint, 151, 152
Church, 8, 9, 313

INDEX

CIO, 25, 32, 34, 37, 53, 60, 67, 68, 74, 75, 127, 128, 138, 174, 266
Circle, 312
City Police, 118
civilizations, 4, 250
classes, 160, 260, 277, 317
Clean Air, 311, 348
Clean Water, 311, 348
Clifford Berry, 296
code, 35, 48, 82, 84, 92, 142, 171, 180, 181, 186, 187, 191, 192, 227, 229, 241, 258, 260, 346, 359
Code & Fix, 227
Code Red, 205
Code Refactoring, 337
coded, 50, 86, 383
coding, 34, 195, 218
Cognitive Science, 322
Cold War, 297
college, 8, 12, 76, 83, 160, 314, 316, 317, 349, 359
College Degree, 26
Color Laser Printers, 152
command line interface, 319
Commerce, 302, 304
commissioned, 10, 300
common language, 10, 73, 351, 352
communication, 10, 11, 41, 45, 70, 88, 90, 103, 105, 130, 157, 192, 230, 231, 238, 239, 248, 254, 290, 292
Communications Escalation Structure, 242
company confidential, 213
company culture, 29
company intranet, 29
company website, 29
Compaq, 11
competence, 15, 34, 56, 77, 78, 84, 148

complacency, 86, 93, 280, 281
Complacency, 93, 159, 280, 281, 282
component tests, 193
components, 39, 141, 159, 179, 180, 184, 192, 194, 209, 259, 261, 263, 322
compromise triangle, 196
computational model, 323
Computer Aided Software Engineering, 228
Computer automation, 324
Computer Engineer, 134
Computer Hacker, 204
computer networks, 141, 303, 308
computer programming language, 323
Computer Science, 26, 27, 322, 382
computer standards, 299
conception, 253
conference calls, 241
configurability, 184
connection points, 209
Cons, 294
consensus, 157, 213
conspiracy theories, 108
Construction, 39, 229
Consultants, 45, 46, 97, 100, 101, 102
consulting company, 33, 68, 99, 100, 109, 111
consumer requirements, 195
Contingency Planning, 294
contractual documents, 304
Controlled Experiments, 307
Controlling the Assault of Non-Solicited Pornography, 304
COO, 128
copyrights, 216
Copyrights, 158
Core Service Offerings, 291
corner stone, 308

corporate asset, 216
corporate partners, 277
Corporate Politics, 16
Counterfeiting, 153
Courage, 289
courses, 316, 317, 359, 382
covert, 106, 107
cowboys, 58
Create Read Update Delete, 227
Creativity, 323
credit card, 189, 327
Credit Card Numbers, 135
Credit Reports, 135
credits, 317
crews, 14, 103
crime, 152, 288
criminal, 151, 288
Criminal Records, 135
CRM, 30, 86, 109, 167, 172, 198, 226
cronyism, 130
Cronyism, 267
crossroads, 327, 328
CRUD, 227
CTO, 37, 53, 56, 57, 60, 68, 74, 75, 127
cultures, 69, 150, 165, 241, 311, 313
Cultures, 313
Customer Relational Management, 30, 86, 109, 167, 172, 198, 226
customizable, 198, 319
Cutting Edge, 264
CYB, 337
cyber, 141
cyber attacks, 141

D

Dale Heatherington, 299
Damage possibilities, 213
dark politics, 31
DARPA, 300

Dartmouth Conference, 323
Data Access Tier, 176
Data Architect, 16, 39, 43, 117, 245, 247
Data Driven, 227
data hub, 254
Data Marts, 117
data warehouse, 109, 227
data warehouses, 53, 110
Database Access Component, 263
database access test, 193
Database Administrator, 17, 35, 43, 75, 383
Database application, 17
database schemas, 181, 188
Database Server, 170
database tables, 199
databases, 16, 17, 110, 112, 179, 226
David Wise, 137, 355
DBA, 238
Deadlines, 269
decoupled, 199
Defending the Faith, 320
defensive strategy, 219
definition of The Elysian Fields of Information Technology, 290
degrees, 213, 317, 349
Deity, 274
delegation, 295
democracies, 26
democracy, 26, 56, 145
Democrat, 347
Democratic Presidential Primaries, 340
demodulate, 299
Denial of Service, 209
Dennis C. Hayes, 299
Dental Insurance, 343

Department of Homeland Security, 142
department stores, 134, 135
Deploy, 85, 194
deployment, 82, 141, 171, 192, 193, 194, 230, 239
Design Concept, 183
Design Development, 38
Design Logic, 184
Design Patent, 219
Design Pattern, 47
design patterns, 181
Design Patterns, 184
Design Physics, 184
designed, 20, 38, 50, 65, 71, 82, 83, 86, 108, 123, 147, 165, 166, 174, 205, 213, 216, 228, 232, 240, 248, 252, 257, 270, 294, 295, 320, 337, 338, 352, 383
Detective, 274
development methodology, 17, 47
development network, 85, 168, 169, 170, 221
Development Server, 169
development standards, 181, 245
diagrams, 9, 88, 181, 190, 213, 244, 245, 247
Diamond versus Diehr, 216
dictatorship, 56, 145
dictatorships, 26
Digital Cameras, 152
digital signals, 299
digital signature verification, 304
dinosaur, 279
Diplomatic Immunity, 128
Direct Deposit, 344
Disability Insurance, 343
disciples, 319
Discipline, 79, 94, 290, 294

Disclosure, 221
Discoverability, 213
Discovery, 220
discriminatory, 136
Disease, 150
Dishonorable Discharge, 61
Disinformation, 137
disrespect, 292
Document Type Definitions, 71
domain, 4, 38, 84, 85, 91, 99, 115, 145, 167, 168, 169, 170, 180, 185, 217, 223, 257, 266, 286
Domain Analysis, 38
domain expert, 145, 286
domain knowledge, 91, 99, 167, 266
Domain Server, 169
dominance, 160, 165, 338
dotcom, 34
Douglas Engelbart, 297
Dr. Presper Eckert, 297
DRAM, 297
DREAD, 213
DREAD model, 213
drill-down, 190
Driver's Licenses, 153
Duplicated, 204
DVDs, 97, 152, 205, 318
Dwight D. Eisenhower, 144
Dynamic Typing, 324

E

E&C, 196, 197
Earth, 4, 13, 14, 150, 153, 154, 302, 312, 313, 326, 348
earthquake, 243
eBusinesses, 170
E-COM, 304
eCommerce, 170

eCommunications, 240, 241, 254
Economics, 313
educate, 105, 180
Education, 27, 136, 150, 302, 341, 342, 344
Educational, 86
ego, 21, 22, 25, 34, 56, 57, 68, 94, 96, 148, 151, 161, 351
Ego-Driven Leader, 272
egotistical personalities, 310
Elaboration, 229
elected, 137, 272
Election Day, 348
electromagnetism, 305
electronic brochure, 252
electronic business, 170
electronic commerce, 170
electronic communications, 240
electronic functions, 297
electronic signatures, 304
Electronic Signatures in Global and National Commerce Act, 304
Electronics, 317
elementary schools, 316
Elevation of privilege, 209
Elysian Fields Project, i, 3, 4, 10, 14, 20, 22, 57, 71, 76, 117, 123, 149, 151, 156, 160, 161, 201, 216, 223, 288, 289, 290, 291, 292, 293, 294, 295, 296, 299, 305, 306, 307, 308, 310, 311, 312, 314, 315, 316, 320, 324, 328, 329, 330, 331, 332, 336, 337, 338, 339, 340, 341, 342, 343, 344, 345, 347, 348, 349
Elysian Fields Vision Quest Guide, 320
Elysium, 3
email, 65, 66, 71, 81, 106, 152, 166, 179, 239, 240, 241, 248, 254, 261, 302, 303, 304, 305, 358

Email, ii, 71, 151, 172, 205, 240, 242, 302, 303, 304, 305, 347
email programs, 303
Emails, 119, 134, 318
Emperor, 147
Employee Discounts, 344
employee turnover, 107, 344
Employee Turnovers, 337
Employment Identification, 153
EMR, 198, 270
encrypted, 304
End-user level requirements, 188, 189
enemies, 21, 31, 54, 56, 97, 140, 278, 336, 337, 339
enemy, 87, 93, 105, 140, 141, 284, 314, 322, 339
Energy, 289, 311, 330, 331, 333, 334, 341
energy solutions, 150, 314, 331
engineering degree, 314
England, 30
enhancement, 290, 291
ENIAC, 296
Enron, 276
enterprise, 17, 29, 30, 31, 36, 38, 53, 71, 83, 84, 92, 99, 157, 160, 176, 179, 180, 188, 198, 199, 223, 226, 234, 238, 253, 258, 259, 261, 262, 263, 314, 318, 319
Enterprise Resource Planning, 86, 109, 167, 198
enterprise software system, 17, 198, 199
entertainment, 3, 46, 234, 266, 325
envisioning, 82, 83, 87, 125, 146, 163, 168, 230, 326
Epictetus, 51, 131, 162
Epicurus, 349
Episode, 236

Episodes, 233, 236
ERMA, 297
ERP, 86, 109, 167, 198, 319
error messages, 262
Ethernet, 298
Europe, 104, 108, 133, 154
Europeans, 154
evening news, 116, 160
Event Handling, 189, 262
event logging, 184
evolution, 4, 217, 218, 250, 251, 264, 278, 290, 296, 302, 305, 320, 324, 325, 327, 328, 329, 345
exception handling, 184, 262
exception tracking, 193
Exchange and Compromise, 196, 197
Executive Management, 26, 53, 65, 67, 69, 75, 127, 148, 180, 256
Executive Officers, 53
exit strategy, 97, 103
Experimental Research, 307, 308
Expertise, 145
Exploitability, 213
extend, 90, 198
Extensible Markup Language, 71
Extranet, 53, 115
Extreme Programming, 226, 227
Extremism, 338, 340
Exxon Mobil, 157

F

face to face meeting, 241
Facial and Speech Recognition, 322
faith, 7, 8, 149, 317
fall guys, 98
fantasy, 250
fast idiot, 295
FCC, 304

Fear of Change, 280
Feature Driven Development, 228
Feature Dump, 235
Federal Communications Commission, 304
Federico Faggin, 297
fifth law, 277
File Downloads, 205
File Uploads, 205
File-Based, 206
Filing, 221
Finance, 26, 157, 172, 174
Finance Department, 174
Financial Accounting, 87
Financials, 290
fired, 30, 59, 69, 75, 78, 140, 255, 256, 280, 286, 292, 309
firing, 75, 98
first binary computer, 296
first digital electronic computer, 296
flood, 243, 272
Floppy Disk, 297
Floppy Disks, 205
Florida, 105
forecasting, 179
foreign oil, 264, 314, 341
forests, 153, 331
formula, 216, 233, 274, 343
Fortune 500, 156, 263, 276, 319
Founder, 276
four different types of departments, 18
fourth law, 277
FP, 186
framework, 199, 201, 244, 256, 258, 259, 263, 294, 330
free resources, 316
freedom of assembly, 136
freedom of information, 302

freedom of speech, 136
free-ed.net, 317, 359
Freeman Miller, 9
frienemies, 140
Function Points, 186
Functional Specifications, 43, 183, 184, 193, 247
Functional-level requirements, 188

G

Games, 79, 152
gap, 51, 100, 231, 280, 351
Gartner, 109
gate keepers, 204
gatekeepers, 41, 204
geeks, 25
Gene Rodenberry, 11
General Electric, 157
General Intelligence, 107
General Motors, 157
General Project Messages, 239
General utility, 219
genesis, 327
Genetically Engineered Humans, 325
Geographical, 136
Geology, 26
George W. Bush, 348
German, 296, 328
Germany, 338
global warming, 80, 312
Global Warming, 150, 153, 154, 327
Gold, 166, 194
Gold Support, 166
gospel, 318, 319, 320
government agencies, 152
government regulatory obligations, 250
Governments, 86, 153
Grace Hopper, 296

Grand Jury, 276
graphical user interface, 319
Graphics Software, 153
Grass-Roots, 347
Great Britain, 108, 313
Greatest Physicist, 309
Greed, 21, 267, 337, 339, 340, 345
Greek mythology, 3
Greek philosopher, 51, 131, 349
green, 80, 243, 248, 249, 342
Greener, 264
Grey Object, 331
grid, 191
GUI, 319
guidelines, 48, 98, 130, 186, 190, 269
Gulf Coast, 276

H

hackers, 141, 201, 204, 206, 211, 212
hacking, 141, 227
Hades, 151, 267, 268, 287, 288, 289
hard drives, 205
Hard Drives, 179
Hardware Architecture, 82
Hardware Patents, 158
hardware platforms, 94, 176
Harry S. Truman, 103
Harvard University, 296
hat trick, 275
Hayes Manufactured, 299
Hayes-Compatible, 299
health insurance, 90
Health Insurance, 343
Healthcare, 150, 329, 331, 333, 334, 341
Hell, 265
help system, 195
Hewlett-Packard, 157, 382
High Priority, 210, 242

INDEX

high risk, 81, 84, 213
High School Diplomas, 26
hi-jacking, 304
Hillary Clinton, 340
Hiroshima, 104
historical map, 266
history of the personal computer, 296
holiday, 90, 135
Hollywood, 46, 105
Home addresses, 135
Home and Studio Recording, 12
hominid, 327
Homo sapiens sapien, 328
Honesty, 8, 94, 273
horizontal array, 179
Horizontal scaling, 179
horizontally scaled, 177
Hospital Administration, 27
hourly rate, 102
Howard Aiken, 296
HR representative, 34
human factor, 20, 22
Human genetic lines, 328
Human Resources, 34, 86, 172
Hunger, 150, 327, 330, 331, 333, 334
hydrogen, 154
Hyper Text Markup Language, 71

I

IBM, 134, 229, 297
IBM 5100, 134
IC, 297
ICBMs, 105
Ignorant Leader, 272
illegal practices, 107
Illinois, 347, 348
illness, 278
Impersonate, 203

Inappropriate encounters, 283
inboxes, 304
Inception, 229
Income, 136, 336
India, 30
Industrial Espionage, 107
Industrial Revolution, 313, 355
industry, 5, 10, 19, 21, 22, 25, 26, 28, 29, 37, 42, 43, 47, 56, 57, 63, 70, 71, 75, 76, 78, 88, 91, 92, 102, 106, 107, 116, 119, 134, 139, 154, 156, 159, 160, 161, 163, 165, 171, 179, 190, 193, 200, 201, 205, 214, 217, 218, 219, 222, 223, 225, 233, 234, 250, 255, 256, 259, 261, 263, 267, 274, 276, 279, 297, 299, 314, 317, 329, 333, 341, 342, 345, 348, 349
Information disclosure, 209
information overload, 146
Information People, 9, 25, 51, 156, 202, 346
infrastructure, 28, 29, 112, 176, 180, 183, 191, 193, 248, 251, 264, 299, 337, 339
inheritance, 260
in-house, 17, 18, 19, 45, 69, 111, 165, 166, 175, 180, 195, 199, 201, 258
input, 53, 204, 209, 270, 295, 309, 310, 346
insanity, 56, 76
installed, 84, 126, 141, 164, 175, 192, 193, 199
instant messaging, 81
Instant Messaging, 240
Insurance Certificates, 153
integrated circuit, 297
Integration, 189
integration points, 184
integration tests, 193

Integrity, 67, 125
Intel, 157, 297
Intellectual Properties, 291
intellectual property, 18, 34, 43, 63, 65, 156, 158, 216, 217, 218, 219, 220, 221, 223
Intellectual Property, 67, 216
intellectual resource, 216
Intelligent Agent, 322
inter-continental ballistic missiles, 105
interfaces, 87, 109, 184
Interfaces, 325
International Patent, 220
internationally, 248, 266
Internet, 34, 53, 65, 67, 71, 72, 86, 107, 112, 115, 140, 142, 151, 157, 170, 171, 172, 173, 176, 177, 180, 189, 205, 238, 240, 251, 252, 253, 254, 263, 265, 270, 274, 276, 297, 299, 300, 301, 302, 303, 304, 310, 316, 347, 352, 383
internet browser, 173
Intranet, 53, 115
intruders, 202
invention, 90, 140, 219, 221, 248, 296, 297, 302, 305, 325, 348, 351
inventions, 159, 217, 220, 298, 305, 311, 358
Inventory, 157, 172, 290
Inventory Management, 157, 172
investors, 159, 219
Iowa State University, 296
IP, 207, 299, 300
IQ, 25
Ireland, 30
isolated network, 170
Israel, 104
IT Director, 35, 37, 66, 67, 68, 69, 74, 138, 163

IT Hades Principle, 288
IT Infrastructures, 19
IT Organizational Charts, 36
iteration, 193, 194, 213, 228
iteration process, 193, 194
ITHP, 288
itinerary, 204

J

J. Presper Eckert, 296
Jack Kilby, 297
jail, 7, 147
jargon, 105, 120, 190, 284
Jewish, 338
Johannes Gutenberg, 328
John Atanasoff, 296
John Bardeen, 297
John F. Kennedy, 4
John Hopkins Bloomberg School of Public Health, 316
John Mauchly, 296, 297
John McCain, 347
John McCarthy, 322
Journalism, 27
jungles, 331
Junior Database Administrator, 35

K

K.I.S.S., 164
Katrina, 276
KB, 236
Keep it simple stupid, 70
Kenneth Lay, 276
keyboard synthesizer, 12
Kindness, 8
KISS, 70
knowledge base, 116, 166, 195
Knowledge Base, 236

Konrad Zuse, 296, 328

L

Labor and Industries, 98, 382
Laboratory Information Management Systems, 198
Lack of Change, 270, 281
Lack of IT Management Experience, 15
LAN, 248, 296
Lancaster, Pennsylvania, 7
Language Barriers, 352
laptop PCs, 295
Larry Roberts, 303
Latinos, 136
Law, 27, 97
law enforcement, 118, 153, 288
laws, 66, 80, 97, 98, 122, 130, 154, 164, 192, 275, 304, 305, 308, 309, 314
lawsuits, 65, 66, 276
Layer, 176
layoffs, 19, 159, 160
Lead Analyst, 117
lectures, 316
Lectures, 318
Legal, 249, 304
legal agreements, 304
legislation, 152, 220, 304
Letter of Grant, 221
liability, 28, 34, 101
liar, 139, 140
librarian, 245
license, 158
licensing, 17, 218, 221, 265
lie, 4, 7, 18, 137, 139
Life Insurance, 343
light bulbs, 154

lightning rod, 150
LIMS, 198
Linguistics, 322
liquidation, 159
LISP, 323
List Processing Language, 323
living business contributors, 235
load balancer, 179
Local and Wide Area Networks, 44
Logic, 176, 322
logical view, 184, 202
Logistics, 290
loosely coupled, 171
Low Priority, 210, 242
Loyalty, 8, 90, 273
Lucius Seneca, 293
Luck, 267
Luther Burbank, 219
lying, 137, 138, 139, 140

M

M.I.T., 303, 316
Macintosh, 319
Macro, 206
magazine article, 352
magazines, 12, 53, 107, 133, 140, 160
Mail Server, 170
MAILBOX, 303
maintainability, 176
Maintainability, 258
malicious software application, 205
Man of the Year, 134
manufacture, 216
Manufacturing, 157, 290, 313
MARK series of computers, 296
Mark Twain, 125
marketing, 66, 86, 135, 304, 319
Marketing, 27, 172, 214, 290, 304

marketplace, 106, 265, 320
marriage, 51, 84, 316, 351
Massachusetts Institute of Technology, 303
Mathematics, 305, 317
Matrices, 189
matrix, 212, 213
Mavericks, 340
Medical Billing, 86
Medical Records, 134, 198, 270, 333, 341
Meetings, 119
Megalomania, 267
Memory, 179, 296, 297
Mennonite, 7, 8, 9
Message headers, 304
messaging applications, 303
Messiah College, 7
metamorphoses, 193
Methodologies, 10, 225, 226, 230, 231
methodology, 225, 226, 230, 231, 233, 234, 236, 243, 244, 245, 246, 254, 263, 306
Metrics, 78, 124
Michigan State, 316
microprocessor, 297
Microsoft, 72, 157, 228, 355
Microwave Oven, 305
MIDI, 12
Mike Boich, 319
milestone review, 194
milestone-driven, 228
milestones, 49, 58, 61, 63, 83, 128, 186, 230, 239, 244, 247
military, 58, 60, 61, 79, 105, 108, 266, 303, 351
Military, 14, 118, 272, 274, 296, 297
mimic human brain activity, 325

Missouri Southern State University, 316
Mistrust, 267
MIT, 297
mitigate, 186, 209, 213
mitigating risks, 213
model-driven, 228
Modeling threats, 208
Modem, 299
modular, 171, 180, 201
modulate, 299
module, 176
monolithic, 70, 134, 179, 180, 230, 233
moon, 4, 151
Morale, 87, 93
mortgages, 91
Motivational Speaker, 318
mouse, 204, 262, 297, 319
movie, 11, 105, 222, 233, 234, 325
MSF, 228
Multipartite, 206
Multi-tiered, 176
murder victim, 147
Murray Hill, New Jersey, 297
Music, 12, 27, 152, 382, 383
musicians, 12, 58
myth, 154, 290, 326

N

NAFTA, 313
Nagasaki, 104
Nanotechnology, 322
napoleon complexes, 32
NAS, 170
nationalism, 338
nationally, 160, 241, 248, 250
NATO, 108
natural disaster, 243, 249, 272

INDEX

Natural Experiments, 307, 308
natural human languages, 323
Natural Language Processing, 323
Naval Base Norfolk, VA, 11
Neanderthal, 328
Neanderthals, 278
Need to Know, 64, 65, 66, 67
Network Architect, 40, 44
Network Area Storage, 170
network bandwidth, 85, 173
Network Engineer, 44
network hub, 204
networking protocols, 299, 300
Neural Networks, 323
neurons, 323, 326
Neuroscience, 322
new age, 32, 326, 348
New York University, 317
newspapers, 5, 107
Newton's Three Laws of Motion, 309, 310
niche, 32, 56, 156, 303
Nobel Prize, 297
non-partitioned data, 179
Non-Profits, 86
Non-provisional (Utility) Patent, 219
Normal Priority, 210
North America, 141
North American Free Trade Agreement, 313
North Atlantic Treaty Organization, 108
North Korea, 302
North Philadelphia, 5, 7
notarized, 304
Notification Component, 261
n-tier, 49, 180, 188
N-Tier, 175
n-Tier diagram, 176

nuclear, 104, 105, 108, 142
nuclear age, 104
nuclear alert, 109
nuclear counter-strike, 109
Nuclear Regulatory Commission, 142
nuclear war, 108

O

Object Oriented, 225, 228, 260, 323
Obsolescence, 281
oil companies, 279, 314
old school, 248
On Demand, 86
OOP, 260, 323
opening summary, 190
operating system, 171, 176, 324
Operating System, 47
Opposing Perspectives, 352
Organizational-level requirements, 188
OS, 171
out of scope, 187, 274
outdated, 81, 111, 248, 254
output, 204, 209, 346
outsourced, 19, 39, 46, 87
Outsourcing, 87, 103
Over inflated Egos, 267
Overcompensation, 282, 283

P

Paid Holidays, 343
Paid Sick Days, 343
Paid Vacations, 343
paradigm, 172
paradox, 199
paranthropines, 327
Parking Privileges, 344
partitioned, 179

Passports, 153
password, 208, 209, 263
Patent and Trademark Office, 219
Patent Cooperation Treaty, 220
patent lawyers, 223
Patent Plaque, 221
patentable, 216, 296
Patents, 158
Patience, 8, 90
pay it forward, 295
Pay It Forward, 310
PC, 11, 80, 134, 157, 168, 173, 205, 295, 296, 299, 305, 319, 348
PCT, 220
Penn State, 317
Pentagon, 141
Perfect Storm, 348
performance tests, 193
Performance reviews, 78
permissions, 115, 203, 232, 233, 238
Personal Computer, 80, 295, 299, 305
Personal Computers, 151, 212, 295
Personal Software Process, 228
Personality, 47, 146
personality types, 47, 48
phases, 99, 179, 181, 192, 227, 229, 230, 233, 270
philosophy, 251, 258
Philosophy, 251, 322
Phone records, 134
Photo Copiers, 152
Physical appearance, 146
physical emotions, 326
Physician, 223, 264, 295
Physics, 297, 305, 306, 307, 308, 309, 356
Planned Pension, 344
planning, 33, 47, 56, 59, 64, 82, 83, 84, 87, 95, 97, 125, 146, 163, 168,
171, 179, 183, 185, 188, 191, 214, 230, 232, 235, 236, 257, 272, 281, 287, 291, 326, 342
Plant Patent, 219
Plant Patent Act of 1930, 219
platforms, 70, 71, 139, 153, 180, 184, 259, 329
Platinum Support, 166
plug and play, 180, 201
Plutarch, 269, 288
PM, 241, 242
podcasts, 316
Podcasts, 318
Poland, 338
Political Clout, 339
Political Science, 27
political suicide, 147, 148, 150
polling, 18, 194
Polymorphic, 206
poor morale, 186
portable device, 297
Positional, 144, 145
Positive Reinforcement, 320
Post Office, ii, 304
post office box, 249
poverty, 7, 14, 136, 338, 342
Poverty, 150
POW, 347
power generator, 142
Power Lunches, 88
power outage, 243
power plays, 31
Powercoat Records, 12, 383
Pre-Design Phase, 38
preemptive nuclear strike, 108
pregnancy, 253
Presentation, 83, 87, 237, 355
Presentations, 119

INDEX

President, 4, 67, 103, 104, 109, 141, 144, 304, 347, 348
Presidential Election, 347
Pride, 268
Prime Directive, 14
Princeton, 317
Principals, 35, 75
principles, 70, 71, 80, 81, 171, 187, 199, 210, 227, 228, 229, 231, 239, 241, 357
Printing Press, 328
Prisoner of War, 347
Probability, 322
problem resolution, 294
Process Management, 82
processing power, 14, 178, 325, 326
Processors, 179
Product testing, 192
Productions Servers, 168
productivity, 15, 18, 39, 40, 78, 80, 87, 241, 242
Professionalism, 290
Profit Sharing, 344
programmer analysts, 30
Programmer\Analyst, 43, 382
Programmer\Analysts, 43, 119
project analysis, 194
Project Deployment, 239
Project Development, 239
project estimation, 186, 271
project failure, 23, 56, 146, 156
Project Management software, 17
Project Manager, 30, 40, 241, 244, 245, 246, 247, 382
Project Methodology, 183
project plan, 26, 29, 60, 183, 185, 239
Project Plan, 185, 239, 247
Project Politics, 20

project requirements, 29, 79, 118, 163, 270, 286, 300
project team, 20, 29, 30, 83, 84, 125, 127, 181, 183, 184, 185, 186, 191, 194, 197, 230, 231, 233, 234, 236, 239, 240, 241, 244, 246, 248, 251, 254, 281, 295
Project Testing, 239
Project Vision, 238
Projects Documentation, 38
Projects Manager, 16
proof of concept, 192, 221
propaganda, 302, 339
proper funding, 267
Proper project planning, 19
proprietary, 11, 110, 138, 165, 198, 285, 352
Pros, 294
protocol, 64, 65, 66, 67, 300
prototype, 192
Prototype, 85, 223
Provisional Patent, 219
PSP, 228
Psychology, 26, 322
public library, 316
publish and subscribe, 172
Publishing, 158
punished, 137
punishment, 79, 140
Punishments, 319
Purchase Order, 87

Q

Quality Assurance, 17, 45, 82, 225, 274
queries, 203
Quest, 93, 320

R

R&D, 214, 225, 308
Race, 135
RAD, 228, 229
Radio Shack, 11
rainforests, 331
raises, 78, 90, 149
Rapid Application Development, 228
Rating systems, 213
Ray Tomlinson, 303
Ready for Change, 233, 234, 263
Receptionists, 249
reckless, 66, 138, 163
reconstruction, 104
Recreation, 302
recycling, 154, 260
redundancy, 179
re-estimation, 186
refactor, 29, 179, 180, 281
Refrigerator, 305
regionally, 241, 248, 250
registered voters, 136
regression tests, 193
regulatory compliance, 258
Regulatory Compliance, 189
re-invent, 218
Reliability, 258
religion, 14, 149, 201, 317, 319
religious, 149, 317
Religious affiliation, 136
Reluctant Leader, 272
Remote Business Management, 263
renewable energy, 316, 345, 348
replicate, 205
reporting, 109, 110, 111, 112, 116, 117, 124, 139, 163, 173, 257, 260, 346
repository, 195
Reproducibility, 213
republic, 147
Republican, 348
Repudiation, 208
reputation, 25, 58, 95, 103, 202, 214, 250
requirements document, 187, 188, 189, 190, 191, 271
Research and Development, 43, 119, 214, 290, 308, 333
Resign, 140
Resource allocation, 179
Respect, 8, 90, 273, 289, 339
Resumes, 135
retirement plans, 90
retroactive, 248
return on investment, 18, 19, 25, 75, 77, 82, 83, 92, 112, 122, 128, 146, 168, 185, 195, 202, 228, 252, 259, 264, 270, 282, 311, 342, 343
reusable, 171
Revenue Based Intelligence, 108
Revenue Limitations, 15
revenue shortage, 249
Rewards, 319
RFC, 225, 233, 234, 235, 236, 237, 238, 239, 240, 241, 242, 243, 244, 245, 246, 247, 248, 249, 251, 252, 253, 254, 258, 259, 260, 263
RFC Project website, 238, 239
Risk Analysis, 183
risk management, 164, 196
Risk Resolution Strategy, 183
Robert Metcalf, 298
Robert Noyce, 297
Robotics, 322
rogue, 281
ROI, 18, 28, 43, 70, 170, 175, 179, 185, 228, 282, 342, 343, 344, 345

role, 8, 38, 39, 53, 58, 106, 115, 117, 181, 203, 214, 232, 233, 238, 263, 351, 357
role-based, 203
role-playing, 58
Roles and Responsibilities, 183, 244
Rome, 147, 293
Ronald J. Sider, 9
royalty payments, 221
RRT Factor, 308, 309, 310
Rules Engine, 34
rules of engagement, 256
RUP, 226, 229

S

SaaS, 172, 173, 174, 175, 242
Safeguard, 202
salaries, 45, 120, 125, 148, 265
Sales, 86, 172, 290, 318
sales pitches, 285
salesman, 285
satellite, 107, 170
scalability, 175, 176, 179, 253, 300
Scalability, 258
scalable, 110, 172, 176, 195
Scanners, 152
Scene, 236
Scenes, 233, 236
schedules, 90, 173, 196, 244, 247
Schematic Design, 38
science, 11, 46, 128, 163, 180, 195, 201, 220, 225, 270, 271, 285, 299, 305, 322, 323, 324, 325, 327, 328, 348, 351
scientific process, 195
Scientist, 223, 264, 295
scientists, 153, 297, 312, 323, 327
scope creep, 99, 129, 235

screen shots, 188
Scrum, 229, 231
SDLC, 9, 17, 18, 19, 20, 163, 180, 181, 185, 189, 191, 194, 196, 197, 214, 222, 227, 233, 234, 254, 264, 326
search and rescue operation, 105
Season, 236
second law, 276
Secure Socket Layers, 173
Securities Fraud, 276
security, 30, 47, 112, 113, 115, 151, 152, 173, 174, 184, 193, 201, 202, 203, 204, 205, 206, 208, 232, 238, 239, 253, 262, 308, 359
Security, 115, 134, 153, 189, 201, 212, 214, 258, 262, 355
security breach, 151
Self Hosting Compiler, 324
Self Righteousness, 320
Self-Replication, 319
Senator, 347, 348
senior management, 30, 59
Senior Programmer\Analyst, 30
Senseless, 275
sensitive data, 136, 202, 209
Service allocation, 172
Service components, 172
Service delivery, 172
Service Interface Tier, 176
Service Oriented Architecture, 171
Service surveillance, 172
Service types, 172
Shadowing, 119
shopping, 135, 266
sick day, 90
side-stepped, 174
Silver Support, 166
Sir Isaac Newton, 309
slide presentations, 97

Small businesses, 31, 32
smart client, 176
snail mail, 304
snap shots, 222
SNDMSG, 303
SOA, 171, 172, 242
Social Security Cards, 153
Social Security numbers, 134
Socialization, 302
Software as a Service, 172
Software Developer, 17, 35
Software Development Lifecycle, 9, 17, 19, 103, 163, 170, 180, 221, 230
software estimate, 185, 186
software patent, 216, 217, 218, 220, 221, 223
Software Patents, 158, 216, 221
Software System Architect, 16, 37, 38, 141, 184, 214, 245, 246, 247, 256, 257
Software System Architecture, 43, 47, 183, 213, 247
Software system support, 195
Software Tester, 44, 75, 383
Software Testing, 45, 87, 214, 269
solar, 154, 302, 314
Soviet Union, 108
Soviet's, 108
Space Shuttle, 21
Spacewar, 297
spam, 152, 304
spamming, 304
spawn, 326
special interests groups, 315
Specific utility, 219
spiral, 228
Spiral, 229
Spoofing, 208
Spread Sheets, 87

SQL, 187, 199
Square, 312
SR&D, 214, 215, 216
SSL, 173
Stabilization, 193
Staffing of Contracting, 39
Staging Server, 169
Stan Mazor invent, 297
Stanford Research Institute, 297
Star Trek, 11, 13
starship, 14, 163
startup, 33, 34, 75
Startup, 28, 33
state, 4, 12, 19, 45, 66, 92, 97, 98, 116, 149, 151, 192, 195, 199, 209, 219, 256, 260, 281, 289, 290, 291, 300, 309, 316, 320, 329, 330
State agency, 98
state legislature, 98
State Police, 118
State Senate, 347
status quoi, 340
Steve Austin, 11
Steve Russell, 297
stock, 78, 90, 93, 160, 182, 183, 276
stockholders, 219
stress, 5, 25, 35, 41, 47, 53, 81, 118, 123, 127, 164, 193, 212, 214, 242, 278
STRIDE, 208, 209
Strings, 324
Strong and Bad, 143
Strong and Good, 143
Structured, 187, 199, 225
Structured Query Language, 187, 199
stupid, 123, 140, 148, 163, 275, 276, 277, 278
Stupid Factor, 275

INDEX

subject matter, 96, 97, 180, 187, 189, 216, 250
submarine, 105
subscriber, 170
Subscribing, 160
super power, 104
superior mind, 325, 326
Super-Nova, 204
Support Manager, 75, 163
support packages, 166
supremacy, 278
synapses, 326
synergy, 291
System Administrator, 207
system architecture, 17, 180, 181, 187, 204, 222, 245
system exceptions, 193
System Performance, 189

T

tampering, 208
Tampering, 208
TCP, 299, 300
TCP/IP, 299
TDD, 229
Team Animosity, 337
Team Lead, 35, 41, 309, 310, 382
Team Leader, 41
teamwork, 180
techies, 25
Technical Evangelists, 317, 318, 319
Technical Specification, 181, 187
Technical Specifications, 185, 247
Technical Writer, 45, 383
Technological Arthritis, 159
Technology cycle, 292
Technology Demonstrations, 318
Ted Hoff, 297

telecommute, 240
telecommuting, 240, 242
Telecommuting, 242, 263
telephone, 106, 195, 248, 254, 299
telescope, 326
television, 11, 13, 25, 53, 58, 80, 107, 133, 233, 234, 324
template, 191
templates, 260
terminology, 70, 130
terrorist threat, 141
tertiary, 101, 127, 159, 331
Test Driven Development, 229
test plans, 44, 79, 181, 192, 193, 239
test server, 192
Test Server, 169
testing phase, 193
Texting, 240, 347
The FBI, 118
The Matrix, 46
The Politics of Lying, 137, 355
The Singularity, 324, 325, 326, 327, 328
The Terminator, 46
Theft, 107, 152
Theology, 26
Theory of Computation, 323
Thieves, 275
third law, 276
third party, 70, 81, 86, 97, 103, 115, 138, 159, 163, 164, 165, 166, 167, 172, 173, 174, 175, 180, 198, 199, 200, 201, 222, 284, 285
third Party Consultants, 18
threat modeling, 202, 209, 210, 211, 212, 213, 214
threat modeling process, 209
threats, 13, 201, 202, 208, 210, 212, 213

three laws, 309
tier, 30, 32, 49, 176, 179, 180
Time Constraints, 15
tourniquet, 83
Tower of Babel, 105
Traffic, 80
traffic patterns, 135
Trainer, 318
Training, 81, 94, 96, 116, 165
training plan, 195
Transient Personnel Office, 11
transistor, 297
Transition, 195, 229
transition process, 194, 195
Transmission Control Program, 300
Transmission Control Protocol, 299, 300
Transportation, 313
Tree Data Structures, 323
Trending, 136
Triangle, 312
Trust, 31, 90, 101, 145, 146, 289, 356
tutorials, 316
types of patents, 219
types of power, 144
types of utility patents, 219
types of virus, 205

U

UAT, 193, 239, 269
UI, 171, 176, 180
UN, 73
unauthorized, 203, 213, 258, 308
understaffed, 83
unethical, 106
unfair advantage, 4, 5, 23, 25, 63, 91, 92, 93, 106, 156, 157, 158, 159, 161, 165, 214, 218, 219, 223, 266, 267
Unified Process, 226, 227, 229
United Nations, 73
United States, 11, 30, 31, 103, 104, 105, 108, 134, 141, 144, 152, 216, 217, 219, 221, 276, 304, 313, 316, 336, 340, 347
United States Navy, 11, 105
United States Post Office, 305
United States Postal Commission, 305
UNIVAC, 297
Universal Automatic Computer, 297
Universal Relay Link, 252
Universal translation, 117
University of Michigan, 317
University of North Carolina, 317
University of Pennsylvania, 317
University of Washington, 317
untrustworthy, 138
upgraded, 81, 91, 171, 177, 198, 199
up-time, 173, 178
Uri Andropov, 109
URL, 252
USB, 205
use cases, 118, 183, 184, 186, 189, 234, 244, 246
Use Cases, 183
User Acceptance Testing, 193
user expectations, 189, 192
user IDs, 207
User Interface Tier, 50, 176
User Interfaces, 171
User name, 263
User Requirements, 183
username, 208, 209
USS San Juan, 105

V

vacation, 90, 133
Value Added Reseller, 198
value-added, 145

INDEX

vanilla, 199, 201
VAR, 198, 258
variables, 46, 233, 306, 353
veins, 302, 340
vendor, 159, 166, 167, 172, 173, 174, 175, 198, 200, 201, 266
ventures, 106, 343
Verizon Communications, 157
version, 57, 71, 72, 124, 163, 166, 185, 192, 194, 198, 199, 201, 226, 234, 236, 285, 326
Vice-President, 67
video conference calls, 241
Video Conferences, 318
video conferencing, 81, 241
Video Conferencing, 87, 240
video games, 11, 76, 250
Video recording, 119
video tape, 135
virtual office, 248, 249, 250, 251
Virtualization, 263, 264
Vision Cycle Diagram, 13, 14
vocabulary, 10, 70, 119, 223, 257, 283, 292
Vote, 341
Voyager, 13, 14
vulnerabilities, 201, 205, 206, 207, 213, 308

W

Wal-Mart, 157
Walter Brattain, 297
WAN, 296
war, 14, 25, 48, 54, 56, 91, 92, 93, 108, 134, 149, 201, 250
War, 91, 104, 108, 296, 338, 341
War Hero, 347
Washington, D.C., 31, 382

waterfall, 228
Waterfall, 230
Weak, 91, 143, 275, 276
Weak and Bad, 143
Weak and Good, 143
weapons of mass destruction, 93
web application, 47, 115, 238, 252, 253, 254, 259, 260, 281
Web Application, 253
web browser, 252
Web Hosting, 172
Web Logs, 240
web master, 245
Web Meetings, 87
Web Services, 171, 172
Web site hosting, 86
Web sites, 115, 240
Web-Portals, 170
Website, 241, 252
Websites, 347
Wellness Incentives, 344
White House, 141, 348
White Objects, 331
white paper, 352
wide area networks, 240
William Jefferson Clinton, 304
William Shockley, 297
Win\Win, 243, 249
Wise and Intelligent, 275
WMDs, 93
Word Processing, 87
work in progress, 92, 191, 234
Working at home, 80, 242
World Economy, 330, 331, 334
World War II, 104, 296, 338
World War III, 108
World Wide Institute of Software Architects, 38, 39, 382
World Wide Web, 71, 251, 254

worm, 205
WWISA, 38, 382
WYSIWYG, 161

X

Xerox Corporation, 298
XML, 70, 71, 72, 73, 188, 245
XP, 226, 227, 229
x-ray, 270

Y

Yale, 317

Z

Z1, 296
Zero Bug Release, 194

ABOUT THE AUTHOR

Mark K. Allen was born and raised in Philadelphia, Pennsylvania USA. He has been a Software Engineer since the early 1990s, and has made the transition into a working Software Systems Architect. During the course of his career, Mark has worked for or served as a consultant with the following companies:

Sears Credit, McCormick-Schilling, Fort-James Paper Mills, Hewlett-Packard, The State of Oregon, Oregon Health and Sciences University (OHSU), The State of Washington, Exodus, Enron, DMR, Comsys, Ciber, Logicalis

Mark is a US Navy Veteran who served in the Persian Gulf. He is also a graduate of the former, National Radio Institute (NRI) Technical School (previously a division of McGraw Hill) Washington, D.C. His courses of study included Electronic Music Technology and Computer Science. He is a member of the World Wide Institute of Software Architects (WWISA) and has been a practicing member since 2003. During his career in IT, Mark has worked in the following roles on various projects:

- **Software Systems Architect**
- **Project Manager**
- **Software Engineer Team Lead**
- **Senior Software Engineer**
- **Programmer\Analyst**
- **Technical Analyst**

- **Technical Writer**
- **Software Tester**
- **Database Administrator**
- **Senior Systems Support Engineer**
- **Network Support Engineer**
- **Help Desk Support**

He has designed, coded, tested, and implemented the following for companies ranging from Startups to Enterprise:

- Client Applications
- Client-Server Applications
- Back-end Server Applications
- Web Services
- Web Applications
- Websites

As an entrepreneur, Mark founded three companies: Powercoat Records, Powercoat Music, and Real Enhanced Decision Technology, LLC. He also a singer/songwriter who has released several music CDs (http://www.powercoatmusic.com) and lives in Washington State. You can contact Mark at mallen@realenhanceddecisions.com.

www.ingramcontent.com/pod-product-compliance
Ingram Content Group UK Ltd.
Pitfield, Milton Keynes, MK11 3LW, UK
UKHW051257180426
11947UKWH00020B/1755